CHRONICLES
OF THE
Civil War

CHRONICLES
OF THE
Civil
War

An Illustrated History of the War
Between the States

MetroBooks

MetroBooks

An Imprint of Friedman/Fairfax Publishers

Library of Congress Cataloging-in-Publication available upon request

ISBN 1-56799-728-7

Editors: Tony Burgess, Ann Kirby, and Nathaniel Marunas
Art Director: Kevin Ullrich
Layout: Charles Donahue
Photography Editors: Valerie Kennedy, Kathryn Culley, and Emilya Naymark
Production Manager: Ingrid McNamara and Camille Lee

Color separations by Bright Arts (Singapore) Pte. Ltd.
Printed in Singapore by KHL Printing Co Pte Ltd.

10 9 8 7 6 5 4 3 2 1

For bulk purchases and special sales, please contact:
Friedman/Fairfax Publishers
Attention: Sales Department
15 West 26th Street
New York, NY 10010
212/685-6610 FAX 212/685-1307

Visit our website:
http://www.metrobooks.com

CONTENTS

INTRODUCTION

What troops
Of generous boys in
happiness thus bred—
Saturnians through
life's Temple led,
Went from the
North and came
from the South,
With golden mottoes
in the mouth,
To lie down midway
on a bloody bed.

—Herman Melville

In your hands, my dissatisfied fellow-countrymen, and not in mine is the momentous issue of civil war. The government will not assail you. You can have no conflict without yourselves being the aggressors. You have no oath registered in heaven to destroy the government, while I shall have the most solemn one to "preserve, protect, and defend it."

—Abraham Lincoln, Inaugural address,
March 4, 1861

I worked night and day for twelve years to prevent the war, and I could not. The North was mad and blind, and would not let us govern ourselves, and so the war came. Now it must go on until the last man of this generation falls in his tracks and his children seize his musket and fight our battles.

—Jefferson Davis,
July 17, 1864

Two widely differing views about the most effective form of government developed during the first eight decades of the existence of the United States. Dividing the competing sections of the young country were several issues—slavery not the least among them. The young democracy took a great deal of pride in having wrested independence from Great Britain, and accordingly such words as "freedom" and "equality" had come to loom large in the sociocultural vernacular; of course, these words meant different things to the different sections of the country. As the larger, more populated, and more industrialized North began to press for the elimination of slavery from national economic operations, the southerners' way of life was threatened. Not surprisingly, these slave-owning agricul-

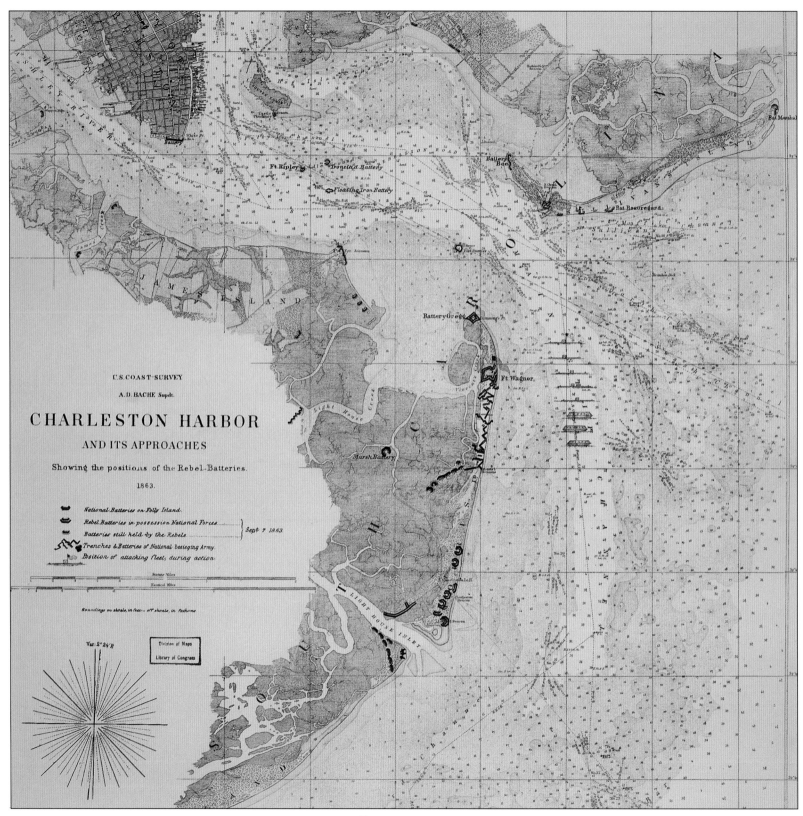

U.S. COAST-SURVEY

A.D. BACHE Supdt.

CHARLESTON HARBOR

AND ITS APPROACHES

Showing the positions of the Rebel-Batteries.

1863.

National Batteries on Folly Island.
Rebel Batteries in possession National Forces
Batteries still held by the Rebels } Sept 7 1863
Trenches & Batteries of National besieging Army.
Position of attacking fleet, during action.

Statute Miles
Nautical Miles

Soundings on shoals, in feet - off shoals, in fathoms

Var: 2° 24' B

Division of Maps
Library of Congress

turalists became increasingly defensive and suspicious of their northern cousins.

As new territories were being shaped within the wide region seized by force from Mexico, battles erupted over whether or not these emerging divisions of land should permit slaveholding. The precarious balance of power that had existed in the U.S. Senate between "slave" states and "free" states began to break down. And as the South's leadership began to feel more and more menaced by the trend moving away from slavery, some southern politicians began to develop their own agendas. These loud, radical politicians made contingency plans that would guarantee them powerful positions within a smaller, independent country that they planned to form. They were quickly matched in the North by the Republicans, a strongly abolitionist party whose star was on the rise as the Whig party began to unravel.

The moderates of the North were outraged by the actions of Stephen Douglas, whose sponsorship of the Kansas-Nebraska Act made possible the spread of slavery north of the line that had been agreed upon in the Missouri Compromise in 1820.

The Missouri Compromise prohibited slavery in any additional states that might be formed from territories lying north of 36 degrees 30 minutes latitude. The Kansas-Nebraska Act changed this by leaving the question of slavery to the states as they were formed, leaving the door open for slavery in previously protected territories. This led to the fierce battles in newly formed Kansas over the issue of slavery that earned the area the epithet "Bleeding Kansas." Douglas' manipulation of the political processes had brought slavery to the fore as a major issue, and there it would remain until the end of the ensuing conflict.

Slavery had gradually died out in the North as many states followed different paths toward emancipation. A few states, such as Massachusetts, freed all of the slaves within their borders immediately; other states, such as New Jersey, freed the children of slaves as they were born. Whichever method was followed, the distinction between "slave" and "free" states was becoming increasingly important. The South began to feel besieged as cries for freedom for all slaves began to ring throughout the North. Soon, abolitionist Whigs began converting to the Republican party.

Southerners were afraid that the agitation for liberation of the slaves would lead to a general revolt, and with good reason. The western hemisphere had recently witnessed the results of the bloody slave rebellion in Haiti, which occurred around the same time as the French Revolution. Following a savage war between the French and their slaves, the slaves emerged victorious in 1803. One of the leaders of the rebellion then led the massacre of most of the whites who had not already fled the island. Thousands of the white refugees from the Haitian fighting had fled to the United States, where their tales of atrocities at the hands of their former slaves quickly spread.

This fear among southerners was amplified by revolt at home, too. Nat Turner's rebellion, for instance, cost sixty white southerners their lives and spread fear throughout Virginia for six weeks in 1831. In addition, the much-publicized mutiny of

blacks on the brig *Creole* had resulted in the deaths of the white crewmen (and the release of most of the mutineers by the British in Nassau). The South's whites felt that they had much to fear, given the history of slave revolts and the fatalities suffered. As a result, the calls for the liberation of the slaves being voiced by the North's politicians served to advance the interests of the southern radicals, who were calling for secession from the United States.

The emergence of violence in Kansas over the issue of slavery further alarmed the people of the South. The acts of political extremism carried out by local abolitionists, undertaken to prevent the spread of additional slave owners into the new territories, terrified the southern populace. In particular, the killings of unarmed proslavery settlers by John Brown in what came to be known as the Pottawatomie Massacre (1856)—a slaughter that went largely unpunished thanks to the intervention of some influential northern politicians—was so outrageous that even the abolitionists began to moderate their tone somewhat. But it was John Brown's next act that attracted national attention and created a palpable climate of fear throughout the slave-holding sections of the country.

On October 18, 1859, John Brown and a small company of men (five of them black and twenty or so white) raided the small community of Harpers Ferry, Virginia. Brown's object was to confiscate arms from the Federal arsenal there, distribute the weapons among slaves, and encourage them to revolt against their oppressors. Although the raid was stopped by U.S. Marines and Brown's goals were not realized, the attack polarized the nation as it had never been before. Once Brown's plans were made public and the thousands of weapons he had amassed were displayed during the trial, a collective shudder went through much of the South. New militia companies were organized throughout the southern states as men prepared to defend their families and their property from any similar raids in the future.

In that tense climate, there was little that the new Republican party could do to calm the fears that had been aroused by the acts of the abolitionists. The country was at a point in its history where it needed a decisive leader along the lines of George Washington or Thomas Jefferson, but instead it was led by the centrist Democrat James Buchanan, who was eager to please both the northern and southern wings of his party. This lack of a single political vision contributed to the imminent fracturing of the nation.

Once the Democratic party had split into various factions in 1860 and Abraham Lincoln, a Republican, was elected president, there was little that anyone could say or do to keep the southern states in the Union. Whereas the Democrats had more carefully positioned themselves with regard to the issue of slavery, the Republicans were the party most closely associated with the abolitionists. In addition, Lincoln had made a name for himself campaigning in an 1858 Illinois senatorial race against Stephen Douglas on an antislavery platform. On February 18, 1861, between Lincoln's election at the end of 1860 and his inauguration in early 1861, seven states seceded and formed the Confederacy. With the nation already beginning to

disintegrate, it was only a matter of time before a blow would be struck that would fatally separate the two increasingly hostile camps.

Lincoln's commitment to nonaggression toward the secessionist states—"the government will not assail you"—had created room for the rebel states to solidify their position politically. But before the southern leaders could take even one step in that direction, they faced a thorny problem. The Federal retention of Fort Sumter in Charleston, South Carolina, and Fort Pickens, near Pensacola, Florida (both southern territories), made it difficult for the Confederacy to be taken seriously by foreign powers—trading partners crucial to southern success. Understanding this, the new Confederacy formally requested the surrender of the garrison at Fort Sumter. That request was rejected, so on April 12, 1861, Brigadier General Pierre G.T. Beauregard ordered his guns to fire on the Federal outpost under Major Robert Anderson. The conflict between the states had begun.

President Lincoln immediately called for 75,000 volunteers from the remaining states with

which to "assail" the Confederacy. This action drove Virginia, North Carolina, Tennessee, and Arkansas—all of which for various reasons had wavered on the issue of secession—to join the Confederacy rather than raise arms against their sister states. With the addition of Virginia to the Confederacy, the capital moved from Montgomery, Alabama, to the more politically and economically visible Richmond, Virginia, and the South had a fighting chance of winning independence.

Meanwhile, the northern states responded to Lincoln's request for troops by sending 100,000 soldiers. But the task before the Federal government—to be the aggressor in a civil conflict—was formidable. Lincoln's hastily assembled army would be forced to attack and subjugate a proud, combative people—many of whom had relatives in the North—occupying an area nearly as large as western Europe. Local newspapers fanned the pride of the southerners into open resentment, and soon even southerners who had been opposed to secession began to join the newly formed regiments that were marching off to defend southern homes and families. Among their greatest fears was what might happen, economically and politically, should their long-suffering slaves be given any degree of civil rights.

It is the process that followed the opening acts of the national tragedy known as the American Civil War that is discussed in the sections of this work. Part One, *Crucial Land Battles*, clarifies the difference between the frequently bloody "transition" battles and the battles that produced the greatest political impact. (According to the definition set forth by strategist and military theorist Carl von Clausewitz, war is a continuation of policy by other means; logically, then, some battles had greater political impact than others.)

Again and again, the South fought invading northern forces to a stalemate in the eastern theater, while in the West, battle after crucial battle were won by the Union army. Perhaps the greatest military mind in the history of the nation, Robert E. Lee, made a great strategic error by defending his

This view of the Capitol was taken on July 11, 1863. Not far from this peaceful scene, one of the decisive engagements of the war, the battle of Gettysburg, was winding up. Despite the tumult of the war, construction on the Capitol continued, as evidenced by the scaffolding in place on the dome, which was completed in 1863. Thomas Crawford's bronze sculpture Freedom *was swung into place atop the dome on December 2 that year.*

On the evening of April 2, 1865, not long before this photograph was taken, the Confederate government abandoned Richmond, which had been the capital of the Confederacy for most of the war. In order to prevent the encroaching Union army from securing any matériel left behind, Lee gave orders to torch the city's warehouses. Soon, explosions rocked the city as ammunition caches caught on fire. When the Union forces rolled into town, they were shocked at the fires that were raging out of control as well as by the general devastation of the city, which had also suffered the ravages of looters. Amazingly, as this photograph shows, the Virginia State House survived the razing of the city with only minor damage.

home state at the expense of the Confederacy's western regions, which were crucial to the continued survival of the southern states. As Union General William T. Sherman said of Lee: "He never rose to the grand problem which involved a continent. . . . His Virginia was to him the world. . . . He stood at the front porch battling with the flames whilst the kitchen and the house were burning, sure in the end to consume the whole."

Part Two, *Naval Warfare*, is a comprehensive survey of the important contributions the U.S. Navy made toward the final Union victory. In rapid succession, new ships or converted civilian vessels were deployed to form an increasingly effective blockade of the Confederacy's ports, many of which were critical to the South's brisk trade with potential European sympathizers. Novel weapons such as rifled cannon and naval mines were utilized by the Confederate Navy in imagina-

tive ways against the blockading Federal squadrons, but the Union Navy ultimately had all the advantages, in particular the powerful support of the heavily industrialized North. Thus, the Union was able to land significant forces on the Confederate coast to neutralize much of the southern states' overseas trade, slowly strangling the emerging nation to death. New and highly mobile army-navy operations penetrated deeply—and nearly at will—into the interior of the Confederacy.

Part Three, *Daring Raiders*, takes a look at the effects that partisan warfare had on the outcome of this momentous conflict. Raids, ambushes, and scouting operations were the defining moments at critical points in the war, but these dramatic exploits are typically overlooked. Yet it was John Brown's raid on Harpers Ferry that effectively launched the Civil War, for instance; had he and his abolitionist sympathizers not whipped up the

fears and outrage of a nation, this internecine conflict might not have started so suddenly or been fought so fiercely by both sides. There are numerous such pivotal operations described in detail here, including the dramatic exploits of such dashing and heroic figures as Confederate ranger John Singleton Mosby, Federal raider William Averell, and train hijacker James Andrews, whose failed raid has become the stuff of legend.

These examinations of the Civil War will be useful to the general enthusiast as well as to more experienced students of the war. Innovative profile maps clearly illustrate the significance of complex terrain features, powerful photographs provide a window onto the realities of living and fighting in the nineteenth century, and insightful, detailed historical paintings re-create the flavor of what is to date the United States' most tragic conflict.

—David Phillips

PART ONE

CRUCIAL LAND BATTLES

The military tasks facing the Federal government in 1861 were considerable because the authority of the National Government had to be reasserted across a very large geographical area—the recently formed southern Confederacy. This enormous region could not be adequately garrisoned to hold the rebelling states in the Union and there were no major objectives that would produce a decisive impact on the morale of the new nation. This rebellion had begun with the seizure by the Confederacy of all of the territory it sought to dominate; in contrast to the complicated task facing Union leaders, the new political leadership of the South had only to defend its territorial boundaries to achieve its political goals.

Northern military strategists were left with no choice other than to establish the Federal government as the aggressor, with the aim of invading and occupying the defended territory of the seceding states. Politically, the role of aggressor was less than desirable: public support, which always runs high for the defense of home and hearth in any society, generally ebbs when a government undertakes an aggressive campaign.

Strategic goals were set for both sides soon after President Lincoln asked for seventy-five thousand volunteers to aid in the suppression of the rebellion. The border states—especially Virginia—refused to become a part of a campaign to attack other southern states

Confederate soldiers began to assemble in large numbers as the winds of war began to blow. Based on volunteer and militia units that had been formed following the John Brown attack at Harper's Ferry, volunteer groups such as this one (Virginia's First Regiment) were made up of men who had drilled and served together— a distinct advantage over their inexperienced Federal opponents.

and eventually seceded. The secession of Virginia was critical in the development of hostilities at this early juncture in what had been, up to then, a bloodless revolution.

Virginia was possibly the most influential state in the country at the time. Nearly one half of the presidents who had served had been sons of the Old Dominion. Many of the settlers who had migrated into newly developed regions in the territories that had become states had originally been Virginians. Proud of their state and its rich heritage, Virginians called the state the "Mother of Presidents" and the "Mother of States." Virginia had a large population, a diversified agricultural system, and levels of industry that could support sustained military operations conducted by large armies in the field. Once Virginia's people had cast their lot with the new Confederacy, the national planners of the South were quick to ensure the Mother of States remained there by moving the capital of the upstart nation to Richmond. Virginia was the key to the rebellion's survival—it gave the rebels the strength that shifted the political and military balance in their favor. Virginia gave the Confederacy a chance for military victory.

Once the stage was set for open warfare, the armies of the North were placed into the uncomfortable role of invader and occupier. The strategic task of the Confederacy was to be that of the defender. One side would invade and the other side would resist. The essentials for Civil War strategy had been set.

The initial strategic planning for the Federal government was conducted by General Winfield Scott, a seventy-five-year-old Virginian soldier who had learned his trade during the Napoleonic period. In the first half of the nineteenth century, however, military strategy had evolved, and up-to-date general principles of warfare had been developed. Younger officers in the national army were skilled in these new approaches to war, but Scott was in command. He began planning the upcoming campaign as if it were an assault on a single fortress, not an entire nation. The initial plan consisted of what was essentially an enormous siege of the Confederacy. Naval forces were ordered into blockade positions and plans were devel-

oped to move armies—once these were raised, trained, and equipped—along rivers in order to divide and seize the South one section at a time. Ridiculed initially, Scott's "Anaconda Plan" would gradually form the foundation of the Union's war strategy.

The most recent military experience of the time had been the Napoleonic wars, a series of quick campaigns by large forces against critical positions or smaller forces of the enemy that had resulted in quick, decisive victories. Northern politicians, concerned about the next elections, and younger officers, who were impatient to get into the field, desired a quick war; soon, the Federal army was prepared for offensive action instead of a prolonged siege. The war was beginning as an enormous chess game with the most valuable position on the chess board—in the eyes of the Union army—being Richmond, Virginia, the heart of the South. The strategy to be used was simple: march south approximately one hundred miles from Washington, D.C., capture Richmond, and end the Civil War. The Federal army would encounter the army of the Confederacy along the route as the southern forces attempted to dispute the passage, and a large, decisive battle—similar to those fought by Napoleon—would occur.

Most of the young officers in either army had received training in military tactics while in such military academies as West Point and the Virginia Military Institute. The curriculum included courses in tactics that were derived from the theories of war that had been developed by a Swiss-born officer who had served on the staff of one of Napoleon's marshalls. This man, Jomini, had studied the campaigns of historical leaders such as Napoleon and Caesar and developed practical guides to war planning, and to combat itself. In the United States, Henry W. Halleck, "Old Brains" of the pre-Civil War national army, had analyzed Jomini's writings and agreed that strategy was

Federal commanders General Henry W. Halleck (top), nicknamed "Old Brains" for his scholarly analyses of tactics, and General Winfield Scott (above, seated, with his staff around him) began to plan for offensive operations against the New Confederacy.

simply the art of directing masses to the decisive points of the enemy. Unfortunately, the Confederacy was large and there were no single, clearly defined points that were critical to the survival of the South. In addition, Jomini had identified approaches to be used by forces entering into combat. One of these, "interior lines," shortcuts that afforded rapid troop movement for attack or reinforcement, presented advantages to the army possessing them. In the eyes of Federal planners, the Confederacy had the advantage of interior lines because it was operating defensively while the Union forces were left with the less useful "exterior lines," which rendered the movement of troops to threatened points more time-consuming. The South could move from one threatened location to another after fighting defensive actions more quickly than the Union army could strengthen attacking columns across the exterior lines it was condemned to utilize. The southern defenders were in the best strategic position and there was little the North could do to change this fact.

Major General Halleck's view of national strategy combined with the Jominian requirement for the maintenance of interior lines of communication produced the planning for the first major Federal offensive of the Civil War. The basic principles of war were closely followed as Brigadier General Irvin McDowell concentrated his force of thirty-five thousand men at Washington, D.C. He and the troops then began to move in the direction of Richmond, a decisive point as defined by their most current theory. The planned march of the Union's concentrated force would give them the advantage of the coveted interior lines while forcing their opponents to move against them along exterior lines.

Unfortunately for the inexperienced Federal strategists, a combination of Confederate intelligence operations, railroads that permitted the rapid movement of rebel troops along those exterior lines, and inexperienced Union units and commanders led to a military and political disaster near Manassas, Virginia, on July 21, 1861. This left the Eastern theater of operations in a stalemate from which it was slow to recover. Meanwhile, Union forces were beginning to move aggressively in the West.

The battle fought at Manassas in 1861, Bull Run, was very important and quite bloody, but like most of the Civil War's battles it was not crucial to the outcome of the war itself. Wars are fought for the impact they have on the politics of either side, and the battles that have the most political impact are the most decisive. Large, complex, and violent battles were frequently fought during the course of the Civil War as each army sought to force the other to move into less desirable terrain or to destroy the enemy. These battles, lacking a strong political impact, are more accurately described as "transition battles," during which the armies maneuvered to locate critical points where a future defeat of the enemy would create substantial political damage.

The Confederacy was able to prevail in many of the early transition battles—Bull Run, Wilson's Creek, and Lexington—but Federal forces would ultimately prove the usefulness of Scott's original strategy of utilizing combined army and naval operations under an aggressive commander at Fort Donelson. A second crucial battle would result in a tactical standoff—but a political victory—at Antietam as large armies were assembled and northern manufacturing capabilities were fully mobilized for a long war.

Largely unprepared for the details of a drawn-out conflict, men from both sides of the Mason-Dixon suffered from the effects of the elements during the winters. Here, troops move to bivouac positions in Sibley tents.

Military academies such as West Point in the North and Virginia's Military Institute in the South provided young officers for the new armies. These West Point cadets are graduating into careers that would see differing degrees of glory, death, and destruction.

chapter 1

FORT DONELSON
A Disastrous Blow

Despite the obvious stalemate that developed along hostile lines on the eastern front, Union military operations in the west were far more successful. Winfield Scott, the commanding general of the United States Army in 1861, had proposed to place the entire Confederacy under siege, a gigantic maneuver designed to prevent the export of cotton, which was a principal means by which the rebels raised the funds needed to import arms and war materials. Scott also planned to use Union naval power along southern rivers to penetrate deeply into the interior of the Confederacy and slowly dismember it. Union politicians and the general population in the North, however, were unwilling to agree to a slow, methodical strategy; instead they pressed for rapid victories.

Scott yielded to this political pressure and agreed to attack Richmond in a plan that resulted in the major military and political defeat at Bull Run. This loss and the timidity of George McClellan—the victor in relatively minor, but highly publicized, victories in western Virginia—who replaced the aging Scott, led directly to the stalemate of 1861.

Federal forces in the Mississippi Valley, however, were soon to begin operations against Confederate defenders in the region. Much as Scott had planned, Union naval forces, combined with large Federal military units, began to move along the navigable rivers that extended deep into the Confederacy. The Tennessee River, in particular, offered great tactical advantages to the invaders: it was large, navigable by large steamers, and presented a virtual highway into the undefended rear areas of Confederate forces in both Kentucky and Tennessee. Once this river system was securely held, Union forces could use it as a vast line of communications to deliver supplies and reinforcements as attackers moved toward either the Mississippi River or to the east to threaten Richmond, the newly established Confederate capital.

"[I felt that] it would be wrong to subject the army to a virtual massacre, when no good could result from the sacrifice, and that the general officers owed it to their men, when further resistance was unavailing, to obtain the best terms of capitulation for them."

—General Simon Bolivar Buckner

Previous Confederate defensive measures along the Mississippi system were designed to prevent powerful Union flotillas from accomplishing the much-desired military goal of splitting the enemy (the Confederacy) into two parts. The Confederacy built powerful fortresses at such strategic points as Island Number Ten, Memphis, and Vicksburg to impede any Federal attempts to attack down the Mississippi from the base of operations at St. Louis. In their rush to defend the obvious route of attack, however, Confederate planners neglected the possibility of invasion along the smaller Tennessee and Cumberland rivers.

It was late in November 1861 when serious attention was given to these rivers by both sides. One defensive position, Fort Henry, was hastily constructed on the right bank of the Tennessee River just to the south of Tennessee's boundary with Kentucky. A second, larger defensive position, Fort Donelson, was just as quickly built at a location on the Cumberland River twelve miles away from Fort Henry. Together, these two fortresses constituted the primary Confederate defenses in the region.

Fort Henry was the first to feel the pressure of the Federal offensive. Naval forces—consisting of newly developed ironclad vessels equipped with heavy guns—moved against Fort Henry and managed to force the small garrison to surrender (without the use of infantry support) on February 6, 1861. Most of the defending garrison, however, escaped capture and retreated to reinforce Fort Donelson.

Federal vessels were soon able to graphically demonstrate the military advantage they had gained on the river systems. Three gun-

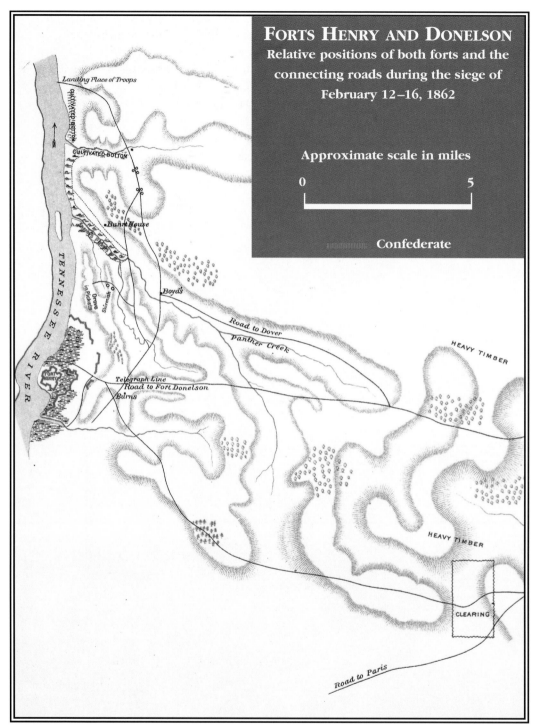

FORTS HENRY AND DONELSON
Relative positions of both forts and the connecting roads during the siege of February 12–16, 1862

Approximate scale in miles

0   5

Confederate

Fort Henry and Fort Donelson were hastily constructed as Confederate strategic planners began to realize that combined Federal naval and army operations could penetrate deeply into rebel territory on the rivers. Boats could move fresh Union troops to new attacking points more quickly than the Confederates could march to oppose them.

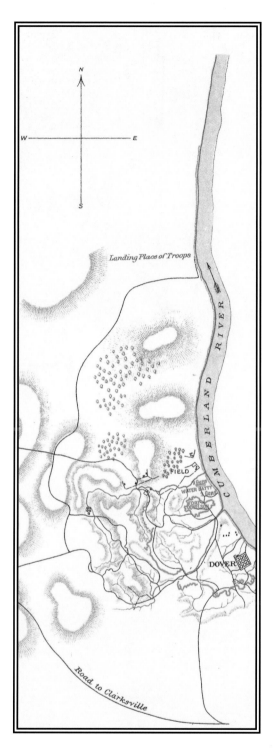

boats moved up the newly opened Tennessee River, past the now-occupied Fort Henry, attacked a vital railroad, destroyed Confederate shipping on the river, and penetrated into Alabama—a state that lay against the Gulf of Mexico. This demonstration showed the danger the defenders were facing as the attacking Federal forces began to gain more and more momentum.

General Albert Sidney Johnston, the Confederacy's regional commander, was placed in an extremely vulnerable position, what with the ability of the Federal navy to conduct unimpeded operations along the Tennessee River, as illustrated by the loss of Fort Henry. There were no defensive positions available to him in Tennessee that Federal forces could not simply bypass to land an army in the defender's rear and then supply them by the river. His defensive line had been easily broken at Fort Henry, and the gathering Union forces could now attack Johnston's remaining forces in Kentucky—at Bowling Green or Columbus—at their leisure. Johnston knew that disaster had

struck and that he must evacuate the forces under his command to new positions below the Tennessee River in Alabama.

The military situation of the Confederate army was complicated by the recent arrival of a new subordinate for Johnston, General P.T.G. Beauregard, the man who had commanded forces at Fort Sumter at Bull Run. The touchy, vain general had quarreled with Confederate President Jefferson Davis and had been transferred to the west. Johnston met with Beauregard in Bowling Green on February 7, 1861, the day after the disaster at Fort Henry. They agreed that there were few options to be considered. First, they could concentrate all of their available forces at Fort Donelson in an attempt to crush the army of Grant, the new fighting general in the Union army. Once this was accomplished, they could shift forces to deal with Buell's army in Kentucky, a separate force that was larger than Johnston's entire army. Second, they could leave a small garrison at Fort Donelson in order to delay the pending attack by Grant as the entire Confederate

Ironclad gunboats, which were relatively new innovations of military engineering, began to appear in large numbers on western rivers. These mobile fortresses could deliver enormous fire power against Confederate defenses and were decisive elements of the Federal attack at Fort Henry.

Defiant Confederate soldiers confidently moved into positions to resist attacks by large numbers of Union troops. Although the Confederate troops were successful in early transition battles, the Union Army's superior numbers and ready access to military supplies and equipment led to a Confederate defeat at Fort Donelson.

General P.G.T. Beauregard was the Confederate commander at Charleston, South Carolina, and ordered the first volley fired in the war, but he proved to be ineffective in the western theater.

army was withdrawn. Remaining in their current location as large Federal armies approached was not an alternative to be considered. The loss of Fort Henry left the Confederate army's lines penetrated and their forces vulnerable.

Curiously, Johnston pursued neither of these options. He was afraid to concentrate his units against Grant because any losses would devastate the entire Confederacy in the West. Rather than assign an expendable rear guard to delay Grant at Fort Donelson, he decided to commit additional troops in an attempt to hold Fort Donelson, a position he feared could be captured by gunboats alone (as had happened at Fort Henry). By the time Grant had closed off the escape route from the fort, Johnston had managed to send

General John B. Floyd, a militarily illiterate former governor of Virginia, was placed in command at Fort Donelson by virtue of his seniority. Under indictment in the North for allegations of fraud while serving in the Buchanan administration, Floyd greatly feared capture by the Federal army.

A former lawyer and a greatly overconfident soldier, General Gideon Pillow became second-in-command at the doomed fortress. He had served in the Mexican War, but Pillow knew little about the art of land warfare.

Like the Confederates, the Federal army at Fort Donelson was burdened with politicians serving as generals. General John A. McClernand would be the first to feel the wrath of the trapped Confederates as they attempted a breakout. Sherman called McClernand, an ambitious person, "the meanest man we had in the West."

nearly one third of his available strength to Donelson's defense.

Johnston's total force of forty-five thousand men had several effective commanders to lead it, but a curious decision was made as to the command at Fort Donelson. Beauregard was an experienced combat commander who was available for command duty, but he was sent to manage the withdrawal from Columbus, Kentucky. Major General Hardee, a West Point graduate, was already in command at Bowling Green, but Johnston nevertheless went there to assist him with the retreat from Kentucky rather than seeing to it that one of them went to Donelson.

Instead, Johnston allowed three brigadier generals to command within the Confederate fortress rather than assign a major general to

manage them. Senior among these was John B. Floyd, recently Secretary of War in the Buchanan administration and a former governor of Virginia. Floyd, totally untrained as a military officer, had recently demonstrated his level of military incompetence by mismanaging a campaign against William S. Rosecrans in western Virginia, a series of minor battles and retreats described by Henry Heth as a "comic opera" campaign. This Confederate loss led directly to the creation of a new Union state, West Virginia, in 1863 and was a major political defeat for the efforts of the South to gain foreign recognition. Having been accused of corruption while serving as Secretary of War, Floyd feared indictment, trial, and the "iron cage" in which the Federal army had promised to

display him, if he were captured. This lackluster brigadier general was senior to the other two generals by virtue of the date he had been commissioned—thus, Floyd was in command at Fort Donelson.

Second in seniority at Fort Donelson was Gideon Pillow, a Mexican War veteran, Tennessee lawyer, and politician. Like Floyd, Pillow was overconfident and poorly suited for command. His commission date gave him the position of second-in-command.

Unfortunately for the officers and men at the doomed fort, the best qualified of the brigadier generals, Simon Bolivar Buckner, was the lowest-ranking brigadier general on hand. He was a West Point graduate—and a personal friend of Grant—who had left the prewar National army to manage his wife's extensive estate in Kentucky. While he was the best of the lot, Buckner had been the last to receive his commission. Their respective dates of rank set the command structure: Floyd was commander of the fort; Pillow, deputy commander; and Buckner, commander of his own brigade.

The fortress was considerably more inspiring than its commanders. Extensive earthworks curved back to rest one flank on the river while the northern end of the works was protected by swamps and a flooded stream. Large artillery positions sited on a high bluff completed the defenses.

Attackers would be moving against Fort Donelson soon. General Grant began to move fifteen thousand men from Fort Henry on February 12, 1862. Unseasonably warm weather induced the troops to discard both blankets and overcoats in the springlike weather. Thus, the Union forces moved quickly, covering the twelve-mile march in a single day, and began investing the Confederate fort by dusk. The perimeter of the Union attackers was large, however, and a large gap was left on the far right of the line. Grant immediately sent for reinforcements that had been left behind to garrison Fort Henry under the command of Brigadier General Lew Wallace. This group of two thousand men was soon marching to close the opening near the river.

Late in the afternoon, the weather began to change dramatically. The springlike conditions of the morning were replaced by sleet as temperatures dropped to 10 degrees Fahrenheit. The soldiers of both sides began to experience what they would later describe as the worst night of the war. Both sides had deployed sharpshooters, and any attempt to build fires attracted bullets. Without fire, all of the soldiers began to feel the effects of the bitter cold.

On February 13, one of Grant's untrained political-appointee brigadier generals, John

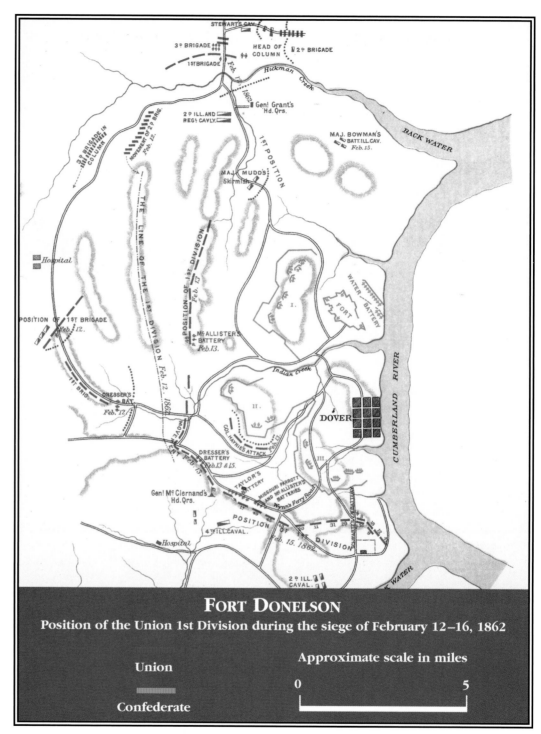

FORT DONELSON
Position of the Union 1st Division during the siege of February 12–16, 1862

Union

Confederate

Approximate scale in miles

0   5

Fort Donelson became a trap for twelve thousand to fifteen thousand soldiers after the breakout attempt of February 12, 1862, failed. Once General Lew Wallace closed off the escape route, the garrison was left with only one option: surrender. Terribly cold weather complicated operations and only a few Confederates escaped capture.

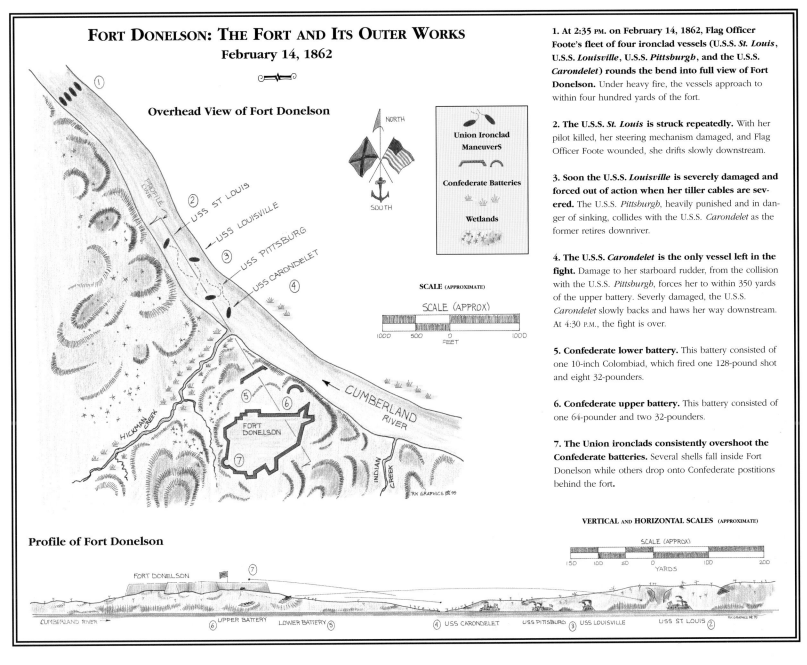

FORT DONELSON: THE FORT AND ITS OUTER WORKS
February 14, 1862

Overhead View of Fort Donelson

NORTH

SOUTH

Union Ironclad Maneuvers

Confederate Batteries

Wetlands

PROFILE LINE

USS ST LOUIS

USS LOUISVILLE

USS PITTSBURG

USS CARONDELET

CUMBERLAND RIVER

HICKMAN CREEK

FORT DONELSON

INDIAN CREEK

RK GRAPHICS BX 99

SCALE (APPROXIMATE)

SCALE (APPROX)

1000 500 0 1000
FEET

1. At 2:35 PM. on February 14, 1862, Flag Officer Foote's fleet of four ironclad vessels (U.S.S. *St. Louis*, U.S.S. *Louisville*, U.S.S. *Pittsburgh*, and the U.S.S. *Carondelet*) rounds the bend into full view of Fort Donelson. Under heavy fire, the vessels approach to within four hundred yards of the fort.

2. The U.S.S. *St. Louis* is struck repeatedly. With her pilot killed, her steering mechanism damaged, and Flag Officer Foote wounded, she drifts slowly downstream.

3. Soon the U.S.S. *Louisville* is severely damaged and forced out of action when her tiller cables are severed. The U.S.S. *Pittsburgh*, heavily punished and in danger of sinking, collides with the U.S.S. *Carondelet* as the former retires downriver.

4. The U.S.S. *Carondelet* is the only vessel left in the fight. Damage to her starboard rudder, from the collision with the U.S.S. *Pittsburgh*, forces her to within 350 yards of the upper battery. Severly damaged, the U.S.S. *Carondelet* slowly backs and haws her way downstream. At 4:30 P.M., the fight is over.

5. Confederate lower battery. This battery consisted of one 10-inch Colombiad, which fired one 128-pound shot and eight 32-pounders.

6. Confederate upper battery. This battery consisted of one 64-pounder and two 32-pounders.

7. The Union ironclads consistently overshoot the Confederate batteries. Several shells fall inside Fort Donelson while others drop onto Confederate postitions behind the fort.

VERTICAL AND HORIZONTAL SCALES (APPROXIMATE)

SCALE (APPROX)

150 100 50 0 100 200
YARDS

Profile of Fort Donelson

FORT DONELSON

CUMBERLAND RIVER

UPPER BATTERY LOWER BATTERY USS CARONDELET USS PITTSBURG USS LOUISVILLE USS ST LOUIS

RK GRAPHICS HE 99

McClernand, ordered an unauthorized attack against some Confederate gun positions that was repulsed with heavy casualties. Those soldiers who had thought war to be an adventure looked on in horror as some of McClernand's wounded burned to death in brush fires that had been ignited by cannon fire.

On the morning of February 14, Grant was reinforced by Andrew Foote's gunboats and an additional ten thousand men sent by General Halleck in St. Louis. Upon the troops' arrival, Grant immediately ordered attack plans to be made, illustrating how different he was from the generals in the East.

Eastern generals saw the maneuvering of their troops as the primary tactic to force the Confederates into positions where they would have to retreat—allowing the Union troops to capture their objectives—or be destroyed (in much the same way as Napoleon had defeated his enemies in the battles they had studied at West Point). These generals had studied the writings of the Swiss-born strategist, Jomini, and many even carried the master tactician's books with them in the field.

Grant was different. Although he had never read the books of Clausewitz, the Prussian strategist and rival of Jomini—Clausewitz's books were translated into English long after the end of the Civil War—there were large numbers of former German officers in Grant's army who would have known about Clausewitz's aggresive theories of strategy. These theories may have been discussed at some point, as some of Clausewitz's philosophy of combat was apparent in Grant's moves. If this was not the case, Grant knew instinctively that regardless of the central feature of the enemy's power—felt to be the city of Richmond in the East—the defeat and destruction of the enemy's fighting forces is the best way to begin any campaign. Eastern generals chose maneuver and countermaneuver as a means to gain a tactical advantage, but Grant generally chose to attack the enemy's fighting capability when he encountered it.

Flag Officer Foote was fresh from his magnificent victory at Fort Henry and Grant ordered him to move against Fort Donelson. Foote had moved his ironclad boats close to the low water–level batteries at Fort Henry and battered them with heavy cannon until they surrendered. His mobile, iron-shielded batteries had proved to be superior to the earthen, stationary guns at Fort Henry; not surprisingly, Foote attempted to repeat this successful tactic against Fort Donelson. He moved his vessels close to the fort as Grant closed the ring of Federal regiments around the besieged Confederates.

Foote moved his ships to within four hundred yards of the twelve large-bore Confederate guns facing him. Shortly after-

Service aboard the ironclad vessels was not without risk. Any exploding shell that penetrated the gunboats' armor plating would deliver deadly, ricocheting fragments throughout the open interior.

ward, the river began to ring like a blacksmith's forge as solid shot from the fort ripped off iron plating and pierced turrets; a 128-pound shot smashed the huge anchor of the *Carondelet*. Several of the Federal vessels in the small flotilla lost their steering control, crashed into one another, and drifted helplessly away from the fort as the totally unharmed Confederate gunners cheered.

Foote made an error in repeating the tactics he had used at Fort Henry: the gun positions he now faced were placed high on a bluff and he had to elevate his guns to hit these targets. Most of his shots passed over their targets, doing no harm until they fell into the Confederate trenches opposing Grant's ground forces.

This initial round in the battle had gone to the Confederates, but there was little, if any, joy at Floyd's headquarters. The three brigadier generals—Floyd, Pillow, and Buckner—were fully aware by this time that they were caught in a trap that would cost

Indiana provided General Lew Wallace for Federal service. His prompt action at Fort Donelson prevented the escape of the entire Confederate garrison. Later, he would write the popular novel Ben Hur.

them their army if they did not get out quickly. The gunboats would undoubtedly return. The lesson of Fort Henry was still fresh in their minds and they knew it was unlikely that Foote would repeat the error he had just made.

Floyd, Pillow, and Buckner were also aware that Johnston had completed his retreat from Kentucky, freeing them from their rear guard responsibilities at Donelson. They began to plan a breakout.

Their plan was bold and good: Pillow would concentrate the bulk of his forces on the Confederate left while Buckner shifted his regiments toward the center of the line to support Pillow's surprise blow against the thinly held Federal right, near the river where McClernand's troops had moved. Each of the attacking regiments was ordered to carry three days' rations in their haversacks—sufficient food to carry them through the entire attack and escape attempt.

The terrible weather, freezing cold, and howling wind masked Confederate preparations for the surprise attack. Federal pickets and nearby sharpshooters, secure in their knowledge that the siege of Fort Donelson had begun, huddled behind what protection from the elements they could find. They knew they had superior numbers, support from naval batteries, and a fighting commander who was unlikely to relinquish the initiative. They were sure that they would be the attackers when the time came.

Grant left his headquarters before dawn to coordinate his next moves with Foote, now suffering from a wound he had received during the earlier attack against Fort Donelson's batteries. As he left his headquarters that morning, Grant issued orders for all of his subordinate commanders to hold their current positions, preventing any repetition of the unauthorized attack ordered by McClernand on February 13. None of the Federal officers suspected a Confederate

Ironclad gunboats and open mortar boats were capable of delivering a tremendous bombardment against Confederate shore defenses.

assault against them and Grant left the field for his conference with Foote without designating an acting commander in his absence.

Shortly after Grant departed, Pillow ordered his regiments to move out of their trenches. Colonel Baldwin's brigade assumed lead positions in the assault, but his men quickly bogged down as they came into contact with McClernand's men. While they had struck hard at McClernand's right, where the Federal lines were most thinly held, the Union soldiers were not caught sleeping. Most had spent a sleepless night in the terrible cold and were in the act of kindling fires that would not attract the bullets of sharpshooters in the daylight when Baldwin's men struck. Their initial fire stopped Baldwin, but his reserve brigade, composed of recently arrived Virginians under Colonel John McCausland, were rushed forward. These hardy men, fresh from the mountain campaigns in western Virginia, attacked ferociously, and heavy fighting erupted around

the Virginians. The cavalrymen of tough Nathan Bedford Forrest secured the left flank of the attackers and McClernand's men were forced back nearly two miles. The Virginians and Forrest's cavalry had broken through the Federal encirclement, secured the main road, and could now escape. The cost in casualties, however, was high on both sides.

McClernand's men fought until their ammunition began to run out. Panicked and repeated messages were sent for reinforcements, but Grant was still away from headquarters. The meeting with Foote to coordinate their next move had temporarily removed Grant from the scene, and lacking an acting commander, the Union officers at headquarters were unable to make a decision in response to the disaster facing them.

Brigadier General Lew Wallace acted on his own authority to release one of his brigades to go to the assistance of the beleaguered McClernand. Errors were made in the confusion and some of Wallace's men accidentally fired into one of McClernand's retreating regiments, a sorely pressed unit that was fighting hard as it moved under pressure to the rear.

Grant returned to the field at approximately 1 P.M. and quickly took decisive action. (It was at this point in the Civil War that Grant demonstrated his great tenacity and decisiveness, which would prove to be precisely the qualities in a commander for which Lincoln would search in 1864.) Most of the commanders in the Union army at this time would have looked at the disaster facing them and would have pulled their men back into a general withdrawal in this lost battle. Grant quickly collected information regarding the enemy's activities and preparations for battle as he just as rapidly ordered troops forward to recapture the lost positions on the right of the Federal line.

After being advised that captured Confederate soldiers were carrying three days' rations with them, he knew the aim of his opponent was not to defeat the Union army in decisive battle but to escape. Grant knew that the ferocity of the attack meant the Confederates had had to shift large numbers of the men from within the defending earthworks into attack formations, so Grant ordered Brigadier General C.F. Smith to attack the fortress' outer works.

Grant's intuition, decisiveness, and ability as a field commander were shortly to receive some much needed assistance from an unlikely source: General Pillow, who ordered the attacking regiments to return to the doomed fort. The trained soldier among Donelson's brigadiers, Buckner, refused to comply with Pillow's order. The militarily illiterate commander, Floyd, heard Buckner's complaint, and agreed to continue with the breakout attempt, but just as quickly reversed himself after a short discussion with the equally incompetent Pillow. As a result of this confrontation, the attackers gave up the field they had captured at so great a cost and returned to the trenches.

As the Confederates withdrew, Union troops followed closely and were soon in their old positions, which had been lost just that morning. Smith's Union regiments followed Grant's order to the letter as they smashed into the trench line on the Confederate left as the rebels retreated; severe fighting to control the breached defenses began. Buckner attempted to expel Smith's men, but Union artillery had been placed into positions from which they could fire on most of the Confederate soldiers who were counterattacking. With General Smith's men occupying the outer works it became obvious to the three generals that the fort could not be defended.

Floyd, Pillow, and Buckner met a second time at their headquarters to debate their next move. Floyd, untrained and inexperienced, was floundering as a commander just as he had in western Virginia the previous fall and winter. Pillow was equally useless, but both agreed with Buckner that the men lacked the strength to fight another battle.

They called the fort's cavalry commander, Nathan Bedford Forrest, who was surprised that surrender was being discussed. His scouts had located an unguarded (but flooded) road over which the entire garrison could escape. The surrender option was selected, however, as the generals felt that

The end was sealed for the Confederates at Fort Donelson as General Smith's men forced their way into the trenches. Smith shouted, "You volunteered to be killed for love of country, and now you can be!" as his men stormed the Confederate defenses.

the men could not survive a march through the deep and freezing waters. Only the choice of commander for the surrender ceremony remained to be decided.

Floyd, the former Secretary of War, had been charged with various criminal actions while in office. Thus, he feared capture, trial, and imprisonment; in fact, he had been the first officer to withdraw from a similar trap at Camp Gauley following a battle with Rosecrans the previous September. He had also led a rapid retreat from a well-planned, but poorly executed Federal trap at Cotton Hill in November. Floyd was excellent in retreat and decided to relinquish command to Pillow.

Pillow, arrogantly overestimating his value to the Confederate war effort, felt the entire Confederacy would suffer a disaster if he were captured. He immediately relinquished command and crossed the Cumberland River in a skiff. Relatively useless, Pillow was the only Confederate officer held in open contempt by Grant.

Buckner, the soldier-officer, would remain in the fort to share the fate of the men under his command. He called for a messenger to carry a message to his old friend, Grant. Meanwhile, Floyd requested permission to escape, once again, from Federal prison—with his Virginian regiments this time. Buckner assented, but with the condition that the escape be completed before the terms of surrender were accepted.

Forrest returned to his cavalry regiment and collected his men. They were going to escape from the doomed fort or die in the attempt. They rode out on the flooded road to safety and many of the cavalrymen carried an infantryman behind him.

Floyd moved his men, two regiments of Virginians and the 20th Mississippi, a regiment placed under his command, to the river bank. Two steamers were approaching the landing at Fort Donelson with loads of

Captain Edward McAllister's Illinois battery moved into positions from where they could fire upon a Confederate artillery position. Conveniently, the recoil from firing these guns threw the gunners and their weapons out of sight of their Confederate targets. McAllister's men fired, recoiled into safety, and then fired again until their opponents' guns were silent.

corn—Floyd would commandeer the two boats and escape with his men. He ordered the men of the Mississippi regiment to secure the boat landing and form a cordon to hold back the deserters and stragglers who were expected to attempt to board the boats in their haste to escape the Union prisons. The men of the 20th Mississippi were also told to hold their positions until ordered to board the boats.

The Mississippians did their duty. Floyd and his Virginia regiments marched aboard the river boats and then left the Mississippi regiment to its fate. Floyd and Pillow escaped the fury of Grant, but they didn't do quite as well with Jefferson Davis, recently a United States Senator from Mississippi. Both were quickly relieved from command for their actions in escaping the fort; only Floyd would receive a

minor command of troops again. Davis never forgave them for their actions at Fort Donelson.

Grant received the note from Buckner, a friend who had loaned him money when Grant had resigned from active service, and quickly considered terms that could be given. After a hasty conference with General Smith, Grant wrote:

Sir;

Yours of this date, proposing armistice and appointment of commissioners to settle terms of capitulation, is just received. No terms except unconditional and immediate surrender can be accepted. I propose to move immediately upon your works.

I am, sir, very respectfully, your obedient servant,

U.S. Grant

Buckner accepted Grant's "ungenerous" terms and was having a sparse breakfast with Lew Wallace when Grant arrived at the Confederate headquarters to accept the final surrender of Fort Donelson.

This was a terrible loss for the Confederates to endure. Grant had captured at least twelve thousand men (and probably more), twenty thousand stand of arms (individual weapons and all associated equipment for each weapon), forty-eight pieces of artillery, the seventeen heavy guns that had held off Foote's gun boats, and large quantities of stores. The Confederates lost over 450 men killed and fifteen hundred wounded against slightly heavier Union losses in killed (five hundred) and wounded (twenty-one hundred).

Unfortunately for the Southern cause, the cost of their loss at Fort Donelson was far greater than the numbers might suggest. The fall of the fort opened the way south into the heartland of the Confederacy and allowed the Union forces to continue with the strategy of splitting the Confederacy along the Mississippi River. More seriously and immediate, however, was the approach of a Federal army at Nashville. As the Confederates evacuated Bowling Green, General Don Carlos Buell moved south from Louisville toward strategically important Nashville. The retreating Confederate army moved through Nashville toward new defensive positions south of the Tennessee River.

Johnston evacuated Nashville and left Floyd in charge temporarily as chaos developed among the city's inhabitants. Soon, Nathan Bedford Forrest arrived and took charge of security: military supplies were saved from looters, food was sent south for the retreating army, and ordinance machinery used in the manufacture of cannon was recovered and also sent south.

Johnston chose to concentrate his forces at Corinth, Mississippi, which bordered precariously close to the Gulf Coast. He could

not afford to retreat any farther because important rail lines at Corinth connected vital areas of the Confederacy. Johnston knew that Corinth would become the next critical target of the Federal offensive and he began to assemble forces. There were approximately forty thousand men in Johnston's army by April 1862, when the western Confederates were planning to make their surprise move.

Grant was the man of the hour throughout the North. He became "Unconditional Surrender" Grant in the newspapers, and reports that he went into battle with his cigar led to the delivery of massive amounts of cigars from his admirers. He was very popular at the time—with everyone except General Henry Wager Halleck. Fort Donelson was the largest battle fought in the western theater up to that point, and Grant was shortly

promoted to second-in-command, under Halleck, in the western region.

Grant had ranked low in his class at West Point and claimed little understanding of the literature of war. Halleck, "Old Brains" of the prewar National army, viewed himself as an intellectual and would not have been attracted to an officer who lacked similar intellectual qualities. Halleck actually appears to have been jealous of Grant's successes and may have attempted to have kept Grant under wraps as his second-in-command. This had little lasting effect, however, because Grant won battles and had proven the strategy of Winfield Scott—assemble a large army, support it with naval forces, and gradually disassemble the Confederacy—to be sound.

Grant was different from most of his contemporaries, who viewed the Civil War as

Nathan Bedford Forrest, a legendary Confederate calvary commander, led his troops out of Fort Donelson. Refusing to surrender, he and his men rode through deep water and intense cold to make their escape.

a series of battles to be won or lost. He was able to rise above the rest of them, see battles as part of a long series of events, and make the outcome of each individual event—win, lose, or draw—serve his strategy equally well. Here was a general who knew how to fight a modern war, could accept the huge losses of men that resulted from the use of new technologies, and employed new strategies that were being developed to replace those that had been prevalent during Napoleon's wars in Europe. More importantly, Lincoln knew he was there and took notice of the new commander and his men in the West.

The impact of the loss of Fort Donelson on the Confederacy was tremendous. Kentucky and territory from which attacks into the North—Ohio, Indiana, and Illinois—could be either threatened or conducted was lost. Tennessee, with its large agricultural capacity and manufacturing capability, was now denied to the South. One of the most strategically positioned of the border states on the western flank, Missouri, was threatened. The Federal forces had proven that their navy could operate successfully on the inland waters: they could attack land positions with heavy guns and deliver battle-ready assault troops and all the necessary supplies, which were being amply produced in the industrial centers of the rapidly mobilizing North.

The new Confederate defensive line was set in the state of Mississippi, resting on the Gulf of Mexico, because Federal gunboats were threatening to split the Confederacy along the Mississippi River. In fact, naval forces were converging from two directions: David G. Farragut's naval squadron was moving north toward the mouth of the Mississippi River and New Orleans, the Confederacy's largest city and principal port, as other gunboats moved downstream to test the South's defenses at Island Number Ten, a fortified position on the Mississippi River.

Albert Sidney Johnston collected all available men in the vicinity to fortify the new defensive line in northern Mississippi as Grant moved forward, waiting for Buell to arrive at Shiloh, Tennessee. Hoping to be able to destroy Grant's army before the arrival of Buell, Johnston and Beauregard attacked the surprised Federal army on April 6. The Union army was steadily driven back,

"The blow [Fort Donelson] was most disastrous and almost without remedy."

—*General Albert Sidney Johnston*

but Johnston was killed and Beauregard suspended active operations a short time afterward. Buell arrived with twenty-five thousand reinforcements and on the following morning Grant regained all of the ground he had lost. The battle was inconclusive, but the Confederates again withdrew to Corinth, Mississippi, and were driven from there on May 30. The Union army now controlled much of Tennessee River, and the Mississippi River, as far downstream as Memphis.

Farragut penetrated the Confederate defenses at the mouth of the river and General Benjamin Butler occupied New Orleans on May 1 as Grant began to plan for operations against the last Confederate stronghold on the Mississippi: Vicksburg.

The taking of Fort Donelson had been the key that unlocked this great series of tactical successes and was one of the most crucial battles of the Civil War.

Federal naval forces continued to press against Confederate strong points. Farragut's squadron soon moved against New Orleans to allow Union troops under General Ben Butler to occupy the city.

chapter 2

PEA RIDGE
Peace for Missouri

"I held the opinion that the immediate possession of the valley of the Mississippi River would control the result of the war. Who held the Mississippi would hold the country by the heart."

—General John C. Fremont

A future general, William Tecumseh Sherman had come to the same conclusion as many others regarding the military importance of the rivers of the Midwest. He wrote to his brother, John, then an Ohio senator: "Whatever nation gets the control of the Ohio, Mississippi, and Missouri Rivers will control the continent." These western rivers had great length, flowed generally north to south, and reached deep into the heartland of the Confederacy.

The winner in the west would be the side that could control the rivers, but the territories gained through river-borne conquests were really the important strategic targets. The balance of power between the two sides depended on the allegiance or control of two important border states. Kentucky and Missouri were the only slave states beyond the Appalachian Mountains that had not chosen sides, and they could go either way. The outcome of their eventual choice was critical to the balance of power.

The population of either of these two wavering states was larger than any Confederate state except Virginia, and either would greatly increase the military manpower of the South. Their true importance, however, was in their strategic location on the crucial river systems: Kentucky's location commanded most of the Ohio River's drainage, but Missouri was the real prize for North or South to claim.

Missouri dominated the region. If it were a Confederate state, troops from there could block or threaten the Union's major routes between the western states and could threaten southern Illinois. Missouri also controlled a large portion of the Mississippi River, including the vital junction with the Ohio River at Cairo. Clearly, Missouri was a vital strategic prize, and both North and South moved to gain control early in the war.

Neither the Unionists nor Secessionists had any special advantage in Missouri. Many slaveholders hoped to avoid war, and

PAGE 35: *The intense fighting at Pea Ridge allowed the Union to retain control of the state of Missouri. More important to the longterm military success in the west was the fact that the Union had control of most of the vital Mississippi River. ABOVE: Republican Congressman Frank P. Blair, the son of a trusted friend of Andrew Jackson, was a commander of Unionist Home Guards. Here, Blair (center) and his staff are planning operations against the secessionists.*

Southern sentiment was greatly offset by the recent arrival of thousands of Germanic immigrants who left their homes in Europe after the failure of the revolutions of 1848, which had been intended to establish a constitutional government in a unified country. These liberal refugees had recently taken an oath of allegiance to their adopted country, the United States, and there was little about the Confederacy that attracted them.

When the Unionists' leader, Frank P. Blair, Jr., a Republican congressman from St. Louis and the brother of Lincoln's Postmaster General, learned of a Secessionist plot to seize the St. Louis Arsenal, he asked for troops to form a guard. Washington sent eighty men under the command of a tough regular army captain, Nathaniel Lyon, from Fort Riley, Kansas. Blair arranged for Lyon to enlist a large Home Guard to maintain order. Soon the Home Guard came into conflict with the pro-Confederate state militiamen.

On May 10, 1861, Lyon and his Home Guards surrounded the militia camp, disarmed the Confederate sympathizers, and marched them through the streets of the city as a form of public humiliation. Tempers were hot and the Home Guard, primarily German immigrants, were soon being cursed by onlookers. Stones were thrown and someone fired a pistol into the German Home Guard formations. The Home Guard returned the fire. As civilians and innocent onlookers began to fall, the situation became a riot during which twenty-eight civilians lost their lives. This riot and the deaths of the civilians galvanized the citizens of Missouri as perhaps nothing else could have done. All thoughts of remaining neutral were forgotten by the time the funerals were over.

As news of the "massacres" in St. Louis spread, recruits for the Confederacy began pouring into camps and training centers. Command of these new soldiers was given to Sterling Price, a former governor who developed a fixation about winning control of Missouri for the Confederacy. He was joined by fifteen hundred cavalrymen, under Jo Shelby, and fifty-four hundred men from Arkansas under a former Texas Ranger, Ben McCulloch. They soon had a force sufficiently large to turn on Lyon's Union soldiers. By July, Price and McCulloch led a joint command of fourteen thousand men and they moved to attack Lyon. They encamped at Wilson's Creek on August 9.

Lyon planned to hit the Confederates before they could bring their superior numbers against him and made plans with the commander of his German element, Franz Sigel. Formerly a professional soldier, Sigel commanded 1,250 Home Guards, whom he had trained intensively for combat. Lyon and Sigel were making a great gamble in the face of superior numbers.

Sigel was to swing wide to the south, approach the left flank of the Confederates, and strike their rear as Lyon attacked them from the front. Sigel was given an artillery battery to accompany his infantry. Luckily, it began to rain hard and Confederate commanders moved their pickets under cover late in the night. As a result, Sigel was able to get his small force into position without detection.

Lyon's regiments were seen at dawn and they began to advance against Confederate positions on a nearby hill. To the south, Sigel's men waited under cover of trees and began to fire into a nearby Confederate regiment. Unfortunately, Sigel soon made an understandable mistake, but one that cost them their position and the battle.

Sigel wrote that he saw a large number of men in gray uniforms approaching and ordered his men not to fire into them. He assumed these were the men of the Union's 1st Iowa Infantry, ex-militiamen who continued to wear gray clothing. These arriving Confederates, clearly not the 1st Iowa, fired into Sigel's men and charged as the Union soldiers broke in confusion. Sigel made his escape, but the Federal force lost both their positions and most of their cannon—weapons that were turned on Lyon's troops.

The battle ended when Lyon was wounded in the head and then killed by a bullet in the chest. It was an appalling defeat for the Union army, but Lyon's aggressive maneuvering had left the Confederates off balance; furthermore, the Unionists had consolidated their positions in Missouri. Sterling Price was able to occupy Springfield, though his position was weakened when McCulloch took his little army back to Arkansas.

German-born Franz Sigel had emigrated to the United States after participating in the failed 1848 revolution in the German states of the Habsburg Empire. Popular with his immigrant countrymen, Sigel remained in positions of authority in the Union army despite blunders that dearly cost the Federals.

General Nathaniel Lyon was wounded in the head and then killed by a chest wound during the battle of Wilson's Creek.

General John C. Fremont, an explorer of the west and the Republican presidential candidate in 1856, was an uninspiring Union commander in the early battles of the Civil War. He was the first Federal commander to order the freeing of slaves—a political blunder at the time.

Price's next target was Lexington, a large town located between Kansas City and St. Louis. He felt it had strategic importance and moved immediately against the town's small garrison. The three thousand defenders fought without support, little water, and no hope or relief from their commander, former presidential candidate, John C. Fremont, in St. Louis. They fought from earthworks for nine days before surrendering to Price on September 20, 1861.

This second defeat in Missouri, coming so soon after the crushing defeat and death of Lyon at Wilson's Creek, created an uproar in the North. The new prisoners were paroled, but the Confederates kept the hero of the siege, Colonel James A. Mulligan of the 23rd Illinois Volunteers, as a prisoner. Mulligan was held until October 30, when he was

escorted to St. Louis under a flag of truce and released.

Fremont was soon relieved of command, but he did provide one excellent service to his country before he disappeared from St. Louis. He selected Ulysses S. Grant to become the commander at Cairo, Illinois. It was Grant's first major command position.

Little changed in the tactical situation in Missouri for the next few months. Price and McCulloch continued feuding with each other until it became obvious that a new commander had to be found. Colonel Henry Heth, fresh from his personal disaster at Lewisburg in western Virginia (where his numerically superior force had been soundly defeated by George Crook), declined the command. Braxton Bragg also decided his military reputation could be enhanced elsewhere. The

new commander selected was Major General Earl Van Dorn. All of the pro-Confederate Missourians were pleased with the selection of a fighter as their commander.

The Union commander in St. Louis, Major General Henry Halleck, had planned a large offensive against several critical points in the region under his authority. Grant would be sent toward forts Henry and Donelson, Pope would move toward New Madrid on the Mississippi, and a third army under the command of Brigadier General Samuel Curtis would attempt to drive Price from Missouri.

Curtis began to march against Price on February 10. Van Dorn, looking forward to the opportunity to destroy Curtis, sent orders to McCulloch to return with his regiments. McCulloch then sent orders to Brigadier

General Albert Pike to assemble his troops and join him to support Van Dorn.

Pike was leading one of the most unusual armies to march during the Civil War. While he had little military experience, the three-hundred-pound lawyer was an expert on American Indians, and the Confederate government had commissioned the Boston-born Pike to negotiate treaties with the Native American inhabitants of the Indian Territory, today's Oklahoma. Treaties were made with the Chickasaw and Choctaw tribes, but half of the members of the remaining tribes were pro-Union and they moved as refugees into Kansas. The treaties signed with Pike obligated the Confederate Indians to fight only in their territory; likewise, the Confederates were bound by their treaties to come to the assistance of the Indians. Pike was less than pleased with the orders to bring his Indian regiments into Missouri and Arkansas to assist Van Dorn.

A battle raged for nearly nine days as Sterling Price's troops fought for the control of Lexington, Missouri, with the men under Union General John Fremont. His inability to recapture this important population center cost Fremont his command.

General Sterling Price, a former governor of Missouri, was determined to win control of his state for the Confederacy.

Price and McCulloch continued their withdrawal from Missouri into the mountainous territory in Arkansas, where they were joined by Van Dorn. The assembled Confederate army had approximately sixteen thousand men to face Curtis' reduced force of about ten thousand. Van Dorn was confident that he could defeat Curtis and ordered the entire force forward on March 3.

Curtis learned of Van Dorn's approach and moved his men into positions on the north side of Little Sugar Creek, where they began to construct earthworks and field fortifications. In the rear of the positions was a high ridge that had peas growing on vines on its slopes, called locally Pea Ridge. Sigel left a rear guard near Bentonville, fourteen miles away, and engaged Van Dorn on March 6 before falling back to the main body at Pea Ridge. Van Dorn, with little reconnaissance, thought he was engaging the primary Union army and made an attempt to encircle

Sigel, but the German officer was able to extract his men and return to the main force in front of Pea Ridge.

Van Dorn, reluctant to attack the strong positions of Curtis, decided to attempt a maneuver similar to that attempted by Lyon and Sigel at Wilson's Creek. He would divide his forces, attempt to flank Curtis' position, and get into the Federal army's rear area to block any attempted retreat. The coordination of widely separated commands at any time is difficult, but was nearly impossible to achieve during the confusion of a Civil War battle. Van Dorn complicated matters by neglecting to explain his plan to the recently arrived Pike, the commander of the Indian Brigade. The movement began successfully enough, but Curtis quickly became aware of the dual movements and moved large elements of infantry with artillery against McCulloch and Pike as they attempted to get to the Union flank and rear.

PEA RIDGE
March 7–8, 1862

1. The original Confederate plan was to swing behind Big Mountain and attack the Union rear. Aware of this Confederate flanking movement, Union troops block the road with trees and other debris.

2. Slowed by the felled trees, General McCulloch turns his forces around and heads down Ford Road with the intention of joining General Van Dorn's troops near Elkhorn Tavern.

3. As the Confederates approach Little Mountain, Union forces open fire with artillery. The Confederates quickly over-run this position.

4. Confederate forces stop in the woods at the northern edge of a large cornfield. Union forces in the woods along the southern edge of this field open fire. The 36th Illinois advances and drives the Confederates back. Confederate generals McCulloch and McIntosh are killed in this action.

5. A final assault from Little Mountain is flanked and turned by Union forces under General Davis.

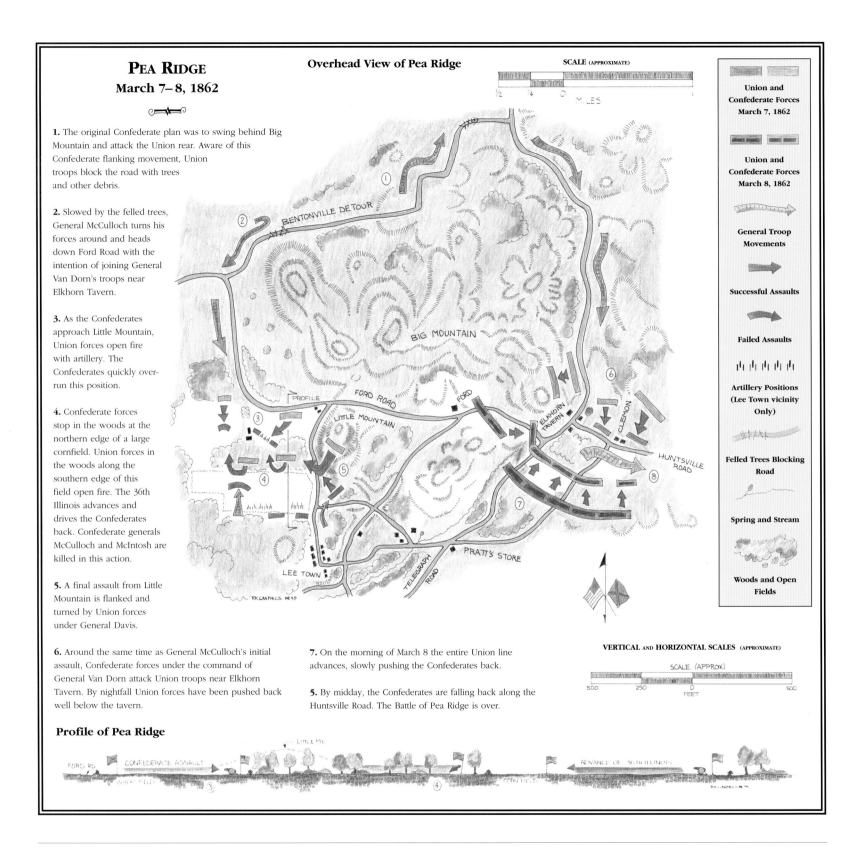

6. Around the same time as General McCulloch's initial assault, Confederate forces under the command of General Van Dorn attack Union troops near Elkhorn Tavern. By nightfall Union forces have been pushed back well below the tavern.

7. On the morning of March 8 the entire Union line advances, slowly pushing the Confederates back.

5. By midday, the Confederates are falling back along the Huntsville Road. The Battle of Pea Ridge is over.

Profile of Pea Ridge

Confederate General Earl Van Dorn attempted to change the course of the war by capturing St. Louis. A smaller Federal force under General Samuel R. Curtis defeated the Confederates at Pea Ridge and forced Van Dorn back to the Arkansas River. While this engraving shows controlled, orderly soldiers in battle, the Pea Ridge combat was actually a confusing, disorganized affair. Van Dorn's supply wagons had been sent to the wrong position and the Confederates were unable to resupply their men.

Van Dorn quickly realized the danger he was in. His divided force could be overwhelmed, one element at a time, by the now alerted Union commander. Van Dorn quickly complicated matters even further by ordering McCulloch and Pike to reverse their courses. This additional confusion was too much for the commanders to manage. Pike and his Indian Brigade ended up in the rear of a Confederate cavalry brigade commanded by General McIntosh.

Soon the Indian soldiers and McCulloch's troops encountered part of the Union army. McCulloch ordered the attack to begin before the Union commander, Osterhaus, could get

his men in motion. John Drew's Cherokees and a regiment of Cherokee mixed-blood soldiers under Stand Watie forced many of the German soldiers to retreat in panic, but it soon was the Cherokee's turn to be scared as the Union soldiers regrouped and fired shells into their midst. Poor luck began to plague the Confederates making the attempt to get into the Federal rear. McCulloch and McIntosh were killed and Pike suddenly found himself the senior officer on the battlefield. He attempted to set up a defensive line out of the Cherokee and some of the remnants of McCulloch's men, but it was a hopeless endeavor: the men were exhausted. Soon after, Pike

received orders to return to the main body of the Confederate army to support Van Dorn.

Price and Van Dorn had done better with the army's main element and had forced many of the Union soldiers to retreat to the slopes of Pea Ridge. They were winning the battle, but luck intervened in favor of the Union army. Through a serious error, Van Dorn's ammunition train had been sent to positions from which it could not be recalled to replenish the artillery with powder and ammunition. Lacking both food and ammunition, the exhausted Confederates could not consider mounting another attack. The Union artillery began the next morning's engage-

Outnumbered and poorly supplied, Confederate soldiers were frequently forced to scavenge for ammunition from their own dead or wounded comrades. Only through valiant efforts by ordinary soldiers did the Confederacy survive for four years.

PEA RIDGE

> *"[The Battle of Pea Ridge] virtually cleansed the South-west of the enemy, gave peace to the people of Missouri, at least for the next two years, and made it possible for our veterans to reinforce the armies."*
>
> —General Franz Sigel

In the distance, Federal troops advance on the Pea Ridge battlefield to reclaim their former positions at Elkhorn Tavern.

ment and, one at a time, the Confederate guns either ran out of ammunition or were disabled by Union fire. It was March 8.

Curtis brought all of his four infantry divisions into position and ordered a general attack. The Confederates made gallant attempts to hold their positions, but the Union infantry and unanswered artillery began to have an impact. The Confederate left began to come apart as additional Federal infantrymen struck Van Dorn's center, and an orderly retreat quickly became a rout. As with Lyon at Wilson's Creek, the decision to divide his force in the face of the enemy—given the numerous difficulties facing any Civil War commander trying to communicate with and coordinate his subordinate units during the confusion of combat—had cost Van Dorn the battle.

Pike, angry with the accusations of atrocities that were made against his Indian Brigade and disappointed with the lack of support given him by Van Dorn, simply left the region to return to the Indian Territory. Van Dorn reported that he had not been defeated at Pea Ridge, but he greatly overstated his impact on the military situation in the wake of his retreat.

Curtis had won a major victory for the Union at Pea Ridge. Price and the Confederates in Missouri had won at Wilson's Creek and Lexington, but now this critical state and her large population were firmly held by the Federal authorities. A large part of the Mississippi River was under Federal control and such northern areas as St. Louis, Kansas, Iowa, and the industrial areas of the upper midwest were now safe from Confederate raiding parties. Coming so soon after Grant's major victory at Fort Donelson, the triumph at Pea Ridge gave considerable levels of comfort to the Union war leaders and their supporters. After Pea Ridge, Missouri remained in the hands of the North for the remainder of the Civil War. And although this border state was to suffer through some of the most severe guerrilla warfare of the entire war (entire counties would be depopulated as a result), in the strategic sense, these ongoing raids were simply a nuisance. Missouri was securely in the grasp of the Union. Price would attempt to invade in 1864, but this would also serve to annoy rather than threaten.

Van Dorn, the handsome, courageous Indian fighter, moved east of the Mississippi and operated there until he was shot dead by a jealous husband in 1863. And Grant was able to turn his full attention from possible threats to Missouri to the campaign against targets in the Mississippi Valley in the continuing effort to split the Confederacy in half.

chapter 3

ANTIETAM
A Bloody, Dismal Battlefield

"[At] Sharpsburg was sprung the keystone of the arch upon which the Confederate cause rested."

—General James Longstreet

The war in the east had been proceeding toward disaster for the Union while the northern armies were showing success in the region to the west of the Appalachian Mountains. Scarce resources, inattention from Washington—preoccupied with the threat to the National capital—and relatively weak Confederate forces (when compared to those in the east) under quarrelsome commanders meant that Federal commanders had to react quickly in a creative fashion or face destruction. This strategic situation led Grant to develop a different view of the war than his eastern counterparts. Grant saw the war as a series of campaigns in which losing or winning decisive victories in individual battles made little difference. He realized that if he could hold on to the initiative as he moved to divide the Confederacy along the Mississippi River, he would later have the opportunity to dismember the western Confederacy one part at a time.

This approach was lost on the Federal generals in command in the east. Engagements had been fought within western Virginia as Federal troops moved in an attempt to secure the Baltimore and Ohio railroad, a vital route from the midwest to the eastern seaboard. The first combat death in the war occurred during the night of May 22, 1861, when a small Union reconnaissance team approached the enemy's pickets at the crossing of the railroad with the Northwestern Turnpike. Thornsberry Bailey Brown, a private, lost his life in this skirmish and became the first Union soldier to die. Shortly afterwards, additional deaths would occur in a cavalry skirmish at Fairfax Station. As the casualty lists began to be posted, the attitudes of the opposing sides in the conflict began to harden.

Ohio regiments, under the command of Union General George McClellan, continued to move into the interior of western Virginia

in what became the first maneuver campaign of the war. The first land battle was fought at Philippi in a surprise attack that resulted in a rout of the Virginia state troops encamped there. The campaign continued to develop, and soon battles were fought at Rich Mountain and at Corricks Ford, where on July 13, 1861, Virginia lost the services of an excellent officer, Brigadier General Robert Garnett. (A West Point graduate, veteran of the Mexican War, and recent officer in the National army, Garnett was the first general officer to lose his life in the Civil War.) Meanwhile, McClellan's Ohio regiments were winning small victories inside enemy territory, for which the general immediately came to the attention of President Lincoln.

The first major land battle of the war, however, was fought a few days after Corricks Ford, on July 21, 1861, when Brigadier General Irvin McDowell ordered an army of thirty-five thousand men to advance toward Manassas Junction prior to moving on toward the newly established Confederate capital, Richmond. The bloody defeat of the

PAGE 45: Thrilled by romantic musings about the valor to be won in combat, Federal volunteers such as this young soldier bravely (if somewhat naively) rushed to the service of their country. ABOVE: Federal Teamsters and frightened Union soldiers fled from the defeat at Bull Run in their first "Great Skedaddle." BELOW: Close-order drill was a constant routine in the life of the volunteer soldier. Noise of battle prevented shouted commands from being heard and commanders kept their men in close formations so they could be maneuvered more easily. Unfortunately, rifled muskets soon took a grim toll on these closely packed formations.

Union forces at Bull Run was made possible by the Confederate use of the Manassas Gap Railroad to move their troops rapidly from the Shenandoah Valley. Even if the Union army had been able to win Manassas, however, it is doubtful that the untrained commands and unskilled commanders would have been able to move successfully against Richmond. If they had, it is equally unlikely that the Confederacy would have capitulated (as was widely believed in the North). The city of Richmond, as the strategic point where a loss would be decisive later in the war, had not yet gained the significance later battles would give it.

Soon after the victory at Manassas had given the Confederacy an opportunity to plan for themselves rather than react to Federal movements, a decision was made to send Jefferson Davis' military advisor, Robert E. Lee, to the region of Virginia's western border, along the Ohio River. Lee had been among the most respected officers in the pre-war National army and had been personally offered the command of the Federal army by

Winfield Scott. But it was as a Confederate commander in the western Virginia mountains that Lee gained his first Civil War combat experience—and this was a dismal failure. Poor weather, mountainous terrain, and quarreling with insubordinate subcommanders (Floyd, Wise, and Loring) rendered Lee's initial campaign a shambles. In fact, it led to a Federal victory that soon after resulted in the creation of a new Federal state, West Virginia.

Lee was accused of incompetence in southern newspapers and he was soon sent on an equally difficult mission. The Federal government had found that Scott's original "Anaconda Plan," which required a blockade against southern ports, was, after all, the best way to win the war. The successful raids against Confederate coastal positions by the Union navy had to be checked, and Davis sent Lee to develop adequate defenses. On the day of his arrival, after reviewing the situation and the loss at Port Royal Sound, Lee decided to abandon the region closest to the sea in favor of new defensive positions to be

constructed at points where rivers were narrow, shallow, and defensible. He knew that Federal "floating batteries"—naval bombardment vessels—would be able to defend any infantry landings. The farther inland he could lure the Federal infantry, the less successful the Union's foot soldiers would be without naval gun support. His ability to defend by trading space for time and good positions was sufficiently successful to halt any additional Federal advances in on the coast until Sherman was able to get in the rear of the defenders at the close of the war. Lee proved himself to be an able engineer, and his experience in the construction of field fortifications would serve him well at later points in the war. Lee was beginning to show his military ability—if not genius.

Lee also learned that defensive positions alone were of little value against a large, mobile force determined to capture them. Large numbers, mobility provided by naval transport, and the use of the deadly floating batteries could be used to concentrate overwhelming force against any point Lee chose

Brightly clad Zouaves, men who had been drilled in assault tactics, fought bravely, their units suffering severe casualties during McClellan's Peninsula Campaign. Here, these men are fighting in the Battle of Gaines' Mill.

to defend. This observation would play a significant role in the formation of his later views regarding defensive combat. He was of the belief that the best defense is undertaken offensively.

Lee was recalled to Richmond in March 1862 to return to his post at Jefferson Davis' side as a confidential military adviser. The Confederacy had just lost at forts Henry and Donelson, and their defenses in the west were beginning to break under unrelenting pressure. It was at this point in the war that Lee recommended to Davis that the Confederacy's defensive strategy must be changed. Because the rebel army was always on the defensive, their Federal enemy was able to develop forces capable of attacking anywhere against an army spread so thin that a Confederate victory was unlikely at any location. The best move would be the concentration of their forces and an offensive strategy that would force the Federal commanders to react against Confederate initiatives. Lee continued to urge offensive action, and out of his recommendations came Jackson's brilliant Shenandoah Valley Campaign of April and May 1862. This campaign served the purpose for which it had been designed by Lee: Federal troops were forced to concentrate against Jackson in the Shenandoah Valley rather than serve as reinforcements for McClellan, the primary Federal threat moving against Richmond in what was to become the Peninsula Campaign.

Following the Battle of Seven Pines on May 31, Lee was able to command the Confederate army, rather than recommend and urge; General Joseph E. Johnston, the army's commander, had been wounded, and Davis placed Lee in command. His first order to Jackson was to move his Shenandoah army to the defenses of Richmond to oppose McClellan's army, which Jackson had indirectly weakened through the battles in the Shenandoah and which now was within

hearing of Richmond's church bells. With the addition of Jackson's small army, Lee had approximately eighty thousand men to oppose McClellan's 117,000. Lee, facing a siege he knew his army couldn't survive, chose to attack the larger army of the timid McClellan in what was to become the Seven Days' Battles for the Confederate capital. Both commanders were soon to learn a great deal about the new style of combat.

In order to control and effectively maneuver infantry formations, commanders had to deploy their soldiers in close, orderly assaults or confusion would overwhelm them when they moved beyond the sight of the units along their flanks. Unfortunately for the men who were called upon to fight the Civil War, the development of new rifled weapons and new artillery tactics resulted in terrible losses for the attackers. Lee continued to believe that only with the offensive could the Confederate army survive and pressed the attack against the Union Army at Mechanicsville, Gaines' Mill, and Frayser's Farm before McClellan arrived at an excellent defensive position at Malvern Hill on July 1, 1862. Lee lost an additional fifty-five hundred casualties at Malvern Hill without damaging the Union army significantly.

Lee became the hero of the Confederacy and would remain so forever, but the losses wrought by his new strategy were horrendous. He lost twenty thousand men out of eighty thousand engaged, but he soon moved from the defenses of Richmond to march toward Washington.

He managed the Battle of Second Manassas very well. Jackson's small army held Pope's Union army in position on August 30 while Confederate General James Longstreet's forces moved against the Federal flank, resulting in another rout. In fact, the entire Union army was forced to retreat into the heavily defended environs of Washington. In a curious turn of events that came as

a result of Lee's ability to take advantage of McClellan's timidity, the opposing armies had moved from lines outside of Richmond to lines outside of Washington in less than two months of combat.

This was the general situation as Lee and Davis began to consider their next moves. Lee preferred a continuation of his offensive tactics and recommended an invasion of the North, to be accomplished by entering Maryland. The risks were great because the Federal armies recovering from their recent losses at Manassas would soon outnumber Lee's victorious forces. Lee could have chosen to return to the defenses in the vicinity of the Rappahannock River and wait for a renewed Union attack, but Lee had few doubts about the need to defend Virginia by attacking into the North. The third option that may have been considered at this time was to remain in northern Virginia, but a shortage of food in the immediate area, extended supply lines, and a shortage of transportation made this option untenable.

Lee's reasoning for the recommendation to enter Maryland was relatively sound. Lee contended that he would be able to feed his men and animals on food and forage that would have gone to the support of the enemy while sparing Virginia's farmers the burden of feeding them. The next series of fights with the Federal army would be fought in their own territory—again sparing Lee's beloved Virginia—and the greater part of the Army of the Potomac would be ordered to pursue the invading Confederates, preventing Union forces from planning and provisioning themselves for another attempt to capture the city of Richmond before the end of the campaign season.

Parallel to the military benefits associated with an invasion into Maryland, there were enormous political benefits to be gained for the Confederacy that were considered. Maryland, a border as well as a slave state, had a strong pro-Confederate minority within its borders. Lincoln had only strengthened their resolve early in the war by placing many of Baltimore's pro-Confederate leaders into prison without trial.

The North had managed to antagonize the two European superpowers of the time, Britain and France, and there were diplomatic reports arriving in Richmond that additional political support might be coming. Victories in the North's territory could have served as an impetus for additional European support or perhaps even outright recognition.

There were even reports concerning the growing antiwar sentiments of many of the Democrats in the North. These citizens and the pro-Southern "Copperhead" movement would take comfort in any Confederate successes in the North and there was a possibility that sufficient numbers would enter Congress in the fall elections to influence Lincoln and his war party, the Republicans. The war was intertwined with the politics of the period, and the Confederate government hoped to take political advantage of any successes that came its way.

Lee had one additional factor to consider as he and his staff began to make their plans for the invasion. His army was in poor condition after long marches, poor food in limited quantities, loss of excellent officers in recent combat, and poor transportation that would limit the amount of ammunition that would be available in the fighting that would certainly develop. These same soldiers, however, had managed to perform near-miracles in the previous campaigns and Lee was certain they would do so again. They would fight against great odds for the entire war—the Maryland invasion would be no different. Only one real concern remained: the men and their officers had been told that they would only be fighting to defend their homes and states. Would they be willing to participate in an invasion of the North?

The Confederacy was rebounding from the battering they had been receiving, primarily in the west, and the autumn campaigns of 1862 showed much promise. Halleck had made a mistake in dispersing his forces in the west and he had over sixty thousand of them spread out in garrisons along railroads from Memphis to Alabama and from Corinth, Mississippi, to Columbus, Kentucky. Buell and his army were making repairs on the railroad as they moved in the direction of Chattanooga. This provided Braxton Bragg with an opportunity to reclaim much of the territory lost after Shiloh, but he chose to attempt to recover the state of Kentucky by mounting a new invasion. This was beginning at approximately the same time that Lee was moving into Maryland. Not surprisingly, the North was becoming alarmed over the dual invasions.

South Carolina's Nathan Evans was given the Nickname "Shanks" at West Point because of his overly skinny legs. After graduating in 1848 he was sent to the frontier to fight Indians. He later resigned in order to join the Confederate army, where he served until severely injured in a fall from his horse in 1864.

On September 5, the decision had been made. Lee's headquarters issued orders and the troops began to move to fords in the Potomac near Leesburg, Virginia. The invading army suffered from many deficiencies as it moved toward the Potomac. Many soldiers had not eaten in several days and the prospect of finding food in the immediate future was remote. As many as one quarter of the army was barefoot, and straggling was at record levels. Some of the stragglers were holding back due to personal politics: they had enlisted to defend their homes and did not want to invade the North.

Other problems began to complicate the operation from the start. John B. Hood and Nathan Evans began a dispute over the possession of captured Federal supplies, which

General A.P. Hill was given command of one of the finest units in the Army of Northern Virginia, the "Light Division." His men rushed from Harper's Ferry to Antietam to enter the fight without delaying to form lines of battle.

resulted in the arrest of Hood for insubordination. A second personal dispute developed between Jackson and A.P. Hill over straggling, and Hill was also placed under arrest. To make matters worse, Lee had been injured in a fall from his horse, Traveller, an accident that resulted in injuries to his hands and forced him to ride in an ambulance as his army spent four days crossing the Potomac near Leesburg.

The news of the invasion spread fear throughout Washington. Recently shocked by the major defeat at Manassas, the Federal government prepared for the worst: clerks were formed into volunteer companies; gunboats prepared to defend the capital; and a boat was prepared to evacuate Lincoln and his cabinet, if that became necessary. Lee had moved into a position from which he could attack Washington, Baltimore, or Harrisburg (a major rail center that was the best of the proposed targets) with relative ease. The Union army commanders began to issue orders to get the Army of the Potomac into motion to check Lee's aggressive moves. The Union was in trouble: Lee was on the doorstep of the nation's capital and Braxton Bragg was massing an army in Kentucky that was threatening to move against Cincinnati.

Lincoln had transferred Pope to the west soon after the loss at Manassas and turned to McClellan. Federal forces were in place at Martinsburg and Harpers Ferry, but their numbers were too small to be able to dispute Lee. Their presence, however, left Lee with a strategic problem that would have to be eliminated if the invasion and subsequent withdrawal were to be successful.

In order to deal with multiple problems simultaneously, Lee divided his already numerically inferior force as McClellan marched to place the Army of the Potomac between Lee and Washington. The Federal commander, as usual, was less than enthusiastic about the need to locate and attack Lee,

Harper's Ferry was the site of a Federal arsenal and the location of John Brown's Raid. Located beneath high hills, the town was impossible to defend from attackers who occupied nearby heights. Stonewall Jackson said he would rather attack it forty times than attempt to defend it once.

General Braxton Bragg was conducting a campaign into Kentucky as Lee moved into Maryland. By October 8, 1862, Bragg was retreating from Perryville after being defeated.

but he was soon to receive the best message delivered to him during the entire war.

Lee had prepared written orders for his commanders on September 9 and copies were made for each of them. On September 13, the 27th Indiana had stopped to rest near Frederick on a campground used earlier by the Confederate army. While resting there, a sergeant and corporal of the Indiana found three cigars wrapped in a piece of paper. Addressed to D.H. Hill, the paper was a copy of Lee's Special Orders No. 191, detailing the plans for the campaign and listing the positions each Confederate commander was supposed to attack. For the first time in the war, McClellan was elated, confident; he wrote to Lincoln that he would "send you trophies."

Harper's Ferry was a clear target whose garrison would have to be eliminated for the Confederate invasion to succeed. Essentially indefensible, the small town was in a deep valley surrounded by high ground. Jackson

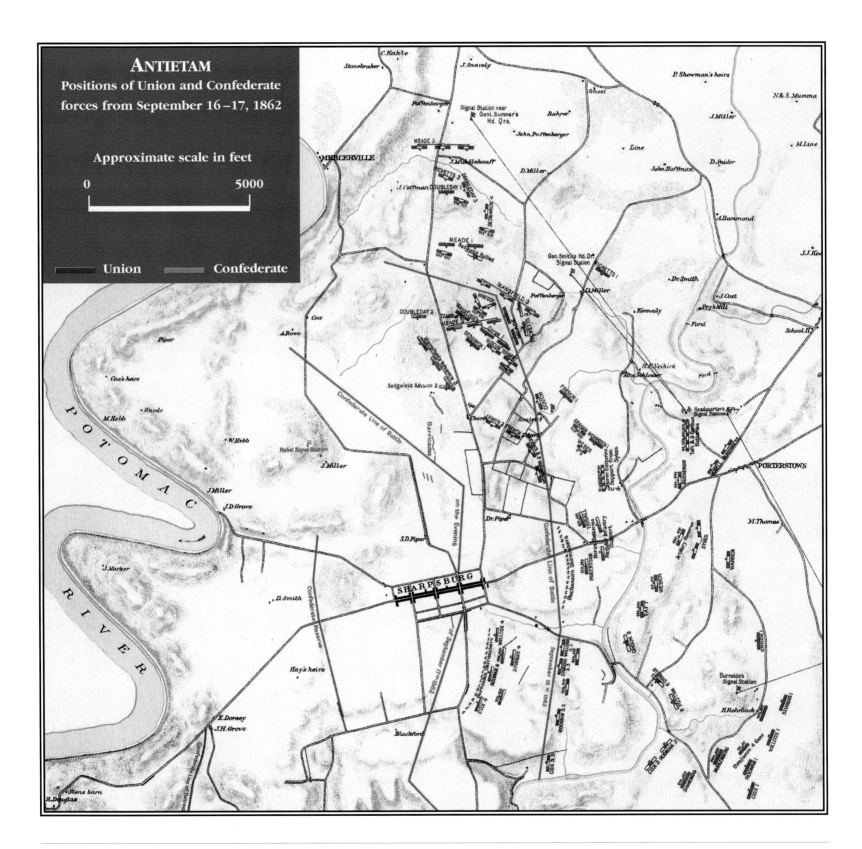

ANTIETAM

Positions of Union and Confederate forces from September 16–17, 1862

Approximate scale in feet

0 ——————— 5000

Union   Confederate

OPPOSITE: The battle of Antietam was fought piecemeal by General McClellan. Fighting began on the northern portion of the battlefield in the morning, and moved to the center of the field by noon. The fighting continued in the southern portion of the battlefield in the afternoon. Caution on the part of McClellan cost him a clear victory. ABOVE: General Lee, with his aggressive approach, had divided his forces to face simultaneous threats from his cautious opponent. Only rapid marching saved his army from certain destruction after McClellan discovered the lost orders.

commented that he would rather take Harper's Ferry forty times than attempt to defend it a single time; the reasons for this sentiment became readily apparent to the defenders who surrendered to Jackson on Monday, September 15. The Union army surrendered seventy-three pieces of artillery, 12,500 men, and thirteen thousand stand of muskets to the victorious Jackson. There was little time to rejoice, however—Lee sent orders for the separated wings of the army to unite as quickly as possible at the Maryland town of Sharpsburg.

As the battle for Harper's Ferry unfolded, Lee was warned that McClellan had a copy of the lost general order and could

be expected to move with previously unheard-of aggressiveness. An operation to relieve the trapped garrison at Harper's Ferry could be expected; the relief force would probably cross South Mountain in the vicinity of Boonsboro, Maryland, at gaps in the mountain, particularly Turner's Gap. Lee sent orders to Longstreet, who was near Hagerstown, to move to defend the gap against a certain Federal attack.

Simultaneously, the Kanawha Division of the IX Corps, under an able commander, Jacob D. Cox, had the lead position as the Federal army approached South Mountain. Cox and his men, toughened by long service and hard marches in the mountains of western

Virginia the previous year, marched swiftly without straggling, but halted when they encountered a familiar figure standing beside the road.

The lone officer, Augustus Moor, had recently been captured by the Confederates near Frederick and had just been paroled. He was making his way back to Federal lines. When Cox told him that their destination was Turner's Gap, Moor forgot for a moment that the terms of his parole prevented him from providing information. A hasty comment, "My God! Be careful," was all that escaped his lips, but Cox was warned. He sent a dispatch to IX Corps Commander, Major General Jesse Reno, a West Point graduate from Wheeling, Virginia, to warn him of the enemy presence on South Mountain.

Severe fighting erupted, but Cox was able to control Fox's Gap by late morning. The cost in lives was heavy (future president Rutherford B. Hayes was severely wounded during this engagement). Cox moved his men toward Turner's Gap, but the arrival of reinforcements for the thin Confederate line delayed Cox and he returned to his position at Fox's Gap. The arrival of reinforcements for both sides led to a general and fierce engagement, with additional combat developing at nearby Crampton's Gap. South Mountain had gradually become the scene of a major battle.

Reno rode out on a commander's reconnaissance late in the evening in an attempt to find a weakness in the Confederate defenses that could be exploited, and was severely wounded in the process. As he was being carried to the rear, the brave Reno announced firmly and cheerfully to one of his division commanders that he was "dead," and soon died of his injury.

The day ended with the Federal army holding the high ground at South Mountain. Lee decided to pull back to positions near Sharpsburg. The news from Jackson that

ANTIETAM

54

OPPOSITE: Terrible casualties were suffered by both sides in the frantic combat to control a twenty-acre field of ripening corn that was adjacent to the Hagerstown Pike. It is remembered in military history simply as "The Cornfield." ABOVE: The romanticism associated with warfare was eliminated from American imaginations after they viewed Alexander Gardner's photographs of Antietam's dead. The terror of the Civil War was driven home to the average citizen by images such as this one of dead Confederates along the Hagerstown Pike.

stage was set for fighting that would surely develop the next morning, September 17.

Amazingly, McClellan ordered a series of separate, piecemeal attacks against Lee's army that Wednesday morning. If he had attacked with the entire force available to him, the Army of Northern Virginia would have been severely defeated. Given the proximity of the Potomac in the Confederates' rear, it is unlikely that very many of them would have escaped capture. A grand opportunity was being squandered along with the lives of many excellent Federal soldiers. Attack after attack across pastures and cornfields against the Confederate left flank was turned back. McClellan next ordered attacks against the center of the Confederate line, but these division attacks also met with a bloody repulse. Entire regiments were decimated in a hail of minié balls and canister. The 12th Massachusetts entered the fight with 334 men, and emerged at the end of the battle with just one hundred of them.

Similar losses resulted among the Confederate army. The Louisiana Tigers, a fierce elite regiment, marched to Sharpsburg with approximately five hundred men, but left 323 of them behind after only fifteen terrible minutes of combat. Jackson's divisions had a large gap smashed into them and their line was about to break when John Bell Hood's division, denied their breakfast by the order to attack, stormed forward and slammed into Hooker's I Corps. Nearly one third of Hooker's men would be killed or wounded as the corps was effectively taken out of the battle. Hood's losses were also horrible to contemplate; many of his men fell to Federal artillery batteries that had been double-loaded with canister before being fired into the Confederate line. Later, John Gordon's men gave their lives to help defend Sunken Road, a feature of the local terrain that would be renamed "Bloody Lane" as a result of their sacrifice.

Harper's Ferry had been captured arrived late on Monday morning. Lee elected to fight McClellan at Sharpsburg, Maryland, though his force would be dangerously small until Jackson arrived. Preparations were made to fight the battle along tree-lined Antietam Creek. Excellent defensive terrain favored the Confederates and a road running north-to-south would allow the commanders to move troops swiftly from one position to another once the battle had begun. There was one dangerous feature of the selected battlefield: the defenders would have their backs against the broad Potomac River and could thus be destroyed if the battle went completely

against them. Lee was the only general in the Southern army who would have been willing to fight a battle against superior numbers from a position such as this. Above all, Lee was a combative general—and he knew his opponent's tendency toward timidity.

As predicted by Lee, McClellan brought his divisions into position slowly. The first arrived in the afternoon on Monday, September 15. He finally arrived in person during the afternoon on Tuesday, September 16, but by then a great advantage had been lost. Three divisions of Jackson's troops had arrived, significantly reducing the numerical advantage held by the Union army. The

The focus of the battle shifted to the Federal left flank, where Ambrose Burnside—through a mistake in orders—shared command with Jacob Cox, the officer who had opened the attack at South Mountain. The valor of the men of Cox's Kanawha Division would be rewarded shortly by Burnside, who gave them the honor of opening the attack on a bridge over Antietam Creek. Three Ohio regiments from the Kanawha Brigade under George Crook were selected to carry the bridge. His attack went wide, missing the approach to the bridge. A second attack also failed. McClellan, growing impatient with the repeated failures, sent a message to Burnside that he was to take the bridge "if it cost him 10,000 men." A third attack was sent forward through the hail of bullets from the defenders on the opposite side. A Georgia brigade held its position at the bridge, pulling back at the last possible moment when the company ran short of ammunition.

McClellan saw a ray of hope for the first time that day. The plan of breaking Lee's northern flank had been abandoned and all of the attacks along Sunken Road were slowing to a halt. The advance across the bridge was the single option remaining—thus, what had begun as a bloody diversion became the focus of Federal strategy. Orders were sent to press forward, but the lead regiments were short of ammunition. Couriers were sent to get reserves to replace the exhausted men who had fought their way across the hotly contested bridge. Burnside continued his buildup along the creek and Lee realized the peril he was in. His final chance to salvage the battle rested with the long awaited arrival of A.P. Hill and his Light Division, one of the best units in the Army of Northern Virginia. The recall order arrived at Hill's position at Harper's Ferry early that morning and he had been relentlessly driving his men toward Sharpsburg. By 2 P.M., Hill's men were crossing the Potomac at Boteler's Ford

General Longstreet described the Confederate dead in their positions in the Sunken Road as, "Mowed down like grass before the scythe." The road became immortalized as Bloody Lane forever.

Union troops pushed to cross this bridge over Antietam Creek. It would be named after Federal commander General Ambrose Burnside.

ANTIETAM: LOWER (BURNSIDE'S) BRIDGE ASSAULT
September 17, 1862

1. The 11th Connecticut loses heavily in the first major effort to take the Lower Bridge. The 11th advances to the stone wall. Captain Griswold and several men attempt to ford the creek but are stopped mistream. Captain Griswold, mortally wounded, dies on the opposite bank.

2. The 2nd Maryland and the 6th New Hampshire are repulsed. Advancing along the road and adjacent fields the 2nd Maryland and 6th New Hampshire reach the bridge but are forced to withdraw.

3. The 2nd Maryland and the 6th New Hampshire fail in a second assault on the bridge.

4. The 51st Pennsylvania and the 51st New York succeed. The 51st Pennsylvania crosses the bridge (a). A portion of the 51st New York fords the creek (b), while the rest follow the 51st Pennsylvania across the bridge.

5. Low on ammunition and facing overwhelming odds, the 20th and 2nd Georgia fall back.

Overhead View of Lower Bridge Assault

Union Positions

Extended Confederate Positions

Failed Assaults

Successful Assault

Post and Rail Fence

Split Rail Fence

Stone Wall

Trees

Orchard

SCALE (APPROXIMATE)

100 50 0 YARDS 100 200

Profile of Lower Bridge

CONFEDERATE POSITIONS

LOWER BRIDGE

FAR RIDGE

H. ROHBACH

PLOWED FIELD

FARM RD.

THREE OUT OF FOUR MAIN UNION ATTEMPTS BEGIN OR END BEHIND THIS SMALL RISE

VERTICAL AND HORIZONTAL SCALES (APPROXIMATE)

100 80 60 40 20 0 FEET 100 200

50 25 YARDS 0 50

---

near Shepherdstown. They had covered fifteen miles in slightly over six hours. Two miles remained, however, between the Light Division and Lee's forces.

Time was short. Confederate defenders were being badly mauled by large, relatively fresh Union regiments and the thin line of defenders was coming apart. Hill's Light Division arrived just in time and didn't stop to form lines of battle. They began fighting as they spread into their customary battle formations and drove back the Federal attack-

ers. Burnside had lost 20 percent of his corps, but he still had more than twice the number of men on the field as did the Confederates. Overcome with doubts, Burnside began to wonder whether he could hold the hard-won bridge, and asked McClellan for reinforcements that would not be sent.

Curiously, the cautious McClellan had the battle won, but he did not know that success was in his immediate grasp. He had two corps in reserve and, if he had

had the nerve, these fresh regiments could have been thrown forward into the thinly held Confederate battle line, which would have been destroyed. He lacked the resolve to throw his last reserves into the battle, however, and lost a grand opportunity to permanently seal the fates of the Army of Northern Virginia, Robert E. Lee, and perhaps the entire rebellion.

One man out of every four engaged had been killed or wounded in the battle fought along the banks of Antietam Creek.

The indecisive engagement, one of the turning points of the entire war, left the opposing forces facing one another on the morning of September 18. The losses of the previous day were the greatest that had occurred in American history: 22,726 men had been killed or wounded.

Lee marched for the safety of Virginia that night—the first invasion of the North had come to an end. McClellan, predictably, refused to attack even though two fresh divisions arrived to reinforce his army, giving the Union commander a two-to-one advantage. McClellan had had enough combat and Lincoln had had enough of McClellan, who was relieved of his command. Little "Mac" reviewed his troops for the last time on November 10 and began to prepare to run for president, opposing Lincoln as a peace candidate.

While the battle at Antietam had technically been a draw, Lee's repulse from northern territory gave Lincoln the opportunity to issue the Emancipation Proclamation. This document would have a great impact far from the area in which the Civil War was being fought. Lincoln had hoped to deprive the Confederacy of much of its economic strength by encouraging many of the South's slaves to escape, but the greatest impact of the Proclamation was felt in Europe.

Britain and France had been waiting to decide on recognition of the Confederacy, but the Emancipation Proclamation's moral impact in countries where slavery had been forbidden long ago ensured that the Confederacy would fight alone against the North. There would be little discussion of foreign help after the battle of Antietam. Lincoln carefully constructed his proclamation to liberate slaves only in the states in open rebellion against the national government. The border states, which were slave-holding areas, could still choose to join the rebellion and Lincoln carefully avoided offending

TOP: Soldiers under the command of General Joseph Hooker attacked Confederate formations near the Dunker Church. Entire lines of men were killed by aimed volleys from either side. ABOVE: This artillery caisson and dead soldiers mark the final position of Hooker's doomed advance.

President Abraham Lincoln met with General McClellan after the bloody fighting along Antietam Creek. Although it was a military stalemate, the Battle of Antietam presented Lincoln with an opportunity for a major moral and political victory: the issuance of the Emancipation Proclamation.

them. This partial liberation of slaves was met with some degree of anger as Lincoln's message seemed to be that someone could not own another human being—unless he was loyal to (or at least neutral toward) the United States during the Civil War. Then, as now, it was impossible for a politician to please everyone.

The tide had shifted favorably once again for the Union. Lee had been repulsed in Maryland and on October 8, Braxton Bragg was driven from Perryville, Kentucky, by Buell. Northern armies had been battering

"It was never my fortune to witness a more bloody, dismal battle-field."

—General Joseph Hooker

the defenses of Richmond in June and July and Lee had won a brilliant battle at Manassas at the end of August, but by October the fortunes of war had shifted once again (at Antietam).

Grant began repairing the mistakes that had been made by Halleck and was busily concentrating his forces in the west for a drive on Vicksburg in an effort to secure for the Union the whole length of the Mississippi River, thereby splitting the Confederacy and denying Richmond precious resources from the Confederate West.

chapter 4

VICKSBURG
Flowing Unvexed to the Sea

"If it should be asked why the 4th of July was selected as the day for surrender, the answer is obvious. I believed that upon that day I should obtain better terms."

—General Joseph C. Pemberton

The Federal army had been doing well in the west after their Confederate opponents had returned to widely dispersed positions and a static defense—the curse of the defender who is responsible for securing every line—following their frustrated counteroffensives at Shiloh and Perryville, Kentucky. General Joseph E. Johnston, now recovered sufficiently from the wounds he had received at Seven Pines, returned to the field. This excellent commander, however, lacked the resources to be able to halt Federal operations as Grant continued to maneuver toward his well-defined strategic goal, the opening of the entire length of the Mississippi River.

Command of the Confederate forces in northern Mississippi was assigned to Lieutenant General John C. Pemberton, commander of weakened forces too widely scattered to be able to resist the concentrated attack Grant was planning. The key to the control of the river was the city of Vicksburg, located on top of a bluff two hundred feet above the river.

Heavy guns on the high bluff located on a great bend in the Mississippi were positioned where they could dominate river traffic for miles in either direction. The lessons learned by naval officers at Fort Donelson would not be repeated here. The powerful batteries and extreme range that the guns of Vicksburg were capable of covering made this bend in the Mississippi a very dangerous place for an attack.

Combined operations conducted by Federal forces on the Mississippi drainage had experienced considerable success up to this point in the war. Farragut and Butler had captured New Orleans in spring 1862; Memphis—the northern extreme of the Confederacy—had fallen in June of the same year. The South still held Vicksburg and Port Hudson, however, along with the 250 miles of the Mississippi River that lay in between the two strongholds.

Lincoln, as any good chief executive would, had defined the military objective in

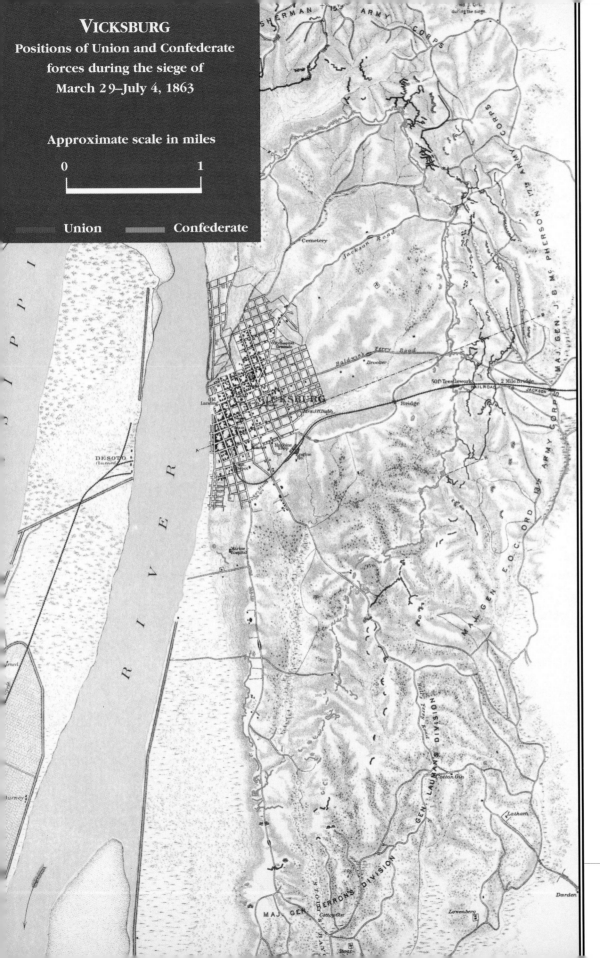

PAGE 61: Federal naval schooners were able to shell Confederate shore positions with newly installed mortars. These large, heavy weapons fired shells high enough into the air that they plunged vertically into the entrenchments at which they were aimed. LEFT: The decisive point of the Confederate defensive along the Mississippi, the critical transportation route for the South, was the city of Vicksburg. General Fremont had claimed that the side "controlling the Mississippi Valley would win the war." Knowing that the loss of the crucial rail and river shipping that went through the city of Vicksburg would threaten the existence of the Confederacy, Grant began to move to claim the fortress city.

grand terms: the Mississippi River should "roll unvexed to the sea." The success of this campaign would yield far more than the symbolic and political results suggested by Lincoln's words. With the securing of the Mississippi, the Federal military would be able to deny the Confederate East the supplies and thousands of reinforcements from the rich states of the Confederate Southwest. Vicksburg was the key—if it should fall, Port Hudson could not be defended.

The strategically important city could have been occupied easily at any time in early 1862, but Van Dorn had been ordered there soon after the battle at Pea Ridge. Since June, fifteen thousand of Van Dorn's men had been busily digging defenses and constructing field fortifications on the heights. Vicksburg was rapidly becoming the "Gibraltar of the West."

Federal troops, gunboats, and vessels carrying large siege mortars began to arrive along the Louisiana shore opposite Vicksburg, and troops were landed to begin to fortify the area. Engineering officers quickly recognized the obvious strength of Vicksburg and suggested a plan to bypass the fortress without a costly battle.

Vicksburg was located at the tip of a large, narrow bend in the river; plans were

made to dig a new channel for the Mississippi through the narrow neck of the peninsula. Soldiers and laborers, many of them African Americans, continuously worked on the canal while Farragut's floating batteries shelled the city's defenses from the river in an unsuccessful attempt to silence the defender's batteries. Farragut raced his vessels past Vicksburg's guns on June 22 and was joined upstream by additional gunboats from Memphis on July 1. Naval engagements against the strong shore batteries continued, but July 1862 was not a good month for the Federal forces.

Halleck was soon promoted to command in Washington, and Grant assumed command in the west. Pemberton was assigned Van Dorn's command in Vicksburg in October

TOP: Prosperity came to the river city of Vicksburg after taxpayers subsidized the construction of railroads linking it to distant markets. ABOVE: The Warren County Courtroom, with its Greek-styled columns, dominated the view of Vicksburg from the river. Steamboats delivered goods and produce to the city's wharves and warehouses, where they were stored until freight cars could move the items to the interior of the Confederacy.

Union forces under General William S. Rosecrans battled Braxton Bragg's Confederates to a bloody draw at Murfreesboro, a battle that took place early on in 1863.

as Grant placed Sherman in charge of a thirty-two-thousand-man army, which moved quickly to attack the city's defensive lines at Chickasaw Bayou on December 20. Pemberton was able to rush reinforcements to the bluffs above Sherman's large army and the ensuing battle cost Sherman two thousand casualties while the Confederates lost fewer than two hundred men.

December was a month filled with additional reverses for Grant's men. Nathan Bedford Forrest, one of the escapees from Fort Donelson, raided deep into the north of Grant's army and cut the Union army's telegraph communications and destroyed nearly sixty miles of railroad.

Van Dorn's Confederates had also been active; they raided the Federal supply depot at Holly Springs, capturing fifteen hundred

men and $1,500,000 worth of military supplies. Grant was left without supplies and communications for eleven days as he marched northward to Grand Junction, Tennessee, a distance of eighty miles. Grant only learned of Sherman's defeat at Chickasaw Bayou, the third of December's reverses, on January 8, 1863.

There was some good news for the Union in December, however, following the standoff between General William S. Rosecrans and Braxton Bragg at the battle of Murfreesboro. This battle, a strategic defeat for the Confederacy, cost Bragg twelve thousand men he could scarcely afford to lose as he was forced closer to Chattanooga.

Grant's reverses were taken in stride as he continued to keep his general objective in view. Lost battles did not mean the end of a

General Joseph E. Johnston, convalescing from a wound he had received at Seven Pines, had left Robert E. Lee in command in Virginia and could spare no troops for the defense or relief of Vicksburg after Grant began his siege.

Very heavy casualties resulted from the Federal attack on Vicksburg's defenses. The color-bearer of the 22nd Iowa Regiment may have planted his colors on the high breastworks, but the attackers were driven back.

VICKSBURG

campaign and Grant continued to press toward Vicksburg with his usual tenacity. Other plans failed and rising water destroyed the channel intended to allow Federal ships to bypass Vicksburg's guns, but these failures only served to increase Grant's determination to capture the fortress.

Grant's next moves were more successful. Gunboats and transports protected infantry regiments that were delivered fresh (i.e. not exhausted by days of marching prior to entering battle). Sherman was sent on a diversion against the doomed city's defenses in late April as Grant prepared to move on a fast-paced campaign into the interior of Mississippi.

Abandoning his base and supply depots at Grand Gulf, knowing that Pemberton could be expected to move against his nonexistent supply lines back to the river, Grant moved out on a three-week campaign inside hostile territory. His gamble permitted his troops to operate on the dry land south and east of the city while his troops lived off the land as they maneuvered between the forces of both Pemberton and Johnston. As anticipated, Pemberton moved to cut Grant's abandoned supply lines with the river rather than unite his forces with those of Johnston to strike Grant in a decisive battle. This error allowed Grant to wage a maneuver campaign between the forces of his two enemies over which he would have had no numerical advantage if they had united their forces. Grant's losses were slight, and within three weeks Vicksburg was completely invested by

ABOVE: While Grant's army attacked Vicksburg from land, the Union navy shelled the town from the Mississippi River. Federal naval officers had accepted the risks associated with sailing their ocean warships into the shallow waters near Vicksburg. RIGHT: The Union navy played a decisive role in securing various waterways important to the Confederacy and shelling strategic cities along southern and western rivers.

VICKSBURG

OPPOSITE: *The 8th Wisconsin Infantry and mascot, an immature bald eagle named "Old Abe," rush into withering fire during the siege of Vicksburg.* ABOVE: *The artillery at Vicksburg turned out to be useless because defenders were unable to lower their muzzles sufficiently to draw a bead on the Union attackers.*

diers surrendered. The "Gibraltar of the West" had fallen.

As predicted, Port Hudson was unable to continue to resist Bank's attacks and the entire garrison surrendered three days after Vicksburg capitulated to Grant. July 1863 was the beginning of the end for the Confederacy. Vicksburg's defenders had ceased to resist on July 3—the same day the final shots were fired at Gettysburg.

Grant had demonstrated his ability to successfully manage his army through military reverses that would have halted other generals in their tracks. He had shown that he was willing to gamble for high stakes when he abandoned his base of operations and entered a maneuver campaign for three weeks inside enemy territory. His excellent Mississippi campaign served as a model for Sherman in the latter's triumphant march through Georgia to the sea. Grant

had proven that the risky project of maneuvering behind enemy lines could be handled successfully.

Losses for the Confederacy were enormous following the fall of Vicksburg. Nearly thirty thousand officers and men surrendered, giving up 172 artillery pieces and approximately sixty thousand muskets. More seriously, the Mississippi River was now open to Federal navigation from New Orleans to St. Louis. The Confederacy had been dealt a near-mortal blow. The new nation had been split, denying the East large quantities of supplies from the West. At the same time, the possibility of recognition from Britain and France was more unlikely than ever following major Union victories and the Emancipation Proclamation. The Union was winning on both military and political fronts.

Union besiegers. His army had marched 180 miles, won five battles, captured Jackson, Mississippi (the state capital), and caused six thousand Confederate casualties.

Grant ordered a general assault on the defenses of Vicksburg by his entire army on May 22, 1863, but the attack failed. The Federal army settled into a general siege: trenches were dug, tunnels were dug beneath the defenders and exploded, and by July 1 the Confederate garrison was using the last of its resources. Vicksburg raised the surrender flag on July 3, and on the following day, the nation's birthday, Pemberton and his sol-

"Port Hudson surrendered because its hour had come. The garrison was literally starving. With less than 3000 famished men in line... what else was left to do?"

— Lieutenant Colonel Richard B. Irwin

General John C. Pemberton served as the Confederate commander at Vicksburg. He came under suspicion from other Confederates because he had been born in Pennsylvania. After marrying a woman from Virginia and serving in the South with the prewar national army, he came to love the region.

chapter 5

GETTYSBURG
Pitting Force Against Force

Following the general standoff between Lee and McClellan at Antietam in September 1862, McClellan was replaced by General Ambrose Burnside. The new commander of the Army of the Potomac returned to the old strategy of invading Virginia, which brought the opposing forces together at the Rappahannock crossings, near Fredericksburg. Lee's army fought a purely defensive battle there from protected positions that allowed the Confederates to receive Union assaults and decimate them. Lee won a lopsided victory at Fredericksburg and would have been well advised to remain in prepared, fortified positions to repel additional invasions as they came. Gradually, the will of the northern population to continue the attack at such a high cost in lives lost might have been sapped. The logic, however, that had led Lee to attempt the invasion of Maryland in 1862 was still active.

Lee had managed to win some decisive victories, but the Union was continuing its advance in the Mississippi region and the naval blockade was beginning to draw tighter daily. He continued to feel that recognition by the North and peace for the Confederacy could be achieved only through large-scale military victories within northern territory. As Lee saw it, the South could win the war only by breaking the political will of the northern population to continue fighting; and this would never happen if Federal reverses occurred only in Virginia. He also knew that eventually Federal success in the west would permit large Union forces to shift against the Army of Northern Virginia and eliminate it.

Before he could prepare for a second invasion, however, Lee was forced to send Longstreet and his three divisions to southeast Virginia and North Carolina's coast to counter a potential amphibious landing that would threaten the railroads connecting North Carolina and Richmond. If Lee had not been forced to send Longstreet south, it is

"Gettysburg was the turning point in the great struggle.... [It] inspired the armies and people of the North.... [It] was at Gettysburg that the right arm of the South was broken."
—General E.M. Law

GETTYSBURG

likely that Lee would have opened the 1863 campaign season with an invasion of Pennsylvania. As it was, Lee and his diminished army remained in position near the city of Fredericksburg.

Following the battle of Fredericksburg, Burnside had been replaced by Major General Joseph Hooker, who managed to surprise Lee with an aggressive crossing of the Rappahannock at the end of April. Lee immediately ordered Longstreet to return with his three divisions, but these were so dispersed that they could not be recalled quickly enough.

On his approach to Fredericksburg, Hooker ordered his army to swing wide to the west to avoid the Confederate defenses, which had caused the dramatic losses in Burnside's attack in December. The circuitous approach gave Jackson an opportunity to make a rapid march and a flanking maneuver against the Federal right. The Federal army, though defeated initially in this attempt, fought hard and reestablished good defensive positions, but Hooker ordered a retreat—back across the Rappahannock.

Lee's sixty-thousand-man army had managed to defeat a force that was twice as large, and they had accomplished this dramatic feat while Longstreet's three divisions were absent from the field. Unfortunately for the South, the great Stonewall Jackson died during this engagement (at the Battle of Chancellorsville), which was a great military and personal (for Lee) loss, but Lee was beginning to believe that his Army of Northern Virginia was capable of accomplishing any task he set before it. On May 9, Longstreet rejoined the army at Lee's Fredericksburg headquarters, and by June 3 the Confederates were preparing for the long march north.

Lee met with his cavalry commander, Major General James Ewell Brown (Jeb) Stuart, near Culpeper, Virginia, at Brandy Station on June 8 and inspected Stuart's five brigades of cavalry. Nearby Federal cavalrymen, eleven thousand strong, attacked early the following morning in what was to become the largest cavalry battle ever fought

on the North American continent. The battered Federal cavalry performed well against the more skilled Confederates and developed confidence in their abilities for the first time in the war.

Stuart paused to repair the damage the fighting had inflicted on his troops, but Lee would wait for nothing. He ordered General Richard Stoddert Ewell to move on June 10, the day after the battle at Brandy Station, in a new, skillfully planned campaign. Ewell marched through the Shenandoah Valley toward Winchester as Longstreet moved on a parallel course on the eastern slope of the Blue Ridge Mountains. A.P. Hill was ordered to follow Ewell's route once Hooker's army began to move. Ewell had only recently been assigned to command Jackson's corps, but he would pass his first test with flying colors.

By June 13, Ewell's lead divisions were approaching Winchester, where Federal Major General Robert Milroy commanded a garrison of over five thousand men. Both Lincoln and Halleck had been trying to convince Milroy of the wisdom of a rapid retreat from Winchester to the (albeit dubious) safety of Harper's Ferry, thirty miles away, but Winchester's commander felt he was safe, particularly since the Army of the Potomac would prevent the enormous Confederate army from moving rapidly against him. Realizing his error as the attack began, Milroy ordered an evacuation during the night, but encountered a large force that had been sent to block his retreat.

A general engagement opened that night at Stephenson's Depot, approximately four miles northeast of Winchester, and by dawn Milroy's small army had suffered 443 casualties and lost 3,358 prisoners to Ewell's corps. The opening battles of the 1863 campaign had gone well for the Confederates, and the long, gray-clad columns continued their lengthy march to the Potomac crossings. Curiously, they would make the move without the scouting of much of Stuart's cavalry.

Stuart had received severe criticism in the Richmond newspapers following the surprise Union attack at Brandy Station. Given his flair for the dramatic, everyone expected him to recover some of his reputation in the upcoming campaign. Stuart wanted to harass Hooker's troops. Lee reluctantly agreed to the plan, but insisted that the cavalry move to the left flank of the infantry columns as soon as Hooker crossed the Potomac. Stuart's best brigades moved out on June 25, and from that point on through much of the upcoming battle they were unable to provide information to Lee as to the location and movement of Hooker and the Army of the Potomac.

Uneventful crossings occurred at the Potomac, and the Confederate army marched into the interior of Pennsylvania. On June 27, Lee learned while he was at Chambersburg—from a report from Longstreet's scout Harrison—of Hooker's move out of Maryland and across the Potomac. He gave orders to have the Army of Northern Virginia concen-

ABOVE: *General Joseph Hooker was given command of the Army of the Potomac following Burnside's defeat at Fredericksburg. Soon, however, he was defeated after a fierce battle at Chancellorsville and George Meade replaced him. OPPOSITE: After winning at Chancellorsville, Lee began to move his army into Pennsylvania in order to locate food and supplies. Their marches would culminate at the small town of Gettysburg.*

trate its forces to meet Hooker's army because a battle would soon develop. Federal leaders knew that the loss of an important city—Washington, Baltimore, or Philadelphia—would be a major victory for the Confederacy and were prepared to fight a major battle to prevent such a loss.

Lee was encouraged by Longstreet to fight purely defensive battles (as they had done at Fredericksburg) in order to inflict severe losses on the Union army, but Lee could not afford to adopt this tactic. He had little room to move about as he had to remain in contact with his extended supply lines in the Shenandoah Valley. His men were able to feed themselves from the rich farms in the area, but an extended stay in a

single area would soon deplete the available food supplies. To construct fortifications and fight a defensive battle in a single location would also seriously deplete the ammunition supply, which was also dependent on the tenuous supply line stretching back through the Shenandoah. The upcoming battle was not of Lee's choosing, but circumstances forced him to fight it. Longstreet had encouraged an attack on the Federal left, placing the Confederate army between the Army of the Potomac and Washington, thereby forcing the Union army to attack. Lee probably felt that the Union army would not be forced to attack, but would play a waiting game as reinforcements arrived daily. Confederate divisions could not move against Baltimore

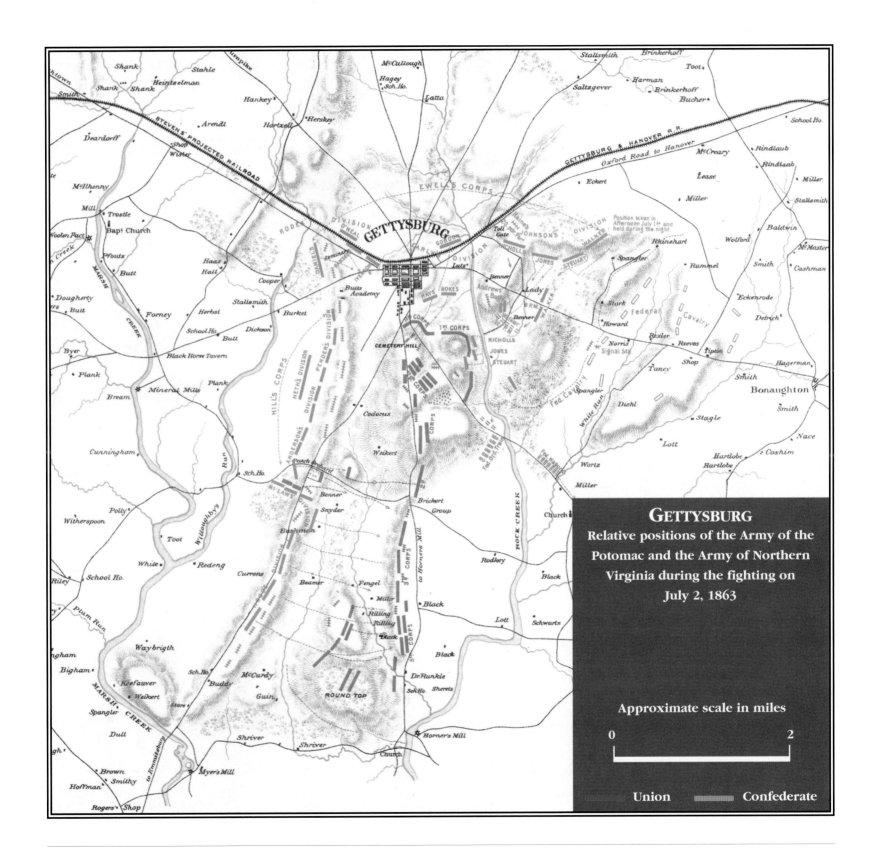

GETTYSBURG

Relative positions of the Army of the Potomac and the Army of Northern Virginia during the fighting on July 2, 1863

Approximate scale in miles

0   2

Union   Confederate

or Washington with an unfought army at their rear, and furthermore the Union army would have no difficulty in feeding its troops, while the Confederate army would be unable to feed itself.

Geography was also against Longstreet's recommendation. Any battle east of Gettysburg would deprive Lee of secure escape routes back through the gaps in the South Mountain range and the prearranged crossings-to-safety in Virginia. Lee felt the immediate and pressing need to fight a battle—a large-scale battle—in Pennsylvania, at a location where a Federal defeat would spell disaster for the Union army, but a Confederate defeat would be manageable for Lee. A movement to the east would put his army in a location where defeat could become a military disaster for the Confederates. Lee had to fight a battle, and Gettysburg was the place where it would be fought.

As the armies drew close to one another, Lee learned from Harrison (a spy, full name unknown) that Hooker had been replaced by Major General George G. Meade on June 28, which was the fifth change of command in the last ten months for the Army of the Potomac. The Confederate army was located northwest of Gettysburg as the Army of the Potomac marched toward them from the southeast. Both armies began to close the gap separating them on June 30 and a severe engagement developed as contact was made in the vicinity of the town.

Meade, a West Point graduate and veteran of the Mexican War, had served competently prior to his recent appointment as a replacement for Hooker and he began to issue orders to his commanders. After learning that Confederates were between Chambersburg and Gettysburg, he ordered three corps of his army to concentrate in the direction of the enemy. John Buford, commanding a Federal cavalry division, entered the excited town just before noon on June 30 and

ABOVE: General George G. Meade, a West Point graduate and veteran of the Mexican War, had received command of a corps after Fredericksburg. Joseph Hooker was overwhelmed by the responsibilities of command and Meade was placed in command of the Army of the Potomac. RIGHT: Confederate James Johnson Pettigrew also charged the Union lines at Gettysburg, but only George Pickett would receive credit for the attack.

found that a Confederate infantry brigade had approached the town and then quickly withdrawn from it. The Confederates, under the command of James Pettigrew, had come to the town to locate shoes, but had withdrawn when the approach of Buford's cavalry was detected. Buford knew the following morning would bring a general engagement in which his troopers would be sorely pressed until the arrival of heavier infantry divisions.

Confederate skirmishers made their initial contact with Buford's pickets at about 5:30 A.M., and severe fighting developed as the Confederates discovered that instead of local militia they were facing the Army of the Potomac. This was a different Union army from the one that had faced the rebel army at Bull Run and in other Virginia battles: poor officers had been replaced as new, experienced officers had risen to command and private soldiers had gained plenty of combat experience. The Federal army had by this time become a large professional army and did not hesitate to engage Lee's upcoming divisions.

Lee gave orders that no general engagement be started on July 1. His army was scattered over unfamiliar terrain within the enemy's territory: Ewell was several hours away to the north and Longstreet's entire corps would need a full day to march in from the west. General Henry Heth (pronounced "Heath") ordered his leading brigades into the town, but they were held up for an hour by Buford's cavalrymen's carbines and horse artillery.

Buford watched the opening rounds of the battle from the top of the Lutheran Seminary building as preparations were made to hold Gettysburg. Additional Union troops—including the Iron Brigade, soldiers who had gained strong reputations for their fighting ability at South Mountain and Antietam—were quickly sent to occupy positions at McPherson's Ridge. As the initial fighting spread, Heth reported that a "heavy force" had been encountered in and around Gettysburg. A short lull developed around noon as reinforcements for both sides began to arrive on the field and soldiers rushed about to occupy various positions.

Men of Ewell's corps, a full division under the command of Major General Robert Rodes, arrived on the field out of the northeast and saw a thinly held line of Federal infantry

TOP: The gatehouse to Evergreen Cemetery on Cemetery Hill. ABOVE: The arrival of General Winfield Scott Hancock on Cemetery Hill during the battle served to rally the retreating soldiers, who rapidly reformed their lines to resist the oncoming Confederates.

in front of them. Sensing an advantage, Rodes ordered an immediate attack. In the rapidly changing situation, additional Federal infantry arrived as Rodes was forming his brigades into attack formations, but at 2 P.M. the Confederate leader ordered an attack. Federal brigades in partially protected positions poured a murderous fire into the Confederate attackers and casualties on both sides were enormous. By the end of the day, Heth had lost fifteen hundred men from his seventy-five-hundred-man division and the Iron Brigade had nearly ceased to exist. Entering the defense of McPherson's Ridge with 1,829 men, the westerners had suffered a staggering 1,153 casualties by the end of the day.

At 3 P.M., the Confederate army began a heavy assault against the Federal defenders in positions north of the town. Ewell's subordinates, Jubal A. Early and Rodes, pressed against the Federal XI Corps from the north and Heth, reinforced by the arrival of William Dorsey Pender's division, attacked I Corps from out of the west. Under this terrible, unrelenting pressure I Corps broke and fled into the town. These men and the soldiers of XI Corps moved through Gettysburg into positions south of the town—Cemetery Hill, Culp's Hill, and Cemetery Ridge—and the two hills at the southern end of the ridge, Little Round Top and Big Round Top.

These were strong positions, but they were long and would require additional reinforcements if the new defensive line was to be held. All available men, including the decimated Iron Brigade, were sent to hold this line as III Corps and XII Corps marched to their aid.

Young Lieutenant Bayard Wilkeson and his small battery, Company G, 4th U.S. Artillery, fire on the Confederate lines from exposed positions. The nineteen-year-old officer lost his life here.

> *"It had not been General Lee's intention to deliver a general battle whilst so far from his base, unless attacked, but he now found himself by the mere force of circumstance commited to one."*
>
> —General Henry J. Hunt

As the tired, bloodied Federal troops climbed into positions at Cemetery Hill, Lee sent his aide Walter Taylor to Ewell with the request that Ewell continue to push forward, "if practicable," and secure the strategic heights. Ewell, a veteran who had served under Stonewall Jackson—a general who had left no ambiguity in orders to subordinates—was new to command at this level and did not drive forward as the aggressive Jackson might have done in this situation.

It was at this point that Longstreet argued for shifting over to the defensive, into positions between the Army of the Potomac and Washington, and forcing Meade to attack them while they were in strong positions. Lee disagreed with this attempt to change the battle plan in the face of the enemy, and

Severe fighting occurred as defenders met attackers in the fields and hills surrounding Gettysburg. Flags, the most recognizable symbols of the individual combat units, were sought-after trophies, and tremendous fights developed over their possession.

Harvard graduate Colonel Strong Vincent led his brigade to Little Round Top, a strategic position that was soon to receive the attention of the Confederate army. He fell, mortally wounded, while rallying his sorely pressed soldiers; they eventually received reinforcements and were able to hold their positions.

after a delay in the anticipated attack by Ewell, Lee rode to Jackson's successor's headquarters. By the time Lee arrived, the possibility of gaining the advantage had been lost—III Corps and XII Corps had arrived at Cemetery Ridge.

Meade had inspected the new defensive line on the low hills just south of Gettysburg and decided to fight the battle from there.

The morning of July 2 opened with additional troop movements. Longstreet continued to suggest that his battle plan be adopted. Lee declined again and began to issue verbal orders to his corps commanders. Interestingly, Lee prepared no written orders. Also, he seemed to be ill as the battle developed. Some officers reported that Lee was suffering from severe diarrhea, but his illness may have been more severe than these observers thought. The commander had experienced sharp pain in his chest and arms earlier in the year, which may have been symptoms of heart disease—angina—brought on by the stress of battle.

This was less than an excellent day for the Confederate commanders. Longstreet, possibly irritated that Lee had rejected his suggestion as to how to fight the battle, delayed in opening his attack. Regardless of the reason for the delay, Longstreet did not get his corps moving until noon. Unity of command—having one commander in charge during battle—is a basic military principle that was in danger at this point in the battle of Gettysburg. Neither Lee's disappointment at the day's progress nor the pain from his illness were improved by the long-awaited arrival of his missing cavalry commander, Jeb Stuart, to headquarters (Stuart showed up just as Longstreet was ordering his corps into motion).

Lee was visibly angry at Stuart and involuntarily raised his hand as if to strike the tardy cavalry commander. By riding around the entire Federal army (in a raid that may

Little Round Top was the critical point in the Union line. If the Confederate attack had broken through there, the result of the Battle of Gettysburg may have been different.

have been planned to recover some of the prestige he had lost at Brandy Station), Stuart had left Lee without speedy and reliable intelligence in the face of a large army while deep within enemy territory. Lee had been forced to send eight separate couriers riding rapidly through Pennsylvania, in all directions, to deliver the message that a great battle was to be fought at Gettysburg and that Stuart was needed. Fortunately for Stuart, Lee soon put aside his anger and asked for his subordinate's help in winning the battle.

After the delay caused by Lee's preoccupation with the plans of his subordinates, the attack was opened on the second day, after

3 P.M., by Longstreet. One of Longstreet's divisions, commanded by Lafayette McLaws, had expected little or no opposition as he moved into his assigned assault position, but was surprised by a large mass of Federal soldiers in his front and on both flanks. These Union regiments were in positions they should not have occupied.

Curiously, part of the Union army had moved from its assigned position along Cemetery Ridge and left the south flank of the Union defensive line, dangerously weakening it. Meade rode to the commander of the out-of-place troops, Major General Daniel Sickles, but it was too late to pull them back.

The attack had begun and Sickles was dangerously exposed.

At nearly the same time, Union General Gouverneur K. Warren discovered a key position, which was undefended, from which artillery, once in position, could fire on the entire Federal line. He ordered the diversion of reserves before Alabama troops could continue their attack from Big Round Top. The war may have been saved for the Union by the aggressive defenders, the 20th Maine commanded by Colonel Joshua Chamberlain, on Little Round Top. Each attack by the Alabama troops was repulsed, but at great cost. The 20th Maine lost 120 men in its defense of Little Round Top.

Sickles' III Corps was forced back from its advanced position with a severe number of casualties, but the main line was secure. Meade was able to shift troops from quiet portions of his line to areas under attack as poorly timed Confederate attacks continued to drive up casualties on both sides. Hill attacked late in the day with minor results and Ewell was unable to get his assault—an

ABOVE: General George Pickett was the commander of the Virginians ordered to attack the Union defenders on Cemetery Ridge. He carried out the order despite the fact that he must have understood the peril his men faced—one of his brigades lost eighty-eight men while waiting to attack. BELOW: Culp's Hill as seen from Cemetery Hill.

attack that should have been timed to coincide with that of Longstreet—launched until around 6 P.M. Ewell's men managed to reach Cemetery Hill, but could not hold their advanced, unsupported positions and were withdrawn. The Army of the Potomac had managed to hold the line against the Army of Northern Virginia.

The third day began with conferences on both sides. Lee was determined to continue with the attack, but Longstreet—as he had throughout the entire battle—had a different opinion. On the Federal side, Meade was unsure of what course to take and made the decision to remain and fight it out on the hills to the south of Gettysburg after a council of his officers recommended that plan.

Ewell would soon be making a diversionary attack at Culp's Hill; the main assault would be made by divisions under the command of Longstreet. Long remembered in history as "Pickett's Charge," the attack against the center of the Union line was composed of three divisions: Pettigrew's, Trimble's, and Pickett's. At 3 P.M., the fifteen

The valiant 1st Maryland Battalion, noted for its extremely brave men, was among the many Confederate forces to be decimated attempting to wrest Culp's Hill from Federal defenders.

GETTYSBURG

thousand Confederate soldiers of these divisions were ordered to march across fourteen hundred yards of open ground toward approximately ten thousand Federal soldiers in protected positions. All of the available Union artillery began to fire into the orderly ranks of Confederate soldiers as they came within range. The effect of the cannon fire was devastating and large numbers of men began to fall. Under fire from artillery as well as volleys from entrenched infantry, the Confederate formations began to entangle as

they were forced to the center. General James Kemper tried to get his men moving toward the correct objective, but he himself was severely wounded.

The mob of Confederates in the center of the attack was massed fifteen to thirty deep as General Richard Garnett rode into it to restore order to the assault. Soon after, he was shot from his horse and killed.

The Union defensive line was broken as the Federal artillery position, Cushing's Battery, fired its last double-shotted canister

into the attackers. Cushing was killed as General Lewis Armistead placed his hat on the tip of his sword and led his men in a breakthrough. Armistead was mortally wounded as he reached Cushing's guns, but his men pressed onward as nearby Union reserve regiments mounted a counterattack.

The attacker in a case like this is in a difficult position. The losses over the open ground had been tremendous and the Confederate reserves were too far in the rear to be able to exploit the breakthrough. The

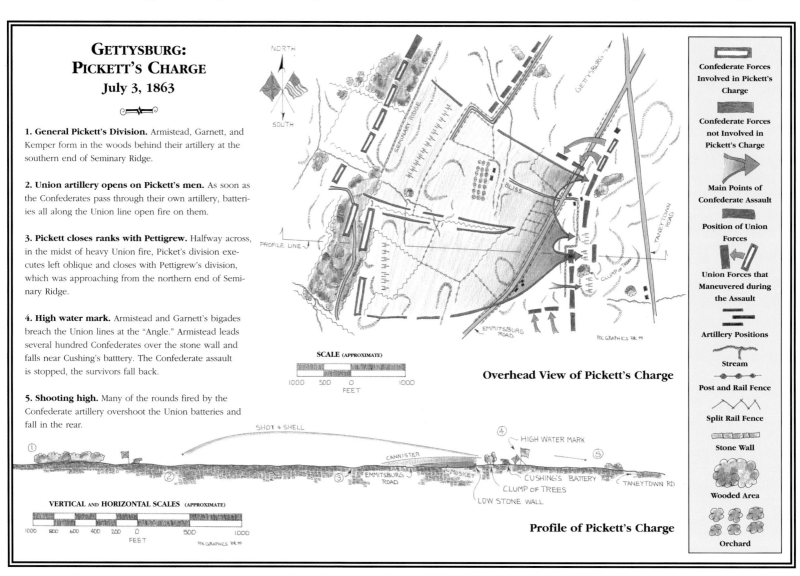

GETTYSBURG: PICKETT'S CHARGE
July 3, 1863

1. General Pickett's Division. Armistead, Garnett, and Kemper form in the woods behind their artillery at the southern end of Seminary Ridge.

2. Union artillery opens on Pickett's men. As soon as the Confederates pass through their own artillery, batteries all along the Union line open fire on them.

3. Pickett closes ranks with Pettigrew. Halfway across, in the midst of heavy Union fire, Picket's division executes left oblique and closes with Pettigrew's division, which was approaching from the northern end of Seminary Ridge.

4. High water mark. Armistead and Garnett's bigades breach the Union lines at the "Angle." Armistead leads several hundred Confederates over the stone wall and falls near Cushing's batttery. The Confederate assault is stopped, the survivors fall back.

5. Shooting high. Many of the rounds fired by the Confederate artillery overshoot the Union batteries and fall in the rear.

SCALE (APPROXIMATE)

1000 500 0 1000
FEET

Overhead View of Pickett's Charge

VERTICAL and **HORIZONTAL SCALES** (APPROXIMATE)

1000 800 600 400 200 0 500 1000
FEET

Profile of Pickett's Charge

Confederate Forces Involved in Pickett's Charge

Confederate Forces not Involved in Pickett's Charge

Main Points of Confederate Assault

Position of Union Forces

Union Forces that Maneuvered during the Assault

Artillery Positions

Stream

Post and Rail Fence

Split Rail Fence

Stone Wall

Wooded Area

Orchard

The valiant 1st Maryland Battalion, noted for its extremely brave men, was among the many Confederate forces to be decimated attempting to wrest Culp's Hill from Federal defenders.

surviving attackers who had penetrated into the Union defenses were too few in number to be able to hold their position in the face of the numerous Federal troops who rushed forward to plug the gap in the line. Within minutes, all of the Confederates who had passed into the Union lines were dead, wounded, or taken prisoner. Meanwhile,

additional Federal regiments began to converge on the point of the breakthrough.

The attack was over. Large groups of Confederates began to move down the slopes of Cemetery Ridge toward the rear. Pickett had lost nearly half of his soldiers in the attack against the center of the Federal line at Gettysburg. He had lost two generals

out of three engaged and the third was severely wounded. Every regimental commander in his division had fallen in the charge. The best of the South's officer corps fell along with very large numbers of soldiers. With the loss of these men, the ability to conduct full-scale offensive operations was also lost to the Confederacy at Gettysburg.

Union artillerymen were instrumental in halting the Confederate Army at Gettysburg. Experienced gunners, well supplied with ammunition, began to decimate Pickett's division as it crossed the broad field at the foot of Cemetery Ridge.

The third day's fighting, however, was not over. General Judson Kilpatrick lived up to his nickname, "Kill Cavalry," by ordering a foolhardy cavalry charge against the right wing of Longstreet. The charge, lead by Brigadier General Elon Farnsworth, resulted in little actual gain, and Farnsworth, who had objected to the plan, was killed in the attack. Stuart was engaged on the other end of the Federal line with his tired troopers

and was repulsed by Federal cavalry as he attempted to attack Meade's northern flank. The battle was coming to an end.

Lee waited for a Federal attack from new positions on Seminary Ridge, but Meade knew the commander of the Confederate army was simply inviting him to attack and avoided the temptation. Moving a company the size of the Union army at Gettysburg from a defensive posture into a counterattack

is extremely difficult and can lead to disaster. Meade had been in command of the Army of the Potomac for only six days and had spent the last three of them fighting one of the most ferocious battles in history. Faced with an opponent who was viewed as a military genius at the time, Meade probably made the correct decision.

A severe storm developed in the afternoon of July 4 and Lee ordered the Army of

Northern Virginia to make its preparations for the return to Virginia. The retreat took days; it was not until July 14 that Lee's army was across the Potomac (his engineers had built a hasty bridge across the river at Falling Waters). With approximately half of the army safely across, the Federal cavalry began its attack. Henry Heth's rear guard, under the command of General Pettigrew, fought tenaciously and broke up the cavalry charge, but Pettigrew himself was mortally wounded. This rear-guard action gave the Army of Northern Virginia the opportunity to escape. The raid into the North had resulted in a terrible loss for the Confederates—one from which they never recovered. As Lee was losing the battle in Pennsylvania, Grant was securing the Mississippi for the Union. The guns fell silent in both places on July 3 and when the dust cleared, it was apparent the rebel states had taken a beating: the Confederacy had been split along the Mississippi while the best army available to the South had been decimated in the North.

Casualties were high on both sides at Gettysburg. Meade lost slightly over twenty-three thousand men, primarily from two of his seven corps—in fact, those two corps ceased to exist at all after the battle. I and III Corps had suffered so many casualties that the survivors were simply incorporated into other commands rather than rebuilt with reinforcements. Confederate losses are estimated differently by various authorities, but they lost at least 20,500 soldiers at Gettysburg. The raw figures, however, don't tell the whole story. Percentagewise, the death count was severe: the Federal army lost 26 percent of its total strength and the Confederates lost approximately 28 percent.

A great deal of controversy remains regarding the conduct of the battle. Lee stated that he would have won the battle if he had had Stonewall Jackson with his army, and this appears to be a reasonable

Federal general Hugh Judson Kilpatrick lived up to his nickname, "Kill Cavalry," by ordering one of his brigades to charge Longstreet's men. The attacking brigade's commander, Elon J. Farnsworth, lost his life in an attack that gained nothing.

> ## *"One mistake of the Confederacy was in pitting force against force. The only hope we had was to out general the Federals."*
>
> —*General James Longstreet*

statement: the aggressive Jackson would not have delayed as Ewell had done on the evening of July 1; Jackson's presence would have held the opinions of Longstreet in check; and the unity of command would have been maintained. The outcome of the fighting might have been different. If Lee had won the battle, however, the strategic outcome would have been similar to what is today in the historical record.

Winning the Battle of Gettysburg would have left the Army of Northern Virginia extremely low on ammunition and encumbered it with numerous wounded soldiers requiring transportation and treatment. The Union army would have lost severely and casualties would have been higher than they actually were, but depleted ammunition and

supplies would have been replaced quickly as the army fell back toward major northern cities. Additional troops would have been mobilized to reinforce the Union army.

Winning at Gettysburg would have been a tremendous moral victory for the Confederacy and would have shaken the resolve of the population of the North; then again, the North had suffered severe defeats

ABOVE: Dead Union soldiers found in areas occupied by the Confederates were normally found stripped of both shoes and equipment. Throughout the war Confederate soldiers had little equipment and often went into battle without shoes. RIGHT: Meade and his forces crept forward carefully and crossed the Potomac River two weeks after the Battle of Gettysburg. The slow movement of Meade allowed Lee to escape.

in the past and continued the fight with increased intensity. Anyway, a victory by Lee would have been offset by the simultaneous and decisive victory of Grant at Vicksburg.

The Army of Northern Virginia moved back into Virginia and the remainder of 1863 saw the North and South in what essentially was a stalemate. Meade was slow to go over to the attack, but actions along the Rappahannock River at Bristoe Station, Rappahannock Station, and Kelley's Ford showed that the fighting ability of the Army of Northern Virginia was no longer what it had once been.

When the Army of the Potomac began its next spring offensive, it was under the command of the man who had been winning the war in the west, U.S. Grant. The Army of Northern Virginia would maneuver openly against him only on May 5 and May 6, in the Battle of the Wilderness. The South had lost so much of its former power that Grant was able to continue his advance toward Richmond while Lee's divisions were forced to oppose his attacks from within entrenchments. There would be an entirely different war in 1864.

chapter 6

MONOCACY
Saving Washington

The spring campaign began under new commanders in 1864. Ulysses S. Grant received the message from Secretary of War Stanton naming him commander of all of the Union armies on March 3, 1863. Soon after, Grant convened a hasty meeting with Sherman and they developed a simple plan: Sherman would concentrate his efforts on destroying the Confederate army, under the command of the capable Joseph E. Johnston, in the west. Meanwhile, Grant would focus his efforts on the destruction of the Army of Northern Virginia, which was under the command of Lee.

Grant quickly took advantage of the recent advance in communications technology—the telegraph—to coordinate the moves of all of the Union armies as if they were a single force with a common goal: the destruction of the armies of the Confederacy. Enormous Union forces were now in motion, presenting multiple and simultaneous problems for Lee. On May 4, 1864, the Army of the Potomac crossed the Rapidan to begin the Battle of the Wilderness as other armies began to move in other areas. General Benjamin Butler moved his Army of the James on transports from Fortress Monroe toward Richmond, but was bogged down at Bermuda Hundred when Confederate resistance stiffened. General Franz Sigel began operations in the Shenandoah Valley on May 2 as generals Crook and Averell began campaigns in southwestern Virginia. Massive operations were in progress against the Confederate army that would continue relentlessly for the next eleven months. If Grant had hoped to get Lee's attention at the opening of the spring campaign, he had clearly succeeded.

Sigel, marching up the Shenandoah Valley (in a southerly direction), presented a threat both to Lee's rear areas and to the vital industrial area of Lynchburg, Virginia. Sigel's march had to be countered, so forces were hastily assembled to oppose him at the small

"[The] situation of Washington was precarious and Wallace moved with considerable promptitude to meet the army at the Monocacy. He could hardly have expected to defeat him,... but he hoped to cripple and delay him."

—*General Ulysses S. Grant*

town of New Market. Confederate General John Breckinridge hurried forces from southwestern Virginia to block Sigel's advance, but in doing so left a weakened force to oppose Crook and Averell as the Union generals moved to destroy the vital transportation link in the area, the Virginia and Tennessee Railroad.

Confederate defenders met Crook at Cloyd's Mountain as Averell and his cavalry moved to the west to attack Saltville. The battle fought between Crook and Albert Gallatin Jenkins, and later John McCausland, continued for only fifty-two minutes before the Confederates were forced to withdraw, but it was filled with tremendous violence that was matched perhaps only by Antietam. This initial battle of the spring campaign was essentially a draw because Crook and Averell were forced to withdraw into the mountains of West Virginia after destroying the vital bridge over New River.

Sigel continued his march in the Shenandoah even as Crook and Averell were withdrawing. He drew near Breckinridge's waiting regiments, which had been reinforced by cadets from the Virginia Military Institute—young men who were about to experience their first battle. By the end of the day, May 15, Sigel was retracing his steps down the valley. He had been beaten by the

PAGE 91: Resolute Union General Lee Wallace led his men in a crucial defense of Washington, D.C., against Confederate invasion at the Battle of Monocacy. RIGHT: This painting of the heroic charge of the cadets of Virginia's Military Institute is located in the Jackson Memorial Hall. It shows the youthful cadets attacking through heavy fire toward a Federal artillery battery. Their participation in the battle—as Breckinridge's last reserves—closed a gap in the Confederate lines and saved the southern army from probable defeat.

TOP: *Virginia's Military Institute cadet Jack Stanard was severely wounded at New Market and died. ABOVE: Cadet F.W. James was also a veteran of New Market.*

These five young men from Virginia's Military Institute were already veterans at the time this photograph was taken; they had served at New Market.

hastily assembled troops under Breckinridge. Grant, in no mood to forgive the failure of the political general from Germany, replaced Sigel with General David Hunter. Grant's plan wasn't working well—he had lost forty thousand men since crossing the Rapidan only a few weeks earlier and there were far too few replacements in the depots to satisfy his needs. In addition, the rest of his strategic planning was not going well. The victory at New Market had allowed Breckinridge to send two of his brigades to reinforce Lee just before the Battle of Cold Harbor, where Grant again lost heavily.

LEFT: Federal General Franz Sigel led his small army against John C. Breckinridge's force on this battlefield. When the guns fell silent, Brecken-ridge had managed to cripple Sigel's army and temporarily save the Shenandoah Valley for the Confederacy. ABOVE: This antebellum photograph shows John C. Breckenridge when he was Vice President of the United States.

General David Hunter was different from most of the other officers available for command at the time. An aggressive Virginian who had remained with the Union army, he was back on the march in the Shenandoah Valley within a week of assuming Sigel's command. Grant had ordered him to unite with Averell and Crook before moving against and destroying the critical rail junctions at Charlottesville and Lynchburg. He was then to return to his base in the northern part of the valley or reinforce the Army of the Potomac.

As he moved through the rich farm areas toward his goal, Hunter freely retaliated against Confederate partisan raiders and ambushes against his supply line by ordering the burning of every rebel dwelling within five miles of each incident. He was able to defeat the Confederate defenders at the Battle of Piedmont and open the rest of the valley for the safe march of his army to Lynchburg. Confederate Brigadier General John McCausland, the man who had led the attempted breakout at Fort Donelson, was the commander of a small cavalry brigade that remained in front of Hunter, attempting to delay his march. By the time Hunter arrived in front of Lynchburg, the small garrison defending the city had been reinforced by Jubal Early and his infantry corps. Hunter, short of food and ammunition by this time, was forced to retreat into the mountains of West Virginia (and on to supply bases in the Kanawha Valley) in order to avoid the destruction of his command.

The Shenandoah Valley clear of Union forces, Early moved to take full advantage of

Major General David Hunter replaced Sigel after the Union defeat at New Market. Known as "Black Dave" by his own men, this evil-tempered general ordered the destruction of civilian homes in the Shenendoah Valley.

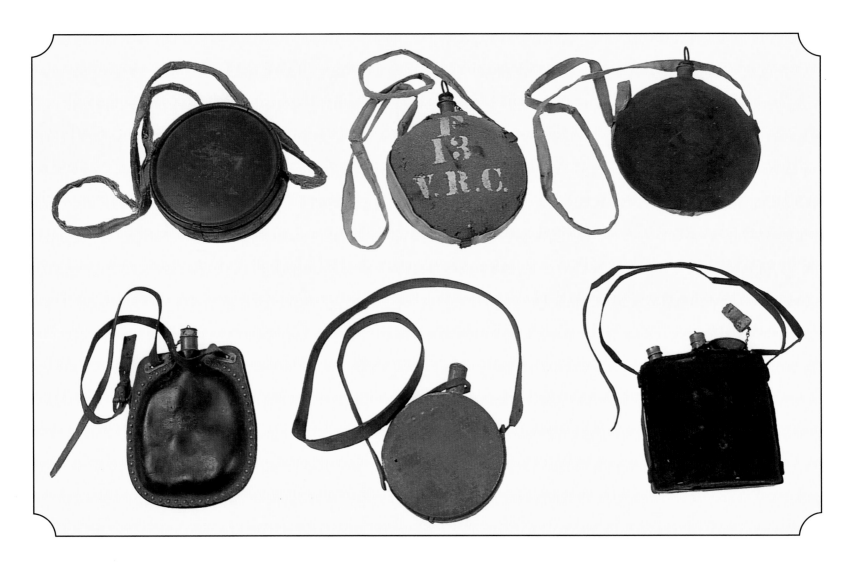

The equipment used by both armies during the Civil War came in a variety of shapes and materials, particularly in the case of the Confederacy. The two canteens on the left are of Confederate issue while the other four are Union products. Occasionally, Confederate soldiers would scavenge for and use Union canteens.

the situation. He moved quickly, hoping to invade Maryland, force Grant to weaken the forces opposing Lee at Petersburg and Richmond, and attack the defenses of Washington. This was 1864, an election year, and the northern population was beginning to show the strains of the ongoing war. Grant's enormous losses and relatively few gains had contributed greatly to this state of affairs in the North. George McClellan had decided to oppose Lincoln in the fall elections as a peace candidate. An attack against the national capital would clearly serve to weaken the administration.

Early ordered his small army forward. He crossed the Potomac at Shepherdstown on July 5, bypassing the frightened Sigel in barricaded positions on Maryland Heights, and marched quickly on Washington before Grant had time to react. Early decided to ignore Hunter as he moved slowly up the Ohio River and then eastward on the Baltimore and Ohio Railroad toward the South's former base in the Shenandoah Valley. Early may have regarded the attack as a "forlorn hope," a suicide operation, but he continued to advance toward Washington.

Hagerstown, Maryland, would be the first to feel the force of the new invasion; John McCausland captured the town and collected twenty thousand dollars as a ransom (instead of burning it). Early had decided to collect money from northern towns captured to pay for the destructive reprisals that had been undertaken by "Black Dave" Hunter.

McCausland would soon face another veteran of the fighting at Fort Donelson, General Lew Wallace. Currently responsible for the defense of Maryland, Wallace was warned of the upcoming attack by a telegram from John W. Garrett, the president of the Baltimore and Ohio Railroad. Wallace began to gather all available units to defend the open approach to Washington. His was a small army of about twenty-five hundred militia and home guards supplemented by a small cavalry unit, the 8th Illinois Cavalry.

Wallace received his first reinforcements on July 8, when the 10th Vermont arrived from the Army of the Potomac. Grant had finally seen the peril facing Washington and quickly ordered the remainder of VI Corps and two divisions from XIX Corps, then arriving at Fortress Monroe, to Washington.

Early's small army was a real threat, especially because there was the danger that one of his subordinates, Brigadier General Bradley T. Johnson, would be able to free the seventeen thousand Confederate prisoners at Point Lookout prison, effectively doubling the size of Early's army. Johnson was from Frederick, Maryland, and was now involved in the capture of his hometown.

Frederick was to receive the same treatment as had Hagerstown. Once the small city was occupied, Early demanded 200,000 dollars from them to pay for the damage done by Hunter in the Shenandoah Valley. The city fathers of Frederick, however, asked for a delay in making the payment. These shrewd

After forcing David Hunter to retreat westward though West Virginia after Black Dave's attack on Lynchburg had failed, Jubal Early marched north through the Shenendoah Valley. By July 9, 1864, Early's Confederates arrived at the Monocacy River, where they found a smaller Union force under General Lew Wallace waiting for them. A quick victory here would have allowed the small Confederate army to occupy the national capital.

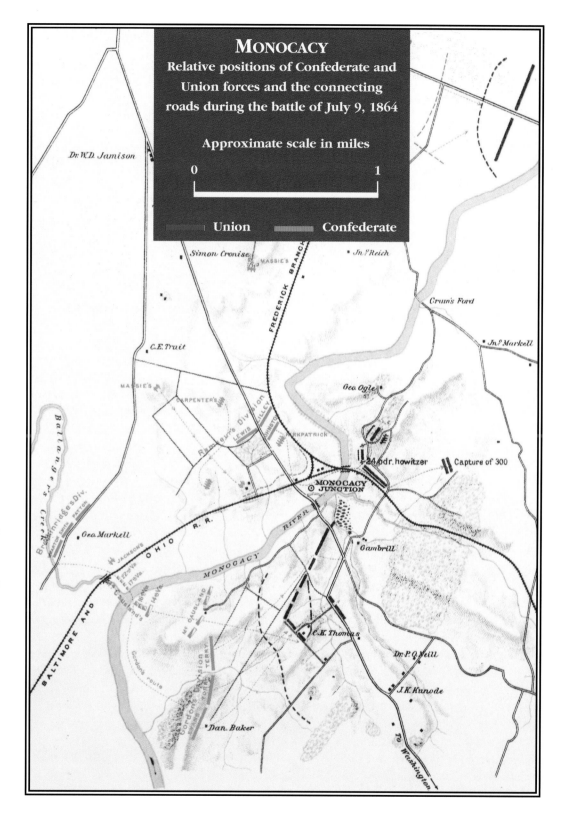

MONOCACY
Relative positions of Confederate and Union forces and the connecting roads during the battle of July 9, 1864

Approximate scale in miles

0   1

Union   Confederate

Courageous Confederate General John B. Gordon had suffered severe wounds at Antietam, but continued to fight. In fact, his division did much of the fighting at Monocacy.

Federal General Lew Wallace had distinguished himself at Fort Donelson and although he was not as successful at Shiloh, he saved the Union's capital at Monocacy.

ABOVE: Confederate General Jubal A. Early had voted against leaving the Union during Virginia's Secession Convention, but soon became an unequivocal supporter of the Confederacy. Criticized by many other Confederates at the time, Early managed an excellent campaign in the Shenendoah Valley in 1864. OPPOSITE: Frequently outnumbered and always poorly supplied, the Confederate army fought valiantly for four years and frequently defeated their opponent's larger armies.

businessmen knew that a battle was about to be fought in the vicinity and they were simply waiting to see who would win. Should the Confederates lose, they would save themselves a considerable expense.

Wallace and James B. Ricketts, a division commander in the Union VI Corps, had their men in the best positions available to them outside Frederick by 4 A.M., but the troops began to worry as they saw the huge dust clouds to the west that announced the approach of a large Confederate force.

Early knew that the Union army near Frederick would attempt to dispute his passage, but he was not worried. Bradley Johnson, unaware of the arrival by rail of Rickett's division, had reported that the Federal force was composed of what was essentially raw militia. Crossing the Mono-

cacy River with a substantial portion of his force was Early's immediate concern. He knew his men would have difficulty making the crossing while under fire and that the few bridges were closely held or threatened with immediate destruction. He sent Bradley Johnson north to cut the railroads connecting Frederick to Baltimore and to raid in the vicinity before continuing on to free the Point Lookout prisoners.

Early sent his other cavalry commander, John McCausland, to the south to cut connections with Washington and to seize the railroad bridge over the Monocacy River. McCausland's men located a ford and crossed the Monocacy River, during which they were engaged by men of the 8th Illinois Cavalry. The Federals were driven off, but McCausland was slightly wounded. His cavalrymen

dismounted, leaving their horses with holders, and continued with the attack—reduced in strength by one hundred men. Seven hundred of McCausland's dismounted troopers were moving against a fence that they mistakenly supposed was being held by local militia. Instead, seasoned veterans from the Army of the Potomac were concealed and waiting.

The horse holders remained in the rear as McCausland's dismounted men began their advance through the waist-high corn toward a force three times their size behind the

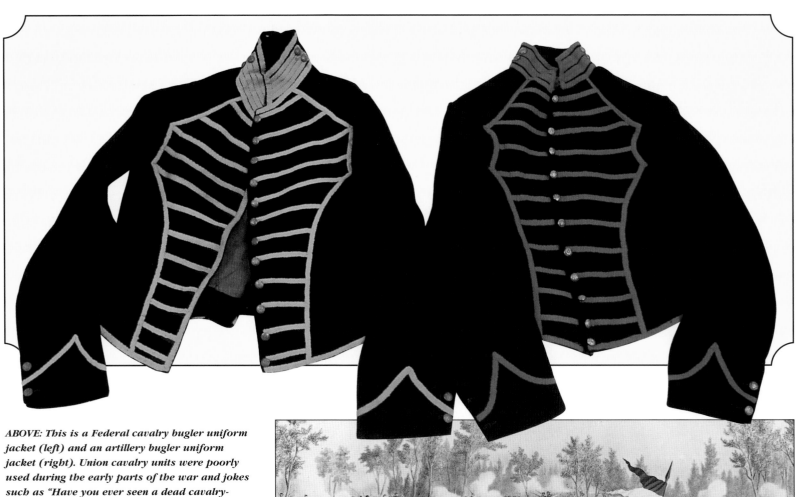

ABOVE: This is a Federal cavalry bugler uniform jacket (left) and an artillery bugler uniform jacket (right). Union cavalry units were poorly used during the early parts of the war and jokes such as "Have you ever seen a dead cavalryman?" were often heard. This attitude, however, changed as new, aggressive cavalry commanders rose in the Union ranks. By the end of the war, Federal cavalrymen operated as highly mobile mounted infantrymen and they made a difference on many battlefields. RIGHT: The 8th Illinois Cavalry engaged McCausland's troopers at Monocacy in a dismounted skirmish. BELOW: Spencer carbine bullets of the type used by Union cavalry.

boundary fence. When the Confederates came into range, the Federal soldiers rose and fired a disciplined volley into the surprised cavalrymen. When the smoke cleared from the cornfield, it appeared to be empty. Survivors of the murderous volley were slipping to the rear, but many were dead or wounded. McCausland made a personal reconnaissance of the Federal positions and gathered his men for a second attempt that was more successful. Only a strong leader in charge of seasoned, disciplined troops would have been able to get his men to attack a second time. Unable to hold the exposed positions they captured, McCausland's cavalrymen again withdrew. Shortly afterward Major General John Gordon crossed the river with his infantry division.

The work of the cavalry was the key to the opening of the battle. Early, though long a critic of the cavalry, wrote that "Gordon moved across the Monocacy on the enemy's flank by a route that had been opened by McCausland's brigade of cavalry in a very gallant manner." McCausland's cavalrymen moved off to the south to block a retreat toward Washington by Wallace or the arrival of Union reinforcements.

Buglers, who were often adolescents, used bugles such as this one to signal commands to widely separated cavalrymen.

Buglers were normally found with the cavalry commanders' staff and many were killed or wounded while serving their country.

Gordon's division was in attack position by 3 P.M. Lew Wallace reassessed the situation. He wanted to evacuate from overextended positions that could be easily attacked on its flank and rolled up, but he could not retreat in the face of an imminent attack by Gordon. They had to remain and fight. Gordon, a veteran of much of the combat up to this point in the war, was eager to accommodate them.

Gordon's soldiers advanced in the face of very heavy fire, losing men every few feet, across a field that was filled with shocks of freshly cut wheat, obstacles that forced them to break their formations. Gordon's attack began to bog down despite covering fire from several guns across the Monocacy under the command of Major William McLaughlin (in whose unit one of the author's ancestors served). These guns were fired at Federal sharpshooters concealed in a house on the battlefield. Reinforcements were rushed to aid Gordon; General Ricketts hurriedly moved his Union soldiers to shore up the threatened line, but this was precisely what the Confederate commanders wanted him to do. The thinned right side of the Federal line could no longer be anchored against the obstacle of the Monocacy River, opening it to a Confederate flank attack. Gordon quickly sent a Virginia brigade against the weakened right side of the Federal line of defense and forced the veterans to pull back, but not before the Federal soldiers inflicted severe casualties on the attacking Virginians. Ricketts was forced to withdraw while under fire, but he and his VI Corps veterans were able to move to the rear without the retreat becoming a retreat. The firing slowed and halted; it was too late in the day for Early to continue the attack.

Lew Wallace, who later wrote *Ben Hur*, had bought twenty-four hours for the defenders of Washington to prepare themselves while they waited for reinforcements to

Exhausted, poorly supplied, and hungry, Confederate soldiers were capable of making tremendous sacrifices in the face of overwhelming numbers of Union soldiers. Regardless of the Confederates' reasons for fighting, the mystique of their heroism lives on to this day.

"If Early had been but one day earlier, he might have entered the capital before the arrival of the reinforcements I had sent."

—General Ulysses S. Grant

arrive. The Battle of Monocacy had cost the Union 1,294 casualties, but the capital was saved. Early lost approximately seven hundred men—who could not be replaced—but continued to advance toward his target.

The Confederates moved down the dusty, hot roads toward Washington. They passed through Silver Spring, and by noon on July 11, Jubal Early was surveying Fort Stevens and planning his attack. His soldiers were exhausted—even the veteran, disciplined troops were worn out after the hot march. They were too tired to assault the Federal defensive line, which was held by hastily organized groups of walking wounded, convalescents, and untrained government clerks. Reinforcements from the VI and XIX Corps were en route, however.

The first men from VI Corps reached the trenches surrounding the capital in the early afternoon of July 11, and Jubal Early had lost his opportunity to win the war for the Confederacy. Severe skirmishing continued as the small Confederate army fought with the Federal reinforcements through July 12, but there would be no general attack. Early had ordered the division commanders to be ready to move in the night and had recalled Bradley Johnson from the raid against Point Lookout.

President Lincoln came out to Fort Stevens to watch the battle and actually came under hostile fire, but there was no large-scale attack on July 12. Early was going back to the relative safety of the Shenandoah Valley before the assembling Federal armies at his rear were able to box his small army up and destroy it. He crossed the Potomac at White's Ford and rested at Leesburg, Virginia, before continuing his march.

Early continued to hold the Shenandoah Valley into the late summer and sent John McCausland north into Pennsylvania in late July. Ordered to capture Chambersburg and collect a ransom or burn the small city, McCausland set torches to the buildings when the townspeople refused (or were unable) to comply. This raid revealed the continuing threat to Washington presented by Confederates in the Shenandoah; Grant ordered substantial forces to move there and destroy Early and his army. Defeated at Winchester on September 19, Early was forced up the valley, but was able to fight a successful battle against enormous odds at Cedar Creek on October 19. His small force was overwhelmed later in the day, ending Confederate dominance in this critical area of Virginia.

The Battle of Monocacy was small when compared to Gettysburg and many of the transition battles of the Civil War. It was, however, possibly the most crucial battle of the war. If Lew Wallace had been unable or unwilling to fight this delaying action, Early would have been attacking the defenses of Washington one day before any substantial reinforcements from VI and XIX Corps could have arrived. The Confederates would have been unable to hold the national capital, but the crucial loss to Early in mid-July would have doomed the Republican administration and Abraham Lincoln in the November elections. George McClellan, the peace candidate, may have been elected, and as president would have witnessed an entirely different outcome to the Civil War.

Lew Wallace and his small Union force were able to delay Early's Confederates for a full day, allowing reinforcements from Grant's army at Petersburg to enter Washington, D.C. Wallace's men saved the nation's capital from occupation and probably saved Lincoln's political career. Years later, veterans of the 15th New Jersey Infantry erected this monument on Monocacy battlefield to commemorate their deeds of 1864.

chapter 7

PEACHTREE CREEK
Breaking Connecting Links

Two rather ordinary looking soldiers met in a Cincinnati hotel room during March 1864; only the stars on their shoulder straps gave a hint as to the importance of their meeting. These two men were Ulysses S. Grant, commander of all of the armies of the United States, and his chief lieutenant, William T. Sherman, now the commander of Union forces in the west, Grant's previous position. The two Ohio-born officers had been friends for much of the war and remained close at this time. Sherman later described the reason for the relationship: "He stood by me when I was crazy and I stood by him when he was drunk; and now we stand by each other always."

The two West Point graduates had planned to press their adversaries relentlessly; the key operations would be in northern Virginia and in northern Georgia. Grant would remain in the field with the Army of the Potomac and engage Robert E. Lee and his Army of Northern Virginia until it was defeated in battle. Sherman was charged with the task of engaging and destroying the other large Confederate formation, the Army of Tennessee under Lee's classmate, Joseph E. Johnston. These Confederate commanders were well-trained, educated and experienced in the arts of war, and their armies were defending their home territories. The tasks the two Union commanders set themselves were by no means easy to accomplish; and to succeed, the attacks had to be coordinated and simultaneous. Sherman told his quartermaster: "I'm going to move on Joe Johnston the day Grant telegraphs me he is going to hit Bobby Lee."

Grant's letter of instruction to Sherman was simple: "You I propose to move against Johnston's army, to break it up and get into the interior of the enemy's country as far as you can, inflicting all the damage you can upon their war resources." Sherman was given no specific target, but Atlanta was an obvious first goal.

"[The] plan, promptly adopted, was simple and comprehensive: To break and keep broken the connecting links of the enemy's opposing armies, beat them one by one, and unite for a final consumption. Sherman's part was plain."

—General Oliver Howard

William Tecumseh Sherman, a trusted subordinate of Grant, was sent to destroy Joseph E. Johnston's Confederate army.

Sad, sleepy-eyed John Bell Hood received his first army command after Braxton Bragg recommended to President Jefferson Davis that Johnston be replaced.

Atlanta had become a vital rail hub, arsenal, and manufacturing center that supported the Confederate war effort. In importance, it was second only to Richmond and its industries turned out war supplies of every description. The railroads from the city carried grain and other forms of food from farms throughout the region and delivered it to Confederate armies in the field.

As Sherman made his preparations to move, Joseph Johnston was also readying his men for the inevitable spring offensive from the Union army. He was prepared for the job in front of him. He had once led the Army of Northern Virginia, but had suffered severe wounds at the Battle of Fair Oaks in 1862, and had been replaced by Lee. This experienced commander brought order and a high state of morale to the Army of Tennessee, the force that had been experiencing extremely high rates of desertion since the defeat under Braxton Bragg at Lookout Mountain and Missionary Ridge that had cost the Confederacy Chattanooga.

Johnston gave a general amnesty to soldiers who freely rejoined their units and developed a system of furloughs to permit his men to visit their families during the winter. But he was also tough: many deserters stood at the foot of their graves while facing

a firing squad. He organized his command into two corps, one under William Hardee, a veteran soldier who had participated in most of the fighting in the west. The other corps went to John B. Hood, a veteran of the Army of Northern Virginia. The Army of Tennessee was preparing for renewed war under tested commanders, one of whom (Johnston) they came to love with a reverence that approached the regard Lee's men held for him. Johnston took care of his men and they trusted him as their commander.

While Johnston may have won the full respect of his officers and men, he was far less popular in Richmond. Jefferson Davis harbored an extreme dislike—which approached distrust—for the general. A dispute developed between the two West Point graduates early in the war during which Johnston's

seniority had been invoked. Johnston had apparently antagonized Davis by not explaining his exact reasons for moving to Richmond following the victory at Bull Run. John Bell Hood entered into this political intrigue by sending a series of secret reports to Davis that painted a picture that differed from the one reported by Johnston. Hood may have been so disabled that he had to be strapped to his saddle, but he was ambitious and managed to undermine the slight amount of confidence Davis had in General Joe Johnston.

Johnston continued to prepare for the invasion he knew would come. He fortified positions on Rocky Face Ridge, a large ridge located a few miles west of Dalton, Georgia, and began the first campaign of the Confederacy with a strategy that matched the resources available. Johnston's strategy was one of defensive maneuver, which permitted his forces to move from one strong defensive position to another while inviting Sherman to make expensive frontal attacks. This campaign was one of the best-managed operations of the entire Civil War.

Sherman moved against Johnston on May 4, 1864 (the same day Grant crossed the Rapidan to begin the Battle of the Wilderness). Fighting occurred each day as Sherman forced his way south, repeatedly encountering strong positions set in his path. Sherman's armies—there were three under his command—would outflank Johnston. Johnston, in turn, would move back to prepared positions and wait for the arrival of the Union army—again.

Hood decided to open an attack of his own on June 22 near a large plantation, Kolb's farm, without the permission of Johnston. Unfortunately for Hood and his men, his preparations for the general assault had been revealed by prisoners and confirmed by skirmishers who were close enough to hear Hood's preparations. The attack struck a Federal force that outnumbered the Confederates. In addition, the Union defenders were ensconced in the relative safety of breastworks constructed just prior to the attack. Cannons fired into the attacking lines with canister and many of Hood's men fell. The Confederates withdrew, re-formed, and renewed their costly attack, then withdrew again. It remains a mystery why Hood ordered the unauthorized attack, but the results are clear: Hood lost nearly one thousand men and failed to report the full results of the error to Johnston.

This slow-paced campaign began to have an effect on the morale of Sherman's command. On June 27, slowed by muddy roads, Sherman decided to attack Johnston in a frontal assault at Kennesaw Mountain, where the Confederates waited in prepared

"I was informed... Thomas was building bridges across Peach Tree Creek.... I percieved at once that the Federal commander had committed a severe blunder in separating his Corps."

—General John B. Hood

positions. The Confederate army was able to fight a defensive battle, evacuate their entrenchments, and move into a new and elaborate line that had been prepared for them by slaves (by contrast, the Union soldiers had to dig their own trenches).

Sherman's plan was simple and was based on the assumption that Johnston had strengthened his vulnerable flanks at the expense of the center. Sherman's entire army would press the whole Confederate line, thereby occupying them while two assault columns would strike into the center of the defensive works. The Union army had not fully absorbed the lesson of Cold Harbor in the east: regiments attacking troops of near-equal strength in defensive positions suffer enormous casualties and gain little. Sherman

lost nearly three thousand men at Kennesaw Mountain while Johnston lost a quarter of that number. Sherman had seen war and knew that men must die while fighting it and planned another attack. Meanwhile, one of his commanders, John Schofield, managed to outflank the Kennesaw Mountain positions that had been causing the Union forces so much trouble.

Anticipating Sherman's move, Johnston moved to another defensive line near the railroad at Smyrna. He then moved again, to the north bank of the Chattahoochee River, with the river at his rear—a location from which no sane man would fight. Sherman saw the slave-built fortifications and pronounced them "one of the strongest pieces of field fortifications I ever saw," but he could also see Atlanta in the distance.

He sent John Schofield upstream, where lightly armed Confederates were scattered, without the loss of a Federal soldier. By midnight, Schofield had built two pontoon bridges and ordered two divisions across into the expanding bridgehead.

Flanked again, Johnston was compelled to abandon his strong positions on the Chattahoochee River and march to new positions on a ridge behind Peachtree Creek. This new defensive line was only five miles from Atlanta. It was at this point that political influence began to have an impact on the operation. Braxton Bragg, Johnston's predecessor, arrived in Atlanta on July 13 on an "unofficial" visit. Bragg was now Jefferson Davis' military advisor. He met with Hood before he went to see Johnston; the disabled

OPPOSITE: *Sherman decided on June 27, 1864, to attack General Joseph E. Johnston's prepared positions on Kennesaw Mountain. Sherman lost three thousand men in this conflict and Johnston was able to withdraw to a new line.*

PEACHTREE CREEK

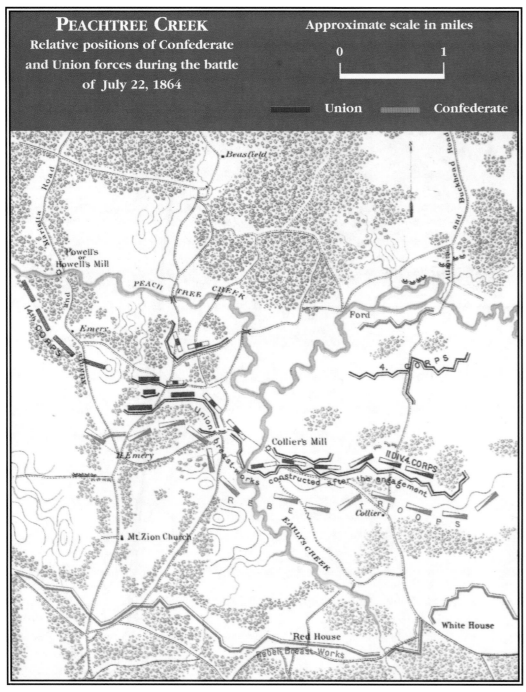

PEACHTREE CREEK

Relative positions of Confederate and Union forces during the battle of July 22, 1864

Approximate scale in miles

0   1

Union   Confederate

Beus field

Powell's or Howell's Mill

PEACH TREE CREEK

Ford

14th CORPS

Emery

4. CORPS

Union breastworks constructed after the engagement

H Emery

Collier's Mill

II DIV 4 CORPS

REBEL TROOPS

Collier

EARLY'S CREEK

Mt. Zion Church

White House

Red House

Rebel Breast-Works

The day after Hood took command, he ordered his men to attack Sherman's forces at Peachtree Creek. Although the poorly executed and uncoordinated attacks caught the Union army off guard, the Confederates lost twice the number of casualties as the Federals—men the southern army could not afford to lose.

but ambitious general bent Bragg's ear, undermining Johnston's postition as commander of the Army of Tennessee and promoting himself.

Johnston had about as much respect for Braxton Bragg as he had for Davis, and said of the Confederate president: "He tried to do what God failed to do. He tried to make a soldier of Braxton Bragg...." The combination of Bragg, Davis, and the reports of Hood were too much for Johnston to defend against and Davis relieved him of command. The combative, and possibly reckless, Hood assumed his command.

John Bell Hood is an interesting historical figure at this point in the Civil War. Always brave and reckless, he had been severely disabled by wounds; in fact, he had lost a leg before being ordered to northern Georgia. Hood was reported to be in extreme pain from his war wounds and may have been taking large amounts of an opiate called laudanum to relieve his discomfort. It is altogether possible that the painkiller interfered with his judgment. Curiously, he had also developed a new interest in religion as he entered into this series of battles and asked Leonidas Polk, a West Point graduate who was an Episcopal bishop of Louisiana and a Confederate general, to baptize him. A case could be made that Hood was preparing for his eventual death, and some historians have felt that his tactics during the remainder of the Civil War hinted tantalizingly of intentions of suicide.

Hood was known to be a bold and aggressive fighter, but he had commanded only smaller units in the past. He was entirely inexperienced at this level of command. Sherman was warned by Hood's West Point roommate, John Schofield, that Hood could be expected to "...hit you like Hell..." but Sherman was pleased with the change of command in the Confederate headquarters. He had been dealing with the delaying tactics of Johnston for over three months and

Benjamin Harrison, a future president of the United States, gained distinction by closing a dangerous gap in the Union line during the Battle of Peachtree Creek.

General Grenville Dodge, a professional railroad engineer before the war, would survive the war and go on to work for the Union Pacific railroad, helping the U.P. to connect the east and west coasts.

General George H. Thomas, a Virginian who remained in the Federal army, had proven his ability in Tennessee. He gained the nickname "Rock of Chickamauga" in the Battle of Chickamauga by saving the Union from total defeat.

was happily anticipating open combat with the Confederate army.

On July 19, the day after Hood took command, the Confederate commander noticed a flaw in the arrangement of the Federal divisions facing him and made some hasty plans. A gap had developed in the alignment of the armies of Schofield and Thomas as they marched into the swampy ground near Peachtree Creek; Hood made plans to attack. His plan was good but the execution was flawed.

Peachtree Creek was Hood's first battle as an independent commander and delays were encountered as the Confederate army moved into positions from which they would attack. The Confederate columns were late and the attack began at 4 P.M. The

attacks were uncoordinated, but the Confederates managed to catch the Federal army off guard as it prepared to stop for the night. Sherman's army, used to doing the attacking against the Confederates in their breastworks, were completely unprepared for the violent attack. Confederate commander William Bate's division charged directly toward a bridge over the creek; once across, he would be in a position to block a Federal retreat.

George Thomas, the Union army commander at that location, was able to move an artillery battery into position to defend the bridge and break up the Confederate attack. Other of his divisions faced the prospect of being flanked and overwhelmed when a counterattack lead by Colonel Benjamin

Harrison, a future U.S. president, closed a break in the Federal defensive line and consolidated the defenders' positions as Hardee, the Confederate corps commander, prepared to order in his reserves.

The reserve division was one of the best in the Confederate army and was under the command of an excellent commander, Patrick Cleburne. Cleburne's men were to be sent in against Thomas' divisions in a last effort to win the battle before dark, but the orders were changed at the last moment.

While Thomas' Army of the Cumberland was under this severe attack, another of Sherman's units, the Army of the Tennessee under Major General James McPherson, had moved within artillery range of Atlanta and fired its first rounds, threatening the

Confederate troops move forward as they march to attack Logan's corps near Atlanta.

off guard. He had been warned of Hood's movements, but the Union commander thought that they were the initial evacuation of Atlanta and was not alarmed. Fortunately for the Union commander, McPherson had ordered one of his corps commanders, Grenville Dodge, to move to positions on the Federal left flank and Dodge's XVI Corps was in position as Hardee's divisions struck.

To the left of this fighting, Cleburne's division located a gap in the Federal defensive line and nearly broke into the rear of the entire Union line before being forced back in severe combat. As the ferocity of Hardee's attack diminished, Hood finally ordered a supporting attack, but it was too late to make any difference in the outcome of the day's fighting. The Federal army lost heavily, however. General McPherson, a young West Point graduate and commander of the Army of the Tennessee, was killed as

Confederate cavalry defending the Georgia Railroad. Cleburne was diverted to support the cavalry, and the battle of Peachtree Creek was over. Hood had lost approximately three thousand men, twice the number of casualties suffered by the Union army, and the attack had gained nothing for the defenders of Atlanta. The impetuous new commander had failed in his initial attack in the open.

Hood faced the dilemma of the defender: he had to attempt to protect all approaches to Atlanta while defending each important target. Sherman had a great advantage and could pick and choose among weaker targets, attacking on his own schedule (as he had done with Johnston). Sherman underestimated the aggressive Hood, however, and

was soon facing a renewed assault by the tired Confederates.

Hood had to contend with the possibility that McPherson would continue his march to the east of Atlanta, bypass the Confederate positions, and march into the city to capture it. Hood briefed his commanders on a plan that would get his troops into the rear of the Army of the Tennessee by attacking around McPherson's southern flank. The orders to begin a long, fifteen-mile march in the dark were issued to Hardee's divisions on July 21, but delays and tired men held up their arrival until noon on July 22. Hardee had made it into a position in McPherson's rear and opened the attack just after noon. Confederate divisions smashed into Federal defenders in an attack that caught Sherman

Major General James B. McPherson was the only Union army commander ever to die in battle.

he rode from Dodge's position to threatened units just to the west. He was shot by skirmishers from Cleburne's division as he tried to avoid capture, becoming the only commander of a Federal army to die in the war.

The battle continued through the remainder of the day, but the combative Hood's repeated attacks cost him nearly eight thousand men, more than twice his losses at Peachtree Creek only two days earlier. Sherman had also lost heavily: 3,722 men died, including General McPherson, for whom Sherman grieved.

By July 28, 1864, the Confederates held only a single railroad supply line into the city, the Macon and Western Railroad. Sherman planned to disrupt the railroad twenty miles south of Atlanta and moved two columns in a converging movement against it.

Hood moved four divisions to stop Sherman and approached Oliver O. Howard,

McPherson's replacement, near a small church called Ezra Church. Howard chose good defensive positions and prepared for an attack. He was cautious and suspected that Hood, always a fighter, would be sending his divisions against him.

Howard's premonition had been right. Hood's men had been lured out of their fortifications a third time in only a few days. Stephen Lee, as aggressive as Hood, drove against the Federal field fortifications again

LEFT: Having earlier fought in the Army of the Potomac, General Oliver O. Howard fought in the Atlanta campaign and survived to become the founder of Howard University in Washington, D.C. BELOW: Union artillery positions surrounded Atlanta.

and again. By 5 P.M., the battle slowed to a halt and the Confederates had again lost heavily. About five thousand Confederates died in this engagement. (Overall, Hood had lost nearly one third of his men in the ten days he had been in command). Federal units, in the relative safety of their hastily constructed breastworks, lost only about six hundred men.

The Union army moved closer to Atlanta and began a heavy cannonade: five thousand shells struck the interior of the city. The citizens tried to survive the shelling by sheltering in dugout "bombproofs," but several died in the first bombardment. Sherman hoped to develop a new tactic to draw the rest of Hood's army out into the open where it could be destroyed, but the fighting settled down into a stalemate.

The doomed city still needed supplies, which had to be delivered over the railroad. Attacks against the railroads had brought Hood out before, so Sherman selected the Macon and Western Railroad as the next target and ordered his entire army to move to Jonesboro. Confederate scouts reported the departure of the Federal army from its positions and Hood thought this was a Union retreat, a grave miscalculation on his part.

Once again, the defenders of Atlanta were ordered to rush against the prepared defenses of the Union army. The Federal soldiers had all the time they needed to dig rifle pits and build fortifications as the Confederate army began to mass at Jonesboro on September 1.

RIGHT, TOP: General William T. Sherman pressed his armies forward in Georgia until Atlanta was besieged. Sherman, a practitioner of modern warfare, struck economic targets that were crucial to his enemy's ability to fight. RIGHT: The railroads that allowed supplies and produce to be shipped to the Confederate army were destroyed. Rails were heated and then bent, rendering the tracks useless.

Hood's ordnance train was destroyed by fire; the flames destroyed a factory near Atlanta.

The fighting was severe and the Confederates suffered many casualties. They were learning the lesson Johnston had taught to Sherman early in the campaign. Union divisions behind the fortifications lost 179 men while the attackers lost 1,725—men Hood could not afford to lose. Worse still, Hardee had to face alone the onslaught of the Federal army. A slow attack using just a single corps cost Sherman thirteen hundred men and an opportunity to trap Hardee's Confederate corps. Hardee's men began to slip away to the south of Atlanta at midnight and the rest of the defenders were also on the march. The city was being evacuated; Sherman had won.

Sherman sent a telegram to Lincoln on September 3, announcing the capture of the city, nearly ensuring the reelection of Lincoln in November. He had captured a vital rail and industrial center that supplied the Confederacy, but he had not been able to destroy Johnston's Confederate army as Grant had instructed him to do.

On November 30, 1864, the volatile Confederate General John B. Hood led the depleted Army of Tennessee against Union defenders commanded by Major General John Schofield in the city of Franklin, Tennessee. The Rebels were repulsed largely thanks to the bravery of Colonel Emerson Opdycke (wielding his spent pistol as a club) and the six regiments under his command.

Atlanta's Peachtree Street was severely damaged during the Federal seige. An important city to the Confederacy because it was a center for industry and a transportation hub, Atlanta was the initial goal of General Sherman's army.

Johnston had shown his skill as a commander when faced with one of the most aggressive of the Union's generals. His strategy had been one of trading space for time while keeping his defenders well concentrated. It was probably the best approach for the Confederacy at this stage of the war. Their manpower and general resources could not sustain a maneuver campaign of attack such as that waged by Hood in the final days of the campaign. Hood had lost more men in ten days than Johnston had lost in the previous 118 days while delaying Sherman's approach toward Atlanta.

The sound of exploding ammunition and locomotives could be heard by the Federal troops at Jonesboro as the Confederate reserve ammunition was destroyed. Hood's army was so weak that Sherman could now virtually ignore it and proceed with his original plan. He sent thirty thousand men back into Tennessee to defend the area against Hood's depleted Confederate divisions while he marched out of Atlanta with over sixty thousand men toward the Atlantic Ocean.

Hood attacked at Franklin, Tennessee, in a hopeless frontal assault against Federal entrenchments that cost the Confederacy the services of Patrick Cleburne, twelve other general officers, and eight thousand men. Hood was attacked at Nashville in a flawlessly planned battle orchestrated by George Thomas. The overextended Confederate line, concave to the enemy's front and denied the coveted interior lines, was severely defeated; in fact, the force was eliminated from the Civil War and the impetuous Hood was relieved from command.

Sherman moved from Atlanta after burning public buildings, destroying all of the railroads in the immediate vicinity, and forcing the city's population to evacuate. He did this to avoid the necessity of leaving a large garrison to control the city, which would reduce his available manpower. He then followed the example of Grant in the Vicksburg campaign by breaking away from his supply lines. He marched forward on a sixty-mile front with emergency rations for twenty days and intentions of living off the country until the Union army reached the seacoast, where they could be resupplied by the navy.

The strategy was simple: wage economic war on a scale similar to that being waged in the Shenandoah Valley by Sheridan, who was marching his divisions toward the Virginia theater of operations to reinforce Grant and eliminate Lee's Army of Northern Virginia. Sherman arrived at Savannah, Georgia, on December 21 and offered the city to the nation as a Christmas present. He continued his destructive march, carrying the destruction and terror of the war directly to the Confederate population.

The key point in the complex Atlanta campaign, however, had been the battle of Peachtree Creek. The decision to replace Joseph Johnston, a man who had designed an excellent strategy that efficiently used the meager resources available, with John Bell Hood, a combative, aggressive commander who had never had an independent command, had proven to be decisive.

Engaging the Union army in the open was suicidal, especially for Hood, who was untried at senior command and experienced only in aggressively executing the plans of others. His army, through poorly timed and often uncoordinated attacks, suffered heavy casualties. Davis' dislike of Johnston, combined with Hood's behind-the-scenes maneuvering, had cost the South dearly at Atlanta. And Hood continued to lose from that point onward in the campaign.

The war was entering the final year.

chapter 8

FIVE FORKS
Carrying Everything Before Them

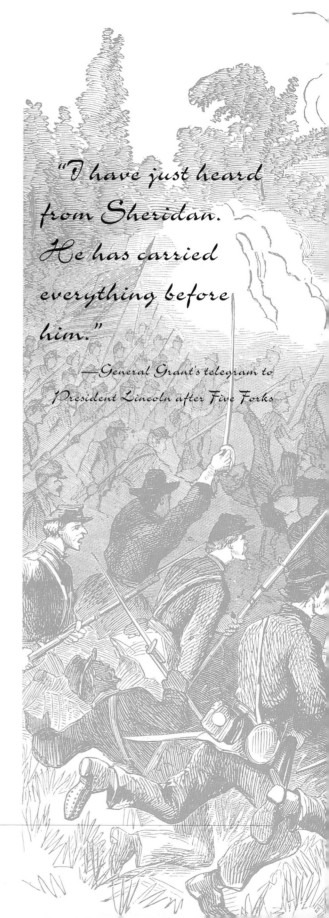

"I have just heard from Sheridan. He has carried everything before him."

—General Grant's telegram to President Lincoln after Five Forks

The last year of the Civil War began and ended in much the same way. Grant was in front of Lee at Petersburg, defending Richmond, the Confederate capital, and Sherman was in Georgia moving to unite his forces with Grant. When Grant had crossed the Rapidan in May, both he and Lee were at the height of their military careers. Grant had won many major victories in the west and Lee had become a legend in the various campaigns in the eastern theater.

After crossing the Rapidan, Grant chose to move along Lee's right flank. Movement along this route allowed him to plan to resupply his forces along Virginia's tidewater rivers and the Chesapeake Bay rather than depend on an enormous wagon train, which would be complicated by the need to care for thousands of horses and mules. Understandably, Grant wanted to concentrate his forces and deploy them effectively in battle rather than use many of them to care for the supply animals.

The two opposing generals met on May 5 in the Battle of the Wilderness, in the same locale where Hooker had lost badly the year before. The fighting consisted of attack and counterattack in tangled brush that caught fire, killing many of the wounded (as had happened at Fort Donelson two years earlier). Lee attacked again on May 6, but neither side was able to gain a clear advantage.

It was at this point in Grant's career that he would show that he was different from all of the commanders of the Army of the Potomac who had served before him. They had always returned to the relative safety of the north side of the Rappahannock after an encounter with Lee, but Grant issued different orders. Ignoring his losses, and relying on his numerical superiority, Grant continued to march southward in an attempt to get between Lee and Richmond. Both armies raced for the vital crossroads at Spotsylvania, but Lee arrived first and began to construct fortifications, defenses behind which his men

PAGE 119: General Philip Sheridan was able to motivate everyone around him to do their very best. Grabbing his personal flag, he led a part of the attack at Five Forks. His magnetic, dynamic personality was irresistible. By illustration, Sheridan once told a severely wounded man to continue forward, which he did until he fell dead from his bleeding neck wound. ABOVE: The disinterment of the Union soldiers' remains from the Cold Harbor battlefield was a gruesome affair.

would fight for the remainder of the Civil War. The Battle of Gettysburg had bled the Confederate officer corps and army to the point that it could no longer maneuver in the open against strong forces like Grant's.

The field fortifications proved strong: the Army of the Potomac attacked them for four days, beginning on May 9, but the Confederates beat back each assault. On two separate occasions, Grant's army was able to break through and each time was unable to exploit the situation. Grant, however, had made a fateful decision at Spotsylvania and wrote to

General Halleck that he intended to "fight it out on this line if it takes all summer." The losses he had suffered and his inability to draw Lee's army into the open convinced Grant that the best strategy lay in moving his army to the south in an attempt to envelop Lee's right flank. This process of slipping south continued for the Federal army while Lee, with smaller numbers, skillfully moved to remain between the invading Federal army and Richmond.

By June 3, the armies faced one another at Cold Harbor, the site in 1862 of the Battle

of Gaines' Mill, where Grant had attacked Lee's entrenched center with his infantry and suffered tremendous losses. Grant later admitted his error in ordering the costly attack at Cold Harbor: "Cold Harbor, I think, is the only battle I ever fought that I would not fight over again under the circumstances." The Battle of Cold Harbor completed a month of heavy fighting that cost the Federal army fifty-five thousand casualties and Lee thirty-two thousand. Grant continued to press his army to the south.

Once the Union army arrived at the James River, Grant's engineers built a twenty-one-hundred-foot pontoon bridge—the longest in history up to that time—and his entire army crossed to the south bank. Following his initial strategy, on June 18 Grant established a supply base, complete with a railroad, at City Point. He then began siege operations against the city of Petersburg, below Richmond, and continued to invest until the following year. Grant was able to view the war as a continuous battle as he clung closely and tenaciously to Lee's army. The war in Virginia had evolved into trench warfare, where siege guns and mortars were used extensively. The firepower and destructive potential of the modern, rifled weapons available to both sides had practically eliminated infantry charges as a battle tactic. Losses were simply too common for either side to attempt this approach. Cold Harbor had taught the commanders well.

Grant continued to move to cross Lee's southern flank and the Confederate army matched each of the Federal movements with new trenches and fortifications. Curiously, these two masters of mobile warfare, Lee and Grant, were reduced to maneuvering their fortifications. Lee had been drawn into a situation that he feared most, a protracted siege in the front of the Confederate capital, Richmond. Earlier in the year Lee had astutely observed to Jubal Early, "We must destroy

Grant proposed to "fight it out on this line if it takes all summer," but his vow was to prove costly to the Federal regiments ordered to attack Lee's entrenched soldiers outside Petersburg, Virginia. The heavy artillerymen who had been converted into infantrymen paid a heavy price in human life under Grant's command.

FIVE FORKS

this army of Grant's before he gets to the James River. If he gets there, it will become a siege, and then it will be a mere question of time."

The stalemate in front of Petersburg continued through the winter. The spring campaign appeared to be the decisive period of the Civil War. Sheridan quickly eliminated Jubal Early's small army in the Shenandoah Valley and then moved his cavalry force to reinforce Grant, whose army required little support. Grant entered the new campaign with a tremendous superiority: 101,000 infantry, 14,700 cavalry, and nine thousand artillery. Lee was attempting to defend Petersburg with forty-six thousand infantry, six thousand cavalry, and five thousand artillery. Grant began to move—again extending to his left in an attempt to fix the position of Lee's flank—on March 29.

Grant had assumed that Lee would soon attempt to evacuate from his entrenched positions and march quickly to combine his forces with those under the command of Joseph Johnston, in nearby North Carolina.

ABOVE: After nearly ten months of deadly fighting in the trenches defending Petersburg, the Union army marched into the evacuated city and stacked their arms for a short, well-deserved rest. BELOW: Preparations had been made in advance for the evacuation of Richmond. Unfortunately, exploding magazines spread fires across wide areas of the city, but Federal infantrymen and impressed civilians soon extinguished the flames.

Bloody fighting occurred when Union divisions began their final attacks against Confederate fortifications in front of Petersburg. Many Confederate soldiers had two rifles—as a rear rank loaded the spent guns, the front rank fired devastating volleys into the Union men.

Richmond had become an arsenal during the war. The capital and government buildings were within sight of arms depots that had been abandoned.

The concentration of these two relatively large Confederate armies could present a threat to the Army of the Potomac until Sherman arrived with his army. Thus, Grant developed plans to prevent Lee's withdrawal. A large infantry flanking force was ordered to press against the Confederate side and rear, drawing them from their trenches in an open battle, and at the same time, Sheridan was ordered to move his cavalry carefully to the rear of Lee and engage the Confederates there. If Lee's divisions could not be drawn out to fight, Sheridan was to destroy secondary targets, especially the Southside and Danville Railroads, thereby blocking a potential escape route and cutting Lee's last supply line.

As at Atlanta, the railroads were targets the Confederates had to defend. Lee reacted immediately to the Union attacks by sending Pickett's division to the threatened area. He also sent all of his available cavalry to assist in the defense of his right flank and vital rear areas. Sent on a reconnaissance in force, a division of Confederate infantry struck Warren's V Corps and general fighting on the southern end of the defensive line began. Grant, sensing an opportunity to bring on a full-scale engagement in which his superior numbers would prove decisive, changed Sheridan's orders. Sheridan's new target was the Confederate rear.

One of Sheridan's cavalry divisions ran into Fitzhugh Lee's cavalry at the road junction Five Forks. Fitzhugh Lee, nephew of the commanding general, deployed his men and skirmishing began as the weather changed. Heavy rain forced Grant to halt operations for the day, but the battle was only postponed for a short period. Sheridan's cavalry found Pickett's division in entrenched positions at Five Forks and the Confederates appeared to be prepared to fight. Grant sent Sheridan infantry support—V Corps under Major General Gouverneur Warren,

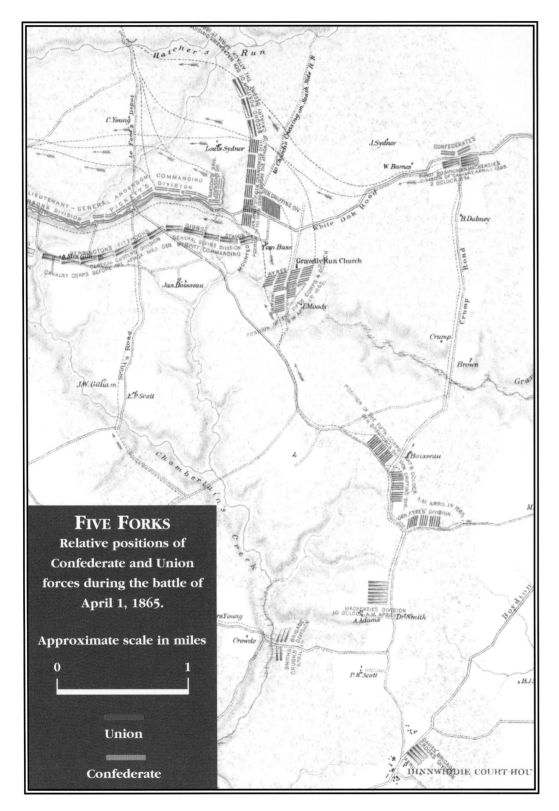

FIVE FORKS

Relative positions of Confederate and Union forces during the battle of April 1, 1865.

Approximate scale in miles

0   1

Union

Confederate

a hero of the battle of Gettysburg—for the cavalry. Sheridan had requested the services of Horatio Wright's VI Corps, a force that had served him well in the Shenandoah Valley, but Wright was too far away to be moved in the rain—especially during the night. Warren would have to do.

Lee, aggressive to the last, ordered Pickett—a general whose sole accomplishment for the Confederate war effort to this point had been leading the ill-fated attack at Gettysburg—to hold the line against Sheridan at Five Forks. The Confederate commander then sent orders to A.P. Hill and Richard Anderson to attack Warren's flank. They intended to fight hard as the rain stopped.

Sheridan, confident and full of fight, suffered from a considerable amount of overconfidence as the rain stopped and roads began to dry. He was soon made aware that Pickett's men, instead of preparing to receive a Union cavalry attack, were in the process of attacking. Pickett was managing a well-coordinated infantry and cavalry attack against the Federal cavalrymen, who were being driven slowly to the south. Less confident by this point, Sheridan called Custer's division from escort duties with the Union wagon train and with his help was able to stabilize his position as darkness fell.

Warren was also having problems in the area. One of his divisions had been sent to White Oak Road, walked into a flanking attack, and were in danger of being routed. Two divisions were hit very hard; only the

The Battle of Five Forks has been described as "The Waterloo of the Confederacy." Believing the Confederate infantry could successfully fight off any Federal cavalry attack, General Pickett attended a "shadbake" in a location where the sound of the battle did not reach him. By the time he and his generals were aware that a battle was being fought nearby, it was too late— Pickett barely escaped capture as his men were routed.

Brigadier General Stephen Dodson Ramseur (seated, right) and the brave men of the North Carolina brigade under his command defended their position against overwhelming odds on May 12, 1864, during the fighting near Spotsylvania Court House.

ABOVE: *Grant, the commander of the entire Union army, remained in the field with his officers. This Mathew Brady photograph, taken after the battle at Spotsylvania, shows his "commander's call." RIGHT: Joshua Chamberlain may have saved the Union army from defeat on Little Round Top. Although severely wounded, Chamberlain fought valiantly again at Five Forks.*

reserve division and Nelson Miles' divisions from II Corps were able to hold the attackers at bay. Warren assigned the responsibility for a counterattack to Brigadier General Joshua Chamberlain's brigade, and the wounded hero of the battle of Gettysburg led a second charge—as he had done in Pennsylvania—and recovered ground lost earlier in the day.

Pickett had handled the Federal cavalry roughly and Sheridan knew there was more to come on the morning of April 1, but there was also an opportunity within his dangerously exposed position. It was clear to Sheridan that Pickett was in more of an exposed position and plans were made for Warren to attack the Confederates on one side as Sheridan hit the other.

Pickett also was aware of his dangerously exposed position and began a cautious withdrawal at dawn on April 1. Sheridan sent immediate orders to Warren: the infantry must move at once. But by the time they were in their assigned positions, the Confederates were gone and Sheridan angrily planned a second plan of attack. His dismounted cavalry would be assigned the task of hitting Pickett's line and holding them in their positions as Warren's infantry struck their left flank. If Pickett's small corps could be driven to the west, Sheridan felt he could cut it off from the rest of Lee's army and destroy it. He met with Warren and reviewed the plan. As Warren later stated about the fateful meeting: "...he was convinced that I understood him," but the infantry commander would be too slow in his deployment and would earn Sheridan's disapproval.

Pickett had wisely prepared his men for the attack and bent his line back along White Oak Road to guard his otherwise exposed flank. He had deployed his forces in the best manner he could; having no evidence that a Federal attack was imminent, he accepted an invitation to lunch from Thomas Rosser, one of his cavalry commanders. Some of Rosser's

men had netted some shad that were running in a nearby river and Pickett, Rosser, and Fitzhugh Lee—on short rations like the rest of Lee's army—accepted the offer of food. Shortly prior to his departure, he was informed by one of his division commanders, Thomas Munford, that Federal cavalry had cut their contact with Anderson's corps to the east. Unfortunately, Pickett disregarded this warning and went to the riverbank to eat fish as an attack on his men developed. Like Grant at Fort Donelson, he compounded his mistake by not informing anyone of his location. And as Pickett and two of his cavalry commanders, Rosser and Fitzhugh Lee, ate shad the Federal V Corps began its attack. The missing commanders could not be locat-

LEFT: Brightly uniformed Zouaves, such as these men of the 155th Pennsylvania Infantry Regiment, dressed like French units operating in North Africa. BELOW: A uniform from a soldier in the 155th Pennsylvania Infantry Regiment. By the end of the war, the 155th Pennsylvania Infantry was one of the few units to retain the Zouave uniforms.

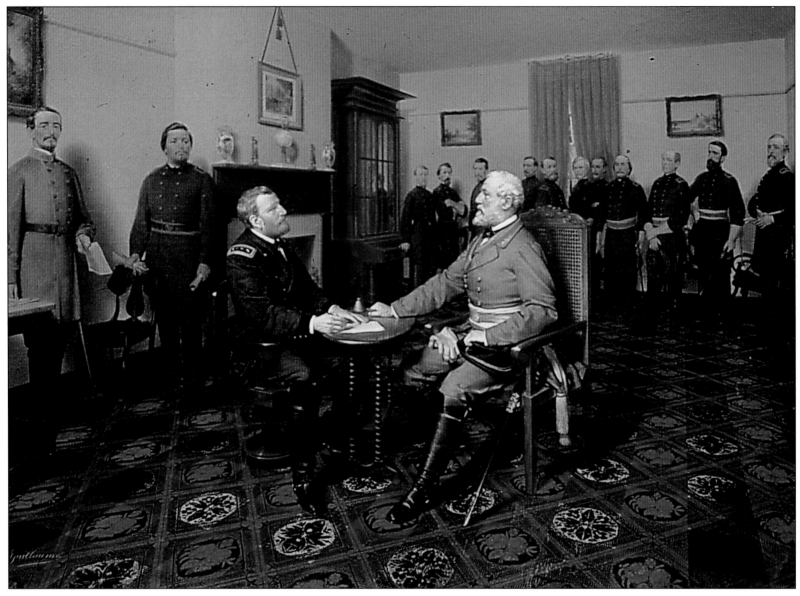

General Ulysses S. Grant met with General Robert E. Lee in Wilmer McLean's home at Appomattox Court House to sign the surrender documents that effectively ended the American Civil War.

ed and an unfortunate atmospheric effect, an "acoustic shadow," masked the sound of the battle as it started only one and a half miles from the riverbank where the missing generals were eating.

The advancing Federal infantry actually missed their opponents in their first attack, wheeled, and accidentally struck the most vulnerable portion of the opposing line, the exposed Confederate flank and rear. Sheridan was reported to be everywhere, waving his personal flag and encouraging his men to attack. The Confederate line began to collapse under the pressure from the multiple attacks that were occurring in the absence of its commander.

Pickett's first warning of the impending disaster was witnessing one of his couriers being captured by Union soldiers. Pickett himself escaped capture, arrived at the site of the battle, and saw that part of his line had been destroyed and that the remainder was being forced to the west—just as Sheridan had planned. Pickett attempted to salvage the

This photograph of Wilmer McLean's house was taken in May 1865, a month after Lee had surrendered his army to Grant.

too slowly. Sheridan relieved Warren, destroying his military career. The dismissed commander requested a court of inquiry, which was eventually held. Warren was finally vindicated in 1882—three months after his death.

Grant renewed the attack on April 2, breaking the Confederate line and forcing the defenders to the North. Lee was forced to abandon Richmond and his Petersburg line, march quickly west to Lynchburg or Danville, and join forces with Johnston—as had been anticipated by Grant. Grant had at last accomplished what he most wished for: Lee was in the open and his tired army was vulnerable. Sheridan hurried west to cut off the Confederate retreat while Grant's infantry pursued relentlessly in a running battle that lasted from April 2 through April 6. Ewell's corps was cut off, surrounded, and captured at Sayler's Creek as Confederate soldiers began to straggle and be captured. When Sheridan moved his cavalry into Appomattox Court House, directly on Lee's line of retreat, the Confederate commander realized that continued resistance was futile. He met with Grant at Wilmer McLean's house in Appomattox on April 9, 1865, and the Civil War in the east was over.

Joseph Johnston surrendered to Sherman on April 26 and Kirby Smith surrendered the last remaining Confederate force in the west on May 26, personally signing the surrender document on June 2.

Lee's excellent defensive line had held Grant's army at bay for months, but once Sheridan was able to defeat Pickett at Five Forks the reduced companies holding the entrenched Confederate positions at Petersburg were unable to resist Grant's overwhelming forces on the day following the battle. Five Forks was the critical point in the Petersburg campaign, and this crucial battle led to the rapid collapse of the entire Confederacy.

The Civil War was over at last.

situation, but it was too late. His entire corps was in the process of disintegrating around him as Warren's V Corps continued to attack. Meanwhile, Federal cavalry attacks swept in from both east and west to eliminate what remained of the Confederate cavalry on the battlefield.

Five Forks had been a military disaster for the Confederacy. The Southern army had lost over five thousand men as prisoners and its weakened line was scheduled to receive a general assault from Grant and his troops on the following day.

Sheridan had managed to win at Five Forks, but he was dissatisfied with the performance of Gouverneur Warren, who had led his V Corps into the rear of Pickett's line—to cut off the Confederates' retreat—

"Grant had been sleeping with one eye open and one foot out of bed for many weeks in the fear that Lee would give him the slip."

—General Horace Porter

PART TWO

NAVAL WARFARE

THE U.S. NAVY AT THE WAR'S BEGINNING

At the beginning of the Civil War, Gideon Welles was appointed by President Abraham Lincoln as Secretary of the United States Navy. The secession of the Southern states was rapid, and Welles was caught unprepared for war. The U.S. Navy (a fleet of fewer than sixty ships) had begun extending its global influence after the War of 1812, and had twenty-eight of its ships located on foreign duty all around the world. Approximately twenty percent of the officers in the U.S. Navy resigned their commissions and offered their services to their native Southern states, and subsequently to the Confederacy. Welles had too few ships, too few officers and men, and too much enemy coastline (about thirty-five hundred miles [5600km]) to control.

President Abraham Lincoln declared a blockade of the South, which had one unintended and undesirable consequence: under international law, this gave the South status as a legitimate belligerent. Had he instead declared that the U.S. Navy was closing the ports of the southern coast in order to suppress an internal insurrection, the Confederacy would not have been able to deal with other nations as an independent warring party.

When the war began in April 1861, Welles had only eight vessels of the Home Squadron immediately available for use, and only four of these were steamers. The rest of the fleet was in foreign waters or laid up in various naval yards and unavailable for duty. By December 1861, however, the industrial

of the North had begun to overcome many of its equipment problems. The U.S. Navy by then consisted of 264 vessels armed with 2,557 guns and manned by twenty-five thousand naval personnel.

Welles began buying up all nature of commercial vessels and converting them for military service. Virtually anything that would float was pressed into service as a blockader. In 1861 alone, 136 vessels were purchased and converted to warships. For instance, the USS *Commodore Perry*, a New York ferryboat, was converted to carry four 9-inch (22.8cm) smoothbore cannon, a 12-pounder (5.4kg) rifle, and a 100-pounder (45.4kg) rifle. The *Commodore Perry* and the rest of the ragtag flotilla was organized and steamed south in early 1862 under the command of Admiral L.M. Goldsborough to seal off portions of the North Carolina coast, a task for which it was hardly prepared.

U.S. NAVY ORGANIZATION

The Union naval officer command structure was composed of regulars and volunteers. Regular naval officers were career navy line officers, nearly all of whom were graduates of the U.S. Naval Academy at Annapolis, Maryland. When war began, Welles ordered the top three classes of midshipmen at the Naval Academy to active duty as officers in the U.S. Navy. Volunteer officers were mostly merchant vessel captains from the North's great mercantile fleet.

Enlisted men in the U.S. Navy were both regular and volunteers. Initially, there were not enough men to service the ships required for all the naval operations. Various enlistment gimmicks were used to entice men to sea. But the navy wound up taking just about anyone who would agree to serve. As early as 1861, former slaves, foreign sea-

Gideon Welles, the iron-willed Connecticut Yankee, was chosen by Lincoln to head the ill-prepared U.S. Navy. Welles, a shrewd politician, put his personal attributes to great use and formed the navy into a world-class sea force.

men, and any others willing to serve were enlisted. As the war progressed and more ships came on line, army units were discharged in large groups to become navy personnel.

Welles organized the navy into squadrons and flotillas. There were essentially six main squadrons during the war: the North Atlantic Squadron (responsible for the Virginia and North Carolina coasts), the South Atlantic Squadron (responsible for South Carolina, Georgia, and Florida's Atlantic coast), the East Gulf Squadron (responsible for all of Florida's west coast), the West Gulf Squadron (responsible for all coastline from Florida to Mexico), the Mississippi River Squadron (responsible for the Mississippi River and all its tributaries down to New Orleans), and the Pacific Squadron, which saw little action. Flotillas

PAGE 133: At the war's beginning, the Union rushed to reinforce critical coastal garrisons. Here, Union troops land at Fort Pickens, on Florida's panhandle, in June 1861. The troop ship has no metal armor or protection; naval warriors had not yet learned the importance of such defenses. ABOVE: The waist-length "shell jacket" worn by U.S. Navy enlisted personnel. It was usually reserved for formal occasions, as combat crewmen preferred a pullover sweater that was also issued.

were detachments broken off from squadrons for temporary duty. For example, the Mississippi Flotilla served in the assaults on forts Henry and Donelson and returned to be part of the Mississippi Squadron after that action had been concluded.

THE CONFEDERATE NAVY AT THE WAR'S BEGINNING

Secretary of the Navy Stephen R. Mallory, Confederate States of America, had a differ-ent problem from that of Welles in 1861. Mallory had no navy whatsoever, and each state was raising its military forces with no coordination with the central government or the other states. Confederate Navy officers came from resignations in the U.S. Navy and from commercial ship captains. Mallory estab-lished a naval academy at Richmond, Virginia, and by the end of 1861 the Confederate Navy had taken form. It had at least thirty-four vessels and eighty-seven officers.

Mallory still lacked ships, however, and he immediately began an ambitious plan to build a navy from scratch. His initial plan involved the construction of ironclad ships to break the blockade, and the construction of raiders to interdict U.S. commerce on the high seas. Mallory's initial fleet came mostly from seizures of U.S. ships. Several ships, most notably the *Merrimack,* were salvaged in whole or in part from the Union's failure to totally destroy them at their respective Union navy yards. Several U.S. Navy ships were seized in southern harbors. Other ships were converted, as in the North, from com-mercial ships.

This cutaway view of an early American man-of-war shows the placement of personnel and stores in the decks below the gun decks. Ships like this one operated mostly in the open sea; the deep draft of their keels made them unsuitable for shallow waters.

Stephen Mallory, Gideon Welles' opposite number in the Confederacy, was a maritime lawyer from Key West and one of Florida's senators before the war. As the chairman of the Senate's Naval Affairs Committee, he gained experience and knowledge that would prove invaluable when he faced the task of building the Confederate Navy from scratch.

The Confederate Navy invented naval mines (called "torpedoes" at the time) and used them in ingenious ways to deny Union ships access to critical ports and channel them into areas where they could be brought under coastal battery fire. These mines are metal canisters filled with powder, floated by empty wooden casks, and fired by electrical fuses.

Mallory, through an intermediary, began making secret arrangements with shipbuilders in England to construct a number of first-class cruisers for use by the Confederate Navy in combat against Union warships and commercial craft. A number of ships were built and delivered to the Confederacy. England came to regret the contract when, after the war, an international court of claims ordered England to pay the United States of America $15.5 million in gold to compensate for damage done by commerce raiders built in England.

Mallory, as former Chairman of the U.S. Senate Committee on Naval Affairs, realized early on the necessity for ironclad ships. In addition to the English-built commerce raiders, he ordered the domestic construction of ironclads, including the former USS *Merrimack,* fated to become the CSS *Virginia.* Ironclad construction began at the various Confederate naval yards throughout the South. By June 1861, Mallory had naval engineers working on construction plans for an ironclad to be built on the hull of the salvaged *Merrimack.*

NAVAL WARFARE IN THE MID-NINETEENTH CENTURY

Understanding any military endeavor, naval or otherwise, must begin with a knowledge of the weapons and tactics used by all partic-ipants. Men in ships do not just sail up to each other and fire away with whatever is at hand. Warfare evolves by invention and research—and sometimes by sheer accident. The American Civil War was no exception to this rule.

For naval purposes, America's most recent serious conflict had been the War of 1812. Although the U.S. Navy conducted extensive scientific experimentation in the 1840s and 1850s, by 1861, most, if not all, of the naval personnel who had combat experi-ence were dead or retired. On the eve of the Civil War, therefore, the U.S. Navy, although made up of professionals, was almost entirely untried in combat. American military person-nel watched the various European conflicts of the first half of the nineteenth century (e.g. the Napoleonic Wars, the Crimean War) with interest. European tactical doctrines

Since almost everything aboard a naval man-of-war had to be made or repaired aboard ship, a crew usually included artisans such as carpenters, ironmengers, and millwrights. These sailors (called "jack-tars" in the old navy) are posed with their work tools on the deck of a warship.

were in vogue in the various American military academies.

Prior to Robert Fulton's application of the steam engine to watercraft, ships moved by the grace of God and the elements. Wind propelled navies to their rendezvous. Sea battles were won and lost with the vagaries of wind and tide. By 1861, however, the steam engine was in common use as motive power (usually in combination with sails) on many boats in inland waters and on the high seas. Steam power propelled a ship through the use of a screw (propeller) or a paddle wheel. Screws were the more efficient of the propulsion methods, and were used extensively on deepwater vessels.

Naval Artillery and Armor
Naval artillery in use during the Civil War consisted of two main types of muzzle-loading guns: smoothbore and rifled. As the name suggests, smoothbore artillery was simply a smooth tube, usually made from bronze or reinforced iron, which fired a round ball. A rifled gun, however, had

The 32-pounder bow rifle on the Teaser, a 64-ton (57.6t.) wooden-hulled tug that was originally in the Confederate Navy, armed with a 2.9-inch (7.4cm) Parrot rifle. Captured by the USS Maratanza in July 1862, it served ably in Virginia rivers until the war's end. Note the shell sitting on the rail: it has two bands, of either wrought copper or lead, that engaged the rifling in the barrel and gave spin, and therefore stability, to the projectile.

grooves, or rifling, in the barrel, and fired an elongated shell. Rifles had several advantages over smoothbore cannon by virtue of the spin imparted to the projectile by the rifling. Rifles had longer ranges and better accuracy, and maintained more of their inertia (or "punch") at greater ranges and, therefore, penetrated better. On the downside, rifles were somewhat harder to load, required specialized ammunition, and took longer to fire than smoothbores.

Naval guns today are identified according to the diameter of their barrels, measured in millimeters, but in the nineteenth century they were designated either according to the weight of their projectile or according to their diameter measured in inches. Thus, a "32-pounder" was a gun that hurled a thirty-two-pound (14.5kg) spherical iron ball from its muzzle, while a "10-inch" gun fired a projectile ten inches (25.4cm) in diameter.

There were several different types of projectiles in use aboard ship during the Civil War. Round shot (also called solid shot) was a solid round or elongated iron ball that was used as a battering projectile. It was fired against land-based forts to knock down walls and at other ships to tear away rigging and sunder wooden planking.

Explosive shells (sometimes referred to as bombs) were hollow, cast-iron spheres filled with black powder. At one point on the shell's surface, a hole was drilled into the sphere to accept a fuse device. When the shell was fired, the fuse was lit, or actuated, by the propelling explosion. When the fuse burned down, the shell exploded, sending shards of the cast-iron casing in every direction. In theory, the fuse burned at a known rate and the gunner, knowing the velocity of his round and the length of the fuse, could time a projectile to explode at a given point. This was rarely true in practice because of the inconsistency of the manufacture of the fuse and the effects of humidity and age on

the explosive contents. Shells were fired at other ships and at troops in the open. The exploding shells destroyed rigging and injured exposed personnel. Obviously, a significant amount of cover could render the shell ineffective. To this end, most forts of the era contained "bomb-proof" shelters.

Antipersonnel rounds come in three varieties: canister (sometimes called "case shot"), grapeshot, and spherical case shot. Canister was simply a can filled with lead balls. When fired, the balls left the can much in the way buckshot leaves the muzzle of a modern shotgun. The spreading balls cut down troops in the open. It was not very effective against covered troops.

Grape shot was a group of iron balls on a wooden stand covered with a cloth bag.

Each group of balls was separated horizontally from the other by a metal disk. In the center of the balls was a wooden dowel holding the whole thing together. When fired from a gun, the bag disintegrated and the balls flew about like common buckshot. This round was very effective against troops in the open and could be put to good use destroying the rigging of a ship.

Spherical case shot was a combination of a fused case shot, or bomb, filled with iron balls and powder. Spherical case shot was sometimes called shrapnel, after a similar invention by a British officer early in the nineteenth century. Upon being fired, the fuse was lit by the propelling charge and, down range, the round exploded, sending the case fragments and the iron balls flying

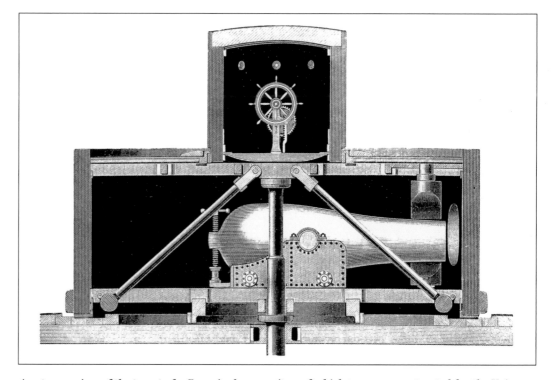

A cutaway view of the turret of a Passaic-class monitor, of which ten were constructed for the Union Navy. Designed by the Swedish naval genius John Ericsson, they were the first iron ships to be built in quantity. The gun shown is a smoothbore cannon. Each Passaic-class monitor had one 15-inch (38.1cm) smoothbore and one 11-inch (27.9 cm) smoothbore, side by side in the turret. The room above the guns is the pilothouse, where the captain and the pilot controlled the ship in combat, sending messages to the engineroom by signals and a speaking tube.

Experienced "jack-tars" of the U.S. Navy aboard the USS Wissahickon, *posed next to an 11-inch (27.9cm) Dahlgren smoothbore cannon on a pivot mount. One of twenty-three Unadilla-class wooden, two-masted schooner gunboats, the* Wissahickon *was built in forty-five days from green, unseasoned wood. It served throughout the entire war, from the Mississippi River to the Atlantic coast. The single pivot gun was set up on rails so that it could be adjusted to fire in any direction.*

*This painting by William R. McGrath shows an underwater view of the CSS **Hunley** as she detonates her spar torpedo against the hull of the USS **Housatonic** in Charleston harbor.*

in every direction. This was used against unprotected troops and sailors on deck.

One other type of projectile deserves mention: the carcass. The carcass was a hollow iron ball filled with pitch and chemicals. The case had holes in it. When fired, the pitch and chemicals would ignite and burn for about eight minutes. Carcasses were fired against wooden ships, powder magazines, and other highly flammable objects.

The Confederate Navy also developed innovative weapons that marked the beginnings of undersea warfare. Spar torpedoes were explosive charges placed at the end of a long pole, or spar. They either were fitted with a contact fuse, which exploded on contact with the side of a ship, or were command-detonated by one of the crew once-contact had been made. Spar torpedoes were fitted to small cutters, sometimes called "Davids" after the first spar torpedo boat, the CSS *David*. In addition, the Confederate Navy developed one of the first operational sub-

marines, the CSS *Hunley*. First placed in service in August 1863, the *Hunley* promptly sank at her moorings. Undaunted, the Confederate submariners raised her from the muck of Charleston harbor and recommissioned her. During a trial run in October 1863, she sank with all hands, killing nine sailors. She was raised and recommissioned again. On February 17, 1864, the *Hunley* crept up on the USS *Housatonic*, anchored in Charleston harbor. She ran her spar topedo against the *Housatonic's* hull, blowing a gaping hole below the waterline and sinking her. Unfortunately, the *Hunley* and her entire crew were also lost during the engagement.

In the early stages of the war, much attention was given to the problem of protecting ships against both naval artillery and ground artillery. French successes using ironclad vessels (notably the *Gloire* in the war against Russia), the destruction of the Turkish wooden fleet by the Russians at Sinope, and the British development of the all-metal war-

ship *Warrior* inspired a change in technology. Military engineers began research and development on armor plating for ships and on weapons capable of penetrating that armor. The generally accepted formula in the mid-nineteenth century was that a fortified land-based gun was equal to five ship-mounted guns on a wooden ship.

Most armor consisted of iron plate, iron railroad rails, or iron bars affixed to a heavy backing of timber. The iron was placed in horizontal and vertical layers over a thick oak superstructure. The iron was usually four to eight inches (10.2–20.3cm) thick, and the wood was usually at least two feet (0.6m) thick. The Confederate ironclads and the Union river ironclads were similarly constructed. Both sides supplemented armor plate with the use of cotton bales, timber, and even chains linked together. (The exception was the series of Union armored vessels of the *Monitor* design, discussed in detail in a later chapter.)

The most vulnerable points on a ship are its motive power plant system, waterline, and steering mechanism. Without power or the ability to steer, a ship simply sits dead in the water and is shot to pieces. If an enemy ship can stay in a blind area away from its opponent's fixed gunports, the ship cannot defend itself. Designs for armoring warships concentrated on these three areas and were paralleled by the development of movable turrets.

Everything that could possibly be plated was plated. For example, the smokestacks of some ships were armored since they had to remain intact to allow proper draft of the boiler fire. If riddled by gunfire, the smokestack would not draw properly, and the boiler fire would not burn hot enough to heat the boiler sufficiently. With reduced steam pressure, the ship's speed and maneuverability would be compromised.

The rudders, which regulate the ship's direction, were controlled from the pilot-

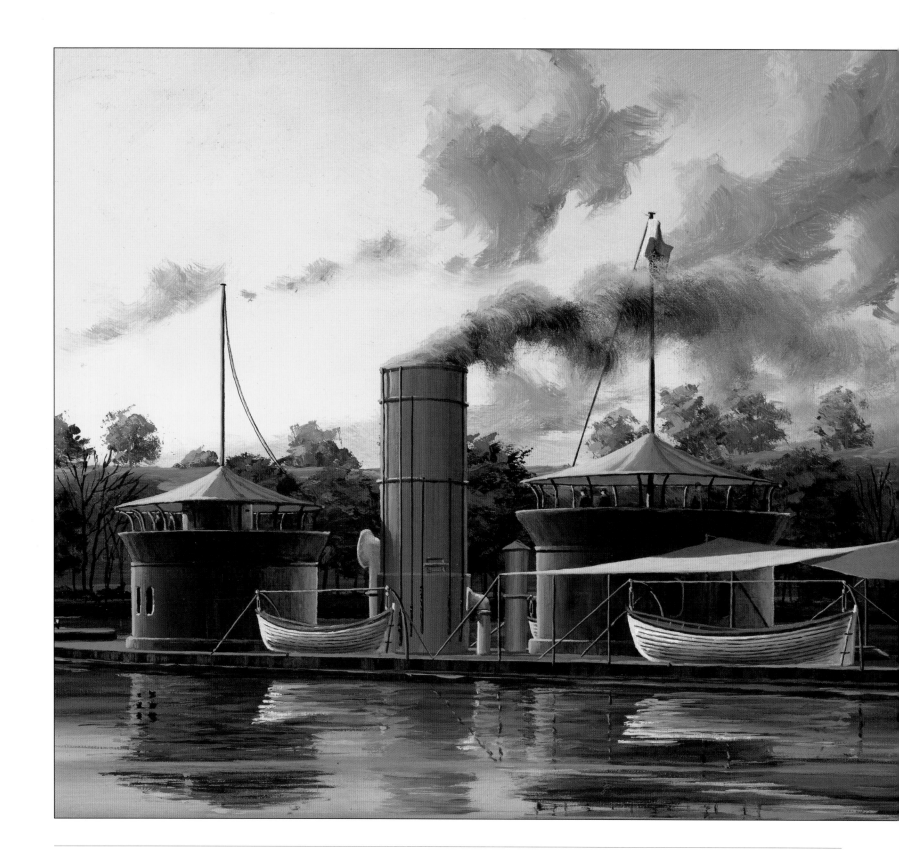

house through the use of chains attached to the rudders. If the chains were exposed, they could be struck and the ship would have no directional movement. If the ship were struck at or below the waterline, water would rush into the ship's interior and sink it. If the hole were not too large and there were time to put corrective measures in place, the ship could often be saved.

Naval Propulsion Systems

Most oceangoing vessels of the era had both a screw, or propeller, and sails to propel them. The screw was used to maneuver in tight places and to propel the ship when there was insufficient wind to use sails. The sails were used in the open ocean to conserve fuel and in the event the steam engine

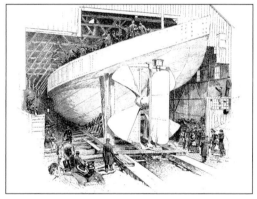

*LEFT: The USS **Onondaga** patrolling on the James River in Virginia. The **Onondaga** was one of the later double-turreted river monitors, commissioned in March 1864. She mounted two 15-inch (38.1cm) smoothbores and two 150-pounder (68.1kg) rifles. She saw action throughout the war and was sold to France in 1867. Painting by William R. McGrath. ABOVE: Stern view of the single-turret monitor USS **Dictator** showing the giant single screw and rudder used to propel and steer the boat. She had a complement of 174 officers and men, crammed into a hull only 312 feet (95.1m) long, 50 feet (15.2m) wide, and 20 feet (6.1m) deep. Built in November 1864, she served in the Atlantic Blockading Squadron.*

ceased to function. The steam engine was driven by a coal-fired boiler. In the Confederate Navy, the fuel of choice was hard, or anthracite, coal, since it gave off very little smoke, making ships difficult to see at a distance on the ocean. Soft, or bituminous, coal was used in Union vessels. Soft coal gave off a dark brown smoke that was easily seen, even at a distance.

Ships used in inland waterway naval operations were usually of the screw-driven or paddle wheel variety. Many naval ships were converted from commercial paddle wheel river steamers. The large paddle wheels were mounted at the stern on one or both sides or amidships, depending on the design of the vessel. The paddle wheel was one of the first motive designs for steam-powered ships. It was very useful in shallow waters where the depth of the keel is critical, but it could also be used on oceangoing craft. When propeller design was understood and implemented, screw-driven ships were used in the open ocean because the screw was more efficient, but had to be set down in the water to do its job properly.

The steam engine took some time to be put into service. Its firebox had to be filled with coal and ignited. The cold boiler, filled with water, had to be heated to a high temperature in order to generate sufficient steam to consistently run the engine at full throttle. One of the worst conditions a ship could find itself in during an engagement was the "steam down" position. In steam down, the boiler was kept at a low pressure, with sufficient fire to keep steam in the boiler, but not enough to move the ship at any significant speed. This was done primarily to conserve fuel on a ship that was not expected to move. If a Confederate blockade-runner passed a Union picket ship that was in steam-down status, there was simply no sense in the Union ship's even attempting pursuit. The time that it would take for the

ship to "steam up" was more than enough to allow the blockade-runner, already under full steam, to get clean away.

Coal was always problematic as a fuel. It was very bulky and very heavy, and it had to be transported to the ships from mining sites in the Appalachian Mountains. Wood was used in early steamers on the rivers, but coal was found to be the superior fuel. Only coal, it seemed, provided a fire hot enough to ensure adequate steam pressure in newer engines. Only in emergencies would other, less desirable fuels such as wood be used. In the open ocean, coaling ships carried the coal to men-of-war, shuttling between the shore and the operating vessels. On the inland waters of the West, such as the Mississippi River, coal barges were towed or pushed up and down the river to the needy vessels. In some cases on the inland waters, a warship would lash a coal barge to its side in order to carry its fuel with it.

Life Aboard Ship

Life aboard a mid-nineteenth-century warship was difficult. There was little room for excess baggage or personal belongings. Men slept in hammocks suspended from interior rigging or on the deck of the ship. Generally, only the captain of the vessel and his officers had private cabins. Space in a warship was needed for survival supplies, munitions, food, and water. Contagious diseases (e.g., smallpox, cholera, and "fever") could and did sweep rapidly through the closely quartered ship's company. Sometimes diseases of malnutrition (e.g., scurvy or pellagra) could incapacitate an entire crew, rendering it ineffective for combat. There was no hospital room aboard ship; the sick lay on the deck until they recovered—or perished. In a couple of situations, there were Union hospital ships available, usually for army casualties, but these ships never had sufficient capacity to handle all the wounded.

The USS Planter, *a supply boat used to transport medical supplies, is shown here at Appomattox Landing, Virginia. The* Planter, *which originally belonged to a Southern plantation owner, was stolen by a slave pilot, John Small, and delivered to Union naval forces in May 1862.*

Medical science, then in its infancy, could do little for the terrible wounds that resulted from most naval combat. The size and type of munitions used created ghastly wounds in naval personnel, and the lack of knowledge concerning proper infection control virtually guaranteed infection, mutilation, amputation, or death for the injured sailor.

In combat, sailors faced the usual hazards of shot and shell. Shot weighed anywhere from six to four hundred pounds (2.7kg–181.6kg) and could crush a man instantly. Shell exploded, sending fragments of hot steel all around. Steam boilers, if struck by a round, would explode, sending scalding steam throughout the enclosed ship. In some instances, the spiraling effect of rounds striking the exterior of the ship, along with the concussion, would send shards of wood flying among the sailors at their gun stations.

On many ships, the interior was painted white to aid vision when the ship was closed up for combat. In addition to the natural darkness, vision would be seriously impaired by clouds of gunsmoke once a battle began. Before a battle, sand would be liberally strewn on the ship's deck because guns were wiped down with water-soaked sponges between shots, and this water on the deck, along with blood from the wounded and killed, would make a shifting deck so slippery that the men could not stand up without the traction provided by the sand. If there were many wounded, the ship's surgeon would not be able to attend to them all. Many would lie moaning and screaming on the deck until the battle was over and they could be attended to by their comrades.

NAVAL WARFARE

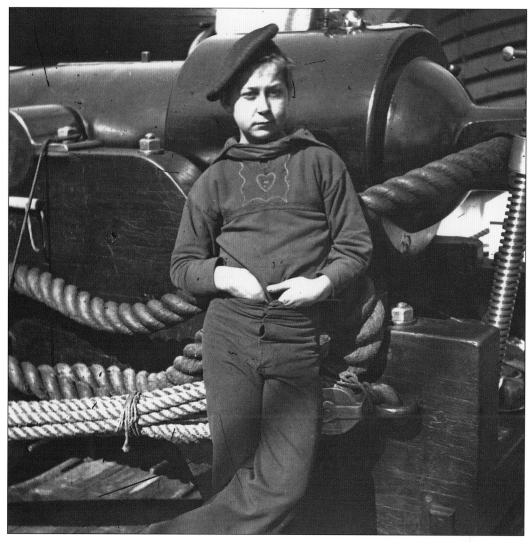

LEFT: Crew of a Sassacus-class, double-ended, sidewheel gunboat posed on her afterdeck. These wooden-hulled boats could steer in either direction thanks to a rudder built on each end of the ship. These lightly gunned, unarmored support ships worked well in shallow, inland waters but were unstable on the open sea. ABOVE: Many a sailor in early nineteenth-century America began his career at sea as a child. This young "powder monkey" had a dangerous job: during combat, he carried ammunition components from the stores to the gunners. He is posed against a rifle that has had its breech reinforced with a band to allow it to fire larger, more powerful powder charges, thus increasing its range and accuracy.

Naval tactics dictated that the vessels get as close to each other as possible and attempt, by smoothbore naval artillery or ramming, to incapacitate the other vessel. For this reason, most early naval battles were fought at very close range. Naval artillery duels sometimes took place with the vessels in physical contact with one another since most naval artillery was of the "battering" kind. A shot fired from too far might not

penetrate a ship's outer hull, or armor, and do the necessary damage. So the closer, the better. Of course, the closer you were, the better the chance the enemy's round had of penetrating your ship.

Once naval rifles came into use on ships, the range and tactics of battle changed. In the battle between the CSS *Alabama* and the USS *Kearsarge*, the two ships, after initially firing at a distance of one mile (1.6km), fought the battle at a range of five hundred yards (457m).

If necessary, sailors and sometimes selected infantry were prepared to leave their own vessel and board the enemy vessel to engage in hand-to-hand combat. While this was only an occasional occurrence, thought was given to the possibility in planning a ship's defenses. For example, in the Union's Mississippi River city-class ironclads, hoses were attached to the steam boiler so that scalding steam could be sprayed on any persons attempting to board the vessel.

A favorite tactic was ramming, and some ships were specially designed to be used as rams. Their prows were armored and their interior structure braced so that they might accept the collision and, it was hoped, escape significant harm. Normally, a collision at sea would put both vessels in danger of sinking, just as a highway collision is likely to wreck both vehicles. Rams had a tactical advantage in that they could try to run themselves into other ships at a strategic point such as the rudder, causing damage that would incapacitate the other ship or sink it.

In this William R. McGrath painting of one of the most famous sea battles of the war, the CSS Alabama, *captained by Commander Raphael Semmes, engages the USS* Kearsarge *off the coast of France. After a lengthy battle, the* Alabama *was sunk, ending her career as a notorious Confederate raider that targeted Union commercial shipping.*

chapter 9

1861
Early Naval Operations

FORT SUMTER

The Civil War is considered to have begun when South Carolina state troops fired on the Union garrison at Fort Sumter in the harbor at Charleston, South Carolina, on April 12, 1861. Prior to this moment, there had not been any serious confrontation between Union military forces and the forces of the seceding states. A lame-duck administration under President James Buchanan stood idly by while state after state seceded from the Union. Buchanan did not want to create any problems.

On January 5, 1861, a Federal force aboard the transport USS *Star of the West* steamed south from New York to relieve the U.S. troops stationed at Fort Sumter under Major Robert Anderson. Upon reaching the Charleston harbor, the *Star of the West* was fired on by South Carolina state militia guns and was forced to turn around and return north without accomplishing her mission. The relief of Fort Sumter was put on hold until the inauguration of Abraham Lincoln on March 4, 1861. Lincoln, newly elected, was also reluctant to force any issue with the southern states, at least until he had a chance to put his cabinet fully in place. Finally, in April, Lincoln ordered a ship of provisions sent to the beleaguered garrison. On April 12, 1861, after negotiations for surrender and evacuation had failed, the South Carolina guns opened fire on the fort, giving Lincoln the excuse he needed to place the United States on a war footing. On April 13, Anderson surrendered Fort Sumter to the Confederates.

The secessionist attack on Fort Sumter was not unexpected. Since Lincoln's election, the pre-election threats of secession by the southern states had begun to be implemented (Florida seceded on January 10, South Carolina on January 11). The U.S. military commanders did what they could in terms of planning for the expected conflict without creating political problems; Lincoln hoped he could keep the country together through diplomacy. As it became clear that armed conflict was inevitable, Union naval commanders began considering those assets in the South that would fall into Confederate hands. Foremost among these assets was the naval facility at Norfolk, Virginia. It contained hundreds of cannon, including more than three hundred Dahlgren guns. In addition to naval stores and a first-class dock facility, it was also the berth for several Union men-of-war, including the USS *Merrimack,* a twenty-two-gun steam frigate.

On April 17, the Virginia legislature voted to secede and the U.S. Navy went into action, its first mission being the destruction of the Norfolk facility. Whether the ineptness of the commanding officer, Commodore Hiram Paulding, the intentional dereliction of loyal southern officers, or both, was responsible, the April 20 attempt to destroy the naval yard failed almost totally. All ships at anchor were burned, including the *Merrimack,* and some stores were destroyed, but, for the most part, the Confederates occupied a nearly intact naval yard. Many of the yard's cannon would be used to arm the forts hastily being constructed by the Confederates along rivers and bays and on the Atlantic Ocean.

SECESSION AND BLOCKADE

As state after state seceded from the Union, it became clear to both sides that war was imminent. Lincoln assigned the task of generating a master strategic plan to an aging but still able General Winfield Scott, hero of the Mexican War. Scott rightly believed that for the North to win, the under-industrialized South had to be kept from supplying and industrializing itself from any outside source. Since raw materials and machinery were scarce in the South and could not be obtained readily from the northern United States, his plan was to choke off the South from the western areas of the United States and from the outside world just as a constricting snake chokes its victim. From this principle came Scott's plan, sometimes derisively referred to as the "Anaconda Plan," which called for a total blockade of all southern ports, complete control over all the river infrastructure in the South, and total naval superiority. Scott felt that without outside supply the South would be forced to capitulate when its supplies ran out (he estimated three years), and combat with the southern states might not even be necessary. Lincoln adopted the blockade aspect of the plan and immediately ordered his tiny national navy to blockade all thirty-five hundred miles (5,600km) of southern coastline and take control of the Mississippi River and all of its many tributaries.

The Union, unprepared for war though it was, began piecemeal implementation of the blockade plan. One by one, southern ports were blockaded, often with only one ship. In the Mississippi River area, Union ships slowly began cruising the waters in an effort to curtail Confederate commerce and test the Confederate defenses at various locations. The rivers in the West were critically important. There was very poor road infrastructure in the South, and most commerce moved on the few railroads and along the many rivers of the area. Control of the river infrastructure was critical if the Union was to have any chance of defeating the Confederate forces in the West using Scott's plan.

The most critical area on the Confederate Atlantic coast was the area of Hampton Roads. Sitting between the Accomack peninsula and Virginia Beach, Hampton Roads controlled all egress from the Chesapeake Bay and Virginia ports to the Atlantic Ocean. Any Confederate ships north of Wilmington and Hatteras would have to put in to these ports; by the same token, any

In the early morning hours of September 9, 1863, landing parties from the blockading Federal fleet attempted a small-boat assault against Confederate forces manning Fort Sumter. The Union raiders met with heavy fire, and the assault failed, with 135 Union casualties.

ships leaving these ports would have to run the gauntlet of Union warships that took up positions in Hampton Roads.

With the announcement of the blockade, the Confederate Secretary of the Navy, Stephen R. Mallory, realized that his naval operations would have a twofold mission: to fight the U.S. Navy and to supply the Confederacy with its material needs. With too much coastline to defend and not enough ships of the line, Mallory decided on a coastal defense strategy that relied on building forts at critical locations while keeping the Confederate navy mobile. In addition to his man-of-war construction scheme, he sought and obtained several ships whose designs enabled them to achieve high speeds in the open ocean. These blockade-runners were to be the lifeline of the Confederacy: they would carry southern goods, chiefly cotton, to European or Caribbean markets (Nassau, Havana, Bermuda), and trade these goods for war matériel. At first the Confederate Navy was heavily involved in

On the night of April 20, 1861, Federal naval personnel at the Norfolk, Virginia, Navy Yard (usually called Gosport) evacuated the facility. Although they attempted to destroy all boats, materials, and docks that could be of use to the Confederates, they failed to destroy the facility completely, and Gosport was put to significant use by the Confederate Navy.

blockade-running. As soon as the trade established itself as profitable, most of the blockade-running business was turned over to private enterprise, although the government continued to receive a percentage of the value of each cargo.

Blockade-runners were operated by businessmen who received large profits from the southern population. The ships were carefully designed and well built, and many of them were paddle-wheelers. Some had telescoping smokestacks, which allowed the ship to change its profile and to lessen its wind drag when under sail. Another technique in use was the removable screw, which was raised out of the water by its shaft once the ship was on the open ocean, further reducing water drag when under sail. The less fuel that had to be carried, the more room for cargo, leading to greater profit.

The reduction and capture of the southern ports, one by one, coupled with the reduction in available landing sites for the blockade-runners, made blockade-running all but impossible by late 1864. It became clear that blockade-running was no longer profitable when the Confederate government ceased to demand its percentage of the value of the cargo, it no longer being worthwhile. During its heyday, however, blockade-running made some people very wealthy; a single trip could pay for the ship, and one runner is known to have made forty-two trips.

PRIVATEERS

To encourage private parties to join the Confederacy's struggle, President Jefferson Davis began issuing Letters of Marque and Reprisal in April 1861. Letters of Marque and Reprisal were individual privateering permits allowing a civilian, under the auspices of the government of a belligerent nation, to attack the commercial and military vessels of the enemy and of neutral nations (if they were carrying contraband bound for the enemy). The civilian ships, called privateers, were allowed to keep the captured ship and its cargo if they could return it to one of their country's ports and have it adjudicated as theirs by a prize court. The ship and its cargo then became a "prize." Prizes were usually distributed on a percentage basis among the ship's owners, officers, and crew. Privateers were generally armed with cannon and small arms.

There was a great deal of concern about privateers in the North, where they were

On March 17, 1862, the cruiser CSS **Nashville** slipped out of Beaufort, North Carolina, to raid Union shipping. In September 1861 she had become the first Confederate warship to arrive in European waters. Late in 1862, she was sold as a blockade-runner and renamed the **Thomas L. Wragg** Early the following year, she was recommissioned as a privateer, the **Rattlesnake**; she was destroyed by the monitor USS **Montauk** on the Ogeechee River in Georgia in February 1863.

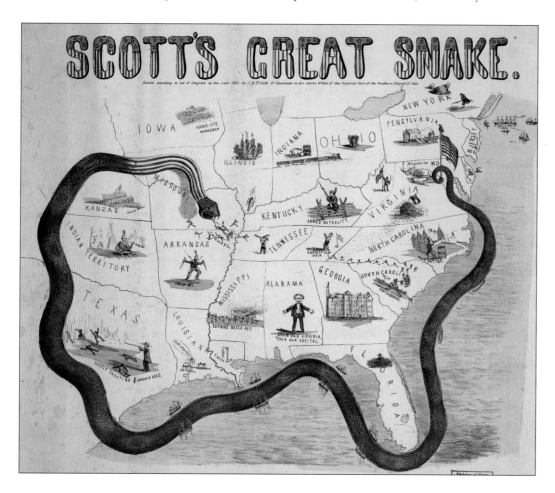

Although derided by many, including the press, General Winfield Scott's plan to economically strangle the South into submission by means of a blockade ultimately succeeded. This pro-Union political cartoon from an Ohio newspaper pokes fun at Scott's plan.

decried as pirates and criminals. Most of the major European nations had abolished privateering against each other in the 1856 Treaty of Paris. After the U.S. Navy had stopped and seized several British vessels coming from southern ports, the British government called on the U.S. government to stop the practice. The U.S. government officially notified the British government that a blockade was in place against the seceding Confederate states and that a state of war existed. Once notified, the major European powers declared their neutrality and opened their ports to both belligerents' navies, including privateers. However, no privateer could discharge or sell its cargo in a neutral port.

Chasing down Confederate blockade-runners at night, especially in bad weather, was not an easy chore. However, as the war progressed and more blockaders prowled the Atlantic ports, Confederate successes dwindled.

The U.S. government tried unsuccessfully to get the British government to reopen the negotiations of the Treaty of Paris so that the United States could join the antiprivateering decision and thereby bar Confederate privateers from using foreign harbors. Some of the privateers were operated by British and other foreign crews, who were quick to recognize that the situation presented immense opportunities for profit.

THE TRENT AFFAIR

One of the war's most anxious moments occurred on the high seas in October 1861. On October 12, the same day the *St. Louis* was launched into the Mississippi River, two Confederate diplomats, John Slidell and James M. Mason, were spirited out of the Charleston harbor on the blockade-runner *Theodora* bound for Havana, a transshipment point to England, where they were to be the emissaries of the Confederate government.

U.S. Secretary of State Seward, upon hearing of their escape from the United States and thinking they were aboard a Confederate vessel, the CSS *Nashville*, ordered that they be captured.

On November 8, the USS *San Jacinto*, under the command of Captain Charles Wilkes, found Mason, Slidell, and their families at Havana, waiting for transportation aboard a British mail packet, the *Trent*. Lying off the Havana harbor, Wilkes waited until the *Trent* had made her exit. On the high seas, the *San Jacinto* forced the *Trent* to heave to and be boarded. Despite the obvious illegality of the act, Union sailors boarded the *Trent*, seized Slidell and Mason, and took them to the *San Jacinto*.

On November 24, Wilkes arrived at Boston with Mason and Slidell, who were immediately imprisoned at Fort Warren in Boston Harbor. Newspapers and politicians were jubilant over the capture. By the end of the next week, England was ablaze with indignation over the flagrant violation of British sovereignty. The British government, through its minister in Washington, Lord Lyons, demanded the release of Mason and Slidell coupled with an appropriate apology. On December 19, Lord Lyons communicated the demand to Secretary of State Seward along with notification that if an answer was

In this contemporary drawing, Captain Charles Wilkes of the USS San Jacinto *boards the British mail packet* Trent *and takes Confederate commissioners John Slidell and James M. Mason into his custody. This incident, commonly referred to as the Trent Affair, severely strained relations between the United States and Britain. At the last hour, Lincoln released Mason and Slidell to continue their journey to England.*

The USS **San Jacinto** *fires a round across the bow of the British mail packet* **Trent***, ordering the foreign vessel to heave to and prepare to be boarded.*

Captain Charles Wilkes, captain of the USS **San Jacinto** *during the Trent Affair.*

not forthcoming in seven days, the British ambassador and his entourage would leave the United States.

Jubilation turned to concern as the U.S. government realized that Britain, already considered friendly to the Confederate States, might feel compelled to take military and diplomatic action against the United States. On December 20, two British warships loaded with troops set sail for Canada to add emphasis to Lyons' demands.

The Confederate government had vehemently protested against the seizure of Slidell and Mason, and used the incident to create a closer bond between the Confederate States and Britain. Lyons met again with Seward on December 21 and 23, underscoring the possibility of Britain entering into a war against the United States. Finally, on December 26, the final day allowed by the British government, the Lincoln administration caved in, admitting that the seizure was illegal, and released Mason and Slidell to continue their trip to England. The Confederate government saw the opportunity to bring the British into the war slip from their grasp.

THE BEGINNING OF COMBINED SEA/LAND OPERATIONS

On the coastal waters of the South, Union naval commanders were beginning the slow, arduous job of working in uncharted waters. One of their first tasks along the Carolina coast was to explore the myriad bays, inlets, and rivers. These relatively shallow waterways provided excellent ports for the shallow-draft blockade-runners. In order to deny their use to the enemy, the Union Navy had to navigate deep-draft warships in these treacherous waters.

In August 1861, in accordance with the blockade order, the Union Navy continued to

Rear Admiral Samuel F. DuPont, an experienced naval officer, was assigned the unenviable task of blockading the South's Atlantic ports at the beginning of the war.

Major General Benjamin F. Butler, a New Hampshire politician and militia commander, assisted in the assault on Fort Hatteras in 1861. After an ill-fated expedition against Fort Fisher, North Carolina, in December 1864, in which he left six hundred Union troops stranded on a beach, he was relieved of command by Lieutenant General U.S. Grant.

carry out its plan to reduce selected critical southern coastal fortifications and harbors. Commodore Silas H. Stringham was placed in command of a squadron composed of seven armed ships and three transports containing nine hundred infantry troops under the command of Major General Benjamin F. Butler. The purpose of this squadron was to destroy and capture forts Hatteras and Clark, which controlled Hatteras Inlet, North Carolina, and the major sounds and rivers within the protection of the Hatteras barrier islands. This area was chosen because it offered the Confederacy a natural blockade-runner port that could supply other southern areas. The two main rivers, the Neuse and the Pamlico, allowed a protected site for blockade-runners to put up and restock.

In this drawing by Alfred Waud, Union troops are shown landing on North Carolina's Outer Banks during the assault on forts Clark and Hatteras in August 1861. This was the first combined sea and land operation in U.S. military history.

The U.S. Marine Corps saw limited action in the great land battles of the Civil War, but marines served an invaluable role as the offensive arm of the Federal blockade of the Southern coast. In this painting, marines advance up a beach on the North Carolina coast in one of the countless amphibious raids that helped to enforce the blockade.

A posed photograph of U.S. sailors servicing a large smoothbore cannon aboard a warship. Each man is at his battle station. Note the gunner, who uses his thumb to cover the primer port on the cannon to prevent an accidental discharge. The sailors wearing the corrugated waist protectors used their body weight to belay the ropes when moving the gun back into position.

On August 27, 1861, Stringham's squadron, consisting of the warships *Minnesota*, *Wabash*, *Monticello*, *Susquehanna*, *Pawnee*, and *Cumberland*, and a revenue steamer, the *Harriet Lane*, bearing a total of 158 guns, arrived in the vicinity of Cape Hatteras. Early on the morning of August 28, they opened fire on the two forts. The transports *Adelaide*, *George Peabody*, and *Fanny* lay offshore out of range of the forts' twenty-five guns. The technique used to reduce the forts was to form the warships in a line and sail in an ellipse within cannon range of Fort Clark, the outermost fort. In this way, the ships were able to fire continuous, though somewhat inaccurate, broadsides into the fort, while at the same time offering more difficult targets to the land-based gunners within the forts. Concurrent with the naval attack, a contingent of infantry was landed north of the forts, where it would be in a position to storm the facilities once they had been sufficiently reduced by the naval gunfire.

TOP: The CSS Florida, a blockade-runner and cruiser, is shown in this contemporary French engraving in the port of Brest, France. ABOVE: The CSS Robert E. Lee was famous for successfully running the blockade twenty-two times before she was captured by U.S. ships off Bermuda in 1863. She was taken into the U.S. Navy and renamed USS Fort Donelson. She went on to work the blockading squadron, chasing down her former comrades. Capable of eleven knots (5.7 m/sec), she boasted telescoping smokestacks and twin paddle wheels.

Having reduced the forts, the Union Army found that occupying them was a little harder to accomplish than they had thought. Within a month, on September 29, three thousand Confederate troops aboard several vessels steamed to Hatteras Island in an effort to cut off and capture six hundred troops of the 20th Indiana who had been sent to occupy Chicamacomico on the northern end of Hatteras Island. The Union troops were warned in the nick of time and managed, through hard marching in deep sand, and with the help of a naval artillery barrage from the USS *Monticello*, to avoid capture and return to the fort.

Following the capture of Fort Hatteras, two naval squadrons were formed in place of the Union's Atlantic Squadron. Admiral Goldsborough was placed in command of the North Atlantic Squadron, responsible for the coast of Virginia and North Carolina, and Admiral Samuel DuPont was placed in command of the South Atlantic Squadron, responsible for the coast from South Carolina to the southern cape of Florida.

BATTLE OF THE MISSISSIPPI PASSES

In late 1861, U.S. Navy operations in the Gulf of Mexico were concentrated on the former U.S. naval base at Pensacola, Florida, the multichanneled mouth of the Mississippi River, and the Confederate ports in Texas. The Mississippi River delta was formed from the river's sediment, which, through the centuries, had reduced the Mississippi's mouth from a single waterway into a series of smaller waterways spread out in the shape of a fan. This geographical situation made it virtually impossible for the USS *Brooklyn* to control the area without additional vessels. In October 1861, four additional ships, the

By midmorning, the colors had been struck by the Confederate troops manning Fort Clark. Union troops moved forward and occupied the fort, which they found abandoned. With Fort Clark in their possession, the attention of the Union armada was turned next to Fort Hatteras. A sandbar across the mouth of Hatteras Inlet prevented the deep-draft Union naval ships from entering the inlet. On the morning of August 29, these ships moved south and set up anchored positions at the southern end of the inlet. From that position, they proceeded to conduct a continuous naval bombardment of Fort Hatteras. Around 11 A.M., the Confederates in the fort sent up a white flag, and an unconditional surrender of the fort and its personnel was effected. The Confederate prisoners were placed aboard the transports and taken to prison on Governor's Island, New York. The forts were then occupied by troops of the 20th Indiana Regiment.

Commissioned just before the war began, the screw sloop USS Richmond *stayed in combat throughout the war, fighting in some of the toughest contests in the West. At the beginning of the war, during the Battle of Sabine Passes, she was struck by the Confederate ram CSS* Manassas.

Richmond, the *Vincennes,* the *Preble,* and the small screw steamer *Water Witch,* arrived to block the passes of the Mississippi. They totaled forty-seven guns, and were considered capable of handling anything the Confederates might have in the area, and of preventing blockade-runners and commerce raiders from gaining the open sea.

On October 13, 1861, in the dark of the morning, a small Confederate flotilla from New Orleans, consisting of the *Ivy,* the *Tuscarora,* the *Calhoun,* the *Jackson,* the ram *Manassas,* and a towboat, the *Watson,* under the command of Commodore J.S. Hollins, steamed their way to the position of the Union Navy. The USS *Richmond* was taking on coal from a coaler and since the ship's crew was busy loading coal, no lookout had been posted. In the nearly impenetrable darkness, the ram *Manassas* took a full head of steam and headed for the position of the Union ships, hoping to ram one or more of them. Suddenly, the *Richmond* and the coaler loomed out of the darkness directly in front of the *Manassas.* Lieutenant A.F. Warley, commanding the *Manassas,* rammed his ship directly into the coaling schooner and the *Richmond,* causing damage to the *Richmond* but crippling his own ship in the process.

Recovering quickly from the surprise, the Union ships came to general quarters and opened a fusillade of cannon fire on the Confederate ships. Warley extracted his now-damaged ram from the side of the *Richmond* and beat a slow but regular retreat to a nearby shoreline. The Confederate ships, some armed with Whitworth rifles, fired into the milling Union ships. In the dark, few of the rounds from either side found their mark. Finally, the *Tuscarora* and the *Watson* delivered five fire barges into the stream floating toward the Union fleet. This succeeded in breaking contact between the two forces.

The oddly shaped but effective Confederate ram CSS **Manassas.** *The first all-metal ship built by the Confederacy, she was cigar-shaped and sat very low in the water. She was run aground by the USS* **Mississippi** *but salvaged by her crew, and she fought at the Battle of New Orleans.*

A fire barge was a device designed for use against wooden ships such as those anchored off the Mississippi passes that morning. A simple floating barge was filled with flammable materials, usually wood, hay, and pitch, and towed to the scene of the fighting. It was maneuvered upstream from the enemy, set on fire, and allowed to float down and into the enemy ships. The size of the fire was so great that any ship that came into contact with it was likely to catch fire. Fire aboard a wooden sailing ship was a great peril, since there were few, if any, methods of putting out a fire, particularly if the crew were at their battle stations defending against other warships.

Morning found the *Manassas* lying concealed along the shore and the *Tuscarora* and the *Watson* grounded on bars. Some miles south, the *Richmond* and the *Vincennes* had gone hard aground on a bar, and the other Union ships had formed into a defensive perimeter to take advantage of the *Richmond'*s guns. The remaining Confederate boats floated to within gun range and

engaged the Union ships in an exchange of cannon fire. However, neither side suffered significant damage, and the Confederates eventually withdrew.

During this exchange of fire, a comedy of errors on the Union side nearly ended in disaster. Captain Robert Handy, commander of the USS *Vincennes,* misunderstood a signal from Captain John Pope of the *Richmond.* Believing that he had been ordered to abandon and destroy his ship, Handy immediately ordered his men into boats and placed a slow fuse on the powder magazine. When Handy arrived aboard the *Richmond* and reported to Captain Pope, he had the national ensign from the *Vincennes* wrapped around his waist like a sash. After a brief inquiry, an apoplectic Captain Pope ordered Handy back to the *Vincennes.* It was discovered that the seaman ordered to light the fuse on the magazine had not done so, and there was no danger of explosion. The next day, the *Richmond* and the *Vincennes* were pulled from the bar and took up their positions on picket duty.

chapter 10

1862
Naval War in the West

"The loss of the rebels must be very heavy; their vessels were literally torn to pieces, and some had holes in their sides through which a man could walk. Those that blew up—it makes me shudder to think of them."

—Lieutenant S.L. Phelps, commander of the ironclad gunboat USS Benton, regarding the naval action at Plum Point, May 10, 1862

IRONCLADS, RAMS, AND TRANSPORTS

Control of the Mississippi River was critical to the Union plan to starve the Confederacy into submission. As long as the Mississippi was not controlled completely by the U.S. Navy, Confederate forces could receive supplies, men, and matériel from the states west of the Mississippi. At the outset of the war, Union strategic planners felt that the gunboats on the Mississippi should be under the operational control of the U.S. Army, since the U.S. Navy was considered to be an exclusively blue-water (oceangoing) navy. Although the navy provided officers to staff the gunboats, it was not until October 1862 that operational control of the ironclads was transferred to the navy.

By the summer of 1861, plans were well under way for the production of twelve to twenty new ironclad river vessels for the U.S. Army. Samuel Pook modified an original design by James Lenthall, and the boats were contracted to be built by James Eads at a new Union shipyard at Mound City, Illinois, near Cairo. Pook's plan called for a massive flat-bottomed paddle wheeler, fifty feet (15.2m) wide by 175 feet (53.3m) long and drawing only six feet (1.8m) of water. On the hull of the boat, a casemate constructed of thick oak and iron plate was to run completely around the vessel. The sides of the vessel sloped at thirty-five degrees, while the front and rear sloped at forty-five degrees. The combination of angle and iron was enough to defeat most cannon.

These new ironclads mounted massive naval artillery. The USS *Cairo*, for example,

PAGE 167: The cotton-clad Confederate Mississippi River Defense Fleet rams crash into the Union ironclad fleet at Plum Point in May 1862. In the ensuing close-quarter combat, several ironclads were rammed and sunk. The Confederates suffered losses as well, presaging the doom of the river defense fleet less than a month later. ABOVE: The only known wartime photograph of the USS Cairo, a city-class ironclad. The Cairo was sunk by Confederate mines on December 12, 1862, in the Yazoo River in Mississippi. She was recovered by the National Park Service in 1964 and put on display at Vicksburg National Military Park.

mounted three 42-pounder (19kg) army rifles, three 64-pounder (29kg) navy smoothbores, six 32-pounder (14.5kg) navy smoothbores, and one 32-pounder (14.5kg) Parrott gun. The guns were arranged three in the bow ports, four on each side, and two in the stern ports. The ship was operated by seventeen officers and 158 enlisted men. After dealing with strikes, supply problems, and other delays, Eads delivered the *Cairo* on

January 15, 1862, ninety days past schedule. In total, only seven of the Eads city-class ironclads were built.

Another novel form of naval vessel in the Mississippi River area was the tinclad. Tinclads were lightly armored river vessels, side and rear paddle wheelers with a shallow draft, many of which had previously been commercial transports. They were armored with quarter-inch (0.6cm) steel around critical

areas, and they used cotton bales, timber, and other materials to help absorb the force of any fire they received. There were a total of sixty-three tinclads on the Mississippi River, each bearing her serial number on the side of the wheelhouse. They were armed with an assortment of cannon. The USS *Marmora* was originally armed with two 24-pounder (10.8kg) smoothbores and two 12-pounder (5.4kg) rifles. The USS *Signal*, dur-

Admiral David Glasgow Farragut, began his naval career as a boy and worked his way to the top of his profession.

ing the same period, was armed with two 30-pounder (13.6kg) rifles, four 24-pounder (10.8kg) howitzers, and one 12-pounder (5.4kg) rifle. The size of the tinclads' crews varied widely depending on the size of the vessel and the number of personnel available.

In 1862 there were two ways to sink a boat with another boat. You could shoot it until it sank, or you could ram it. There was, of course, a serious downside to the latter option: unless the ramming boat was specially prepared, it usually suffered as much damage as the boat rammed. A U.S. Army officer, Charles Ellet, came up with the idea of reinforcing certain boats and using them to intentionally ram enemy ships. Logically enough, these special boats were called rams. Ellet convinced the army's Quartermaster Department to purchase seven river steamers and have them converted to his specifications. The interior frames of the rams were

reinforced so that they would survive the shock of hitting another vessel at speed. The bows were reinforced and filled with timber. The rams were somewhat unusual in that most of them carried no naval artillery. Ellet commanded the ram fleet, and it remained a U.S. Army unit throughout the war, operating as an independent command. Although Ellet's rams operated under naval orders, there was some resentment on the part of naval officers over the fact that army officers had been placed in command of boats in a naval flotilla.

Yet another of the specialized river vessels was the mortar scow. The mortar scow was a raft with sides carrying a mortar. A mortar is a weapon with a high angle of fire, used for indirect fire on protected targets. By firing its round high into the air, it can strike areas which are protected from direct cannon fire, such as the interior of a fort. These mortar scows were not self-powered, and they had to be pulled into position by other craft.

In addition to the mortar scows, there was a small fleet of powered schooners that carried mortars. These, originally commanded by Admiral David Dixon Porter, U.S.N., at the Battle of New Orleans, were kept with the fleet of Naval Officer David Glasgow Farragut, and were used repeatedly on the lower end of the Mississippi River and in the Gulf of Mexico.

After General Ulysses S. Grant's victory at forts Henry and Donelson, the idea of moving troops by naval craft and using naval gunfire in support of the infantry became an integral part of his strategy. In the summer and fall of 1862, in preparation for further operations against Southern strongholds, the government purchased or leased numerous commercial paddle wheel river steamboats. These boats were used as troop transports and bore neither armor nor cannon.

Even as early as 1862, the Union advantage in men and matériel was beginning to show in the West. Large Union forces pushed

The USS Cincinnati, *another of the city-class ironclads built by James Eads, was twice sunk and raised during the war, and saw action in the western theater. The colored bands on the smokestacks identified the city-class ironclads.*

Lieutenant General Ulysses S. Grant, commander of land forces in the western theater, later went on to lead all the Union armies and to accept Lee's surrender at Appomattox.

Captain David Dixon Porter became commander of Union naval operations in the Mississippi River after Henry Walke fell ill.

Confederate General Lloyd Tilghman, commander of the defenders at Fort Henry, was killed in action at Champion's Hill, Mississippi in May 1863.

the Confederates out of Kentucky by March. Although General Henry Halleck was in overall command of the western district, Grant was the major tactical commander. Grant knew that the lack of interior lines of communication in the rural South meant that he had to depend significantly on naval transport. This dependency led, in part, to a friendship between Grant and Porter. This friendship in turn contributed greatly to the development of the doctrine of combined army and naval operation.

In late January 1862, President Lincoln took a bold step to get the inactive Union forces into combat. He issued General War Order Number 1, declaring that all Union forces should move against the enemy on February 22. Modifying Scott's "wait and starve" theory, Lincoln hoped that a concerted drive against the Confederates would strain

their limited resources and bring about their surrender. He was to be very disappointed, however, as most of his commanders showed a lack of resolve and an inability to take the offensive, while the enemy displayed tremendous spirit and tenacity.

FORTS HENRY AND DONELSON: CONTINUED DEVELOPMENT OF COMBINED OPERATIONS

Grant told Halleck that his plan was to proceed against Fort Henry on the Tennessee River. With Halleck's approval and the support of the navy, Grant embarked on his campaign. His plan was to assault Fort Henry from the land side with ten thousand troops

while the navy's new ironclad gunboats shelled the fort from the river. On February 5, 1862, a cold and rainy day, Grant's operation began. His troops were delivered in two groups because of the shortage of transports. The naval forces under Commodore William D. Porter consisted of three of the new Eads ironclads (the *Carondelet*, the *Cincinnati*, and the *St. Louis*), a converted river steamer, the *Essex*, and three wooden ships (the *Conestoga*, the *Tyler*, and the *Lexington*). Fort Henry commanded a straight two-mile (3.2km) stretch of the Tennessee River. This forced the Union ships to fight the fort bow on, which meant that only their bow guns could be brought into action. Fort Henry had seventeen guns, twelve of which were trained on the river. The Union fleet could only bring about seventeen of their total seventy-six guns into action.

*The USS **Lexington** was one of the timberclad gunboats that gave naval gunfire support to Union army forces at Shiloh.*

The Union gunboats moved to within a third of a mile (0.5km) of the fort and began their cannonade. For an hour and a half the duel between the fort and the ironclads raged. Finally, the Confederate commander, General Lloyd Tilghman, his guns dismounted and his crews wounded by the continuous bombardment from the fleet, sent up the white flag. The shooting ceased, and Tilghman surrendered his garrison to the U.S. Navy. Captain Henry Walke went ashore and took custody of Fort Henry until Grant, whose troops had been seriously delayed by the flooded lowlands and by Confederate infantry, arrived some time later and took control.

During the battle for Fort Henry, the first fight in the West between ironclad gunboats and land-based weapons, the utility of the ironclad vessels was proven once again. The gunboats were struck repeatedly by accurate Confederate fire, but their armor held up against the onslaught. Only one, the *Essex*, suffered any serious damage, when she was hit by a shot that pierced the boiler and sent scalding steam through the ship, killing or wounding twenty-nine men.

Immediately upon taking control of Fort Henry, Grant reorganized his forces and declared his intention to take Fort Donelson, a nearby Confederate bastion located on the Cumberland River. Flag Officer A.H. Foote, U.S.N., reformed his fleet and replaced the damaged *Essex* with another Eads ironclad, the *Pittsburg*. On the afternoon of February 14, his fleet began the bombardment of Fort Donelson. The fort was defended by sixty-five guns and twenty-one thousand men. It was situated on top of a hundred-foot (30.4m) bluff and was protected by well-designed fortifications.

Foote's fleet moved to within four hundred yards (365.7m) of the fort and suffered severe damage. The *St. Louis* and the *Louisville* had their steering shot away and went adrift. The *Pittsburg* and the *Carondelet* were not able to withstand the fire from the fort's batteries and were severely damaged. After an hour and a half, the fleet withdrew from the fight. Each of Foote's vessels had been struck about fifty times with heavy shot, and the fleet had suffered fifty-four men killed or wounded.

On February 16, Grant's troops occupied Fort Donelson and took twelve thousand prisoners, pushing the Confederate line of defense further south. On February 17, a delighted President Lincoln appointed Grant commander of the new military territory of Western Tennessee. For the Confederacy, the loss of forts Henry and Donelson was a disaster. Their loss forced the evacuation, on February 20, of the fortifications at Columbus, Kentucky, which controlled part of the upper Mississippi River.

It was obvious by this point that the Union strategy was to work toward the complete closure of the Mississippi River. The collapse of the Confederate line in Kentucky opened the way for Union incursions deep into Tennessee and, collaterally, along the Mississippi River. The next step for the Union

forces was to begin the point-by-point reduction of Confederate strongholds at both ends of the Mississippi.

SHILOH, OR PITTSBURG LANDING

By early April, Grant's army had moved into lower Tennessee and encamped near Pittsburg Landing, close to a small church called Shiloh Meeting House. Confederate forces under General Albert Sidney Johnston, recently forced out of Kentucky, regrouped at Corinth, Mississippi, south of Grant's position. On April 2, Johnston ordered his forty thousand soldiers to march against Grant's position at Pittsburg Landing.

Grant had used river transports to move his troops to Pittsburg Landing, and the ironclads used the landing as a staging point for further reconnaissance down the Tennessee River and its tributaries. One such reconnaissance went as far as Chickasaw, Alabama, and Eastport, Tennessee.

On April 6, Johnston's forty thousand troops fell upon Grant's unsuspecting infantry force of forty-two thousand, and the battle was on. Initially, the Confederates made significant gains, but they were eventually prevented from destroying Grant's army or occupying Pittsburg Landing. One key ingredient in the Union victory was Grant's ability to use navy transports to land infantry reinforcements at the landing, placing fresh troops near the fighting.

A contemporary popular depiction of Grant's army standing against the onslaught of Confederate infantry at Shiloh.

At the critical juncture of the battle, when Confederate forces massed for a final attack on the beleaguered Union troops, the USS *Tyler* and the USS *Lexington* took up positions near the bank of the Tennessee River and the left wing of the Union defenders. As the attack began, the ships opened fire with their guns and howitzers, pouring nearly four hundred rounds into the Confederate line between 6:00 P.M. and 5:00 A.M. the following morning. Some historians maintain that without the naval gunfire supporting them, the Union infantry would have been overrun. Whether or not this is the case, the utility of combined naval and infantry operations was clearly demonstrated.

BATTLE OF NEW ORLEANS

Prior to the outbreak of hostilities, New Orleans, the largest city in the South, was a major shipbuilding depot for the U.S. Navy. Its ideal location at the mouth of the Mississippi River made it a natural harbor for the transshipment of materials from ocean-going vessels to river vessels, and for the construction and repair of ships. The Confederates lost no time in putting these facilities to good use when they seized the naval yards and forts in January 1861. After the skirmish at the passes of the Mississippi River in October 1861, Lincoln knew that he had to take New Orleans to control the mouth of the Mississippi River ab move the passes. In November a plan was drawn up, set for execution in April 1862.

At New Orleans, the Union naval attack was expected. Two large forts, Fort Jackson and Fort St. Phillip, guarded a bend in the Mississippi River fifteen miles (24km) below New Orleans. Confederate defenders based their defense on these two old but substantial structures, combined with a makeshift blockade constructed of old ship hulls strung

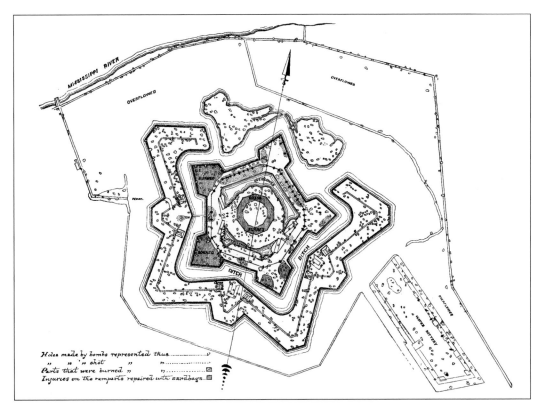

In an early form of bomb damage assessment, this engineer's drawing of Fort Jackson, which guarded the Mississippi River south of New Orleans, shows the locations of shell holes, marks, and other damage caused by the Union naval bombardment.

together on a chain across the river. If the Union fleet approached and passed the forts, the chained ships were to stop it and make it a sitting target for the forts' guns.

The original plan for the attack on New Orleans was conceived by Commodore Porter. This officer, however, was too junior in rank to lead the attack, and he was given responsibility only for the mortar schooner fleet. President Lincoln chose David Glasgow Farragut to lead the assault on the lower Mississippi River. Farragut was one of the navy's most experienced senior officers; he had begun his career in the War of 1812 as a ten-year-old midshipman aboard a naval man-of-war.

In secret, Farragut and Porter began assembling the necessary men and ships for the expedition. Naval Secretary Welles, to cover Farragut's assignment, divided the Gulf Blockading Squadron into two parts, East and West, assigning Farragut responsibility for everything from the Rio Grande River at the Texas-Mexico border to Saint Andrew's Bay in Florida.

The New Orleans task force set out, and by February 1862 most of the fleet was assembled in the Gulf of Mexico. On March 1, Farragut sent a party into Biloxi, Mississippi, to raid the local post office and other shops for information. Through this, he received word of the Union victories at Fort Donelson and Fort Henry, and of the advance against Island Number 10 (see page 56). The way was paved for an assault on the Mississippi River and New Orleans.

NAVAL WAR IN THE WEST

OPPOSITE: *Admiral Farragut's flagship, the USS* Hartford, *runs the guns in front of Fort Jackson, Louisiana. Painting by Tom W. Freeman.* ABOVE: *The Union fleet passing forts Jackson and St. Phillip below New Orleans. Most noticeable is the ram CSS* Manassas *at the extreme right side of the engraving. In the center of the engraving, the USS* Hartford *is attacked by a fire raft on her port side.*

It took the better part of a month to get the entire Union fleet over the sandbars at the mouth of the Mississippi River. By the beginning of April the fleet was finally over the bar and in position to begin the reduction of New Orleans and its two forts. Porter's twenty-one mortar schooners were brought to within one mile (1.6km) of the forts and anchored. Their masts were camouflaged to reduce the potential for counterbattery fire. At 9:00 A.M. on April 18, Porter gave the order to open the mortar barrage on the forts. Each 13-inch (33cm) mortar fired one round every ten minutes; and more than three thousand mortar rounds were fired over the course of ten hours.

At nightfall, Farragut called a cease-fire and sent a small force forward to assess damage. The team found the forts on fire, but realized that a long period of siege would be necessary to reduce them. The next day, with ammunition running short, Farragut slowed the mortar schooners' rate of fire to two rounds every hour.

A bird's-eye view of the Union fleet passing the forts below New Orleans.

If Farragut was to run the river past the forts and get above them, the chain and hulk blockade had to be dealt with. He ordered a couple of gunboats to attempt a breach of the blockade with electrically detonated explosives. Intense Confederate artillery fire from the two forts prevented the explosives from being set, but sweat, axes, and saws accomplished the desired end, and the blockade was breached sufficiently on the eastern side of the river to allow the fleet to pass.

The Confederate naval forces, led by Commander John K. Mitchell, were augmented by the Confederate Army's River Defense Fleet, which remained independent from the navy, and the Louisiana State Navy, which was completely independent. Mitchell, in disagreement with the Confederate ground commander, Brigadier General Johnson Duncan, kept the majority of his fleet north of the hulk blockade and out of mortar range. The Confederate fleet, consisting of

several ironclads and other river steamers, would await the Union fleet north of the blockade line and attack it as it attempted to move upstream against the river current and around the bend at the forts. It was decided that each individual Confederate ship captain would make his own decisions in the upcoming battle.

Farragut's plan called for his fleet, which was divided into three sections (red, blue, and red-blue), to run past the forts in that

Farragut brought Union mortar boats up to bombard Fort Jackson before attempting to pass it with the fleet. The masts were camouflaged with trees to help conceal the mortar boats from Confederate observers directing counterbattery fire.

Union Captain Theodorus Bailey and Lieutenant George H. Stevens on their way to the city hall to accept the surrender of New Orleans. Confederate forces had evacuated the city to prevent its destruction, leaving its citizens at the mercy of the occupying Federal troops.

order, negotiate the breached hulk blockade, and fight the Confederate ships above the forts. The red segment, commanded by Captain Theodorus Bailey, consisted of the USS *Cayuga*, the USS *Pensacola*, the USS *Mississippi*, the USS *Varuna*, the USS *Oneida*, and three gunboats. The blue segment, commanded by Farragut, would consist of the heavy frigates USS *Hartford*, USS *Brooklyn*, and USS *Richmond*. The final red-blue segment, commanded by Captain Henry Bell, was composed of the USS *Iroquois* and five gunboats.

In the early morning hours of April 23, the fleet set off in order up the river. The night was pitch black as the fleet approached the forts and began the battle. Although raked by heavy fire from the forts, the van-guard red segment negotiated the hulk

*TOP: The sloop of war USS **Brooklyn**. Commissioned just before the war, in 1859, the **Brooklyn** fought in every major engagement in the West. She continued to serve in the U.S. Navy until 1889, when she was decommissioned and sold. ABOVE: The Union fleet attacks Fort St. Phillip below New Orleans.*

blockade and was the first to come into contact with the Confederate fleet. The iron-clad ram CSS *Manassas,* commanded by Lieutenant A.F. Warley, surged among the wooden Union ships, but was sunk after ramming only two of them and inflicting serious, though not fatal, damage. The CSS *Governor Moore,* with Lieutenant Beverly Kennon commanding, managed to ram and sink the USS *Varuna* before being so badly shot up that, like many others, the boat had to be burned to prevent her capture.

Ship by ship, the Union fleet negotiated the forts, the hulk blockade, and the Confederate Navy. The death toll was high and the damage significant, but the fleet finally got past the forts. Ships stopped for their crews to repair them, bury the dead, wash the gore from the decks, and prepare for the next engagement: taking the city of New Orleans. On April 25, Union troops entered New Orleans and reoccupied the Federal buildings. On May 1, all hostilities in New Orleans were brought to an end with the formal surrender of the remaining Confederate land and naval forces in the city.

ISLAND NUMBER 10 AND MEMPHIS, TENNESSEE

Between the confluence of the Ohio and Mississippi Rivers at Cairo, Illinois, and the mouth of the Mississippi River below New Orleans, there are a number of islands. During the Civil War, these islands were numbered consecutively from Cairo to New Orleans. In the bend of the Mississippi River near New Madrid, Missouri, was Island Number 10. The Confederates had made this choke point in the river into a formidable fort, defended by seventy-five cannon and six thousand troops.

At the same time that Farragut was approaching New Orleans, the Mississippi

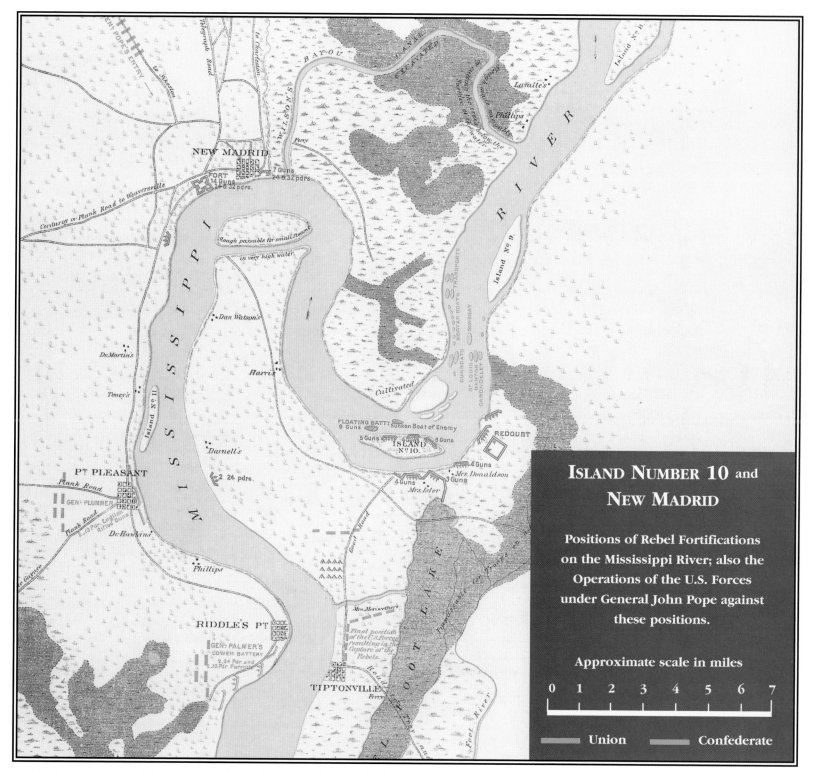

This contemporary map of the area around Island Number 10 shows Confederate fortifications.

NAVAL WAR IN THE WEST

LEFT: During a violent thunderstorm on the night of April 1, 1862, a handpicked raiding party of forty men from the 42nd Illinois Regiment assaulted the upper battery at Island Number 10 and spiked the Confederate cannon there, making them useless to oppose the passage of the Union fleet. ABOVE: On June 6, 1862, the citizens of Memphis, Tennessee, watched as the Union fleet completely destroyed what was left of the Confederates' Mississippi River Defense Fleet. The way to the key city of Vicksburg, Mississippi, was now open.

River Fleet, with Foote commanding, was anchored off Island Number 10. In early March, U.S. Army General John Pope attacked and seized New Madrid with twenty-five thousand infantrymen. If the Union Navy could get some gunboats past Island Number 10, Pope's infantry would be able to cross the river and invest Island Number 10 from the south.

On April 4, Walke, commanding the USS *Carondelet,* volunteered to run the gauntlet past Island Number 10. On a pitch-black night, the specially prepared boat began its secret passage. A sudden thunderstorm lit up the night as the boat slid past the Confederate batteries. To make matters worse, the coal dust residue in the *Carondelet*'s stacks caught fire and lit up the boat. Confederate batteries opened up, but to no avail. The *Carondelet* was safely past. The

feat was duplicated on April 6 by the USS *Pittsburg.* On April 7, without delay, the two gunboats patrolled while Pope's infantry crossed the river and landed below Island Number 10. By late afternoon the fort had surrendered, and the Mississippi river was open all the way to Memphis, Tennessee.

North of the key port of Vicksburg, the only remaining Confederate stronghold was Memphis. The Mississippi River Fleet, accompanied by Pope and his infantry, eased down the river, anchored at Plum Point, and began their usual mortar bombardment of Fort Pillow, north of Memphis. Captain Charles Davis replaced the injured Captain Foote on May 9. On May 10, the USS *Cincinnati* deposited a mortar scow at the bank and anchored nearby, steam down. Suddenly, eight ships appeared steaming up the river. They were cottonclad rams of

The USS **Pittsburg***, one of the city-class Eads ironclads.*

the Confederate Army's Mississippi River Defense Fleet, commanded by Commodore James Montgomery and his companion, General Jeff Thompson, a Missouri guerrilla leader.

The *Cincinnati*'s crew tried desperately to get her steam up, but she was struck almost instantly by the CSS *General Bragg*. Within a few minutes she was struck twice more by the CSS *Sumter* (not the raider of the same name) and the CSS *General Sterling*

Price. The *Cincinnati*'s 32-pounder (14.5kg) smoothbores blew holes through the lightly clad rams as she filled with water and sank to the bottom.

Nearby, the Union gunboats *Carondelet* and *Mound City* heard the cannon fire and steamed toward the action. The rebel steamer CSS *General Van Dorn* rammed and sank the *Mound City*. The *Carondelet* fired a 5-inch (12.7cm) Dahlgren rifle round through the CSS *Sumter*'s boilers, blowing her up. Sam

Phelps, commanding the USS *Benton,* fired an 8-inch (20.3cm) shell through the CSS *General Lovell*, hitting her boilers. He then turned on the CSS *General Van Dorn,* hitting her boilers as well. With the arrival of the heavy gunboats, the lightly armed Confederate River Defense Fleet broke off the engagement and headed south to the protection of Fort Pillow's guns. For the first time on the river, the Union fleet had been severely bloodied by Confederate naval forces.

On May 25, Colonel Charles Ellet arrived with seven rams of the U.S. Army's Mississippi Ram Fleet, an organization completely independent of the navy. The vessels were designed for the specific purpose of ramming, and initially carried no armor or weapons. Later in the war they were armed with light cannon. On May 30, Confederate forces were forced to abandon Fort Pillow, blowing it up before withdrawing to Memphis.

Memphis was virtually defenseless. These men and boats that could be spared had been sent to defend New Orleans. The entire garrison at Memphis consisted of about two hundred troops and the eight ships that remained of Commodore Montgomery's River Defense Fleet after the fight on May 10.

In the predawn hours of June 6, the Union Navy came to Memphis. Montgomery's eight ships stood across the river in two lines abreast. Ellet's rams competed with Davis' ironclads for the honor of reaching the Confederate fleet first. In the smoky dawn, the Union rams and gunboats destroyed Montgomery's fleet with virtually no losses of their own. Only the CSS *General Van Dorn* managed to escape destruction and run to Vicksburg. At 11:00 A.M. that same day, Union troops landed unopposed and took control of Memphis.

1862
Naval War in the East

"*After firing for two hours I find I can do the enemy about as much damage by snapping my fingers at him every two minutes and a half.*"

—*Gun Division Officer aboard the CSS Virginia to Lieutenant Catesby Jones when asked why his gun crew was standing at ease during the battle with the USS Monitor*

THE *MONITOR* AND THE *MERRIMACK*

By all rights, the battle between the USS *Monitor* and the CSS *Virginia* should never have taken place. Neither ship was ready for battle, and both ships barely made it to Hampton Roads that fateful day.

The CSS *Virginia* was built using the hull of the former USS *Merrimack*, which had been burned at Norfolk when the Union forces evacuated. Although officially named the CSS *Virginia*, the ship is almost always referred to as the *Merrimack*. Confederate Secretary of the Navy Mallory asked for designs for an ironclad ship capable of at least coastal water operation. After some discussion, a design conceived by noted ordnance expert Lieutenant John Mercer Brooke, based on the hull of the *Merrimack*, was selected. The novelty in Brooke's design was

that the armor on the *Merrimack* would extend below the waterline, with the decks awash. One great flaw, however, was that her anchor and screw were exposed and vulnerable to ramming or cannon fire. Naval Constructor John L. Porter and Engineer-in-Chief William P. Williamson were directed to build the ship, while Brooke was made responsible for her armor and weapons.

In spite of delays, changes, material shortages, lost shipments, strikes, and the other problems usually associated with government contracts, the *Merrimack*, using her flawed original steam engines, was finally launched on February 13, 1862. Brooke had altered his designs so that the vessel now had a casemate of twenty-four inches (60.9cm) of pine and oak planking, and four

PAGE 185: A somewhat fanciful depiction of the battle between the USS Monitor and the CSS Virginia. On the left, the USS Cumberland sinks. ABOVE: Tom W. Freeman's painting of the CSS Virginia, the ironclad built on the recovered hulk of the USS Merrimack, in drydock. There are no known photographs of the Virginia, but several contemporary drawings survive.

NAVAL WAR IN THE EAST

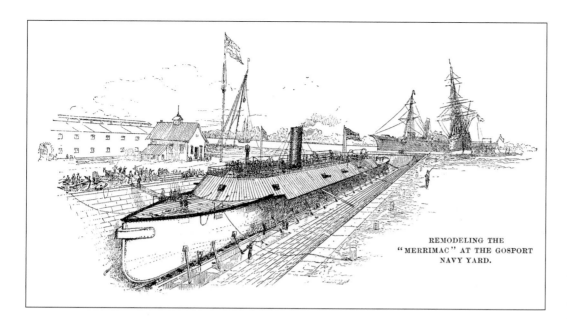

REMODELING THE "MERRIMAC" AT THE GOSPORT NAVY YARD.

TOP: *A contemporary drawing of the CSS* Virginia *in drydock at Gosport Navy Yard, Norfolk, Virginia.* ABOVE: *Two Union naval officers survey the damage to the* Monitor's *turret caused by gunfire from the* Virginia. *Note the two large dents in the turret to the left of the left-hand gunport.*

inches (10.1cm) of iron plate. The casemate was open to the sky and covered with a grating of two-inch (5cm) iron bars, leaving it highly vulnerable to plunging fire.

Brooke armed the *Merrimack* with two 7-inch (17.7cm) rifles fore and aft, 6.4-inch (16.2) rifles at the forward corner ports, and six 9-inch (22.8cm) Dahlgren smoothbores, three on each side. To complete her armament, a two-foot-long (0.6m), fifteen-hundred-pound (681kg) iron ram was affixed to her bow. She was now the most dangerous warship afloat. One major disadvantage, however, was that she had a twenty-three-foot (7m) draft, very deep for inland waters. Her draft was made deeper by the fact that two hundred tons (181.6t) of pig iron had to be put in the bilges to keep the boat upright in the water. By the time a full complement of ammunition and one hundred fifty tons (136.2t) of coal were on board, she wallowed, and was barely steerable at her top speed of nine knots (4.6 m/sec).

To crew the *Merrimack*, a call was sent out for volunteers, and a few trained seamen were found. The rest of the crew, some two hundred men, were taken from a nearby infantry unit. Mallory personally selected Captain Franklin "Old Buck" Buchanan to command the ship, with Lieutenant Catesby Ap. R. Jones as his executive officer. Mallory's orders to Buchanan were simple: steam into Hampton Roads, sink the Union vessels there, and break the blockade.

At the same time that the Confederacy was rebuilding the *Merrimack* as an ironclad, the Union navy was seeking its own design for a series of ironclad ships. Secretary of the Navy Gideon Welles asked for plans for an ironclad vessel. Initially, two designs were submitted. The first, by Cornelius Bushnell, was for an armored ship to be called the USS *Galena*, while the second, by Merrick & Sons of Philadelphia, was for a wood-framed steam frigate with an iron casemate, to be

OPPOSITE: *Port side of the experimental ironclad USS* Galena *looking forward. An early experiment in ironclad design, the* Galena's *armor failed when struck at right angles by plunging fire. The armor was removed in 1863, when the* Galena *was converted to a three-masted screw sloop.* ABOVE: *Officers of the USS* Monitor *pose for a group photograph before the famous battle against the CSS* Virginia.

Captain John Worden commanded the USS Monitor. Worden was severely wounded during the battle when a round from the CSS Virginia struck the pilothouse and blinded him.

Captain Franklin "Old Buck" Buchanan, commander of the CSS Virginia, was a longtime U.S. Navy officer who resigned his commission in order to serve his native state of Virginia.

called the USS *New Ironsides*. Welles' board asked Bushnell to submit some guarantees that his design for the *Galena* would actually float and move. Bushnell sought the advice of John Ericsson, an eccentric but distinguished boatbuilder. Ericsson told Bushnell that the *Galena* design would indeed work, and he asked Bushnell to take a look at his own design for an iron ship. Ericsson's design had previously been submitted to Napoleon III of France, but had been dropped when the Crimean War ended. The design was for an armored flat raft with a rotating cupola on top. One large gun mounted in the rotating cupola would be able to fire in any direction.

Impressed by Ericsson's plans, Bushnell took them to Welles, who was also captivated by the novel idea of the turret. The turret

was to become a standard element in the design of naval men-of-war for the next hundred years, but the board was still not convinced. Certain that Ericsson's was the best design, Welles and Bushnell convinced President Lincoln to support the plan. In a final showdown, Ericsson, backed by Welles and Lincoln, appeared before the board. The board finally acted, deciding that all three designs would be built: the *Galena*, the *New Ironsides*, and Ericsson's *Monitor*.

The *Monitor* was 172 feet (52.4m) long and forty feet (12.1m) wide, and had a draft of ten feet (3m). She had a wooden hull below the waterline, and her overhanging deck, five inches (12.7cm) above the waterline, was a twenty-six-inch (66cm) layer of white oak covered with five inches (12.7cm) of laminated iron plate. The turret was a

massive metal can, nine feet high (2.7m) and twenty feet (6m) in diameter, made of eight-inch-thick (20.3cm) laminated iron plate except at the gunports, where the turret was protected with an extra inch (2.5cm) of iron plate. The structure was open at the top, with an iron grate across the opening. It sat on the raft, held down by its own weight, and it was arranged so that it could be lifted from the deck slightly and rotated with the use of gears driven by a separate engine. In trial runs, it was found that the small steam engine could turn the turret two and a half revolutions per minute. Ericsson asked for two guns to be mounted in the turret side by side, and was given two 11-inch (27.9cm) Dahlgren smoothbores capable of firing 166-pound (75.3kg) shot.

Ericsson's design incorporated several novel features besides the turret. The anchor was enclosed in a recess in the bow of the ship, allowing it to be raised or lowered under fire without exposing the crew. There were two steam engines running a single drive shaft that turned a four-bladed screw nine feet (2.7m) in diameter. The screw was protected underwater by the boat's armored stern. The engines' boilers drew air through two shafts which terminated flush with the deck. These shafts were connected to two giant belt-driven blowers which, at least in theory, would move fresh air into the engine and living compartments while exhausting toxic, stale air from the ship. The pilothouse was on the front of the bow, preventing the *Monitor*'s guns from firing directly forward.

On January 30, 1862, the *Monitor* slid down the ways at the Continental Iron Works in New York City and, to the amazement of some, she floated. Several more weeks of finishing work were required, and her newly named commander, Lieutenant John L. Worden, went about gathering a crew. By February 19, the *Monitor* was ready to be turned over to Worden. He fired up her boil-

the threat to the fleet in Hampton Roads was real, and the Union needed the *Monitor* there as soon as possible to deal with the threat from the *Merrimack*.

On March 6, the *Monitor*, pulled by a tug, the *Seth Low*, and accompanied by two gunboats, the *Currituck* and the *Sachem*, steamed down the East River and into the Atlantic Ocean. For some unknown reason, Welles cabled the naval commander and ordered the *Monitor* to come directly to Washington instead of Hampton Roads. Fortunately, the *Monitor* had already sailed.

On March 7, on the open ocean, the *Monitor* was hit by a major storm. Seawater came over her two-foot (0.6m) freeboard and cascaded down the air ventilator shafts, fouling the blowers and killing the boiler. Without the blowers, the crew spaces filled with noxious fumes, and crew members dropped unconscious. Topside, Worden attempted to signal the tug, but no signal flares were available and the tug paid no attention. Several efforts were made to get the pumps started and the blowers working, but to no avail. Luckily, the wind and waves died before the situation could become truly disastrous. The crew of the *Monitor* was able to repair the damage, and she was once again under way.

At Norfolk on March 6, Buchanan had planned to make his way out of the yard and into Hampton Roads during the night hours, arriving on station at daybreak. The pilot, however, would not run the river without channel lights, all of which had been removed by the Confederates as a precaution against invasion. On March 7, the pilot refused again to sail, as Norfolk was being buffeted the same storm that was battering the *Monitor* farther out to sea. Buchanan could only fume and wait.

March 8 dawned bright and clear. Buchanan ordered the *Merrimack* to head for Hampton Roads. As a final preparation for

Abraham Lincoln meeting with civilian and military leaders aboard the U.S. revenue steamer **Miami**.

ers and set out on the East River. Within a short time, however, one of her engines failed, and it took several hours to return the vessel to the docks for a week's repairs. Following the repairs, the *Monitor* was ordered out again, but this time it was found that she would not respond to the wheel. After careening rather comically around the river and running into the banks, she was returned once again to the docks. Finally, in testing the boat's two 11-inch (27.9cm) guns,

Worden discovered that they could only be fired one at a time because of the manner in which the gunport shutters were rigged.

In Washington, meanwhile, rumors were rampant concerning an imminent attack by the *Merrimack*. At one point, members of the White House staff panicked and ran to the windows to see if the *Merrimack* was coming up the Potomac River, only to be reminded that her draft was too deep to cross the bar several miles downriver. Still,

NAVAL WAR IN THE EAST

192

battle, her sides were covered with fat and tallow in the belief that it would make the cannon balls slide off more easily. The engineering officer confidently assured Buchanan that although the *Merrimack* had not had a shakedown cruise, the ten-hour trip down the river would serve the purpose well, providing the opportunity to identify problems and make any necessary repairs. The iron-clad boat steamed into the bay accompanied by two smaller boats, the *Raleigh* and the *Beaufort*. The Union fleet lay at anchor, stretched from Newport News around the end of the peninsula to Fortress Monroe. The U.S. Navy's largest men-of-war—the *Congress, Cumberland, Minnesota, St. Lawrence,* and *Roanoke*—watched in silence as the *Merrimack* lumbered slowly toward them. It was unthinkable that any ship could withstand the thirty-five-gun broadside from one of these huge ships. Yet the *Merrimack* came on, headed toward the *Congress*.

Aboard the *Congress*, the crew waited silently over their guns until the *Merrimack* was a mere one hundred yards (91.4m) away, point-blank range. Finally the *Congress* delivered a full broadside into the

OPPOSITE: On March 8, 1862, the Confederate ironclad CSS Virginia, *seemingly impervious to cannonfire, swept past the USS* Congress, *a frigate commissioned in 1842, and set her on fire. The* Congress *burned down to the waterline. Painting by Tom W. Freeman. ABOVE: The USS* Monitor *(left) and the CSS* Virginia *(right) move in close to fire at each other in the famous battle at Hampton Roads, Virginia, on March 9, 1862.*

Merrimack. As the smoke cleared, the *Congress*'s crew was amazed to see that the Confederate ship had suffered no damage at all. Lieutenant Jones then ordered the *Merrimack*'s starboard guns to fire, and the *Congress*'s wooden side was instantly blasted into kindling.

The *Merrimack* continued on, moving toward the *Cumberland.* Buchanan steamed in at an angle from which the *Cumberland*

ABOVE: *Lieutenant W. N. Jeffers, the officer who took charge of the USS* Monitor *during its battle with the CSS* Virginia *after Captain Worden was wounded, continued to command the* Monitor *through most of the rest of her short career.* RIGHT: *Another artistic rendition of the battle between the ironclads* Monitor *and* Virginia *at Hampton Roads.*

could not bring any of her twenty-two 9-inch (22.8cm) Dahlgrens or her 10-inch (25.4cm) pivot gun to bear. He fired one round from a forward 7-inch (17.7cm) rifle, which exploded among the *Cumberland*'s contingent of marines, killing and wounding several of them. The *Merrimack* then rammed the *Cumberland* at full speed, striking her just behind the bow and tearing a hole in the hull below the waterline. Instantly, the *Cumberland* fired a point-blank broadside into the *Merrimack*. The *Merrimack*'s ram was caught in the *Cumberland*'s side, giving the *Cumberland* the opportunity to blast the *Merrimack* with three more broadsides. The *Merrimack* at last showed some damage, and some of her crew were killed, but more importantly, the sinking *Cumberland* was threatening to pull the *Merrimack* down with her. Finally, however, the fifteen-hundred-pound (681kg) ram ripped itself from the bow of the *Cumberland,* and the *Merrimack* was able to back off.

While the *Merrimack* was engaged with the *Cumberland,* tugs began moving the remaining Union men-of-war into the fight. The *Minnesota,* the *St. Lawrence,* and the *Roanoke* were all run aground on the sandbars in the bay. Another tug came to the assistance of the *Congress,* now heavily damaged, and ran her aground as well. All of the Union ships were now helplessly stuck and could only await the fatal attack of the massive ironclad.

The *Merrimack* turned back to the *Congress* and began raking her with cannon fire. For two hours the *Congress* accepted the punishment, while making feeble attempts to return fire. With his crew nearly all wounded or killed, the acting captain of the *Congress,* Lieutenant Austin Pendergast, ordered the colors struck and white flags raised. The Confederate *Beaufort* was ordered to come alongside, remove the wounded, and burn the *Congress.* While she lay alongside, Union

NAVAL WAR IN THE EAST

infantry and artillery, perhaps not understanding or seeing the surrender, opened up on the *Beaufort*, wounding many of her crew. This apparent violation of the law of naval warfare enraged many of the Confederate officers. The *Beaufort* pulled away out of range of the shore-based guns. Buchanan, standing on the deck of the *Merrimack* and firing a rifle at the *Congress*, was himself wounded by a rifle shot, and he had to turn command of the *Merrimack* over to Jones. Jones then fired repeated rounds of hot shot into the *Congress,* setting her ablaze.

It was about 5:00 P.M. now. Jones wanted to finish off the *Minnesota* before steaming to rest under the protection of Confederate guns at Sewell's Point for the night. But it was getting late, and he did not want to risk running aground in the dark. The *Merrimack* had taken a few good hits from the *Cumberland*. She was leaking a little water, a couple of her guns had been disabled, and some of her crew, including Old Buck, had been wounded. Jones reasoned that the ships would all be there tomorrow, so he turned the *Merrimack* and headed for Sewell's Point.

During the night, the burning *Congress* served as a beacon and a notice of what the next day might hold for the U.S. fleet. Around midnight, the watching Confederates saw the chugging form of a boat, but it was a boat unlike any they had seen before. It looked like a water tank on a raft.

The *Monitor* had arrived at Hampton Roads too late to save the *Congress* or the *Cumberland*. Worden anchored the *Monitor*

and reported to the senior commander, Captain John Marston on the *Roanoke*. Marston's only order to Worden was to protect the *Minnesota* when the *Merrimack* came down, as she surely would the next morning. Worden steamed the *Monitor* to the wounded *Minnesota* and anchored next to her. Aboard the *Monitor*, the crew, without sleep or food, kept busy all night helping the *Minnesota*. The *Congress* finally exploded. Meanwhile, at Sewell's Point, after the wounded had been tended to and repairs to the *Merrimack* made, her crew slept and, on the following morning, ate a hearty breakfast.

At 6:00 A.M. the following day, March 9, 1862, the *Merrimack* fired a shell from one of her forward batteries into the battered *Minnesota*. Worden ordered the *Monitor*'s crew to battle stations and began an indecisive engagement that would forever change naval warfare.

Worden decided to engage the *Merrimack* as far from the *Minnesota* as possible, hoping to keep her occupied and prevent an attack on the stranded, vulnerable wooden man-of-war. As the two iron ships closed in on each other, they began to steam in an ever-decreasing circle, until they were firing into each other at point-blank range. Suddenly, the *Merrimack,* whose draft was thirteen feet (3.9m) deeper than the *Monitor*'s, ran hard aground on a sandbar. Jones ordered the engineer to lash down the engine's safety valves and get her off the sandbar or blow her up in the attempt. Everything that could burn was thrown into the furnace, increasing the boiler's pressure to dangerous levels, and the churning screw finally backed the boat off of the bar. Jones then ordered his crew to prepare to ram the *Monitor*.

Aboard the *Monitor*, Worden saw the boarding party forming on the *Merrimack*'s hurricane deck. He ordered his men to prepare to repel boarders and to load the 11-

inch (27.9cm) Dahlgrens with canister shot. Worden's gunner reported that both guns were already charged with solid shot, and Worden ordered them fired. The first round struck the *Merrimack* hard and tore away some of her armor, but the second gun would not fire, having been improperly loaded. Worden ordered the *Monitor* into shallow water where the *Merrimack* could not follow, giving his gunners the fifteen minutes they needed to repair the gun. But the *Merrimack* gave chase and struck a glancing blow against the *Monitor*, doing more harm to herself than to the other ship. Nonetheless, the *Monitor* was able to get into the shallows and repair her gun, returning thereafter to continue to battle.

The two ironclads continued to rake each other. Aboard the *Monitor*, the gunnery officer could not see the *Merrimack* because of his enclosed position inside the turret, and he could not tell what direction he was pointed in. Moreover, the machinery used to rotate the turret had been damaged by seawater, so that the turret could not be stopped with any precision. The turret's guns had to be fired on the fly each time the turret rotated past the *Merrimack*.

Worden once again ran the *Monitor* into shallow water to replenish ammunition in the turret and conduct a damage check. He found the boat to be in good shape despite the intense fire from the *Merrimack*, so he ordered her off the shoal and back into the action. Within minutes, the two ships were hammering each other again. A shell from the *Merrimack* struck the pilothouse on the *Monitor*, blinding Worden and knocking down the others with him. Worden, not knowing the damage to his ship, ordered the helmsman to sheer off. As soon as the executive officer came on the scene, Worden put him in command and ordered him to save the *Minnesota*. In the confusion, however, the helmsman received no further orders and

This contemporary engraving shows the crew of the Monitor *abandoning ship as she founders in a gale off the coast of North Carolina on December 31, 1862. Her tug, the USS* Rhode Island, *is shown in the background.*

After the battle at Hampton Roads, Confederate fortunes in the Norfolk area took a turn for the worse. In order to prevent her capture by Union forces, the crew of the CSS Virginia *blew her up and burned her on May 11, 1862.*

NAVAL WAR IN THE EAST

continued to widen the gap between the two warships. Finally, the executive officer ordered the *Monitor* around and in pursuit of the *Merrimack.*

Jones saw the *Monitor* break off the engagement and head for the shallow waters. His men were tired and his ship had been battered heavily by the *Monitor*'s 11-inch (27.9cm) guns. Also, the tide was running out, and if he did not get to safer waters he would have to spend the night in the sound with the Union ships. He finally ordered the pilot to head for the Elizabeth River and Norfolk. The *Monitor* briefly gave chase, but declined to run up under the Confederate land-based guns. The first battle between ironclad ships was over.

During the next month the *Merrimack* came down three times to battle again with the *Monitor.* However, William Jeffers, now commanding the *Monitor,* was under orders not to engage the *Merrimack,* and he refused to bring her out from under the protection of the Union's land-based guns. The blockade was preserved, and the South's one chance to break it was now lost.

Union victories in the Peninsular Campaign made Norfolk untenable. With Norfolk lost, the *Merrimack* had no place to go. Finally, in May, she was intentionally run aground and burned.

After the success of the *Monitor,* the United States Navy ordered new monitors of the Passaic class. The Passaic-class monitors were larger and heavier than Ericsson's original *Monitor.* In addition, certain innovations had been made based on the *Monitor*'s experiences. The pilothouse was now atop the turret rather than sitting in front of it. Also, inside the turret there was now one 11-inch (27.9cm) and one 15-inch (38.1cm) gun, instead of the *Monitor* 's two 11-inch (27.9cm) guns. The first of the class, the USS *Passaic,* was launched in November 1862. Others would follow in short order.

The *Monitor,* meanwhile, saw her last action in May 1862. Accompanied by the USS *Galena,* she steamed up the James River to Drewry's Bluff. There a hot battle ensued. The fort blasted the two ships and the *Galena* was severely damaged. The *Monitor* could not sufficiently elevate her 11-inch (27.9cm) guns to fire into the fort and was worthless in the fray. The ships broke off the battle and retired downriver. The *Monitor* would not see action again.

In late December, she was ordered to Charleston, South Carolina, for bombardment and blockade duties. While she was under tow on the Atlantic Ocean, a storm came up and she sank along with sixteen of her crew.

The Union blockade was successful. The *Merrimack*'s failure to break it only heightened expectations that the South would soon be sealed off from the outside. Charleston was one of the few ports that posed any threat to the blockade. Blockade-runners came and went from Charleston. With iron-clad monitors, the U.S. Navy thought, Charleston could be brought to her knees.

Admiral Samuel DuPont was pushed by Welles to take a fleet of ironclads, steam into Charleston Harbor past the forts, and demand

The crew of this Passaic-class monitor poses on deck after a battle. Before them is the ship's retreat gun, a small cannon used for ceremonial purposes. Note the pilothouse mounted on top of the turret, an innovation based on the **Monitor's** *experiences in its fight with the* **Virginia***.*

The double-turret monitor USS Onandaga. *The crew in the foreground are shown rowing one of the ship's cutters. The enlisted men wear infantry-style kepis, while the officers wear the popular straw boaters.*

the surrender of the city under threat of naval bombardment. By early 1863, the U.S. Navy had a number of ironclads. The first post-*Monitor* ironclad, the USS *Passaic,* had finished her trials and was ready for action. She was followed in short order by the USS *Weehawken,* the USS *Nantucket,* the USS *Montauk,* and the USS *Patapsco.* These vessels, along with the oddly built USS *Keokuk,* the USS *New Ironsides,* the USS *Nahant,* and the USS *Catskill* steamed into Charleston Harbor on April 7, 1863.

Immediately, things began to go wrong for the Federal fleet. The lumbering ships milled around, uncertain about mines and shallows. Finally, they fell into a position and began firing on Fort Sumter. Over the next few hours, the Confederates would pour more than two thousand rounds of every kind imaginable into the grouped ironclads. For their part, the ironclads would manage to fire a total of about one hundred fifty rounds from their 11-inch (27.9cm) and 15-inch (38.1cm) guns. Without doing any damage to Fort Sumter, the monitors were collectively shot up so badly that several were forced to withdraw from the fray. The *Keokuk* was hit more than ninety times and ultimately sank.

As evening arrived DuPont withdrew his ships with the thought that he would try again the next day. That night, at a meeting of his captains, he found that they unanimously felt that to go against Charleston the next day would be disastrous and lead to the loss of the fleet. The test of *Monitor*-type ironclad against fort had finally taken place and had found the ironclads no match for carefully emplaced and protected fortress artillery.

TOP: This contemporary drawing shows the use of the monitor fleet against Confederate shore defenses at Charleston, South Carolina, late in the war. ABOVE: The single-turret monitor USS Canonicus *receiving coal from a supply ship on the James River before the battle for Richmond, Virginia. The large ironclads required constant refueling with coal to ensure full power from the boilers.*

1863–1864
The Confederacy Divided in the West

VICKSBURG, PORT HUDSON, AND ARKANSAS POST

By early 1863 only two Confederate strongholds, Vicksburg and Port Hudson, stood in the way of the Union's drive to cut the Confederacy in half and deprive it of the supplies, food, and men it got from the states west of the Mississippi River. Lincoln demanded that Vicksburg be taken at all costs. If Vicksburg fell, the reasoning went, Port Hudson would be easily invested and taken as well. The Union would then have complete control of the Mississippi River plus the Atlantic and Gulf coasts, and would quickly starve the Confederacy into submission.

But taking Vicksburg was not to be that easy. Farragut, following his victory at New Orleans in April 1862, was under strict orders from Welles to proceed to Vicksburg and take the city. In early May, Farragut ordered his ships upriver to Vicksburg, though he was not keen on taking deep-draft ocean vessels so far up a river. He was further dismayed that the army had given him only twelve hundred infantrymen with which to assault and occupy Vicksburg.

With Captain Samuel P. Lee in charge of the expedition, Farragut's ships sailed with army transports in tow to Vicksburg. On May 18, 1862, Lee, under a flag of truce, demanded the surrender of the city. He was firmly rebuffed by the Confederate commander, Martin L. Smith. Lee was stymied. The Union troops, commanded by Brigadier Thomas Williams, were sick with malaria, dysentery, and scurvy. The army had not supplied rations for the infantrymen, so the army troops were fed from navy rations, putting

PAGE 205: When Union ships ventured up the southern rivers, they found it tough going. Trees, vermin, snakes, Confederate snipers, fires, and insect-borne diseases made the effort hazardous and miserable for the crews of the boats. Here, sailors from Admiral David Porter's flotilla on the Red River use a makeshift log raft to clear the channel. ABOVE: This is the earliest known photograph of ironclads in action. Taken by Confederate photographer George S. Cook from the parapet of Fort Sumter, it shows the monitors Weehawken, Montauk, and Passaic as they fire on the Confederate batteries at Fort Moultrie.

In this contemporary drawing, Porter's fleet is shown running downriver past the Vicksburg batteries on April 16, 1863. Note that coal barges and other unarmored vessels are lashed for protection to the city-class ironclads on the side opposite the bluffs. The burning stacks of logs at left were ignited by Confederate soldiers on the opposite shore to backlight the ships for the gunners on the bluffs.

everyone on half rations. There was no hope that they could storm up the cliffs at Vicksburg, which measured two hundred to three hundred feet (60.9m–91.4m) high, and take the Confederate positions. In addition, some of the ships' guns could not elevate high enough to fire at the uppermost land batteries. Finally, on May 25, Farragut, sick with dysentery, arrived at Vicksburg. All of his commanders counseled against trying to take the city with so few boats and troops. Farragut agreed and, leaving a token force to blockade the river at that point, fell back to New Orleans. The first attempt to take Vicksburg had failed.

Lincoln and Welles were outraged. Lincoln sent new orders to Farragut demanding that he assault Vicksburg. Farragut

regrouped his ships and, with his infantry reinforced to a total strength of thirty-two hundred men, returned upriver to Vicksburg. Farragut also recalled Admiral David Porter and his fleet of mortar schooners, which had been blasting away at Mobile and Pensacola since the taking of New Orleans. With the mortar schooners present and his fleet at anchor below Vicksburg, Farragut began his bombardment of the town in late June.

Using a courier, Farragut notified Flag Officer Charles Davis, whose Mississippi River Fleet was now at Memphis, that Farragut would run the batteries at Vicksburg and join with Davis above the city. Davis replied that he would leave Memphis immediately with his fleet.

On June 28, 1862, Farragut's fleet began the run upriver past the Vicksburg batteries. Porter's mortar schooners opened fire from below the city, and the army artillery units,

now stationed across the river, added supporting fire. Farragut's plan was similar to his New Orleans one: he would run upriver in double columns with the men-of-war spaced so that the gunboats could fire between them. By midday, the fleet, less one or two ships that failed to make the run, was above Vicksburg. Yet Farragut knew that the exercise was futile. Without sufficient supporting infantry, the flotilla could do nothing to reduce Vicksburg. The Confederates had an estimated three thousand troops in heavily fortified positions atop the bluffs, and twelve thousand additional troops within a day's march of the city. To send Williams's thirty-two hundred men against them would just result in pointless slaughter.

On July 1, Davis and the Western Gunboat Flotilla arrived at Farragut's position north of Vicksburg. The whole western navy was now assembled there: Davis' gunboats,

Commander Isaac N. Brown, C.S.N., a former U.S. Navy officer, joined the Confederate Navy at the war's beginning. In one of the most daring episodes of the war, he steamed the ironclad ram CSS Arkansas *through the entire Union fleet at Vicksburg.*

was completing the construction of the iron-clad ram CSS *Arkansas*, after she had been saved from destruction upriver after the fall of Memphis. Brown, an able commander formerly of the U.S. Navy, was one of the Confederacy's senior officers. Brown scavenged iron and timber from every source imaginable to make the *Arkansas* impregnable against the Union ironclads. He gathered a crew from Confederate ships that had been destroyed. He assembled a motley group of cannon and built carriages for them. There was not enough armor to cover the whole boat, so portions of the ship, such as the pilothouse and stern, were left unarmored. Finally, in mid-July, Brown, eager for combat, started the incomplete *Arkansas* down the Yazoo River toward the Mississippi.

During the trip down, the steam boxes leaked steam into the magazine and got the gunpowder wet. Brown stopped the boat

and had the crew take all the wet gunpowder onto the river bank and dry it in the hot summer sun. By evening, the powder was dry and back aboard the boat. From time to time during the trip, Brown stopped along the riverbank to gather intelligence about possible Union naval activity. He was told that the Union fleet was still in the Mississippi above Vicksburg. What Brown did not know was that Farragut had ordered three Union boats—the ironclad *Carondelet* and the tinclads *Queen of the West* and *Tyler*—on a reconnaissance mission up the Yazoo that very day. Farragut knew that the *Arkansas* existed, but he believed that she would never appear, and that she did not pose a threat.

In the early morning hours of July 15, 1862, the *Arkansas* ran into the three Union ships. Immediately, the *Arkansas* opened fire on the ironclad and the two tinclads with her

Ellet's rams, and Farragut's fleet. But with insufficient infantry support, the massed fleet could still do nothing. What was more, the river was falling, and Farragut knew that he had to get below Vicksburg before the water became too shallow for his men-of-war. Staying where he was ordered, he cabled Washington for instructions, noting the fact that if he did not move soon his blue-water fleet would be stuck in the Mississippi River until next year. Finally, Welles relented. He ordered Farragut and his fleet to the Gulf of Mexico, and ordered Davis and the gunboat flotilla to remain at Vicksburg and continue the assault.

Unbeknownst to the Union, the Confederate Navy was preparing a problem for the Union fleet. At Yazoo City, Mississippi, Commander Isaac Newton Brown, C.S.N.,

The CSS Arkansas *under construction at Yazoo City, Mississippi.*

This painting by Tom W. Freeman depicts the CSS Arkansas *running among the Union fleet lying at anchor in the Mississippi River above Vicksburg on July 15, 1862. She deliberately came in very close to the Union men-of-war so as to prevent them from getting up to ramming speed.*

THE CONFEDERACY DIVIDED IN THE WEST

A contemporary photograph of the timberclad USS Tyler *lying at anchor. The timberclads were converted sidewheel towboats with a very light armoring of wood. Timberclads had a very shallow draft and made good reconnaissance vessels in the shallow waters of the western rivers.*

forward rifles. Initially, the Union ships tried to fight bow-on against the oncoming ram, but the commanders soon realized that they were no match for the Confederate ironclad. Captain Walke, aboard the *Carondelet,* ordered the ships turned back toward the Mississippi. But fire from the *Arkansas* cut into the ironclad, severing her steering gear. The *Carondelet* drifted into shallow water and received another broadside from the *Arkansas.* Seeing the ironclad disabled, Brown turned the *Arkansas* toward the two tinclads, which were waiting in the river to see the outcome of the ironclad battle.

The *Tyler* and the *Queen of the West* turned and fled toward the Mississippi and the security of the Union fleet. Brown had been wounded and his pilot killed by a shot

from the *Carondelet,* but he remained at his post. Fire from the *Tyler's* stern guns had no effect on the *Arkansas's* armor, but did damage the smokestack to the point where the boiler fires would barely draw. This served to cut the *Arkansas's* speed to almost nothing and nullify her ramming ability.

In the Mississippi, the Union sailors heard the firing and thought the three-ship force was firing on Confederate guerrillas along the bank. Within minutes, however, they observed the *Queen of the West* and the *Tyler* steaming toward them at full speed. Behind them, the *Arkansas* limped along slowly, belching cannon fire. The fleet was caught completely unprepared, its crews asleep and its boilers cold. Watch officers beat to quarters and, though immobile, the

fleet opened fire on the *Arkansas* with every gun available.

For half an hour, the *Arkansas,* with almost no motive power besides the river current, drifted among the Union ships, trading shots with the most powerful fleet on earth. Round after round cut into the *Arkansas,* peeling off the armor plate and riddling her with holes. Floating among the unmoving Union fleet, the *Arkansas* could fire all her guns as rapidly as possible. Finally, she cleared the fleet and drifted under the guns on Vicksburg's bluffs. Brown was given a hero's welcome.

Farragut was beside himself with anger. His repeated insistence that the *Arkansas* would never appear was recalled silently, if not out loud, by everyone in his command.

Ironclad ships were not invincible. In this depiction of action in February 1863 on the Mississippi River, the CSS Queen of the West, *a former Union ram captured and used by the Confederates, attacks the city-class ironclad USS* Indianola. *With the help of two other vessels, the ram CSS* William H. Webb *and the cottonclad CSS* Beatty, *the* Queen of the West *forced the ironclad to run aground. Her crew abandoned her, and she was burned by the Confederates the following day to prevent her recapture. Painting by Tom W. Freeman.*

He became a man possessed, and ordered an attack on the *Arkansas* that afternoon. But by the time he got the *Hartford, Sciota, Sumter* (salvaged by the Union Navy), and *Winona* under way it was dark, and the ships passed Vicksburg without sighting the *Arkansas* laid up at the wharf. The following day, Farragut conferred with Davis. Farragut wanted a combined daylight assault on the *Arkansas* using both fleets. Davis declined, fearing that

he might be caught below Vicksburg, cut off from his base at Memphis. An alternate plan was agreed upon.

Davis moved three of his gunboats to the bend in the river and began to fire upon the Vicksburg batteries with those boats and with his mortar scows anchored to their rear. Davis then sent the *Essex* and the *Queen of the West* toward the *Arkansas*, while Farragut sent the former Confederate ram *Sumter* up

to her. As the *Essex* closed in, the fire from her 10-inch (25.4cm) forward cannon tore into the *Arkansas*. With Brown unavailable for duty and only forty-one men capable of manning battle stations, the *Arkansas* continued to fight. One lucky 10-inch (25.4cm) shell from the *Essex* killed or wounded half the crew when it entered a gunport.

The *Essex* attempted to ram the *Arkansas*, but struck only a glancing blow and ran into the bank. The *Sumter* then ran in and struck the *Arkansas* broadside, but did little damage. The *Queen of the West* made the final ramming attack, but lost speed in maneuvering and also did little damage. All three ships were riddled by cannon fire from the bank and drifted away from the *Arkansas*, which remained defiantly afloat.

On July 24, Farragut finally turned south with his fleet and headed for the Gulf of Mexico and New Orleans. Davis took his gunboat flotilla and fell back all the way to Memphis. Vicksburg had once again proved to be too much for the Union Navy to take.

After a long, hot, and very difficult summer, Lincoln was perplexed by the fact that Vicksburg still stood. He ordered a political appointee, General John McClernand, to raise a force of men and take Vicksburg by land. Generals Grant and Sherman feared the intervention of the inexperienced McClernand, who was senior to Sherman. They conspired with Admiral David Porter, who had replaced Davis and was now commanding the western gunboat fleet, to beat McClernand to the punch. Their plan was simple: Grant would move down the Mississippi and engage Lieutenant General Pemberton's troops north of Vicksburg. At the same time, the gunboat fleet and Sherman, with thirty thousand men, would take Vicksburg by storm. It was December 1862 before the force was fully assembled and ready to make the assault.

Before Grant could get very far, Confederate cavalry destroyed his lines of supply, and he was forced to fall back to protect them. Sherman and Porter, however, did not know this. They plowed down the Mississippi with the gunboat fleet and eighty-five troop transports. Part of the fleet had been stationed at the mouth of the Yazoo River in early December. These boats were under orders to conduct reconnaissance up the Yazoo to determine the location of Confederate forces and artillery. On December

12, a task force of five boats was moving in the vicinity of Haines' Bluff when one of them, the USS *Cairo*, ran over a mine and became the first warship ever to be sunk in combat by a submerged mine.

On December 27, 1862, Sherman ordered the transports on the Yazoo River to a point about eighteen miles (28.8km) upriver from Vicksburg. From there, his troops disembarked from the transports into a swamp. Four infantry divisions slogged through the swamp, dogged by Confederate snipers, for a day and a half. Finally, they arrived at the base of a two-hundred-foot (60.9m) bluff, now manned by close to twenty thousand Confederate troops. Valor alone was not enough to carry

*TOP: A contemporary photograph of the giant ironclad USS **Choctaw**. She weighed 1,004 tons (910.8t) and was 260 feet (79.2m) long. She was converted from a steamer according to plans by William D. Porter. Her armor and armament were too heavy for her hull, making her slow and difficult to maneuver. An experimental two-inch-thick (5.1cm) rubber armor was constructed on her forward casemate but proved to be useless. ABOVE: The city-class ironclad USS **Essex** was captained by William D. Porter, elder brother of Admiral David Porter. The structures on the bow are privies for the crew to use while the ship is docked. The **Essex** was the vessel that finally finished off the CSS **Arkansas**.*

THE CONFEDERACY DIVIDED IN THE WEST
212

LEFT: On December 12, 1862, the USS Cairo, a city-class ironclad on a reconnaissance mission up the Yazoo River with four other boats, hit a Confederate naval mine and sank to the bottom in twelve minutes, becoming the first man-of-war ever sunk by a mine in combat. Painting by William R. McGrath. ABOVE: In 1964, the USS Cairo was raised from the bottom of the Yazoo River by the National Park Service and placed, with its contents, on display at the Vicksburg National Military Park. Here the pilothouse of the Cairo sees the light of day for the first time in 102 years.

the day, and on December 30, Sherman, having suffered 1,776 casualties, ordered his men back to the transports. Sherman and Porter planned to move farther upriver to Haines' Bluff and make another assault there, but bad weather prevented their attack. In abject defeat, Sherman fell back down the Yazoo River and turned his command over to McClernand, who had arrived during the battle. The third attempt to take Vicksburg had failed.

McClernand and Sherman decided to make a quick effort to take another Confederate position, known as Fort Hindman or Arkansas Post, which sat on the Arkansas side of the river just above Vicksburg. Regrouping the gunboats and the infantry, they stormed the small fort and occupied it within a couple of hours.

By this time, Vicksburg had become a truly irritating thorn in the side of the Union.

Tom W. Freeman's painting of the USS Choctaw. *Note the narrow bow and wide stern, designed to help stabilize the unwieldy boat. Her 11-foot (3.4m) draft was unsuitable for very shallow waters.*

It symbolized the Confederacy's stubborn resistance to the Union's best military efforts. Beginning on May 18, 1863, Grant, determined not to fail again, invested Vicksburg from the south and east, laying a protracted siege to the garrison. On July 4, after enduring incredible hardships, the Confederate forces at Vicksburg finally surrendered the city. On that same day, at Gettysburg, Pennsylvania, General Robert E. Lee was withdrawing to the South after an epic, three-day battle that would later be considered the turning point of the war, the "high-water mark of the Confederacy." And on July 9, Port Hudson, completely surrounded after the fall of Vicksburg, surrendered. The Confederacy was now cut in half, denied the support of its western states.

THE RED RIVER CAMPAIGN: COMBINED OPERATIONS GO SOUR

The Red River winds slowly and tortuously from Shreveport, Louisiana, southeast across the state until it enters the Mississippi above Port Hudson. After the collapse of Vicksburg and Port Hudson, there was little of military value in Louisiana, and few military men thought it worth any effort. However, the conduct of any war is guided by politics, and this one was no exception. Two important political matters concerned the administration in Washington. First was the fact that Napoleon III had established a government in Mexico under Maximillian of Hapsburg. The Confederacy had lines of communication open to the French through Mexico, and there was some concern that a French incursion into Texas, with Confederate complicity, might create a problem requiring a significant diversion of resources. Perhaps more importantly, the blockade of the South had created

A great danger to deep-draft sailing vessels was becoming grounded in a river under the enemy's guns. On Friday, May 13, 1863, the USS Mississippi, *an old side-wheel frigate that had served as Commodore Matthew Perry's flagship during the Mexican War, ran aground directly under the guns of Port Hudson, Louisiana. Her crew set her on fire and abandoned her. Her magazines later blew up, finishing her completely. Painting by Tom W. Freeman.*

a shortage of cotton, causing prices to soar to about $400 a bale. The Red River ran directly through Louisiana's cotton country. A valuable crop of Confederate cotton lay on the ground ready to be harvested by anyone who could get to it. The twin aims of the

Red River Campaign were to establish a Union military presence in western Louisiana that could deter a French incursion, and to sieze the valuable cotton crop.

In February 1864, President Lincoln ordered General Nathaniel Banks to depart

New Orleans, with naval support from Admiral David Porter and his gunboats, ascend the Red River, and seize the western Confederate capitol at Shreveport. General Banks's plan was to move his infantry along the river roads and have the Union Navy,

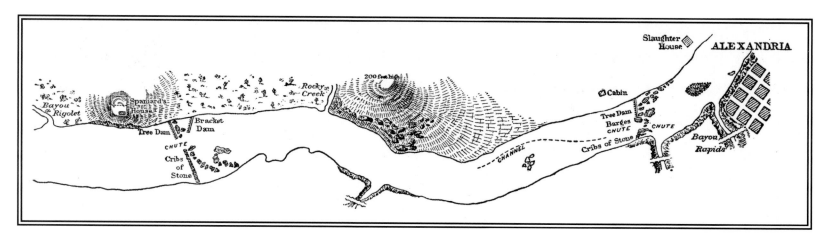

TOP: *In one of the most amazing engineering feats of the war, Union troops from Wisconsin constructed a dam to raise the Red River sufficiently so that the Union flotilla would not be trapped above the falls. This contemporary map shows the location of the dams above Alexandria, Louisiana. ABOVE: Once the dam was built and the water was high enough, each Union warship ran the chute over the falls to safety below. No ship was lost in the action.*

with troop transports in tow, ascend the river. That way they would be able to trap any Confederate force they encountered in a pincer, crushed between Banks' infantry and Porter's gunboats.

The plan worked well on March 14, when the Union forces met their first resistance at Fort DeRussy. The gunboats fired into the fort, while the infantry attacked its weaker land side. The Confederate forces immediately withdrew northward, abandoning large quantities of weapons and stores. By March 16, Union troops occupied Alexandria, Louisiana. It was here that the seeds of disaster were sown.

Porter released several vessels and their crews to scour the Louisiana countryside for cotton. They were accompanied by numerous speculators who had been given passes by President Lincoln, creating a climate of corruption and profiteering. More than two thousand bales of cotton were gathered and shipped to the military garrison at Cairo for auction. Meanwhile, however, Banks and his infantry continued to slog their way up the single roadway that paralleled the river, pulling ahead of Porter's fleet.

Porter could not get all of his boats past the falls north of Alexandria. He decided to establish a support base at Alexandria, and the *Eastport*, four ironclad gunboats, and a couple of tinclads were left to protect the site. By April 3, the task force had reached Grand Ecore. Here again certain vessels could not make the move upriver and were left behind to protect the lines of communication. Porter surged ahead with two monitors, the *Osage* and the *Neosho*, the tinclads *Cricket* and *Fort Hindman*, the timberclads *Lexington* and *Chillicothe*, and a string of transports carrying an infantry regiment from Sherman's army. The plan was to meet with Banks' force at a small landing located below Shreveport and coordinate their attack. But when Porter arrived at the designated meeting point, Banks' infantry was nowhere to be found.

General Nathaniel Banks, commander of Union forces during the Red River campaign to seize Shreveport, Louisiana, nearly brought on a disaster when he allowed his infantry to become separated from their supporting naval craft. The infantry became engaged with Confederate forces and the naval craft were left too far up the river. Only determination and luck prevented the entire task force from falling victim to the Confederates.

Late that afternoon, a runner advised Porter that Banks' force had been set upon and routed by Confederate forces at Sabine Crossroads, sixty miles (96km) to Porter's rear. Banks was in full retreat. Porter realized that he was now in a desperate position, where his flotilla could easily be cut off and destroyed piecemeal by Confederate land forces. He had to get out of the Red River as quickly as possible.

Porter turned around and made a dash for the south. All along the way, the fleet was under attack by Confederate forces. Several ships were damaged, abandoned, and blown up; others, including the *Osage*, ran aground but were saved. Finally, after eight days of flight, Porter reached Grand Ecore. Gathering up the boats stationed at Grand Ecore, he then made a run for Alexandria.

In the ten days that it took to get from Grand Ecore to Alexandria, Porter's boats were constantly harassed by Confederate forces along the shore. Banks' retreat had left the Confederates unhampered in their efforts to slow and destroy Porter's fleet. The *Eastport* headed upriver to support the main fleet, but was lost when she ran aground and had to be blown up. The crews of several ships were killed by intense Confederate artillery fire. On April 28, Porter dragged into Alexandria to find his entire gunboat flotilla above the falls. The river was dropping rapidly, and as a result the falls had risen to four feet (1.2m), too high for many of the boats to go over safely. The Eads city-class ironclads *Carondelet, Mound City, Baron de Kalb,* and *Pittsburg*, the monitors *Osage* and *Neosho,* the *Chillicothe, Lexington, Ozark,* and assorted transports were all stranded.

With Confederate forces converging on him, Porter was in big trouble. As he contemplated the choice between surrender and a hopeless fight, an infantry officer, an engineer in civilian life, proposed creating a dam to raise the water and allow the boats to float over the falls. Despite the fact that the river was more than seven hundred feet (213.3m) wide, the dam, begun on May 2, was finished on May 8. By May 12, after many a heart-stopping moment, the entire fleet was over the falls and headed for safe waters.

The Red River expedition, an audacious plan driven more by economic and political concerns than by strategic considerations, was over. Despite the successful seizure of much valuable cotton, the mission was a dismal failure, and only ingenuity and a great deal of luck had kept it from becoming a total disaster.

A contemporary photograph of the Red River dam constructed above Alexandria, Louisiana, by Wisconsin troops.

chapter 13

1863–1864
Confederate Raiders on the Open Seas and the Final Forts

"To act as a private armed vessel in the service of the Confederate States, on the high seas against the United States of America, their ships, vessels, goods and effects, and those of her citizens during the pendency of the war now existing."

—From the Letter of Marque authorizing the privateer Savannah, the first to be commissioned by the Confederate government

CONFEDERATE COMMERCE RAIDERS

Early in the war, Confederate Secretary of the Navy Mallory knew that his navy was at a serious disadvantage against the Union's naval forces. He had no ships of the line able to go toe to toe with the Union Navy. Instead, he decided to strike at the North's vulnerable mercantile fleet. It was a plan with several advantages: it would harm the North's economy by hampering trade with Europe; the Union would have to send men-of-war in pursuit of the Confederate commerce raiders, drawing resources away from the main fighting; the conflict would become more clearly international, and neutral European nations such as England and France would see that the Confederate States of America was more than a local insurrection; and, perhaps most importantly, the

raiders could seize needed supplies and redirect them to the South.

Between June 1861, when the CSS *Sumter* steamed out of the Mississippi River, and November 1865, when the CSS *Shenandoah* surrendered in Liverpool, England, a series of Confederate commerce raiders brought U.S. oceangoing commerce to a virtual standstill. During that period, the major raiders, including the *Sumter, Florida, Alabama, Nashville, Shenandoah, Georgia, Tallahassee*, and *Chickamauga*, captured 211 commercial ships as prizes. Most prizes were emptied and burned. Several were paroled to return prisoners from captured ships. A few were recommissioned as Confederate raiders.

The first raider, the CSS *Sumter*, operated in the Caribbean Sea and in the Atlantic. Captained by Raphael Semmes, former U.S. Navy officer and lawyer, she took eighteen prizes in her relatively short career (June 1861 to January 1862). In truth, at 437 tons (396.8t), and with her small coal bunkers, the *Sumter* was too small and lacked the range to be truly effective as a raider. But by being the first raider on the high seas, she became a symbol of the threat posed by such raiders. As soon as she began taking prizes, foreign shippers stopped using U.S. carriers for their cargoes, and representatives of the merchant shipping industry besieged Washington with complaints. Some merchant ships sailed under foreign flags to reduce the danger of capture. Crews for the *Sumter* and other raiders were composed of foreign seamen, crews from prizes who enlisted after capture, and a few Confederate naval personnel.

As soon as Semmes reached Europe, he discovered the tangled labyrinth of diplomatic intrigue instigated by U.S. government representatives to the European nations. Depending on the political climate, Britain, France, and Spain supported or failed to support Confederate ships seeking refuge and repair in their harbors. Sometimes the law of

PAGE 219: *Illustrating one of the great dangers of naval combat, this contemporary engraving shows a cannon exploding aboard the USS J.P. Jackson in Mobile Bay, Alabama. Explosions were caused by overloading, metal fatigue, and poor construction. RIGHT: The CSS Florida approaches a United States merchant ship to seize it as a prize. The general signal to heave to and surrender was a shot across the bow of the merchant ship. Painting by William R. McGrath.*

neutrality was strictly adhered to, while at other times it was ignored. Sometimes provisions and coal could be obtained, other times not. When Semmes sailed into Gibraltar, a diplomatic storm ensued. Semmes knew that the *Sumter* was rotting and half her crew had deserted. So he sold the ship, paid off the remaining crew, and sailed to London, where he eventually took command of the CSS *Alabama*.

Of all the raiders, the *Alabama* was by far the most successful, bringing down sixty-nine prizes between August 1862 and her battle with the USS *Kearsage* in June 1864. The *Alabama* was one of several ships that the Confederate government obtained through their secret agent in England, Commander James Bulloch, C.S.N. Bulloch's mission was to obtain commerce raiders, built in England, for the Confederate Navy. However, Bulloch had to navigate around England's official neutrality and internal laws prohibiting such ventures. So, a diplomatic ruse was developed. The ship would ostensibly be built as a commercial vessel under British registration. Her armament would be purchased from other quarters and sent as freight aboard a second ship. When the ship was ready for sea, the two vessels would meet outside the territorial waters of any nation and the ship would be turned over to Confederate officers, commissioned in the Confederate Navy, and armed with the guns from the second ship. In this way Semmes obtained his second command. He enlisted

The USS **Brooklyn** *after the Civil War. Her funnel can be seen lowered just forward of the mainmast. She served the U.S. Navy until 1889.*

eighty-three foreign volunteers to serve as crew aboard the *Alabama*.

The *Alabama* operated throughout the sea lanes of the world, seizing and destroying U.S. merchantmen. In January 1863, Semmes sailed the *Alabama* to Galveston, Texas, only to find the city under fire from several Union warships. Semmes, flying the British ensign, lured one of the ships, the gunboat USS *Hatteras*, away from the protection of the other ships. When challenged,

Semmes ran down the British ensign and ran up the Confederate naval ensign. He fired a broadside into the *Hatteras* and got her to surrender before he burned her. Her crew was taken prisoner and transported to the island of Jamaica, where they were paroled.

The *Alabama* sailed the Caribbean, the Atlantic, the Cape of Good Hope, the Indian Ocean, and the Dutch East Indies taking prizes wherever she went. After two years afloat, she was in serious need of repair and

maintenance. Also, the crew was becoming dissatisfied with the long periods at sea and the declining numbers of prizes. In June 1864, Semmes steamed to the coast of France and docked at Cherbourg. Within a short period, the U.S. ambassador had cabled every U.S. station in Europe, notifying them that the *Alabama* was in Cherbourg. Off the coast of England, the USS *Kearsage*, under the command of Captain John Winslow (formerly a naval officer in the Mississippi

A clipper ship (foreground) lays on the sails to escape the CSS Alabama (background) in hot pursuit.

Kearsage, the crew was at Sunday services. They had watched the port for seven days without any activity, and were not expecting the *Alabama*. She was soon sighted, and the crew beat to quarters. Winslow decided that he would run the smaller, lighter *Alabama* down and ram her, but before he could do so, the *Alabama* opened fire. Soon the range was only five hundred yards (457.2m). Each ship held her rudder hard to starboard to prevent the other from having an opportunity for raking fire. This forced the two ships into a series of concentric circles, twisting around each other. The *Alabama's* largest gun was a 7-inch (17.7cm) Blakeley rifle, while the *Kearsage* had two 11-inch (27.9cm) Dahlgrens and four 9-inch (22.8cm) Dahlgrens. As the range closed, the larger guns began to tell. Their massive charges ripped into the *Alabama*, killing several of her crew and disabling her engines. Finally, Semmes was forced to strike his colors. The surviving crew abandoned the sinking *Alabama*, and about half of them were picked up by several British and French pleasure craft that had observed the fight. These sailors, including Captain Semmes, were safely released in England, while the remainder were captured by the *Kearsage*.

Another of the British-built raiders, the CSS *Florida*, was commissioned in August 1862. She was placed under the command of Lieutenant John Maffit, C.S.N., who was only able to get about twenty men to enlist out of the one hundred twenty he needed to run the ship. Worse followed, however; as soon as Maffit took command, the ship's company was swept with yellow fever. Maffit had no surgeon and no medical supplies aboard. He realized that if he waited, he might lose the whole crew, including himself, to the disease. Maffit made directly for Mobile Bay, then under blockade by two Union ships. With only four hands well enough to man the ship, he ran the colors of the British Navy

Gunboat Flotilla), received the word and steamed for Cherbourg, where he anchored outside the harbor to await the *Alabama*.

Semmes was urged to avoid a fight with the Union man-of-war if possible. However, he determined to fight the *Kearsage*, and

announced his intention by issuing a challenge to the U.S. Consul in Le Havre through a Confederate agent there.

At midmorning on Sunday, June 19, 1864, Semmes steamed out of Cherbourg and straight for the *Kearsage*. Aboard the

LEFT: Tom W. Freeman's painting of the action between the CSS Alabama (foreground) and the USS Kearsage off the coast of Cherbourg, France. ABOVE: This contemporary engraving depicts the gun-crew of the 11-inch (27.9cm) forward pivot gun of the Kearsage preparing to fire at the Alabama.

until challenged, and then struck the British colors and made for the Mobile harbor. He easily outran the blockade ship and suffered only minor damage from gunfire. Once in Mobile, he recruited a crew sufficient to man the *Florida* properly.

Four months later, five days after the *Alabama* took the USS *Hatteras* off Galveston, Maffit and a fully crewed *Florida* shot out of Mobile Bay in the dark of the night and sped past the blockaders. The fact that the two most famous Confederate raiders were both roaming the high seas reflected badly on Secretary Welles, and in Washington there were calls for his resignation. Maffit roamed the Caribbean and the Atlantic at will, seizing prizes. But after five continuous months at sea, the *Florida* was in dire need of overhaul. Maffit headed for the port of Brest, France.

In France, most of the enlisted crew deserted, and Maffit, weakened by his bout with yellow fever, was replaced by Lieutenant Charles Manigault Morris. In England, the Confederate agent Bulloch managed to enlist sixty men for her crew. By February 1864, she was ready to sail again and slipped into the Atlantic Ocean.

Morris ran up and down the Atlantic coast wreaking havoc among U.S. commercial vessels. Late in the year, he decided to head for the Pacific and attack the whaling

CONFEDERATE RAIDERS ON THE OPEN SEAS AND THE FINAL FORTS

Commander Raphael Semmes, captain of the Alabama, *addresses his crew just prior to their engagement with the* Kearsage.

trade there. But on October 4 he first stopped in Bahia, Brazil, for overhaul and shore leave for the crew. The day following her entry into port, the USS *Wachusett*, a wooden screw sloop of ten guns, eased into port behind her. Two belligerents were now together in a neutral port. International law prescribed that only one vessel could leave within a twenty-four hour period. Thus, if the *Florida* left, the *Wachusett* would have to wait a day before pursuing her.

Commander Napoleon Collins of the *Wachusett* decided that the raider would never leave port. In a blatant violation of international law, Collins, in the dark morning hours of October 7, got a full head of steam and rammed directly into the starboard side of the *Florida*. Immediately, a boarding party from the *Wachusett* swarmed over the lightly manned *Florida* and took control. By that morning, the *Wachusett,* with the *Florida* in tow and under sail, left Bahia for the United States. Brazil was suitably outraged and demanded the return of the *Florida*, but the boat was improvidently sunk in an accident with an army transport ship a short time later. Collins was court-martialed

*The surrender team from the **Alabama** rows up to the **Kearsage** to announce the surrender and to request assistance for the Confederate crew of the sinking vessel.*

of the *Alabama*, lost in June, the *Florida*, lost that same month, and the *Tallahassee*, decommissioned after her spectacular cruise along the northeastern coast of the United States. Her captain, James Waddell, took her on a cruise along the South Atlantic to Cape Horn and into the Indian Ocean. In January 1865 he stopped in Melbourne, Australia, to rest and refit. After several weeks, he continued to hunt for U.S. flag vessels in the north Atlantic, at one point coming within miles of the Arctic Circle. Waddell pillaged the Pacific whaling trade. On June 28, 1865, more than two months after Lee's surrender at Appomattox, Waddell took eleven vessels, sinking them all. Waddell seized a steamer

with newspapers on board, somewhat out of date, which told of the fall of Richmond and Jefferson Davis' vow to fight on. Within a month, however, he hailed a British merchant-man and was told the truth of the collapse of the Confederacy. Waddell dismounted his guns and sailed around the Cape of Good Hope to Liverpool, England, where he surrendered the *Shenandoah* to the Royal Navy on November 5, 1865. The last Confederate had surrendered.

One unique vessel should be noted. A Danish vessel, the *Staerkodder*, was an iron-clad ram sloop of fourteen hundred tons (1271t) with a 300-pounder (136kg) rifle at her bow and two 5-inch (12.7cm) rifles. The

for the incident, but Welles declined to accept the verdict and sentence of the board, and Collins was allowed to retire some years later as an admiral.

The CSS *Tallahassee*'s career lasted a little over a month. Yet during that time she took thirty-eight prizes and successfully out-ran Union blockaders. After outfitting, this English-built ship ran from Wilmington, North Carolina, up the northeast coast. In August 1864, she put in at Halifax, Nova Scotia, for repair. The U.S. fleet attempted to bottle her up, but with the help of friendly Canadian pilots she slipped into the Atlantic from a little-used tributary. After more pillaging, she reentered Wilmington harbor and was decommissioned. She was recommissioned the CSS *Olustee*, made a brief foray into the Atlantic, and was then made into a blockade-runner.

The cruise of the CSS *Shenandoah* was the final chapter in the story of the Confederate commerce raiders. Commissioned in October 1864, she followed in the footsteps

*The CSS **Stonewall**, one of the ironclads built secretly in France and then embargoed by the French government. After the war, she was turned over to the U.S. government, which sold her to Japan.*

Danes, recent losers in the Schleswig-Holstein War against Prussia, needed to sell the ship, and found a willing buyer in Confederate agent Bulloch. In January 1865, she left port with a Danish crew and was transferred to the Confederate navy on the high seas. Her captain was Thomas Jefferson Page, and she was commissioned the CSS *Stonewall*. But the new, unwieldy ship needed repairs, so Page put in at the Spanish port of La Coruna. Within days, word got out and two U.S. warships, the USS *Niagara* and the USS *Sacramento*, appeared in the bay.

Page was not concerned. The *Stonewall* was an ironclad ram and the *Niagara* and the *Sacramento* were both wooden. When he was ready to go out, he would be glad to take both ships on. In March, the *Stonewall* made several forays toward the two wooden ships, but they declined to stand and fight. In late March, Page, now ordered by the Spanish government to leave the port, fired up the *Stonewall*'s boilers and went to do battle. All day, Page steamed back and forth waiting for the two warships to attack, but neither did. The commander of the *Niagara*, Thomas Craven, feared the loss of both ships if he attacked the ironclad ram. Finally, at nightfall, Page steamed off for the South Atlantic and Nassau. Arriving at Nassau on May 6, Page discovered the surrender of the Confederate government. He sailed the *Stonewall* into Havana and sold her to the Governor-General of Cuba for $16,000, without once having tested her in battle.

BATTLE OF MOBILE BAY

By the late summer of 1864, only three Confederate ports remained unconquered: Mobile Bay, Charleston, and Wilmington. Grant, now commander of all Union ground forces, was of the opinion that a victory at Mobile Bay would allow the Northern forces to slice off several more states from the Confederacy and join with Sherman's campaign in Georgia. Farragut was ordered from New York to make the attack.

A complicating factor was the presence of the ironclad ram CSS *Tennessee* being built in Mobile. Welles feared that the *Tennessee*, commanded by Buchanan, recovered after his wounds aboard the *Merrimack*, would leave the bay and strike at the wooden fleet in blockade. But that was not Buchanan's plan. He knew, as did everyone, that an attack on Mobile Bay was imminent, and his job was to defeat the Union Navy when it came. Buchanan had help in the form of submerged mines, multiple piling lines, a narrow channel, and sunken hulks.

Farragut ordered four of the latest Monitor-class ships sent to him. By July, the USS *Tecumseh*, the USS *Manhattan*, the USS *Chickasaw*, and the USS *Winnebago* were on their way to Farragut. The *Tecumseh* and the *Manhattan* were improved Canonicus-class monitors, each carrying two 15-inch (38.1cm) guns and eleven inches (27.9cm) of armor.

I am going into Mobile Bay in the morning if "God is my leader" as I hope he is;

D. G. Farragut

ABOVE: Admiral Farragut's letter home just before the Battle of Mobile Bay. "I am going into Mobile Bay in the morning if 'God is my leader,' as I hope he is." RIGHT: The Confederate ram CSS Tennessee and Farragut's flagship, the USS Hartford, engage at close quarters in Mobile Bay, Alabama. Painting by Tom W. Freeman.

A contemporary engraving of the action in Mobile Bay.

The *Chickasaw* and the *Winnebago* were new four-screw, twin-turret Milwaukee-class monitors, each carrying four 11-inch (27.9cm) guns, two in each turret, and eight inches (20.3cm) of armor. In addition, Farragut had fourteen more men-of-war, including side-wheel gunboats and rigged ships.

At the crack of dawn on April 5, 1864, the Union fleet started into Mobile Bay. The four monitors, led by the *Tecumseh*, were in the starboard column. The remaining fourteen wooden ships, lashed together in pairs, made up the port column. Almost as soon as they entered the bay, the *Tecumseh* veered to port, struck a mine, and went down immediately, with the loss of all but eight hands. Terror

struck, and the captain of the *Brooklyn,* fearing she was among the mines, began backing to avoid them. Farragut, lashed to the rigging of the *Hartford*, his flagship, saw the *Brooklyn's* movement and knew that unless something was done, his whole fleet would come to a halt directly under the Confederate guns. Farragut uttered the now-famous command, "Damn the torpedoes! Full speed ahead!" The Union fleet steamed forward. Several officers aboard other ships reported hearing their vessels pass over the mines and hearing the firing mechanisms snap shut; but the mines failed to detonate.

As the fleet passed Fort Morgan, the fort's batteries cut into the wooden ships.

Raking fire from the Confederate naval vessels, including the *Tennessee* and the *Selma*, could not be answered because of the angle. As the column passed the forts, the weakest vessels in the rear were cut to pieces by the fort's guns. The *Hartford* cut out across the mined area and was followed by the others in column.

The monitors steered immediately toward the *Tennessee*. The Confederate gunboats accompanying the ram pulled away and headed for the shallows, knowing they were no match for the monitors or the heavy gunboats. There then occurred a lull in the battle as each side took stock of its position and regrouped. Aboard the *Tennessee*, Buchanan ordered the crew to breakfast, but continued a two-knot (1.3m/sec) crawl toward the Union fleet.

When lookouts saw the oncoming *Tennessee*, the fleet went to her. Farragut ordered all ships to attempt to ram the Confederate ironclad. The big wooden frigates began firing on the ironclad, but caused no damage at all. The *Brooklyn* missed in her ramming attempt and was shot up by the *Tennessee*. Next, the *Monongahela* with the *Kennebec* lashed to her side rammed into the ironclad. Other than spinning the *Tennessee* around, the blow did nothing. Once again the *Tennessee's* gunners blew holes through the wooden ships. Suddenly, the monitor *Manhattan* appeared and fired a 15-inch (38.1cm) solid shot weighing 350 pounds (158.9kg) that completely pierced the *Tennessee's* iron siding. Immediately, the *Lackawanna* steamed in to ram the ironclad, but missed. Following shots from the *Lackawanna* severed the *Tennessee's* steering chains on the quarterdeck, and she lost steerage. The *Hartford* then made a run at her, but also missed and was gored by the *Lackawanna* after passing the Hartford. The monitor *Chickasaw*, meanwhile, fired rounds into her continuously.

Finally, Commander James Johnston, the *Tennessee's* captain, conferred with Buchanan, whose leg was broken. Buchanan ordered Johnston to haul down the colors in order to prevent further bloodshed.

By late morning, the Battle of Mobile Bay was over. Farragut's armada had suffered over 325 casualties against the Confederates' thirty-two. Within days, the forts capitulated to the combined power of the gunboats and Union infantry. The Gulf of Mexico was now completely in Union hands.

WILMINGTON, NORTH CAROLINA: THE FINAL FORT

Only one location kept supplies open to the Confederacy. After the fall of Mobile, Fort Fisher, at Wilmington, remained alone in defiance of the Union blockade. As long as she stood, blockade-runners had a safe haven to enter and deposit their goods. By late 1864, Welles had decided to reduce Fort Fisher, and had appointed David Porter to command the expedition. But Porter knew that Fort Fisher could not be taken by naval action alone, and he implored Grant to provide infantry to make the final combined assault. Grant finally sent Major General Ben Butler with sixty-five hundred men under Godfrey Weitzel.

Butler had a plan that involved the detonation of a large explosive to shock the fort's inhabitants, followed by a land assault by infantry. Porter, always willing to try something new, agreed and provided an old ship, the *Louisiana*, filled with more than two hundred tons (181.6t) of powder. On Christmas Day, 1864, the *Louisiana* was pushed to within a half mile (0.8km) of the fort and, in the dark hours of the morning, exploded. The effect was less than spectacular. Undisturbed inside Fort Fisher, the Confederates thought that a Union gunboat

TOP: The battered CSS **Tennessee**, *her smokestack gone, surrenders to Farragut's naval forces in Mobile Bay. ABOVE: The* **Tennessee**, *shown here after her capture in Mobile Bay and her recommissioning as a Union ship.*

The Federal fleet bombarding Fort Fisher, south of Wilmington, North Carolina. After a later assault, it was discovered that the bombardment had had little effect.

had hit a mine and blown up. The plan called for the infantry to be landed on the beach and immediately assault the fort while the navy provided gunfire support. But by noon, no troops had landed on the beach. Porter had his ships open fire.

Within several hours, Weitzel, with the navy's assistance, had twenty-five hundred men, about one-third of his force, on the beach five miles (8km) from the fort. After a reconnaissance, Weitzel knew that his small

force could not possibly take the fort, which, for all the bombardment, was relatively undamaged. Butler had queried Porter on the possibility of the navy steaming into the Cape Fear River and taking the fort from the rear. A reconnaissance showed that this was not possible either. Butler ordered the troops back aboard the transports and headed back to Hampton Roads. Amazingly, he left six hundred infantrymen behind, stranded on the beach in enemy territory. It took two

days, but Porter eventually managed to remove the men safely.

Butler was sacked for the fiasco, and Grant reassured Porter that Fort Fisher would be a primary target. Within two weeks, Grant sent eight thousand troops under General Alfred Terry, with "do or die" orders, to Porter. On January 13, the bombardment opened and, presaging the combined operations of World War II to come eighty years later, more than two hundred boats filled with infantry headed for the shore. Within four hours, all eight thousand troops were ashore and entrenched. The naval bombardment continued for another two days.

Porter, anxious to be involved in every single fray, formed a naval landing party made up of two thousand sailors and marines. This naval landing party would assault the fort from the opposite side at 3:00 P.M. on January 15, when the official assault was to begin. With the signal, the men of the naval landing party began their assault. They were closer than the infantrymen, and the fort's defenders thought they were the main attack. In the open, running down a beach with no fire support and only small arms, the naval party was cut to pieces, with more than three hundred men killed.

The naval assault may have helped. Within minutes, the infantry dashed against the fort from the opposite side. Too close for naval gunfire support or the use of cannons inside the fort, the battle was waged hand-to-hand. Finally, at 9:00 P.M., Terry sent a signal rocket up from the fort announcing the fort's surrender and its occupation. The Union blockade of the South was now complete. From this time on, nothing would come into or out of the South by water.

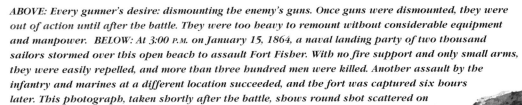

ABOVE: Every gunner's desire: dismounting the enemy's guns. Once guns were dismounted, they were out of action until after the battle. They were too heavy to remount without considerable equipment and manpower. BELOW: At 3:00 P.M. on January 15, 1864, a naval landing party of two thousand sailors stormed over this open beach to assault Fort Fisher. With no fire support and only small arms, they were easily repelled, and more than three hundred men were killed. Another assault by the infantry and marines at a different location succeeded, and the fort was captured six hours later. This photograph, taken shortly after the battle, shows round shot scattered on the beach.

chapter 14

THE NAVIES AT WAR'S END

UNION NAVAL SUCCESSES

With all her ports blockaded and her navy in ruins except for the odd raider at sea, the Confederacy lost the ability to supply, and thus defend, herself. During the four years between 1861 and 1865, the Union Navy's might expanded tremendously. Swifter ships with more powerful guns were being produced. In 1861 the United States was at best a second-rate force on the high seas; by the war's end, it had become the world's foremost naval power. At Mobile Bay in 1864, Farragut had at his command the most powerful naval battery on earth. But, as has usually happened in peacetime, the U.S. Navy was allowed to decline in power during the years between the Civil War and the turn of the century. However, the Spanish-American War and for- eign expansion once again spurred growth.

The Union's most remarkable feat during the war was the building of the largest navy in the world from scratch. This buildup was not a slow, methodical pursuit of more modern naval craft, but a sudden, rapid technological expansion involving the construction of mod- ern, multipurpose naval craft suitable for the wide variety of missions that were thrown on the navy by the war government. This modern fleet successfully blockaded more than three thousand miles (4,800km) of coastline, includ- ing large ports; defeated every Southern war- ship; attacked and destroyed Southern coastal forts; gained control of all major rivers and trib- utaries; and supported the land operations of the Union army.

This success was due in large part to an unusual willingness to experiment with new naval technology. From a wood and steam

navy in 1861, the Union, within four years, effectively produced modern steel warships carrying the largest naval ordnance produced and capable of going head to head with any known warship on earth.

Welles showed remarkable insight in his use of naval officers and their promotion. The old navy was steeped in tradition, particularly where the promotion of officers was concerned. Welles, knowing that his war situation did not allow for the niceties of the old navy's promotion system, promoted and used commanders he knew could get the job done. Admiral David Porter, a loudmouthed firebrand who should have been court-martialed and drummed from the service under the naval etiquette of the times, was instead promoted and used extensively by Welles, who knew he was a very able commander and got results regardless of his personality. Welles also used a junior flag officer, David Farragut, when other, more senior officers were available. Welles knew that Farragut would complete his missions.

UNION NAVAL FAILURES

Despite its tremendous successes, the Union Navy also had its share of shortcomings and failures. As the Union Army did on several occasions, the Union Navy failed to adequately follow up on its coastal victories at Hatteras,

A rare photograph of the building of the ironclad USS **Indianola** *She was later captured by Confederate forces, but was of little use to them since they had to destroy her a month later to prevent her recapture.*

Port Royal, Pensacola, and New Orleans by not having a sufficient infantry force available to press the victory inland.

Farragut and the other commanders suffered from a belief that nothing could withstand the powerful guns that a fleet could bring to bear; some called it "bombardment fever." Yet, they ultimately did come to realize that while the navy could perform certain siege and reduction tasks, it could not achieve major military objectives alone.

Welles suffered from his own fever: "iron fever." He initially believed that the ironclad was the answer to all of his naval problems, without giving adequate consideration to additional factors such as naval firepower, adequate support from ground forces, and deepwater operations.

Whether or not the blockade was truly effective is open to question. There is a historical perspective that holds that the

UNION NAVAL OFFICERS.

REAR AD. S.F. DUPONT.

REAR AD. L.M. GOLDSBOROUGH.

COM. DAVID D. PORTER.

REAR AD. A.H. FOOTE.

LIEUT. JOHN L. WORDEN.

COM. CHAS H. DAVIS.

REAR AD. D.G. FARRAGUT.

ABOVE: The Federal blockade fleet off the Confederate coast. Blockade duty was boring, with occasional moments of excitement when chasing a blockade-runner. LEFT: A contemporary engraving of the seven senior officers of the U.S. Navy.

Southern ports should have been bombarded and captured through combined naval and ground operations. The blockade was extremely costly in terms of men and ships. Yet, statistically, the main objective of the blockade, stopping blockade-runners, was not achieved. Until 1864, the chances of a blockade-runner being captured were less than one in four. Until mid-1864 the blockade was only marginally effective in terms of economic impact on the South. And by the time it became truly effective, the land war had progressed to the point that the outcome was no longer in doubt.

In spite of the successes of the combined operations conducted during the war (e.g. Vicksburg, Wilmington), the primary focus of the Union was on land warfare. Halleck, and later Grant, being army men, felt that the true objective of the war was meeting the enemy on the battlefield and defeating his army. This, of course, was at odds with Scott's plan for the economic strangulation of the South. Perhaps some of the blame for this can be laid on President Lincoln, who felt that the early inaction of his land forces was cause for great concern.

William R. McGrath
© 199[?]

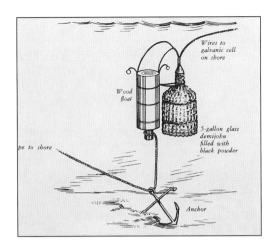

CONFEDERATE NAVAL SUCCESSES

The South was incredibly fortunate to have Stephen Mallory, a true visionary, available to be its Secretary of the Navy. Like the Union command, Mallory was asked to start from scratch and build a formidable fighting force complete with equipment, personnel, lines of supply, lines of communication, arsenals, docks, yards, and ships. The precise extent to which he succeeded is subject to debate, but he was without question far more successful than might reasonably have been expected.

The Confederate Navy employed a half-dozen or so spar torpedo boats, or "Davids," so called for the first one, named CSS **David** *These were semi-submersible boats that sank their targets with a spar torpedo (a long rod with an explosive charge at the end) extending from the bow, then backed off and moved away. They were not very safe, and several of them drowned their crews.*

Prior to the Civil War, the South was a primarily agrarian economy with very little industry. When the war came, the South began a rapid industrialization to the degree allowed by the materials it had available. This industrialization allowed for the construction of an ironclad navy with capable armaments.

The South's lack of an established navy was in some ways a blessing from a technological standpoint. With a severe lack of equipment and technology, individual efforts at technological innovation were encouraged and rewarded. As a result, the Confederacy was the first nation to build and use underwater mines, the first to build an ironclad warship, and the first to build and use a successful submarine.

CONFEDERATE NAVAL FAILURES

Secretary Stephen Mallory's reliance on large, costly ironclad warships for attack and defense purposes was not successful under the circumstances of limited time, money, and materials. Federal ironclad and wooden-hulled ships were equally vulnerable to ramming. In retrospect, it seems clear that a fleet of fast, cheap Ellet-type rams might have been more effective in the long run.

Mallory's reliance on the expensive commerce raider fleet provided a great deal of publicity, but in the end was not very useful to the South, since the raiders could not bring their prizes into southern ports and benefit the South economically. Mallory's hope that the raiders would draw off major portions of the Union fleet was not fulfilled. Welles assigned some ships to chase the raiders, but this effort was designed mostly to quiet the criticism he received from the civilian mercantile class.

The South failed miserably to exploit its technological advantages. It failed to coordinate and devote the resources necessary for an aggressive mine-laying program in southern

ABOVE: Two Confederate ironclads of the James River Flotilla, CSS **Fredericksburg** *and CSS* **Virginia II,** *though built late in the war, saw repeated action in the defense of Richmond, Virginia. Both were blown up to prevent capture after the evacuation of Richmond.* **RIGHT:** *Sailors and marines aboard the USS* **Miami** *open fire on the CSS* **Albemarle** *as she rams and sinks the USS* **Southfield** *at Plymouth, North Carolina, on April 19, 1864. Both paintings by Tom W. Freeman.*

harbors and rivers. Mines were developed, built, and emplaced by engineers like Zere McDaniel, Matthew Fontaine Maury, and others on an *ad hoc* basis. Experiments with small, fast, shallow-draft boats armed with explosive torpedoes on spars proved them very effective. Yet none of this innovation was coordinated at any level; the inventors were simply left to ply their respective efforts wherever they felt they would do the most good.

NAVAL INNOVATION

If anything can be said of the American Civil War, it is that it allowed individual initiative to be brought to the fore. Naval warfare was completely revolutionized. Iron ships replaced wooden ships forever. Muzzle loading, smoothbore cannon disappeared in favor of more powerful and accurate breech-loading rifled cannon. Faster, more powerful steam engines were developed, not to be replaced until gasoline, diesel, and eventually nuclear power replaced coal.

Most importantly, the army and the navy found that, through cooperation, the tactical advantages of each could be combined to make an imposing assault force. With the navy's ability to bring large-caliber weapons to bear and the infantry's ability to maneuver on land, no fort was safe. The lessons learned at Fort Henry, Fort Donelson, Shiloh, Vicksburg, Hatteras, and Fort Fisher would well serve men later landing at Normandy, Iwo Jima, and Inchon.

PART THREE

DARING RAIDERS

Much has been written about the myriad aspects of the Civil War, from the illustrious leaders and little-known players to the remarkable battles and inconsequential events, from the country's economic conditions and the delicate balance of power of the North and South that existed before the war to the bold actions of a few brave and zealous individuals who agitated an entire nation into bloody conflict. However, missing from many of our histories is an examination of a now-familiar tactic that had a profound impact on the war, on military strategy studies, and especially our understanding of violent political force to this day: the raid and reprisal attack. These strategic innovations forever changed the nature of war.

There were many raids and reprisal attacks that were conducted by both sides during the Civil War, and it would be impossible to document all of them in this single volume. This work will focus on representative raids—some entirely unknown to the general historian—that were ordered against specific targets. While army-size raids, such as Sherman's March to the Sea and Grant's earlier operations in the vicinity of Vicksburg, are great raids, these maneuvering armies are beyond the scope of this book.

Daring John Singleton Mosby had a quick temper and a great deal of courage that often got him in trouble before the war, but served him well as a guerrilla commander. He and most of his men lived within the region in which they operated, and so were able to obtain food, shelter, and information from the population, as well as outmaneuver enemy troops operating in unfamiliar territory.

Many of the famous raider attacks carried out in the Missouri region were planned and conducted without traditional military objectives in mind. These raids and reprisal operations, while frequently bloody, did little to attain the military objectives of either side. For this reason, these are also considered to be beyond the scope of this book.

Raids that were conducted with true military goals in the minds of those who planned them—rather than raids executed simply to destroy property—these are the subject of this examination. The raids found here were generally conducted by small groups of patriots who had an impact well beyond their numbers. For example, the raid that resulted in the capture of Harry Gilmor is perhaps as well planned a raid as has ever been attempted and deserves study in the military's war colleges. With this raid and the use of scouts, a new tactic—the utilization of special operations forces—entered American military strategy in an impressive way.

Here also are the raiders themselves—soldiers of fortune, zealots, pirates, murderers—all men of conviction who often used incredible violence to achieve their political goals. One of these raiders, John Brown, would become a nationally recognized personality and as great a hero to much of the population of the North as he was a villain in the South. Other raiders—like John Singleton Mosby—have become legends. Mosby's guerrilla operations enabled him to capture a Federal brigadier general from within his own Union camp, an act so daring that it was reported directly to President Lincoln.

Raids also encompassed the full theater of operations of the war at large. Noteworthy and included here are a few of the raids conducted by rail, some involving great train chases and hijackings of locomotives; maritime raids utilizing battleships at sea; cavalry raids struck with speed and accuracy deep into enemy territory; and land maneuvers accomplished with spies, co-conspirators, and legions of self-serving partisans.

Newspaper accounts of wartime events and the sketches that accompanied them were frequently inaccurate or misleading. In "Recapture of a Train from Mosby's Guerrillas," the Confederates are shown using muskets as they attempt to defend their booty. However, Mosby's men relied primarily on the new revolvers and shotguns, seldom using a saber, much less a long musket with a bayonet attached.

chapter 15

A POLITICAL EXTREMIST RAIDS HARPERS FERRY

Terrorists usually band in small and relatively weak groups that utilize random acts of repeatable violence against helpless (and sometimes only symbolic) targets to accomplish political goals that they have insufficient power to accomplish through traditional political or military means. John Brown and the members of his small group were able to effectively use such an approach in Kansas and later in Virginia to create a political atmosphere that served as a catalyst for the emergence of the American Civil War.

Brown was a singular figure who had been drawn to the cause of the Northern abolitionists who sought to free all of the nation's slaves—a goal he adhered to strictly once he had begun. This violent political extremist was eloquent in speech and tenacious in action once he had selected his course, and he was soon to become a hero. Brown knew that he could not lose as he set out: if he were successful and survived the initial actions, he could gain additional sup-

port for the continuation of his efforts, but if he were to lose he would become a martyr to the cause he had chosen. Curiously, he was to lose his life after a highly publicized state trial as he became a national hero to the Northerners. Equally curious, this political extremist risked and lost the lives of some of his sons for the cause he followed as zealously as any terrorist with conviction.

After developing an intense hatred of slavery and all things associated with it, John Brown embarked on a personal crusade against it. He had failed miserably at several attempted business ventures, but where he had missed the mark in business, he had managed to fulfill his goals within the abolitionist movement. After entering into abolitionist activities as early as 1846, Brown arrived in the territory of Kansas to join five of his sons in 1855.

A crisis was developing in the area—one that had been gathering momentum since the previous year, when the Nebraska Territory

"You had better, all of you people of the South, prepare yourselves for the settlement of this question. It must come up for settlement sooner than you are prepared for it, and the sooner you commence that preparation, the better for you. You may dispose of me very easily; I am nearly disposed of now; but this question is still to be settled—this Negro question, I mean."

—John Brown

Armed men on both sides of the Slavery issue in the new territory began to conduct reprisals, which were followed by counter-reprisals in a spiral of violent acts by extremists who would be labeled terrorists by today's standards. Such extreme bloodshed and violence gave rise to the appellation "Bleeding Kansas"

"Break the jaws of the wicked.... Without the shedding of blood there is no remission of sins...."

—John Brown

was preparing for statehood. The whole region was north of the old Missouri Compromise line, where slavery was automatically excluded by law. The region was expected to become two new states; since both would be in free territory, they would enter the Union as free states, which would upset the precarious balance within Congress. Southerners were also concerned that the entry of Kansas into the Union as a nonslave state would leave Missouri, a slave state, surrounded on three sides by territory into which slaves could easily escape and expect to be assisted by abolitionists. The loss of an expensive slave was a severe financial blow to the slaveowner, and there was a great public outcry in Missouri over the anticipated statehood of Kansas and the threat that it posed.

The Kansas-Nebraska Act of May 1854 was cleared through Congress, and the com-promise over the entry of new states into the Union was eliminated as the radical elements on either side of the slavery issue began to take over the political processes of the nation. The trouble between the two sections that had been feared for so long was about to break into the open.

Congress had left the question of slavery in the new territory to the Kansas territorial legislature. This left the decision to the voters from the side who arrived in Kansas in the greatest numbers before the vote to form the legislature. Both groups began to encourage settlers from their side of the issue to move into Kansas, and as Missouri was immediately adjacent to the new territory, it should be no great surprise to learn that the proslavery forces crossed the border in large numbers from Missouri to vote. They won control of the new territory's legislature and began to lead the political processes as well.

New laws were rapidly enacted to protect the property of slaveowners. It quickly became a hanging offense to hide a fugitive slave. In addition, the victorious proslavery forces managed to expel the few Free State legislators who had managed to get elected. By the end of 1855, one of the antislavery settlers was killed in a dispute with a man who supported slavery. Angry Free State men assembled and soon burned the home of the man responsible for the killing, who had gone unpunished. Once the brutal series of attacks and reprisals was under way, the cycle of violence began in earnest.

Leaders of the Free State movement called for their supporters to assemble in Lawrence, a town controlled by antislavery men, and John Brown arrived as a volunteer to fight the Southerners. Open combat between the two factions was avoided, but by May 1856 "Border Ruffians"—as the proslavery forces were labeled in Northern newspapers—attacked Lawrence and destroyed newspapers, the Free State Hotel, and the home of the governor.

This anarchic attack resulted in angry denunciations by Northern congressmen, and in one speech in particular Senator Charles Sumner of Massachusetts angrily denounced the raid and slavery, and spoke harshly about an absent senator from South Carolina. The following day, Representative Preston Brooks of South Carolina walked up to Sumner and began to beat him with his cane for Sumner's vituperative remarks made the previous day.

It was the devastating attack of the Border Ruffians on Lawrence, combined with the lawless attack on Senator Sumner, that managed to provoke a heated response from John Brown and his closest supporters. Brown decided that a lesson had to be taught to the attackers and their supporters, and he decided to give them a demonstration that would not soon be forgotten.

Brown selected his targets carefully from a list of personal and legal opponents he had developed in the short time he had been residing in Kansas. His supporters began to prepare their weapons for a raid that would be soon glossed over by the Northern press and overshadowed by the larger events that were to come, but that served to foster an atmosphere of suspicion and fear between the two opposing sections for much of the remainder of the nineteenth century.

Within two days of the beating suffered by Sumner, John Brown and a small party of supporters made their way to the nearby home of James Doyle, a man who had expressed proslavery views. After forcing their way into Doyle's cabin, they shoved Doyle and two of his young sons outside. The raiders responded to the begging of Doyle's wife and allowed the youngest son, who was fourteen, to remain inside with her.

After leaving the cabin, Brown and his men hacked their three unarmed victims to death with swords. The skulls of the boys were split, the arms of one body were severed, and the gruesome reminders of the visit of John Brown and his allies were left lying on the lonely prairie. Brown had sent an unmistakable message—and challenge—for the proslavery forces to consider.

The raiders immediately left the Doyle farm to locate another victim. Soon they captured Allen Wilkinson, a member of the proslavery Kansas legislature, and hacked him to death as his wife stood nearby, helplessly pleading for the life of her husband.

Wilkinson's skull was also split open, and a fourth grim reminder of Brown's anger and politics was left dead.

The raiders were to make one more murderous visit, in the early morning darkness of May 25, 1856. Seeking a local proslavery saloonkeeper, they learned that their intended victim was away, but that his brother, Dutch Bill, was staying in the saloonkeeper's house for the night. Dutch Bill's skull was split and he was stabbed. In a final brutal act, one of the attackers severed one of the innocent man's hands.

An unbelievable series of acts along Potawatomi Creek in eastern Kansas had

PAGE 251: John Brown was born in Connecticut in 1800, and was raised in a household of passionate Calvinism, a faith determined to resist all forms of evil and wrongdoing. After failing at several business attempts, he joined his sons in Kansas in 1855. He had been drawn naturally toward abolitionist causes and as early as 1851 his violent tendencies began to express themselves. At one time he told friends that blacks should kill anyone trying to enforce the Fugitive Slave Act. Brown had made a choice that would occupy the remainder of his life—militant opposition to the institution of slavery. ABOVE: Once he became nationally recognized, Brown soon had the financial backing of prominent citizens in the North, his "Secret Six," who provided funds for organization, training, and a large future operation. These wealthy abolitionists paid for both muskets and the thousand pikes soon to be in use at Harpers Ferry.

occurred. Brown had been recognized by several of the survivors of the night of terror, and there was a general outcry in Kansas for his arrest and punishment. Unfortunately for those from both sides of the slavery issue who wanted to see justice served for the

dreadful deeds of Brown and his party, nothing was done to apprehend him.

Equally unfortunate for the nation, the Eastern press chose to ignore the facts of this series of atrocities, and several newspapers began to claim that no murders had occurred

at all. Northern newspapers began to shield Brown and some actually began to defend his actions. In addition to the snow job by the Northern press, a congressional committee investigating the killings managed to ignore the series of brutal murders, as did local legislators, and much of the North. The propaganda war surrounding Brown's actions further divided a strained nation.

Despite its unnecessary brutality, the slaughter of the five proslavery men, the Potawatomi Massacre, came to be viewed by much of the North as a noble act against an oppressive society that held human beings in bondage. One man's terrorist had become another man's hero.

The acts of Brown and his followers, however, were entirely without justification. Unarmed civilians had been gruesomely murdered to achieve political aims. Unfortunately, the Northern press and the antislavery majority in the congressional investigating committee contrived to shield Brown from either punishment or criticism. He succeeded beyond what were probably his own best expectations: John Brown won national attention for his violent crusade against slavery, and with the encouragement he received, Brown began to plan a second, more spectacular raid.

For a while, John Brown remained quiet and conducted no further operations against his hated enemies, the proslavery forces of Kansas, but he had not given up on his overall goal of freeing the slaves of the South. Realizing that he would need arms—and these would cost money—he began a series

OPPOSITE: Brown's ferocious opposition to slavery in Kansas culminated in August 1856, when he and a band of followers hacked several proslavery settlers to death. RIGHT: With the financial support of well-to-do abolitionists, Brown organized a group of twenty-two men— including a few African Americans and several of his own sons—with the intention of capturing Harpers Ferry, the location of one of the only two Federal arsenals in the entire country. His plan involved the capture of the arsenal, confiscation of muskets and ammunition, and escape into the nearby mountainous region, where he expected slaves to rally to him in large numbers to fight for their freedom.

Harpers Ferry, located at the junction of the Shenandoah and the Potomac rivers, lay within one of Virginia's deep valleys where abundant water power and inexpensive river and rail transportation had allowed small industries to develop and thrive. Brown—under the alias of Isaac Smith—relocated to a leased farm in the vicinity of the little town as final plans were developed for the attack.

of ambitious fund-raising trips to the Northeast. Wisely obtaining a letter of recommendation from the leader of the Free State movement in Kansas, Brown began an extended series of trips between the Midwest and the Northeast, primarily Boston, where

he met with most of the more prominent abolitionists of the country. He managed to visit Senator Charles Sumner, still recovering from the attack by South Carolina's Preston Brooks, and soon began to receive small sums of money from his various supporters.

Brown, four of his sons, and about a dozen followers began to prepare for future operations against slaveholders. He was able to use the money collected in the North to purchase arms and supplies for his men, and he obtained the services of Hugh Forbes, an

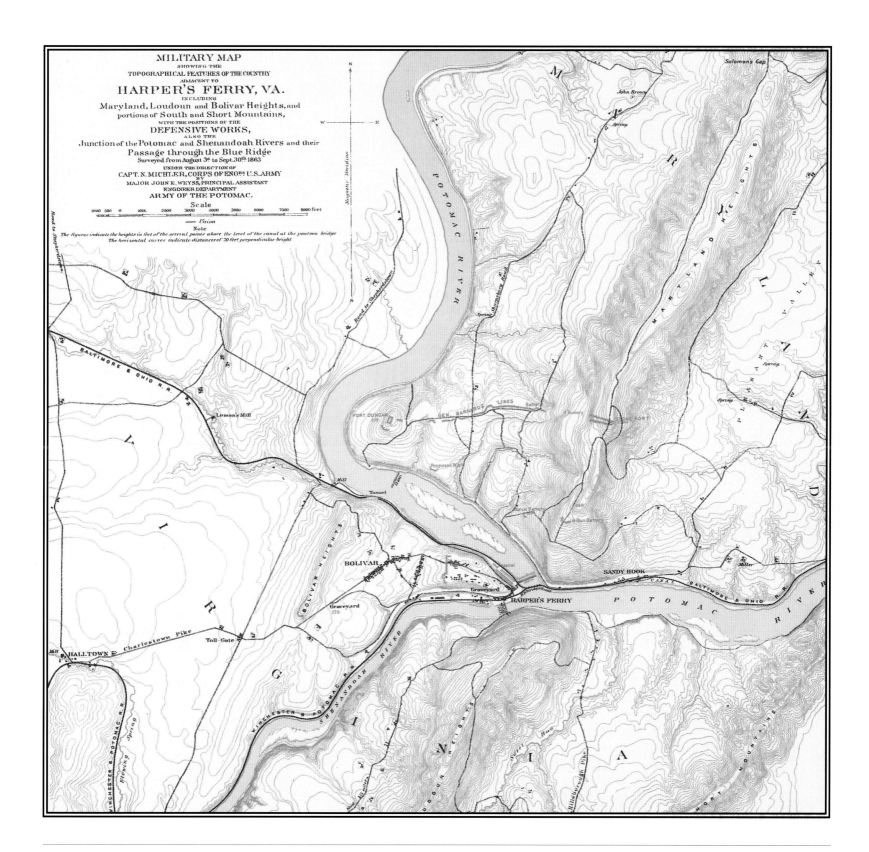

A Political Extremist Raids Harpers Ferry

English mercenary, who was hired to train the small group. In addition to his supplies, Brown ordered one thousand pikes—long, heavy, archaic, spearlike weapons—but he didn't reveal his plans for these primitive weapons to anyone.

By May 1858, Brown was able to assemble a provisional constitutional convention for the United States that clearly stated his faction's intentions in its preamble:

Whereas slavery, throughout its entire existence in the United States, is none other than a most barbarous, unprovoked, and unjustifiable war of one portion of its citizens upon another portion…. Therefore, we, citizens of the United States and the oppressed people who…are declared to have no rights which the white man is bound to respect…ordain and establish for our-

selves the following provisional constitution and ordinances, the better to protect our persons, property, lives and liberties, and govern our actions.

Immediately afterward, Brown disbanded the convention, moved the Kansas men to Ohio, and sent John Cook of Connecticut to Harpers Ferry, Virginia, with orders to collect information on the town, its citizens—especially the slaves—and the layout of the surrounding countryside. The foundation for a major raid was being carefully prepared and Brown's supporters began to follow his instructions faithfully.

He had decided not to tell any of his financial backers of his specific plans, but he did inform Forbes that his initial operation would involve a raid on the U.S. arsenal at Harpers Ferry in an attempt to obtain modern firearms that could be used to arm slaves who would rally to his small insurrection. Forbes, unpaid by Brown, soon informed two abolitionist senators, Massachusetts' Henry Wilson and New York's William H. Seward (soon to be Lincoln's secretary of state), of the planned attack. Both kept the secret, but they were able to convince Brown's abolitionist supporters in the Northeast that they were involved in a scheme that had considerable personal risk for them. The Secret Six soon began to withdraw open support for Brown, but there is little doubt that they still hoped he would be able to strike an effective blow that would lead to freedom for the nation's slaves.

Well known throughout the country, Brown moved into the immediate vicinity of Harpers Ferry under an assumed name, Isaac Smith, and he rented the Kennedy farm in Maryland. Brown had quietly moved his base of operations to within five miles (8km) of the intended target. Some of his men remained in Chambersburg, Pennsylvania, where they received arms and supplies that

John Brown understood the fact that he could lose his life in the Harpers Ferry raid, but he also realized his very public death could serve to galvanize public opinion in the North against slavery as nothing else had done to this point in history.

were sent on to Brown in Maryland in smaller, less noticeable shipments.

On October 10, 1859, John Brown issued his "General Order No. 1," from his "Headquarters War Department, Provisional Army, Harpers Ferry," and, with his raiders, began to transfer the arms to a schoolhouse closer to town. At 11 P.M. on Sunday, October 16, John Brown ordered his small Provisional Army, composed of sixteen white men, four free blacks, and one escaped slave, to collect their arms and begin their long-planned "march to the Ferry."

It began with remarkable ease. Once the party of armed men crossed the covered bridge over the Potomac River, they entered Harpers Ferry, captured the night watchman at the arsenal, occupied Hall's Rifle Works, and abducted some of the more prosperous citizens of the region as hostages.

The forty-odd captives, including Colonel Lewis W. Washington, a relative of the nation's first president, were confined to a single room in the fire engine house at the arsenal where Brown had decided to develop his primary point of defense. His plan from that point depended upon the arrival of thousands of slaves, which he would lead into combat against their oppressors.

It was at this point that Brown's plan began to crumble. The slaves did not come; Brown, having no alternate plan, remained inactive as large forces were arrayed against him as the use of weapons revealed the presence of the Brown party.

An arriving train was halted and one of Brown's men fired at a railroad porter, mortally wounding him. Curiously, and as if a hidden hand were involved in managing this affair, the men who had come to save slaves had just killed a free black man. The townsmen, fully aroused by now, began to assemble with their firearms, and the raiders were forced to retreat into the arsenal buildings to escape the heated volley of bullets.

Once the presence of Brown and his raiding party was discovered by the townspeople, the men of the town and immediate vicinity took up arms to defend themselves. Their firepower forced Brown and his men to withdraw—taking with them several prominent citizens as hostages—into the relative safety of the engine house where they prepared to withstand a siege.

Drinking townsmen continued to fire at the raiders whenever an opportunity presented itself, and after several hours Brown lost his first man, Dangerfield Newby. A black man lost his life in his attempt to free others, but his noble sacrifice was unnoticed by the besieging forces as his body was dragged to a nearby gutter and left for hogs to consume.

Brown realized that he was trapped. He withdrew as many of his men as possible to the engine house, where he barricaded his party with his hostages and sent two men— one his son Watson—under a flag of truce to negotiate. Both were rapidly shot down, but the injured Watson was able to return to the relative safety of the improvised fort before dying. Soon another raider was killed as he attempted to flee, and three others were forced from Hall's. Two were killed; the third was captured and nearly lynched before he

was saved by a local doctor. The mayor of Harpers Ferry, Mr. F. Beckman, was killed in the free-for-all and the captive raider was murdered, his body used for target practice.

Local militia companies arrived and established a cordon around Brown's position from which there could be no escape. By sunset on the first day, a company from Winchester, Virginia, arrived, along with three additional companies of soldiers from Frederick, Maryland. Later in the evening, more companies arrived, this time from Baltimore, along with a small detachment of U.S. Marines. Two regular officers who were on leave from their regiments were ordered to take charge of the operation to subdue John Brown and his Provisional Army. Colonel Robert E. Lee, of the Second United States Cavalry, and Lieutenant J.E.B. Stuart, of the First United States Cavalry, had been sent to restore order and recapture the national armory.

Lee rapidly established order within the ranks of the volunteers and militia, even halting the Baltimore troops at a point nearby once the true numbers and condition of the raiders were known. Lee positioned the volunteers in a way that made any escape impossible and then waited for daylight before acting.

At dawn, Lee sent Stuart forward under a flag of truce with a written demand that Brown and his men surrender immediately and release their hostages, and that "if they will peaceably surrender themselves and restore the pillaged property, they shall be kept in safety to await the orders of the President...That if he is compelled to take them by force he cannot answer for their safety." Stuart was instructed to accept no counterproposal from Brown, who rejected Lee's terms. When Stuart signaled Brown's refusal, Lee ordered an immediate attack.

Lee sent a dozen marines under the command of Lieutenant J. Green into concealed positions near the engine house. Three of the men were equipped with sledgehammers to break down the doors of Brown's fort and begin the assault immediately. Lee ordered his men to attack using only bayonets in order to protect the lives of the hostages, but the initial assault failed to breach Brown's defenses; the raiders had placed the fire engine against the doors and tied them shut with heavy ropes. Lee next ordered his reserves to use a heavy ladder like a medieval battering ram to smash a portion of the door and gain entry.

Until now, Brown's firing had been harmless, but soon one marine, Private Quinn, was mortally wounded. The marines rapidly subdued Brown's surviving raiders, using bayonets to kill two who resisted, and Green struck Brown with the blunt edge of his sword after the abolitionist was pointed out to him by a hostage. The hostages and the slaves who had not participated in the fighting were soon released to return in safety to their homes. The active portion of John Brown's raid into Virginia was completed, but the political phase—the trial and the national publicity drawn to the infamous Brown—was just beginning.

Brown's raid was a small, timely spark, that when applied to the highly combustible mixture of fear and national politics, hastened the process toward conflict that in retrospect appears to have been inevitable. And he had one final goal: to become a martyr to his chosen cause.

The new Republican Party and its abolitionist members were quickly blamed for this raid by apprehensive Southerners. Virginia, in particular, had been sensitized to the effects of slave rebellion and had experienced the fear and terror of Nat Turner's rebellion, which left defenseless white civilians dead in the wake of black insurgency. Once the weapons collected by Brown—especially the cruel-looking pikes intended for the hands of escaped slaves to be used to kill their masters and their families—were displayed, a collective shudder went through Virginia. Accusations were directed toward the Republicans that suggested that the political party had plans to destroy the South in an enormous slave rebellion to be paid for by Northern interests. The fear of a slave rebellion and the hatred of the Republican Party for its suspected complicity in these acts would loom large when Abraham Lincoln won the next presidential election.

Brown was indicted for murder and treason in the regular session of the Circuit Court of Jefferson County, Virginia. His attacks, while on a federal installation, had violated state laws and his trial was swiftly under

Brown's men had securely barricaded themselves inside the engine house, but Lieutenant Green's men were able to use a fire ladder as a battering ram to smash through the doors to gain entry. Once inside, the marines were able to bring the hostage situation under control, even though they were ordered not to use their muskets, and had to face gunfire with only their bayonets.

way. Brown's intention to become a highly publicized martyr was soon to receive unexpected support from an unlikely quarter.

Virginia's governor, Henry A. Wise, arrived on the scene to take charge of this highly visible case and to use it for his own advancement. Wise, who had his sights set higher than the Virginia governor's mansion, hoped to transform the trial into a nationally recognized event that would provide publicity for him. Wise's interference with the events surrounding the trial played directly into Brown's own plans to promote himself as a sacrificial victim.

Brown won admiration even from his most unappeasable political foes as he revealed his total commitment to his goal. He desired martyrdom, and on the occasion of his sentencing (to death by hanging) gave a powerful speech that was widely read throughout the North. In part, the defiant abolitionist said:

Now, if it is deemed necessary that I should forfeit my life for the furtherance of the ends of justice, and mingle my blood further with the blood of my children and with the blood of millions in this slave country whose rights are disregarded by wicked, cruel, and unjust enactments, I say, let it be done.

A powerful man had determined to lead the slaves to freedom or die in an attempt to draw supporters to his cause. His strong, eloquent speeches were widely distributed in both sections of the troubled country and resonated with a vastly different effect in each. In the North, he was recognized as a martyr to the teachings of the abolitionists, who were so greatly despised in the South; indeed, his name eventually became a part of a battle hymn that was sung as Northern soldiers invaded Southern territory to accomplish his goals.

Governor Wise, in anticipation of threatened attempts from Northern forces to mount a rescue of Brown from the Jefferson County jail where he awaited execution, ordered one thousand state troops to Charlestown to guard the execution. At least one member of the large contingent was moved by the historic event. Thomas Jonathan Jackson (soon to become known as "Stonewall" to the nation) wrote:

LEFT: Lieutenant James Ewell Brown Stuart, soon to be known as Jeb to friend and foe alike, was on leave from his regiment, the First United States Cavalry, when John Brown and his Provisional Army attacked at Harpers Ferry. Stuart was immediately recalled to duty and sent to assist Colonel Robert E. Lee—who was also home on leave—to subdue the insurrectionists.

Lee and Stuart swiftly gained control of the local volunteers and militia companies surrounding Brown and the engine house. Stuart was sent forward with an ultimatum from Lee demanding immediate surrender, but this was rejected and Brown sought to negotiate. On receiving a signal that Brown had refused to surrender, Lee ordered an immediate assault by a detachment of U.S. Marines. As Lieutenant Israel Green ran inside the engine house, one of Brown's hostages immediately pointed the leader of the raid out. Green had been ordered to avoid gunfire so that innocent hostages wouldn't be hurt accidentally, and he rushed Brown, beating him to the floor with the blunt surfaces of his sword.

...altogether it was an imposing but very solemn scene. I was much impressed with the thought that before me stood a man, in the full vigor of health, who must in a few moments enter eternity. I sent up the petition that he might be saved. Awful was the thought that in a few minutes [he would] receive the sentence, "Depart, ye wicked, into everlasting fire!" I hope that he was prepared to die, but I am doubtful.

John Brown walked toward the hangman's scaffold. He had no final words, but he passed a note to a guard in which he wrote that he was certain that "the crimes of this guilty land will never be purged away but with blood." He had worked long and hard, sacrificed several of his sons, and gave his own life for his beliefs.

The goal was admirable, though the methods he used hastened a national disaster, the greatest in U.S. history. Brown's use of terror to accomplish political goals served

to galvanize much of the North, especially the new Republican Party, and abolition of slavery became a widely recognized goal. In the South, fear of political domination by Northern politicians and the simultaneous dread of additional raids designed to provoke slave rebellion created political unrest, which was capitalized upon by politicians with extreme views—such as secession.

The raid on Harpers Ferry by John Brown and his Provisional Army had far-reaching consequences for an entire nation.

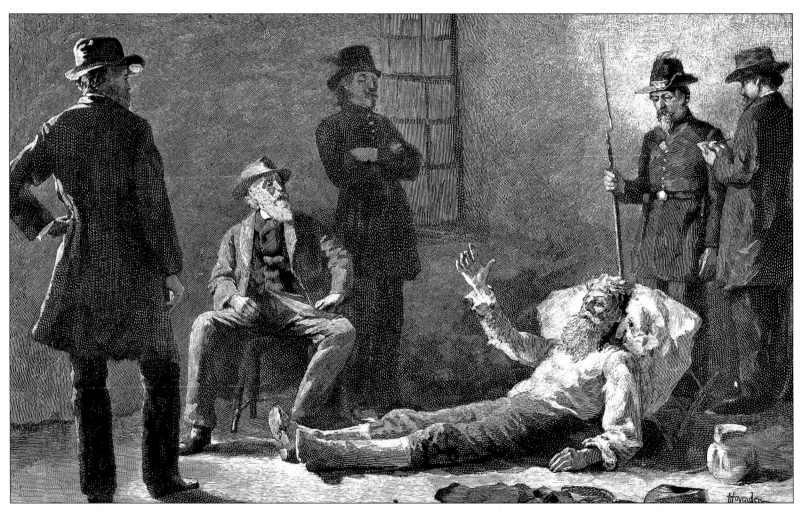

Once captured, John Brown shifted from his role of avenging angel to that of a persecuted Christian awaiting an unjust end at the hands of cruel tormentors. Brown brought the abolition movement to the front of national politics in a very dramatic fashion. He and one of his Northern backers, Thomas W. Higginson, agreed that his execution would do more for the success of their movement than his raid would have. The intense newspaper coverage of both raid and trial brought the issue of slavery and abolition to the attention of nearly every citizen in the country.

A POLITICAL EXTREMIST RAIDS HARPERS FERRY

"The result proves the plan was the attempt of a fanatic or madman, which could only end in failure; and its temporary success was owing to the panic and confusion he succeeded in creating by magnifying his numbers."

—General Robert E. Lee

John Brown's demeanor while awaiting his execution was selfless and rational. He understood his actual worth to the abolition movement, and said, "I am worth inconceivably more to hang than for any other purpose." His death resulted in the small, limited abolitionist effort becoming a general uprising of supporters in the North— many of whom would be wearing blue uniforms in a very few years as they prepared to invade the South.

A POLITICAL EXTREMIST RAIDS HARPERS FERRY

chapter 16

THE LOCOMOTIVE RAIDS

> *"The line that connects an army with its base of supplies is the heel of Achilles—its most vital and vulnerable point."*
>
> —John Singleton Mosby

Early on in the Civil War, both sides recognized that railroads were a decisive advantage to the side utilizing them most effectively. Northern and Southern strategists alike had been trained in the same academies with the same textbooks, and they had similar thoughts about warfare. Henry Wager Halleck, called "Old Brains" in the prewar national army, had translated from French the works of Henri de Jomini, a military strategist who served with Napoleon.

All the skilled officers of the period were familiar with the twin concepts of "interior lines" and "exterior lines," which referred to the distances to be traveled by troops seeking to reinforce a threatened section of defenses. Obviously, the side having to travel the shortest distance—possessing interior lines—had a distinct advantage over its adversary.

It became apparent rapidly that physical distances were less important to the general concept than was the time-to-distance ratio, which could be shortened through the use of a more rapid means of transport. Railroads thus became a key factor in Civil War battles, and the side controlling the most rail mileage and rolling stock had a distinct advantage over the side lacking this modern form of transport. In this arena, the North had a clear advantage.

The Confederacy needed additional locomotives and cars for their railroads but lacked the industrial capability to manufacture them. Early in the war, the forward-looking General Thomas J. "Stonewall" Jackson developed a good plan to obtain a generous supply of locomotives from the nearby Baltimore and Ohio Railroad (B&O)— at the expense of the North.

Jackson had occupied Harpers Ferry, but he had not ordered any attacks on the railroads, despite the fact that there were many trains filled with coal being moved from the mines at Cumberland, Maryland, to the east-

"To move swiftly, strike vigorously, and secure all the fruits of victory, is the secret of successful war."

—General "Stonewall" Jackson, 1863

PAGE 265: The nation's railroads were generally composed of two vital components: the rails and the rolling stock that ran on them. These critical transportation elements were utilized effectively by both sides during the Civil War and were attacked as legitimate targets of war. The Confederacy had fewer railroad systems, and the Union army made frequent attempts to cripple the South's ability to deliver military supplies by destroying their railroads. Attacks were most common against the most precarious of the system's components, the railroad bridges. LEFT: Thomas J. Jackson, known as "Stonewall" to both sides after the Battle of Bull Run, managed a dramatic, but often forgotten raid on the Union's most crucial railroad, the Baltimore and Ohio, inside his native Virginia. Jackson was able to capture fifty-six locomotives, which were in short supply within the new Confederacy. Lacking rail connections with Southern railroads, Jackson ordered his men to use draft animals and their own muscles to pull the captured locomotives overland for nearly twenty miles, to where they were placed back on rails and sent off to support the Confederate war effort.

ern seaboard, where supplies were being stockpiled for possible emergency shortfalls in the future. There were double tracks on the B&O between Point of Rocks, Maryland, and Martinsburg, Virginia, a distance of some twenty-five to thirty miles (40 to 48km).

Jackson complained to Garrett, the president of the railroad, that the night trains were disturbing his troops as they tried to rest and requested that the eastbound trains be scheduled to pass Harpers Ferry between 11:00 A.M. and 1:00 P.M. Garrett, not wanting to be difficult with someone who had the power at hand to order his railroad blockaded, promptly agreed to this request. But since the empty cars were still sent back west at night, Jackson complained that it was just as noisy, and he asked that Garrett schedule his empty trains to pass on the double track during the same period. Garrett did as requested, and for a brief period each day the short distance between Point of Rocks and Martinsburg was filled with trains.

Jackson had created the perfect situation for a major train hijacking, perhaps the largest in history. As soon as his schedule was working and the rails were filled with trains, he ordered John Imboden to cross the Potomac River to the Maryland side and allow trains to pass freely until 12:00 P.M., noon, but Imboden was not to permit any additional eastbound trains to pass afterward. At that time, he was to destroy the rails.

Simultaneously, Jackson sent another force west to do the same at Martinsburg, catching all the trains that were going either east or west between these two obstructing forces. Jackson ordered all of the captured trains to be taken on the branch railroad to Winchester, Virginia, for safekeeping until additional arrangements could be made. Jackson had managed to collect fifty-six locomotives—more than three hundred cars—in a single hour.

As there were no additional rail connections south from Winchester, Jackson ordered that his captured locomotives be hauled overland by horse and manpower from Winchester to the connecting rail line at nearby Strasburg. In a single crafty stroke, Jackson had simultaneously enriched the Confederacy's stock of locomotives and cars while nearly crippling the B&O for an extended period.

The railroads were used to great advantage in the war by both sides, and their value to military operations was quickly recognized. Defenders sought to protect their railroads as the attackers attempted to destroy rails and, whenever possible, the rolling stock that carried both men and supplies. The railroad systems became critical targets that had to be attacked or defended, depending on the perspective of the two armies. Control of strategic rails became crucial.

One of the more interesting but hare-brained raids of the Civil War involved a strategic attack on a railroad that was believed to be critical to the successful

James J. Andrews, like Jackson a native of western Virginia, developed a bold and innovative plan to destroy one of the South's major railroad systems early in the Civil War. He and his Ohio volunteers commandeered an entire train while its passengers and crew were having breakfast. As nearby Confederate troops watched, the raiders took control of the train and ran it toward the North with the intention of burning strategic bridges along the route.

General Ormsby Mitchel was the Federal officer who approved Andrews' daring plan to raid along the entire railroad. Mitchel accompanied Andrews to several Union encampments as they sought volunteers for this dangerous mission.

defense of Chattanooga, Tennessee, in early April 1862. The Western and Atlantic Railroad was the connecting link between supply and recruit depots in the vicinity of Atlanta, Georgia, and Union commanders in Tennessee believed that Chattanooga would swiftly fall under their control if the railroad were rendered inoperable.

The entire operation arose from the suggestion of a courageous and seasoned part-time Union spy, James J. Andrews, who was very familiar with the area considered for the raid. Andrews, a Virginian, had made a number of trips into Confederate territory under the guise of a contraband smuggler. He had been able to pass as a dealer in medicines and other scarce supplies, thereby gaining the confidence of Southerners, and he had made more than one trip into Confederate-controlled Tennessee.

The Union army was moving south to the site of what would become known as the Battle of Shiloh. Andrews proposed a plan to facilitate the troop movements that involved destroying the railroad from Atlanta to Chattanooga. Once the line was inoperable, the Federal army could move forward without fear of encountering a coordinated response from the Confederates to the south.

Andrews and General Ormsby Mitchel visited the camp of several infantry regiments to request volunteers for this hazardous operation, and twenty-four men from the 2nd, 21st, and 33rd Ohio Infantry regiments volunteered in spite of the risks involved. They would be traveling in civilian clothing behind enemy lines. Exposure and capture would undoubtedly result in hanging by the Confederate authorities. All of the volunteers were enlisted men, except for one man: William Campbell. Campbell was a civilian who was in camp visiting his friend, Private Philip Shadrach, and when his friend stepped forward as a volunteer, Campbell also volunteered for the perilous raid.

James J. Andrews, the bold Union spy who conceived the dangerous raid along the railroad, had operated deep within the Confederacy on previous expeditions. Posing as a smuggler and war profiteer, the gentlemanly Andrews had been completely accepted by his unwitting acquaintances in the South. He was the last man they would have expected to be a Federal agent in their midst.

The men were divided into small groups with instructions to meet Andrews in Marietta, Georgia, on April 10. Three men were lost on the initial leg of the trip, but Andrews was able to assemble twenty-one raiders in Marietta on April 11. Andrews briefed them on the plan.

The volunteers were to purchase tickets on a northbound train from Marietta and wrest control from the railroad crew as they went along. The raiders would then burn the bridges they crossed as they rolled back toward Tennessee. Unfortunately for the plan, Andrews and his band saw more Confederate soldiers along the route than they had anticipated, and Andrews gave each man an opportunity to withdraw from the

operation. They all agreed to proceed with the operation as planned, but two men didn't choose to make the rendezvous with the others to purchase tickets.

Andrews and nineteen raiders bought their tickets on the Western and Atlantic Railroad in Marietta at 5:00 A.M. the following day, and the raid was under way. The initial stop was at Big Shanty, seven miles (11km) from their starting point, where there was a breakfast stop. At Big Shanty the train's conductor, William C. Fuller, the engineer, Jeff Cain, and the rest of the passengers left the train. Andrews and his nineteen men remained aboard as the others left for their morning meal.

At about the same moment, Andrews ordered that the locomotive, tender, and three cars be uncoupled from the rest of the train. Privates Wilson Brown and William Knight, both engineers in their civilian occupations, climbed into the engine with another Union soldier to act as firemen. Curiously, they did all of this while being watched by Confederate soldiers camped beside the tracks, but the first realization that something unplanned was happening occurred when Fuller and Cain heard their train pulling swiftly away from Big Shanty. Andrews' raiders had succeeded in capturing the locomotive, the *General,* and the raiders raced toward the bridges that were their targets and the safety of Tennessee.

Unluckily, Andrews and the Ohio volunteers hadn't taken into consideration the courage and persistence of William C. Fuller and Jeff Cain. Initially, the two railroad men simply ran after the train on foot, but after the first few miles, they found a handcar and used it to follow the stolen train until they found an old locomotive, the *Yonah,* sitting on a siding.

Andrews' steps to ensure the success of his plan were almost perfect. He had ordered rails removed on the run from Big Shanty for

Andrews would have successfully completed his mission on the railroad if it hadn't been for the efforts of William Fuller, the train's conductor. Enraged by the theft of his train, Fuller pursued Andrews' men on foot, with a railroad pushcart, and aboard trains, forcing the Union raiders to push on without stopping to burn the bridges that would have effectively halted any further pursuit. As the chase continued, Andrews and his men were forced to abandon their engine, the General, *and attempt to escape on foot.*

the first twenty miles (32km) to Kingston, and he cut the telegraph wires. Once he had done all this, he felt that pursuit would be unlikely. But he made a fatal miscalculation when he passed the *Yonah* without stopping to disable it.

Fuller had encountered southbound freight trains in the vicinity of Kingston and was forced to abandon the old *Yonah,* but he ran along the track until he was able to locate another locomotive, the *William R. Smith*. Another break in the tracks halted Fuller, but he again dismounted from the train to run an additional three miles (5km) until he was able to board another train

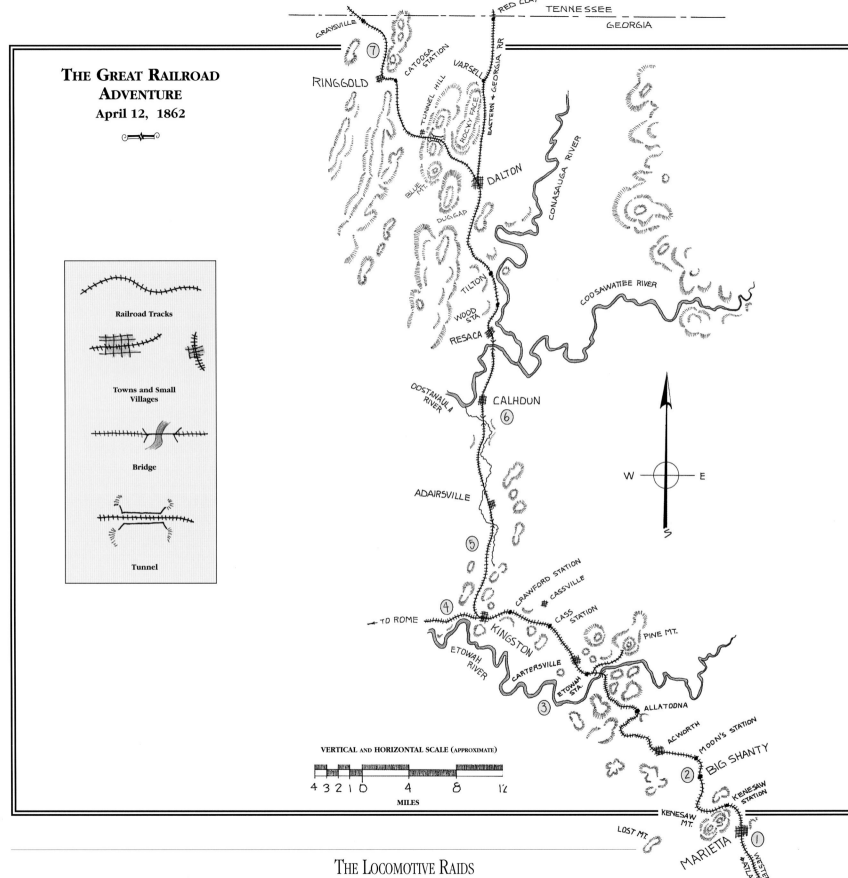

THE GREAT RAILROAD
ADVENTURE
April 12, 1862

Railroad Tracks

Towns and Small
Villages

Bridge

Tunnel

TENNESSEE
GEORGIA

GRAYSVILLE
RED CLAY
RINGGOLD
CATOOSA STATION
TUNNEL HILL
VARSELL
ROCKY FACE
EASTERN + GEORGIA RR
BLUE MT.
DALTON
DUGGAP
CONASAUGA RIVER
COOSAWATIEE RIVER
TILTON
WOOD STA.
RESACA
OOSTANAULA RIVER
CALHDUN
ADAIRSVILLE
CRAWFORD STATION
CASSVILLE
TO ROME
KINGSTON
CASS STATION
PINE MT.
ETOWAH RIVER
CARTERSVILLE
ETOWAH STA.
ALLATODNA
ACWORTH
MOON'S STATION
BIG SHANTY
KENESAW STATION
VERTICAL AND HORIZONTAL SCALE (APPROXIMATE)
4 3 2 1 0   4   8   12
MILES
KENESAW MT.
LOST MT.
MARIETTA
WESTERN ATLANTIC

THE LOCOMOTIVE RAIDS
270

1. On April 12, 1862, James Andrews and eighteen volunteers from the 2nd, 21st, and 33rd Ohio Infantry and one civilian volunteer, boarded the *General*, a northbound train, in Marietta, Georgia. Their goal was to take control of the train and destroy track and bridges while en route to Tennessee.

2. At Big Shanty, when the crew and other passengers stopped for breakfast, Andrews and his men took control. Under the eyes of Confederate soldiers camped along the track, they uncoupled all but three cars and took off. The *General's* conductor, William Fuller, and several others started after the raiders on foot. Along the way they found a push car, which they used until they reached Etowah Station.

3. At Etowah Station Fuller commandeered the *Yonah*, which was working on a side track. The *Yonah* was used to pursue Andrews as far as Kingston.

4. The Raiders had blocked the tracks at the Kingston yard. Undaunted, Fuller's party continued on foot until they came across the *William R. Smith*, which had just come from Rome, and continued the pursuit.

5. Six miles north of Kingston the raiders removed a rail from the track. Forced to abandon the *William R. Smith*, Fuller and his party set out again on foot. Two miles south of Adairsville, Fuller's footsore group intercepted the southbound *Texas*. Running her in reverse, they renewed the chase. Andrews had encountered the *Texas* at Adairsville and had argued her onto a side track under the guise that they were a "special" loaded with powder for General Beauregard, so that he could pass.

6. At the village of Calhoun, ten soldiers from the 1st Georgia Volunteers joined the chase.

7. About two miles north of Ringgold, water and wood ran out and the *General* lost steam. The raiders, one by one, dropped off the train and ran into the forest. Five miles from Tennessee the *General* was abandoned.

Within a week all the raiders were captured. Andrews and seven others were hanged. The others were later exchanged. The survivors from this raid, all enlisted men, were the first to be awarded the newly authorized Congressional Medal of Honor.

Conductor William Fuller followed Andrews' men on a construction pushcart that had been used by men repairing the rails. Pressing it into use, Fuller and his men, including the train's engineer, continued their chase until derailed. Andrews had ordered his men to break the rails at strategic but inconspicuous points, such as on curves, in an effort to slow any pursuers.

pulled by the *Texas*. Once Fuller had abandoned the *Texas'* cars on a siding, he ran the locomotive in reverse as he chased the raiders aboard the *General*. The tenacious Conductor Fuller was soon closing in on the Union raiders, who were racing for their lives as the *Texas* and the *General* engaged in what has become known as the Great Locomotive Chase.

As the Union soldiers dropped cross ties onto the rails in front of Fuller's locomotive, halting him only momentarily, it became obvious that they would be unable to return to the safety of Tennessee, and one by one the men began to drop off the train to run into the nearby forest. With their supply of wood and water needed to power the locomotive dwindling, Andrews and the last of the raiders abandoned the *General* five miles (8km) from the Tennessee border.

Conductor William C. Fuller disrupted the Union sabotage mission when he undertook his personal pursuit of the men who had robbed him of his train. The operation was a complete failure. Within a week, all of Andrews' raiders were in Confederate custody and imprisoned. James J. Andrews was tried as a spy and executed by hanging in Atlanta on June 7, 1862. On June 18, another seven of the raiders were hanged—including Private Phillip Shadrach and his civilian friend, William Campbell. The two men who had declined to board the *General* at the last moment in Marietta were also captured, and fourteen of the original twenty-two raiders remained in Confederate prisons.

The Confederate authorities underestimated their prisoners, who managed a daring escape in October. Eight of the men evaded capture: four were able to reach Tennessee; two others made their escape to Federal territory in Mississippi; and two more reached the safety of the Union navy that was blockading the Gulf Coast. The remaining six were recaptured quickly and held until they were exchanged for Confederates held in Federal prisons. These brave raiders were awarded the new medal that had been authorized by Congress for military heroism, the Congressional Medal of Honor. Curiously, the highly regarded medals were awarded to men who were on an espionage operation in civilian clothing.

Andrews and Campbell, the two civilians, were hanged and received no decorations for their hazardous service and sacrifice. Nor was Private Shadrach awarded the medal—he had enlisted, had served, and was hanged under an assumed name.

The raid was well conceived and boldly executed, and would have served as a model for future raids along the line had it not been disrupted by the valiant efforts of Conductor William C. Fuller. It was entirely due to his remarkable tenacity that the Union's brazen

ABOVE: Once they were out of both wood and the water needed to develop steam for their engine, Andrews' men were forced to abandon the train and flee into nearby Tennessee. Within a week, all of the raiders would be captured and placed in Confederate prisons. Andrews and seven of his volunteers would eventually be hanged as spies. RIGHT: The Confederate locomotive General was brazenly stolen by Andrews and used to withdraw toward Union lines along the Tennessee border. During their bold raid, Andrews' men traversed most of the length of the Western and Atlantic Railroad, but the tenacious pursuit of Conductor Fuller prevented them from completing their mission, the destruction of the crucial bridges along the route they were using to escape. Fuller's grit doomed the raid to failure, and resulted in the execution of eight of the brave raiders.

raid deep into the interior of the Confederacy was thwarted.

The hastily conceived plan had no contingency provisions to allow for the unexpected—like Fuller's pursuit and the increased number of soldiers along the route. The Union army learned from this devastating failure, and rash operations like Andrews' raid would not be repeated in any such amateurish fashion.

chapter 17

AVERELL'S DECEMBER RAID

The Union army made many errors in strategy and execution of plans during the first two years of the Civil War, and as a result were able to claim relatively few victories. Perhaps it was due solely to an unknown source of inner courage and morale that the Union soldiers remained in the field and the Northern population continued to support their efforts despite their grim losses. The Confederacy had done remarkably well with its limited resources up to this point in the war, but the Union army was rapidly sorting out poorly qualified officers and replacing them with men who knew how—and were willing—to fight.

Operations continued against railroads and the supply depots and camps that were frequently associated with the rail lines. These raids, like the operation that resulted in the Great Locomotive Chase, were planned to accomplish more than simply the destruction of military property and an increased cost of continuing operations.

It was just this type of operation that developed in the mountains of West Virginia in December 1863, just after the region had entered the Union as a new state. This raid, like most of the others, had more than a local significance, but deserves a special place in history as one of the best planned, best executed, and most successful raids of the Civil War.

Following the battle of Gettysburg, Confederate General James Longstreet and his divisions were sent into Tennessee, where they proceeded to lay seige to the Federal garrison in the city of Knoxville. The garrison, under the command of Ambrose E. Burnside, was hard pressed and in danger of being forced to surrender.

Longstreet was receiving much of his supplies over the Virginia and Tennessee Railroad, which wound through the hills of southwest Virginia before entering Tennessee, and Federal tacticians felt that a raid against this vital supply artery could

"I would define true courage to be a perfect sensibility of the measure of danger, and a mental willingness to incur it."

—General William T. Sherman

result in a general weakening of the Confederate besiegers of Knoxville and relieve some of the pressure on Burnside before he collapsed. All of this was occurring at a time when the Union army was beginning to shift over to the offensive operations planned for 1864, and a Federal setback in Tennessee could easily have tilted the military initiative back in favor of the Confederacy and prolonged the war.

Brigadier General William W. Averell was positioned in northwestern West Virginia at a position providing some additional security to the exposed Baltimore and Ohio Railroad. He had recently completed the training and refitting of three West Virginia mounted infantry regiments and formed the 4th Separate Brigade. Having inherited his command from General Robert H. Milroy, Averell drilled his new corps until he was satisfied with its performance.

Averell and his troops, a single brigade of mounted infantry, were directed to cut the Virginia and Tennessee Railroad at some vulnerable point and interrupt the transport of troops and supplies between Richmond and

PAGE 275: William Woods Averell was appointed to West Point in 1851 and as an early army assignment served in New Mexico territory, where he gained practical experience in the art of the cavalryman. Soon to be a cavalry commander in the Union army, Averell fought his former classmates at Bull Run, and alongside McClellan during the Peninsula Campaign. He later took command of several regiments of mounted infantrymen in West Virginia, which he refitted, trained, and drilled to create the 4th Separate Brigade. With these men, Averell conducted brilliant raids deep within Confederate territory. LEFT: General James Longstreet, one of Lee's commanders at the Battle of Gettysburg, had been sent into the western theater as the East settled into a general lull following the Confederate defeat in Pennsylvania. After fighting at Chickamauga, Longstreet was sent by Braxton Bragg to besiege the Union's Ambrose Burnside at Knoxville.

Knoxville. Averell was unambiguously ordered to accomplish this assignment despite the obvious risks to the men of his command. The situation in Knoxville was judged to be sufficiently critical to justify a dangerous midwinter raiding party against the Confederate railroad. Although General William Tecumseh Sherman was able to raise the siege on December 3, 1863, Averell's raid was allowed to go forward in an attempt to further deflate the Confederate advantage.

Averell met with the department commander, Brigadier General Benjamin F. Kelley, at department headquarters in Cumberland, Maryland, where Averell devised an excellent plan that called for deception at every turn.

First, E.P. Scammon's brigade in the Kanawha Valley would move eastward to occupy Lewisburg on December 12. Scammon and his troops would remain in position until December 18, but he was instructed to press in the direction of the Confederate base of Brigadier General John Echols at the nearby town of Union. Colonel Augustus Moor would be sent south to Marling's Bottom by December 11 and push forward to threaten Lewisburg but remain in the vicinity of Frankford until December 18. General William Sullivan would be positioned in Woodstock within the Shenandoah Valley on December 11, and he would move to threaten Staunton on December 20 and 21. Colonel Joseph Thoburn would move on to the Parkersburg pike once he reached

Rhode Island's Ambrose Burnside had led brilliant amphibious attacks against North Carolina's Outer Banks early in the Civil War, commanded a corps at Antietam, and served briefly as commander of the Army of the Potomac at the disastrous battle at Fredericksburg, Virginia. Sent west to a new command, he was trapped in Knoxville as his men began to go hungry. The Confederates had broken their "cracker line."

Union General Benjamin F. Kelley had been involved in the war since its beginning. Wounded in the chest in the first land battle of the Civil War, Philippi, Kelley went on to become the commander of the entire region. His responsibilities included the defense of a crucial transportation route, the Baltimore and Ohio Railroad.

Monterey. His command would head for Staunton as well, in a feint to trick Confederate defenders into believing that Staunton was the object of the combined attack.

Averell's predeparture preparations were now complete. He had arranged for "demonstrations," or threatened attacks, against Confederate forces in Lewisburg from two possible directions, and two other forces were deployed into locations from which they could threaten Staunton. Averell hoped that Sullivan's movement toward Staunton and Scammon's threatened movement toward Union would provoke the defending Confederates into concentrating their forces, thus producing a wide gap in their lines through which his entire force could ship into the area, disrupt the railroad, and then ship back out without a fight.

All of the various units associated with Averell's plan began to move at one time. His mounted units left the post at New Creek near the Maryland border on December 8. Colonel Thoburn split from the main force on December 12 and moved according to plan. Obviously confused by the multiple movements of large Federal forces, the Confederate defenders began to react to these vaguely defined threats. Lewisburg and Union were obvious targets and it appeared that Staunton and its large store of supplies might be the intended point of these unusual midwinter moves.

Averell traveled over seldom-used back roads during a severe rainstorm that lasted two days, but the Union column made good progress and was able to penetrate deeply into Confederate territory without being detected. Travel was particulary difficult for the mounted men as most of the streams they had to cross did not have bridges. The majority of Averell's supply train, composed of wagons and ambulances, was sent along with Colonel Thoburn's infantry, and the sol-

Colonel Eliakim P. Scammon led a diversionary movement toward John Echols' base at Union, West Virginia, to add to the South's confusion about Averell's intended target. Soon, Scammon—promoted to general—fell victim to another raider, however, when Confederate Major Knowing snatched him from a riverboat anchored deep within Federal territory and delivered Scammon to Richmond. Soon, every mounted man in southern West Virginia was engaged in a search for Scammon.

diers were without the sparse comforts that they would have had.

Part of Averell's success to this point was due to the active patrolling that was done by his mounted scouts. Averell had been fortunate when he inherited a portion of Milroy's old command, including a scouting company that had been organized in St. Louis at the outbreak of the war. General John Frémont had ordered the formation of the scouts—who were expected to operate in the uniform of the enemy—at the urging of his wife, Jessie Benton Frémont. Once the scouts were organized, they were named "Jessie Scouts," in honor of the general's wife.

While many of these scouts, including their first commander, Charles Carpenter, were freebooters who were involved in the Federal war effort for what can be best described as "personal enrichment motives," several of the survivors had gained real military skills. Dressed in a Confederate uniform as often as they wore Federal blue, these scouts operated freely in a broad screen well to the front of Averell's primary column. Averell wrote in his report: "The head of my column was preceded by vigilant scouts, armed with repeating rifles, who permitted no one to go before them....My scouts thrown out kept me informed of the enemy's movements and positions."

Disguised in Confederate uniforms, the scouts were often able to approach and capture enemy couriers, and their dispatches were soon in Averell's hands. At least one message detailing troop movements, written by Major General Sam Jones, was captured and taken directly to Averell. Jones' dispatch had special instructions with the captured message: "The operator at Jackson's River will use every effort to get the above to General Early and a copy to Colonel Jackson. Colonel Jackson must have a copy of it."

Obviously, the message was not delivered to the local telegraph operator and both General Jubal Early and Colonel William Jackson were deprived of the advantageous early warning of Averell's movement. Without Jones' instructions, Confederate pursuit remained confused amid all the Federal maneuvering of troops.

It was thanks to his scouts that Averell was able to approach Salem, Virginia, and the target, the Virginia and Tennessee Railroad, before being detected. Four miles (6.5km) from Salem, a Confederate patrol met the lead elements of Averell's column. Without providing any details of the encounter, Averell reported that he learned from them that General Fitzhugh Lee had left

The Confederacy's John Echols maintained a significant force at his base near Union, West Virginia. Any movement by Averell would have to take Echols' presence into account, but the Federal plan actually took advantage of his presence by developing a feint toward him as Averell moved south toward the Virginia and Tennessee Railroad.

Lynchburg with the intention of intercepting the "Yankees" and that a train filled with troops was expected momentarily to guard the supplies accumulated at Salem for Longstreet's use in Tennessee. The Jessie Scouts had probably been able to intercept the Confederate patrol and engage them in conversation to gain this information. Based on this knowledge, a 350-man forward element rode into Salem on December 16 just before the arrival of the train filled the reinforcements from Lynchburg. Averell wrote in his report:

I hastened my advance, consisting of about 350 men and two three inch guns, through the town to the depot.

The telegraph wires were cut first—the operator was not to be found, the railroad track torn up in the vicinity of the depot, one gun placed in battery, and the advance dismounted and placed in readiness for the expected train of troops.

A train from Lynchburg, loaded with troops, soon approached. My main body was not yet in sight, and it was necessary to stop the train; a shot was fired at it from one of the guns, which missed; a second went through the train diagonally, whch caused it to retire, and a third and last hastened its movements.

Averell was reinforced with the arrival of the rest of his column, and parties were sent along the tracks in both directions to destroy as much of the railroad as possible in the short time before additional Confederates arrived. Depots and their contents were burned and cars on the track, the "water-station," the "turn-table," and five railroad bridges were destroyed by the raiders. Averell reported that private property was left untouched by his men and the citizens "received us with politeness."

After approximately six hours of destruction, the entire 4th Separate Brigade rode out of Salem to a position about seven miles (11km) from the town where they stopped to rest for the night. They had covered the last eighty miles (129km) to the doomed Confederate depot in an impressive thirty hours, and rest was needed by all. Averell's men planted misleading information by telling a few of the "polite" locals that they were planning to retreat from the area by way of the town of Buchanan, which was several miles to the east. The false information soon found its way to Fitzhugh Lee, who, believing it to be valid intelligence obtained through a lapse in security on the

part of some of the Union cavalrymen, led his men to the east and permitted Averell to escape from the noose that was being drawn tightly around him.

The Union commander was beginning to manage a near-miraculous escape from deep within a fully aroused and angry Confederate region. The earlier feints in the direction of Lewisburg and Staunton as well as a false advance by his men toward the town of Fincastle had confused the pursuit and spread the pursuers widely apart. Even so, the Jessie Scouts needed to secure the services of a local guide to take them through obscure country roads to safety.

Scouts rode into the small community of New Castle, Virginia, after discussing who in the region would be the best guide for the nearly trapped Union column. There were approximately twelve hundred Confederate troops in the vicinity under experienced commanders like Fitzhugh Lee, John Echols, John McCausland, and William L. "Mudwall" Jackson, so called to clearly distinguish him from his relative, "Stonewall."

Once the decision was made to impress a local guide, the scouts chose someone who would be in the best position to know all of the area's more obscure roads and trails: "Dr. Wylie," a man who would have ridden all of the back roads during the worst of weather. The country doctor was selected and advised that if he wanted to survive the war's current dangers, he would have to lead the entire command to the relative safety of West Virginia.

Leaving the campfires burning in the night, Averell was able to escape once more from the closely drawn Confederate traps that had been set for him. His corps reached the bridges over Jackson River near Covington and crossed at a gallop as the bridges had been filled with combustible materials and were set for destruction. One of Averell's regiments remained on the south

AVERELL'S DECEMBER RAID ON SALEM, VIRGINIA
December 6–24, 1863

THE DECEPTION

A. E.P. Scammon's brigade in the Kanawha Valley was directed to move on Lewisburg and then to press toward the Confederate base of General Echols at Union.

B. Colonel Moor was to threaten Lewisburg from the north and hold near Frank Fort.

C. General Sullivan was ordered to move from Woodstock south toward Staunton.

D. Colonel Thoburn was detached from the main column at Monterey and demonstrated in the direction of Staunton.

THE MAIN ASSAULT

1. General Averell's force of mounted infantry departed New Creek on December 8, 1863.

2. As planned, Colonel Thoburn split from the main force at Monterey and advanced in the direction of Staunton.

3. Four miles (6.4 km) north of Salem, lead elements met a Confederate patrol and learned that a troop train was en route to Salem. A 350-man force immediately rode into Salem on December 16. The train was forced back and when the rest of the force arrived, the depot and contents were burned.

4. Averell's raiders burned the bridges over the Jackson River near Covington.

5. After riding over four hundred miles the march concluded at Beverly on December 24.

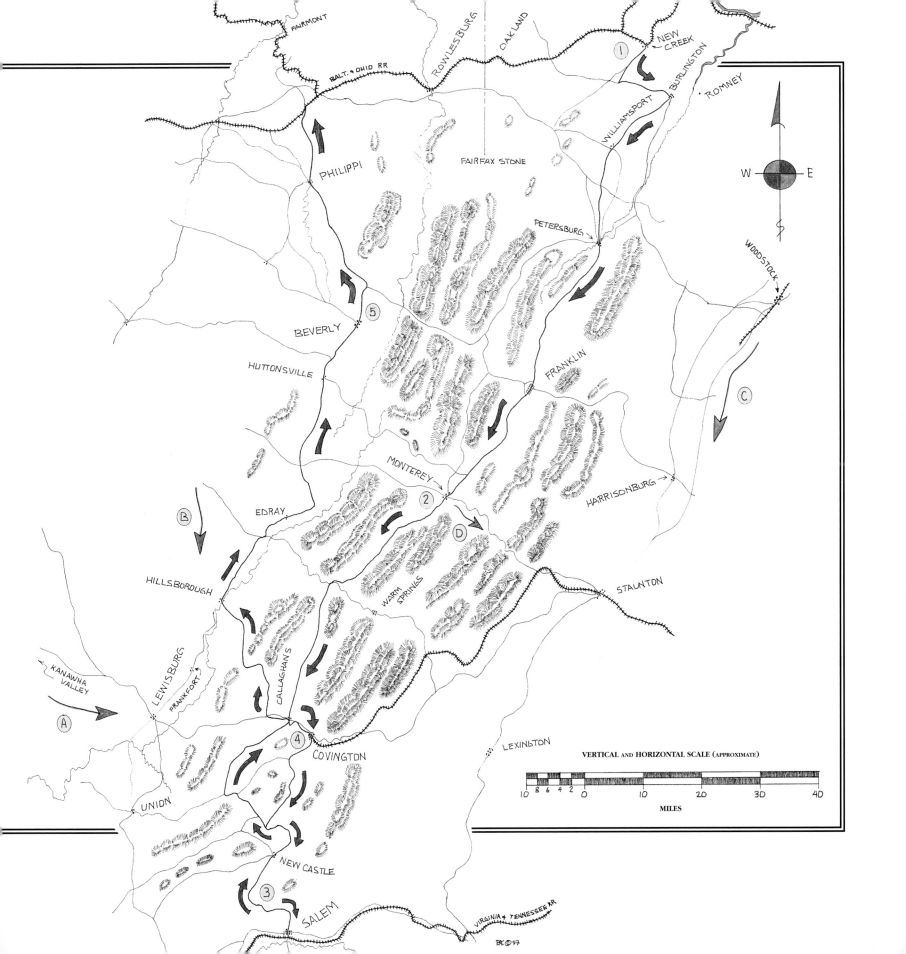

AVERELL'S DECEMBER RAID

side of the river to provide security as their wagons and ambulances crossed, but these were trapped when the Union commander ordered the bridges burned. Averell ordered the trapped regiment to swim their horses across the freezing, ice-filled river after destroying the wagons; four men drowned. A night attack against the regiment before the escape had cost the lives of five officers and 119 men.

Due to confused orders from General Kelley, the regiments that had been placed earlier into positions from which they would have been able to support Averell's retreat were no longer there. Nearly trapped, the Union column was nevertheless able to ride over obscure roads and trails to the Greenbrier River Valley, just inside the eastern boundary of West Virginia, as they continued north toward their base areas.

Averell's report illustrates best the conditions faced by his men:

> *On the way to Edray my rear guard experienced some trifling attacks on the 22nd. The road thence to Beverly was a glacier... traversed with great difficulty and peril. The artillery was drawn almost entirely by dismounted men during the 23rd and 24th. Couriers had been sent forward to Beverly to bring out subsistence and forage, which we succeeded, after*

Averell (second from left), and his officers developed an excellent plan of attack against a critical transportation route, the Virginia and Tennessee Railroad, which connected Virginia with the western theater of operation. Averell led bold cavalry raids against Confederate units and targets—at one stroke at Moorefield, West Virginia, he nearly eliminated Jubal Early's cavalry as an effective fighting force—but he was later relieved by Philip Sheridan, possibly to make room for a rival commander, Torbert. This photograph was taken during McClellan's Peninsula Campaign.

> *extreme hardships, in meeting on the 24th.*
>
> *The officers and men undertook all that was required of them, and endured all the sufferings from fatigue, hunger, and cold with extraordinary fortitude, even with cheerfulness. The march of 400 miles [644km], which was concluded at Beverly, was the most difficult I have ever seen performed.*

The raid across the entire length of the new Union state, West Virginia, by twenty-five hundred Union soldiers had been more successful than anyone had ever hoped when the excursion into Confederate territory was ordered. Averell, through skillful planning and the careful deployment of his scouts, had managed to ride deeply into hostile territory for two weeks to destroy a major Confederate depot and disrupt a primary railroad communications route between Virginia and Tennessee. He lost relatively few men on the freezing trip, and his men were soon to receive the thanks of a grateful government. Secretary of War Edwin M. Stanton ordered that all the men on the raid be provided new suits, gratis, to replace those ruined by the rigors of the long trip.

With Averell's successful raid, the Union army had come a long way from James J. Andrews' failed raid on a similar railroad target early in the previous year.

Grierson's Raid

An unlikely leader was finding his true vocation during the early part of the Civil War. Benjamin H. Grierson had been making his living as a musician and a music teacher when the war erupted; when he was assigned to the cavalry, he objected vigorously. He had been kicked by a pony as a child, hated horses, and desired nothing more than service far away from them. Nevertheless, the unlikely cavalry commander learned his trade as well as anyone else in the Union army, and he was soon recognized as a superb cavalry commander.

During the early spring of 1863, Ulysses S. Grant was in the process of developing his attacks against the Confederate strong point, Vicksburg, the last major obstacle preventing the Union from grasping total control of the length of the Mississippi River. Union control of the river would effectively split the Confederacy into two isolated sections. Defending against this major campaign was the Confederacy's General John Pemberton and a force that outnumbered Grant's attackers. The plan was audacious and Grant was faced with the loss of his entire army if he failed.

Pemberton was responsible for the defense of a broad area and Grant took advantage of

Benjamin Grierson was an unlikely cavalry commander. A music teacher who hated horses, this Federal officer was soon to lead effective, well-planned raids into the Confederacy. During Grant's Vicksburg campaign, Grierson led a raid that crossed the entire breadth of the Confederacy as large Rebel units searched for him in all directions. His masterly use of deception prevented his apprehension and the destruction of his command.

this by sending out large forces to keep his Confederate opponent confused as to the true intentions of the Union army. Division-sized elements of Grant's army were dispatched to the north and northwest of Vicksburg, but Grant's most daring diversionary move would be a cavalry raid from La Grange, Tennessee, across Mississippi to link up with Federal forces in the vicinity of Baton Rouge, Louisiana. The commander chosen for the dangerous operation was Benjamin Grierson.

Grierson's orders were given as broadly as possible to allow him to modify his plan as needed as the military situation facing him changed. With the Union army positioned in west Tennessee and northern Louisiana, Grierson's raiding party would be able to disrupt the Confederate lines of communication—actually cutting the Confederacy temporarily in half—while leaving the Confederate army under Pemberton confused as to his intentions. Pemberton's staff planners would anticipate a deep strike into their territory before the raiding party would ride swiftly back into Tennessee. The Union plan assumed that Confederate forces would react to Grierson's presence by concentrating along his probable line of withdrawal rather than by attempting to cut

him off from his true destination, a link-up with Federal forces far to his south. The plan was good and the commander was brave and capable of completing it.

He was ordered to ride from La Grange, Tennessee, in a general southerly direction through Mississippi along a route that would allow him to strike at the region's two north-south railroads and permit the destruction of the major east-west railroad that connected Vicksburg with the eastern part of the Confederacy. The tactical goals of the raiding force included the burning of military supplies found along the route while they provoked reactions from local Confederate commanders—preventing them from concentrating against Grant.

Grierson and his seventeen hundred cavalrymen left their camps at La Grange on April 17 and moved south. They quickly encountered small groups of Confederate militia and regular soldiers who were easily brushed aside by the large Federal cavalry force. On the fourth day, Grierson used an excellent deception maneuver to throw his pursuers off of his trail. He sent a report back to his headquarters that outlined his intentions:

At 3 o'clock the next morning, April 20, I

detached 175 of the least effective portion of the command, with one gun of the battery and all the prisoners, led horses, and captured property, under the command of Major Love, of the Second Iowa, to proceed back to La Grange, marching in columns of four, before daylight, through Pontotoc, and thus leaving the impression that the whole command had returned.

Grierson had decided to confuse his pursuers. His "less effective portion of the command" included his sick and injured men who would slow his march as they moved south. These men, called the "Quinine Brigade" by the remaining cavalrymen, returned to Tennessee in a column that rode four abreast to make their numbers appear larger than they actually were. The sick men were sent on the route that the Confederates assumed Grierson would be taking as he returned to the safety of La Grange and they quickly set off in pursuit—giving Grierson an additional ten hours' head start.

The following day, April 21, Grierson repeated his successful deception by sending another large group, an entire cavalry regiment—the 2nd Iowa Cavalry—off to the east toward

a Confederate base area before turning north to safety and Tennessee. Grierson reported:

The following morning at 6 o'clock I resumed the march southward, and about 8 o'clock came to the road leading southeast to Columbus, Miss. Here I detached Colonel Hatch, with the Second Iowa Cavalry and one gun of the battery, with orders to proceed to the Mobile and Ohio Railroad in the vicinity of West Point, and destroy the road and wires; thence move south, destroying the railroad and all public property as far south, if possible, as Macon; thence across the railroad, making a circuit northward; if practicable, take Columbus and destroy all Government works in that place, and again strike the railroad south of Okolona, and, destroying it, return to La Grange by the most practicable route.

Colonel Hatch and his 2nd Iowa Cavalry had to make a fast march of 175 miles (282km) before they reached La Grange, but Grierson's ruse worked flawlessly. Hatch was pursued closely by the only major Confederate force in the area and Grierson continued to move south as his Confederate pursuers marched north after Hatch and his Iowa cavalrymen, believing that this was the entire Federal raiding force. Hatch actually outnumbered those in pursuit and could have defeated them in open battle, but he merely engaged in a fighting withdrawal in order to continue the illusion that the entire force was returning to La Grange.

Remaining unchallenged, Grierson continued on his march deep into Southern territory. He had developed a very effective scouting capability and his scouts, dressed in Confederate uniform and subject to execution as spies if captured, moved freely to Grierson's front and flanks as they rode swiftly to capture strategic points prior to the arrival of the Federal main body. They captured bridges before they could be destroyed and scouted for the presence of the enemy before Grierson could be attacked by larger forces that could possibly eliminate his raiders.

Colonel Grierson was actively sending out small parties in several directions to deceive the Confederates as to his real intentions. On April 22, he sent thirty-five men of the 7th Illinois Cavalry to the east toward the town of Macon to destroy telegraph lines there.

He made careful use of all of the assets at his disposal, occasionally relying on single brave scouts:

I sent a single scout, disguised as a citizen, to proceed northward to the line of the Southern Railroad, cut the telegraph, and, if possible, fire a bridge or trestle-work. He started on his journey about midnight, and when within 7 miles [11km] of the railroad he came upon a regiment of Southern cavalry from Brandon, Miss., in search of us. He succeeded in misdirecting them as to the place where he had last seen us, and, having seen them well on the wrong road, he immediately retraced his steps to camp with the news. When he first met them they were on the direct road to our camp, and had they not been turned from their course would have come up with us before daylight.

Grierson had been saved by the actions of a single brave man who would have been hanged had it been discovered that he was a Union soldier in civilian clothing. The oncoming Confederates would have caught Grierson's command

"before daylight" in their night camps and would have decimated the Union soldiers.

The remainder of Grierson's "Butternut Guerrillas" moved in advance of the regular troops and entered the town of Newton Station on April 24. Disguised as Confederates, they were able to learn that there were two trains due to arrive at the strategic town and one of them, a freight train bound for Vicksburg and loaded with supplies for the garrison there, was captured as it pulled on to a siding. Grierson soon ordered his men to burn all of the military supplies, and destroy as much track as possible. Grierson further ordered that two captured locomotives be blown up. The commander described the scene in his report:

Lieutenant-Colonel Blackburn dashed into the town, took possession of the railroad and telegraph, and succeeded in capturing two trains in less than half an hour after his arrival. One of these, 25 cars, was loaded with ties and machinery, and the other 13 cars were loaded with commissary stores and ammunition, among the latter several thousand loaded shells. These, together with a large

quantity of commissary and quartermaster's stores and about five hundred stand of arms stored in the town, were destroyed. Seventy-five prisoners captured at this point were paroled. The locomotives were exploded and otherwise rendered completely unserviceable. Here the track was torn up, and a bridge half a mile west of the station destroyed.

By early afternoon, his command was back in the saddle and moving west.

It was at this time that Confederate General Pemberton began to take Grierson seriously and he sent units throughout the region to trap him—just as Grant had hoped when the raid was ordered. The overall tactical picture, however, was muddied by the presence and actions taken by the independent commands sent out from Grierson's column. Colonel Hatch was still moving back toward La Grange, Tennessee, and the thirty-five men of the 7th Illinois Cavalry were still in the vicinity of Macon and confused the situation for the Confederates.

Grierson and the main column continued to move westward as Colonel Hatch retreated slowly back to Tennessee and the men of the 7th Illinois attempted to locate and rejoin the main force. By April 27, the small detachment had found Grierson, and Hatch had reached safety in Tennessee, but the Union commander knew that time was running out for his command. They were deep within enemy territory, exhausted from riding thirty-five miles (56km) each day, and living off the land. They were within fifty miles of their planned destination, Grand Gulf, a town on the Mississippi River that Grant had planned to use for an amphibious landing, but there were no indications that the landing had actually happened. There were no rumors, refugees, or prisoner reports of any Federal landing in the vicinity, and Grierson was concerned that he could lose his entire force by capture. He wrote in his report:

> *Hearing nothing more of our forces at Grand Gulf, I concluded to make for Baton Rouge to recruit my command, after which I could return to La Grange, through Southern Mississippi and Western Alabama; or, crossing the Mississippi River, move through Louisiana and Arkansas.*

He had taken the decision to make his escape, but the safety of Baton Rouge was still 150 miles (241km) away. His worn-

Kicked by a pony as a child, Benjamin Grierson feared horses as much as he disliked them. Fate, however, had placed him in the Federal cavalry, and Grierson soon developed himself into a dashing, able cavalry commander in the western theater of operations. His raid across Mississippi left General Pemberton, the Confederate commander at Vicksburg, confused about Grant's intentions until it was too late for Pemberton to concentrate Confederate forces against him.

out men and their horses were suffering from the extended march they had been forced to make, although they replaced their mounts from local sources whenever they had an opportunity. But they had managed to avoid any direct combat with the Confederate forces that were spreading throughout the region to trap them. After two full weeks in the saddle, Grierson ran into trouble on May 1 at a bridge guarded by Louisiana Partisan Rangers and suffered five men wounded and an additional five men captured. Grierson was forced to leave his wounded men behind at a local plantation as he continued the retreat. Confederate forces in large numbers were swarming in the area and he and his exhausted regiments had to continue riding if they were to reach safety. They rode all night, many of the men so exhausted that they had to tie themselves to their saddles to remain mounted, but they arrived within four miles (6.5km) of the Union lines at Baton Rouge the following day, where the men were allowed to stop for rest. They had successfully pulled off a daring and ambitious raid across the width of the Confederacy.

Grierson described the results of his raid:

These two historic photographs were taken by a Confederate secret agent, Lytle, within minutes of one another. They show Grierson's command safely arrived at Baton Rouge, Louisiana, after an epic raid that covered 600 miles (965 km) through hostile territory over a period of sixteen days. The photograph on the left was taken first.

During the expedition we killed and wounded about 100 of the enemy, captured and paroled over 500 prisoners, many of them officers, destroyed between 50 [80km] and 60 miles [97km] of railroad and telegraph, captured and destroyed over 3,000 stand of arms, and other army stores and Government property to an immense amount; we also captured 1,000 horses and mules.

Our loss during the entire journey was 3 killed, 7 wounded, 5 left on the route sick; the sergeant-major and surgeon of the Seventh Illinois left with Lieutenant-Colonel Blackburn, and 9 men missing, supposed to have straggled. We marched over 600 miles [965km] in less than sixteen days. The last twenty-eight hours we marched 76 miles [122km], had four engagements with the enemy, and forded the Comite River, which was deep enough to swim many of the horses. During this time the men and horses were without food or rest.

chapter 18

A Gray Ghost Captures A General

T he Confederacy was blessed with men who had practically grown up in the saddle. For this reason, the South's cavalry was able to dominate its Federal counterpart during the first half of the Civil War. There were, however, many men who for a variety of reasons did not adjust well to the discipline and regimentation of the regular army. These rugged individualists were more than willing to ride deeply into Federal country at the head of a Partisan Ranger band and do battle behind their opponent's lines.

One of these men was John Singleton Mosby, a 125-pound (57kg) twenty-seven-year-old with a bad temper and a poor attitude toward his West Point commander, Fitzhugh Lee. Mosby had done well in the cavalry, rising from private to lieutenant in a short time, but the discipline of the regular

officers was too much for him. After he had incurred the wrath of Fitzhugh Lee for calling a bugle a horn, Mosby realized that his career opportunities within the First Virginia Cavalry could be limited. He resigned his commission, as officers were permitted to do, and volunteered to serve as a scout for Jeb Stuart, the officer who had assisted Robert E. Lee with the resolution of John Brown's attack on Harpers Ferry.

As a scout, captured then released shortly after, Mosby demonstrated to his superior officers that he was quite capable of collecting intelligence on enemy activities. This ability, combined with his desire for independent duty far from senior officers, convinced Stuart that Mosby and nine men should be left in northern Virginia to begin operations as a Partisan Ranger in December 1862.

"In one sense the charge that I did not fight fair is true. I fought for success and not for display. There was no man in the Confederate army who had less of the spirit of knight-errantry in him, or who took a more practical view of war than I did."

—John Singleton Mosby

PAGE 291: John Singleton Mosby, photographed in 1863 at the height of his activities against the Union army, bears himself with the confidence of a soldier at the peak of his skills. He was the commander of a battalion of accomplished Confederate cavalrymen who had carried the war into the previously secure rear areas of the Union forces, in the immediate vicinity of Washington, D.C. Early in Mosby's guerrilla career, he planned a raid with the goal of capturing a British officer, Percy Wyndham (left), who had belittled him publicly. Wyndham was absent, but with the assistance of a Union army deserter, Mosby was able to capture Brigadier General Edwin H. Stoughton, the youngest general in the Union army. It was Mosby's inability to adapt to the military discipline demanded by West Point graduate Fitzhugh Lee (above) that led the future raider to independent service. Lee, demanding strict adherence to all traditions and customs of military life, became angry when he heard Mosby call a bugle a "horn."

A GRAY GHOST CAPTURES A GENERAL

John Mosby and a few of the men who served with him in the 43rd Battalion of Partisan Rangers. Most of his men lived in Loudoun County, Virginia, the area where the majority of their operations were conducted, and they all received support and intelligence on enemy activities from a network of friends and relatives spread throughout the region.

Mosby's achievements were such that by the middle of January, he was attracting unwanted attention from Union commanders in the area. His swift, silent raids on isolated sentry positions had netted twenty-two prisoners in a very short period. In response to this new challenge, Colonel Percy Wyndham, an experienced British soldier of fortune, began sending large forces into the area in an effort to locate and eliminate the disruptive guerrilla force.

"No human being knows how sweet sleep is but a soldier."

—*John Singleton Mosby*

An odd feud between the partisan leader and the former soldier of fortune began when the frustrated Union colonel was told by paroled prisoners that the man who had captured them had sent a verbal message. The Union horsemen were advised that if they weren't better armed and equipped, it wouldn't pay to capture them.

Mosby had been scouting the region around the Federal camps near Fairfax, Virginia, for some time. In his efforts, he was

John Singleton Mosby enjoyed posing for photographs during the war. This was taken in Richmond in January 1863, and a note on a print written later by Mosby states, "The uniform is the one I wore on March 8th, 1863 on the night of General Stoughton's capture."

each rider was armed with a saber and two pistols when captured.

The personal feud between these two enemies became more personal as Mosby's raids continued and Wyndham found that he was unable to halt them. In early March, Mosby captured another nineteen officers and men near Middleburg, and the newspapers let out a howl of protest over the poor management of the cavalry that permitted these disasters to continue.

Mosby, aided by a recent deserter from the 1st New York Cavalry—"Big Yank" Ames, who had deserted from his regiment over the Emancipation Proclamation—approached the sleeping village where Percy Wyndham was living. Mosby and twenty-nine of his men decided to make a night call on the outspoken Englishman who had challenged them from a distance.

Nearby, there was a house where the commander of the 2nd Vermont Brigade, Edwin H. Stoughton, slept after a late party. Stoughton had recently become the youngest

general officer in Federal service at the age of twenty-four; the Vermont native, a member of a wealthy family, was a West Point graduate. Unfortunately, he enjoyed entertaining the ladies—one twenty-year-old woman had been quartered in a well-guarded tent located near Stoughton's headquarters—and this night had been special. His mother and sister were visiting from Vermont and had attended an evening champagne party planned for the occasion. All of Stoughton's officers had been there and the pleasant night had been enjoyed by all.

Colonel Wyndham, the recipient of only bad luck since Mosby had been left in his area of responsibility by Stuart the previous December, was finally to be lucky. He had been summoned unexpectedly to Washington and, with regrets, missed Stoughton's party.

Late in the night, as the last of the revelers had departed to their homes and quarters, riders approached the single sentry who was slowly patrolling in the small town. With the enemy at least twenty-five miles (40km)

aided by a young woman, Antonia Ford, the daughter of a local merchant whose brother was serving in the artillery. Mosby disguised himself as a citizen and remained in the Ford home for three nights as they collected information on the enemy.

After reporting to Stuart that the Federal cavalry was isolated from the rest of the Union army at Fairfax and vulnerable to attack, Stuart urged that an attempt be made to capture Wyndham. Late in February, Mosby, with twenty-six men, was able to capture an outpost of forty Union cavalrymen and their horses, an act that infuriated the already frustrated Wyndham. He continued the verbal feud with the partisan leader by publicly denouncing him as an ordinary horse thief. Mosby responded to the charge by dryly noting that all of the horses he had stolen had riders to go with them, and that

Mosby and his men seemed to be everywhere and the large section of northern Virginia where they operated most frequently became known—especially among Union soldiers—as Mosby's Confederacy.

Mosby and his men became a painful thorn in the side of the Union army in northern Virginia. Long rides, sudden attacks, and swift withdrawals became the hallmarks of these Confederate Partisan Rangers as they sabotaged the Union army's lines of communication.

A GRAY GHOST CAPTURES A GENERAL

A Gray Ghost Captures a General

ABOVE: Fairfax Court House, Virginia, photographed in June 1863. It was in this small town that General Stoughton had decided to host a champagne party—at the time of Mosby's arrival, Stoughton was sleeping off the effects of his party in a bedroom. LEFT: Mosby and his raiders struck swiftly, without warning, and frequently escaped without losses. Lonely outposts were normally their targets, but they often raided against Federal supply lines. Careful scouting operations ensured successful attacks.

away and roads that were bottomless mud holes, the picket didn't bother to sound an alarm. These lonely riders had to be returning Union cavalrymen. Slowly, they split into smaller groups; one went to the telegrapher's tent while another rode directly to the lonely picket, surprising him by brandishing pistols directly in his face. One group rode to the house where their English quarry was reported to be sleeping.

Stoughton's aide opened the door of his residence when the men outside announced that dispatches had arrived for the general. He was more than mildly surprised when a short man with a plume in his hat shoved a pistol into his chest and hushed him. Immediately afterward, John Mosby was inside Stoughton's bedroom, where he raised

the nightshirt of the sleeping general and whacked him across the rear to awaken him.

More than a little confused, Stoughton asked Mosby if Fitzhugh Lee was present. Lying behind a smile, Mosby said that his former senior officer was there. Stoughton asked to be taken to him as "I knew him at West Point."

Mosby had missed his intended target, Colonel Wyndham, but he had captured a brigadier general instead. The total yield from Fairfax Court House was larger than anticipated: the raiders left with a brigadier general, two captains, thirty privates, and fifty-eight horses.

When advised of the results of the raid, President Lincoln came out with one of his more memorable statements on the war:

"Well, I'm sorry for that. I can make new brigadier generals, but I can't make horses."

Antonia Ford, Mosby's co-conspirator within the Union camp, was soon arrested for her complicity in the raid, and she spent months in a Federal prison. Subsisting on a diet of rice and poor-quality meat, she was pale and thin by the time she was sent through the lines to Richmond. A year and a day after the successful raid, she married Major Joseph Willard, a Union officer who had been quartered in her home early in the war, but she was dead within seven years, possibly a victim of the poor diet she had lived on while in prison.

Mosby continued his active military career for the remainder of the Civil War. By late spring, he had attacked a train delivering supplies for Joseph Hooker's army that was located to the north of the Rappahannock River, and fought a major battle with an overwhelming force of Union cavalry. The partisans escaped after fierce hand-to-hand combat with their pursuers and enjoyed the supplies looted from the train. The men had done such a good job fighting behind the enemy's lines that the Confederate War Department officially designated them the "43rd Battalion of Virginia Cavalry" on June 10, 1863.

The men of the 43rd Battalion continued their fight against the Union army, striking where they were least expected. They were in near-constant motion and their success was noticed by both General Lee and the Confederate War Department. Lee wrote that in the previous six months Mosby had killed, wounded, or captured twelve hundred Federals and had taken more than sixteen hundred horses and mules, 230 head of cattle, and eighty-five wagons and ambulances.

Mosby and his men continued to conduct successful operations even as the Confederate Congress ordered all of the Partisan Ranger companies disbanded. They

"It is just as legitimate to fight an enemy in the rear as in the front. The only difference is in the danger."

—*John Singleton Mosby*

had become havens for able-bodied men seeking to avoid the draft, and as often as not, they would rob Confederate citizens as readily as they would Union sympathizers. Only the 43rd Battalion of John Mosby and the men serving to the west under Hanse McNeil were exempt from the order to disband.

Some of Mosby's major operations included attacks against the Federal crews seeking to repair the Manassas Gap Railroad, a supply line that, when opened, would have permitted General Sheridan to move south toward the vital railroads that passed through Charlottesville. In early October 1864, guerrilla raids resulted in derailed and wrecked trains and captured Union guards. Repairs to the line were never completed. By the middle of October, the raiders had set an ambush for another train, this time on the vulnerable B&O. After loosening a rail from its cross ties, the men settled down to rest, but were roused by a loud explosion from a rupturing steam-engine boiler. They captured an army payroll that was on the train, and Mosby's men rode from the scene with $170,000 in Federal greenbacks.

Speedy riders and good intelligence collected from supporters and family members living within their area of operations enabled Mosby's men to engage in sudden attacks that were especially dreaded by Union soldiers. They knew Mosby seldom struck without a high probability of success.

A GRAY GHOST CAPTURES A GENERAL

Mosby nearly died of wounds that he sustained when a Union cavalry patrol fired at him through a window in a house where he had stopped to have a late dinner with friends one December evening. Quickly removing his officer's insignia, he lay on the floor—bleeding from what should have been fatal injuries—and gave a false name to the officer who came to interrogate him. Left to die, Mosby nevertheless recovered and continued his activities for the remainder of the Civil War.

He disbanded his men at Salem and they went their different ways. The battalion had suffered severe casualties. Somewhere between 35 to 40 percent of the command was killed, wounded, or captured during the war. Eighty-five of the men were either killed or mortally wounded, or were executed when captured by their enemies. More than one hundred men were wounded in combat and another 477 were captured.

After the war, Mosby was denied the opportunity to surrender, and lived as a fugitive. He evaded capture for nearly two months by hiding near the homes of family members until he was paroled through the direct intervention of Grant at the end of June 1865. He resumed his law practice at home with his family. He became friends with Grant, became a Republican and was condemned in the South for it, and was appointed to positions in the Federal government, including consul in Hong Kong for eight years. At the age of eighty-two in 1916, John Mosby died after a long, adventuresome life.

Confederate veterans, survivors of Mosby's 43rd Battalion of Partisan Rangers, were proud of their hazardous service and they met at reunions with family members.

"To destroy supply trains, to break up the means of conveying intelligence, and thus isolating an army from its base, as well as its different corps from each other, to confuse their plans by capturing despatches, are the objects of partisan war."

—John Singleton Mosby, 1887

Mosby survived the dangers of war, but he was initally refused the opportunity to surrender after Appomattox. General Grant intervened and Mosby was able to return to his law practice in Virginia. Mosby never forgot Grant's gallant act; he later became a Republican and served as U.S. consul in Hong Kong.

chapter 19

JONES' AND IMBODEN'S THIRTY DAY RAIDS

> "I have often thought that their fierce hostility to me was more on account of the sleep I made them lose than the number we killed and captured."
>
> —John Singleton Mosby

Large numbers of Union soldiers were about to lose a great deal of sleep as the spring campaign of 1863 opened in the mountainous region of what was then north-western Virginia, and today is part of West Virginia. This region of Virginia had fallen under the control of the Union army after the bumbling campaigns led by former Virginia governors Henry A. Wise and John B. Floyd in late 1861. Their personal feuding combined with their lack of military ability had resulted in a general evacuation from the strategic, resource-filled Kanawha Valley. Confederate General W.W. Loring's invasion of the region in September 1862 also failed when the fractious officer chose to ignore—or misunderstood—his orders, and after great initial successes his small army was forced to retreat from the area.

Local Unionists, backed by strong contingents of Federal soldiers, were encouraged sufficiently by Confederate failures in the region to form a "loyal" government as well as a "New State Movement." With a new government in the northern city of Wheeling, the Union supporters were close to the formation of their new state, West Virginia, which would be a major political victory for the hard-pressed federal government in Washington, D.C. The splitting of a major Confederate state, Virginia, would represent a political and moral victory for the national government at a time when it was sorely needed.

The success of a raid into Federally controlled western Virginia would have several benefits for the Confederacy. First, the New State Movement would be shaken to its core

PAGE 303: John D. Imboden began the Civil War as an artillery officer and fought gallantly at Henry House Hill during the Battle of Bull Run. Soon, he was organizing the 1st Virginia Partisan Rangers, and commanding a full cavalry brigade. After the raid into western Virginia, he participated in Lee's Gettysburg Campaign by raiding along the Baltimore and Ohio Railroad, assisting with wagon-train escort duties, and fighting as part of the rear guard as the Confederate army withdrew from Pennsylvania. ABOVE: General William W. Loring had served in the Mexican War as a major, a conflict in which Robert E. Lee served as a captain. Loring's loss of an arm and his reputation as a warrior produced unrealistic expectations of success when he took the field. He led a successful invasion of the strategic Kanawha Valley in western Virginia during the summer of 1862, but he failed to hold the area for the Confederacy.

as the raiders moved at will through its territory—a demonstration of a capability that could be repeated at any time in the future. A new Federal state would not necessarily become a safe area for Unionists, and the raiders planned to show their Unionist enemies that there would be a price for their betrayal of Virginia. Second, the attackers intended to destroy as much of the property of the Baltimore and Ohio Railroad as was possible. The strategic rail system was the southernmost line of supply that linked the western Union states with the battlefields in the eastern theater, and its destruction would delay the arrival of supplies and reinforcements that would be detoured over railroads further to the north. Finally, the region to be invaded was a rich source of horses, cattle, general supplies, and, most important, new recruits who could be added to the rolls of the Confederate army.

Two experienced officers—William E. Jones, who was known as "Grumble" to his men, and John D. Imboden—would lead the two small armies that would operate independently for most of the incursion. From the time they left their camps, which were located just to the east of the mountainous region, on April 20, 1863, until they returned on May 22, their Union opponents would have little opportunity to catch up on the sleep they were missing. The Union force garrisoning western Virginia was spread thinly in several isolated outposts, and reinforcements were slow to be ordered to march to the assistance of threatened points. A general panic had seized the Union commanders as Jones and Imboden began their independent marches. Swift movement—even by the largely infantry and dismounted cavalry forces of the Confederates—confused the Federal commanders, and each key point felt threatened. The overall commander in the area, Brigadier General Benjamin S. Roberts, was unable to order his scattered men to

concentrate at a single location to face the raiders in a decisive battle. Each small, isolated detachment of Union soldiers had to face the raiders alone, and the raiders appeared to be everywhere simultaneously.

Imboden was the first to move. He marched his invading force out of his camp on Shenandoah Mountain on April 20, the day before Jones' planned departure. This force, made up chiefly of infantrymen, would naturally be expected to move slower. It was composed of the 22nd, 25th, 31st, and 62nd Virginia infantries, the 18th and 19th regiments, the 37th Battalion, some Virginia Cavalry, and McClanahan's Battery. The total force was 3,365 men and six guns, but only seven hundred of the cavalrymen were mounted. The remainder were expected to obtain mounts during the raid by either capture or purchase.

The first four days of the long march were among the worst as the tired men struggled forward along the Parkersburg pike's and Staunton Turnpike's soaked roads during drenching rainstorms. They arrived at Huttonsville in the Tygarts Valley after the first seventy miles (113km), where within only a few miles the first major Federal garrison, at Beverly—the 2nd West Virginia Infantry Regiment and a few soldiers from the 8th West Virginia, in all about nine hundred men—waited in complete ignorance of the Confederate army that was advancing against them.

Imboden ordered an attack on April 24. The surprised Federal soldiers put up a stiff resistance. They were able to hold out until late in the evening, when their commander, Colonel Latham of the 2nd West Virginia, ordered a retreat toward Philippi, the location of the first land battle of the war, after ordering that fire be set to all government supplies that could not be easily moved. Part of the town was unfortunately burned as well, but Latham's men escaped. Imboden ordered a cavalry pursuit, and the retreating Federal soldiers were chased for only a short distance. There were few casualties in this first skirmish of the extended incursion: no one was killed and only a few men received wounds.

"Grumble" Jones ordered his small army from its camp at Lacey Springs, Virginia, on April 21. His force was composed of the 7th, 11th, and 12th Virginia Cavalry regiments and White's, Brown's, and Witcher's cavalry battalions. Jones had a few small infantry units and artillery attached to his force. They arrived at Moorefield in West Virginia's Hardy County and found that the south branch of the Potomac River was so swollen by the recent spring rains that they could not cross. After ordering his infantry and artillery support back to their base areas in the Shenandoah Valley, Jones led his column south to Petersburg, where they were able to cross the dangerous river.

The following day, Jones took a side road that would take his men to the Northwestern Turnpike, where they could travel quickly to their selected targets. Once they entered Greenland Gap, a force of eighty men from the 23rd Illinois and the 14th West Virginia Infantry regiments disputed their passage. The greatly outnumbered Union soldiers took cover in a log church and house, and a brisk but hopeless fight ensued. In a short time, the defenders were forced to surrender after two of their men were killed and several wounded. Jones had lost four men; ten were wounded.

When the Confederate raiders began to be reported over a broad region in western Virginia, the Union's commander in the region, General Benjamin Roberts, was unable to concentrate his widely dispersed men at a single point to face them. Unable to react, Roberts and his men were forced to remain in place to face Jones' or Imboden's attacks alone.

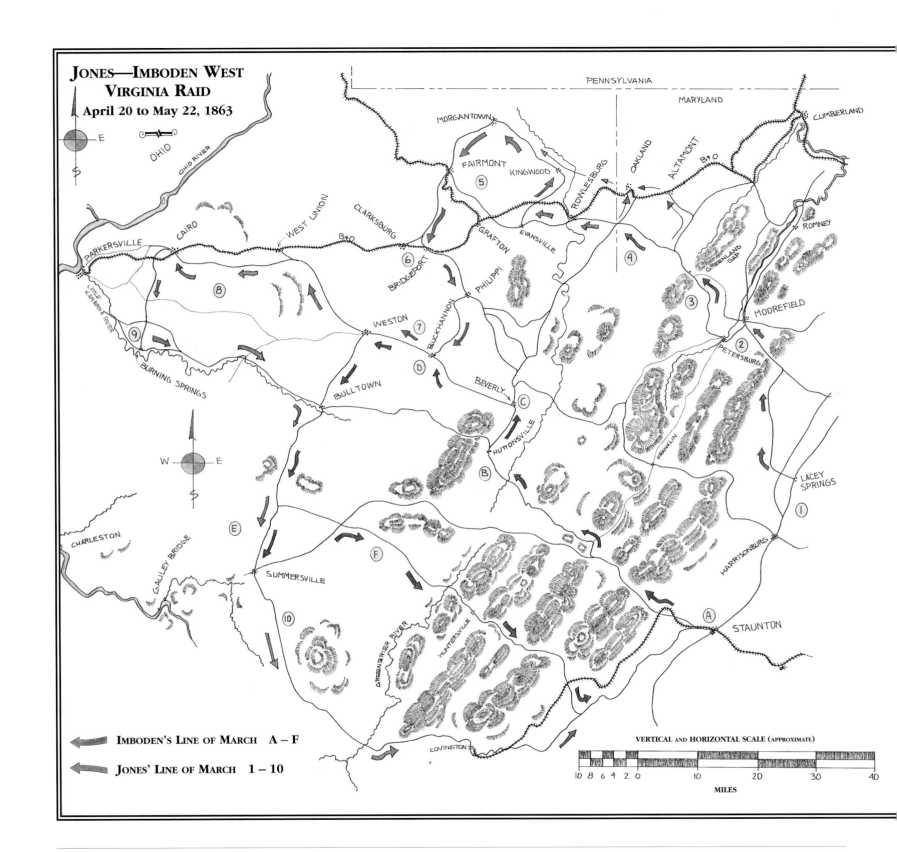

JONES—IMBODEN WEST VIRGINIA RAID
April 20 to May 22, 1863

PENNSYLVANIA
MARYLAND
OHIO
OHIO RIVER

MORGANTOWN
CUMBERLAND
FAIRMONT
KINGWOOD
ROWLESBURG
OAKLAND
ALTAMONT
B+O

WEST UNION
CLARKSBURG
CAIRO
PARKERSVILLE
B+O
GRAFTON
EVANSVILLE
ROMNEY
GREENLAND GAP
MOOREFIELD

BRIDGEPORT
PHILIPPI
BUCKHANNON
PETERSBURG
WESTON
LITTLE KANAWHA RIVER
BURNING SPRINGS
BULLTOWN
BEVERLY
HUTTONSVILLE
FRANKLIN

LACEY SPRINGS

CHARLESTON
GAULEY BRIDGE
SUMMERSVILLE
GREENBRIER RIVER
HUNTERSVILLE
HARRISONBURG
STAUNTON

COVINGTON

IMBODEN'S LINE OF MARCH   A – F

JONES' LINE OF MARCH   1 – 10

VERTICAL AND HORIZONTAL SCALE (APPROXIMATE)

10 8 6 4 2 0   10   20   30   40
MILES

JONES' AND IMBODEN'S THIRTY DAY RAIDS

306

A. Imboden departed Staunton on April 20 en route to Beverly.

1. Jones departed Lacey Springs on April 21.

B. On April 23 Imboden's forces reached Huttonsville

2. Jones reached Moorefield on April 23. High water on the South Branch of the Potomac forced Jones to leave behind his infantry and artillery.

C. After a two-hour struggle Imboden captured Beverly on April 24.

3. On April 25 Union forces delayed Jones for over four hours at Greenland Gap.

4. Jones split his force into three sections. The main section went to Rowlesburg and two smaller sections went to Oakland and Altamont. On April 26 Jones failed to capture Rowlesburg and marched through Evansville and Kingwood to Morgantown. On April 28 the Oakland and Altamont groups rejoined Jones near Fairmont.

D. On April 28 Imboden occupied Buckhannon and waited for Jones.

5. On April 29 Jones attacked Union forces at Fairmont and destroyed the suspension bridge over the Monongahela.

6. On April 30 Jones captured a company of Federal soldiers at Bridgeport. May 1 he passed through Philippi.

7. On May 2 Jones rejoined Imboden at Buckhannon. Both then moved to Weston. On May 6 Jones headed northwest toward Parkersville.

8. Part of Jones' force attacked West Union while the other damaged a rail tunnel and burned bridges at Cairo.

9. On May 9, Jones burned the oil fields at Burning Springs along the Little Kanawha River.

10. Jones rejoined Imboden on April 14 at Summersville. Both agreed little more could be accomplished and returned to the Shenandoah via seperate routes; Jones through Lewisburg and Covington.

E. Imboden went south to Summersville, captured a Union wagon train, and waited for Jones.

F. Imboden returned through Huntersville.

Very real danger lay in wait for the solitary courier. Raiders would often ambush or sweep up as captives unfortunate soldiers assigned to this perilous and unpleasant duty.

As they ascended into the high, freezing mountain, Jones began to send selected detachments to destroy their targets. Colonel Harman's group, composed of the 12th Virginia Cavalry, Brown's Maryland Battalion, and McNeil's Rangers, were sent to cut the telegraph wires and destroy the railroad bridges at Oakland before marching west to rejoin the main column at Morgantown. Others were sent to burn railroad bridges twelve miles (19km) east of Oakland. The widely spread detachments made Jones' column appear larger than it actually was and panic spread throughout the region.

Harman rode along the Pennsylvania border, spreading panic as he went, and he entered Morgantown during the afternoon of April 27. After a short occupation of the town, they left and rejoined Jones, but the entire force returned to Morgantown again at noon on April 28. Many of the men who had fled the town with their horses returned only to lose their mounts to the invaders. The men were on their best behavior and guards were posted at local saloons to ensure that they remained sober. They left Morgantown after dark and rode south to Fairmont.

Gaining the opposite side of the town before the Federal garrison could retreat, the Southern cavalry was soon charging through the streets. The few soldiers assigned there, 260 of them, were soon secured as prisoners and the town was occupied. A train loaded with troops and artillery arrived from nearby Grafton, but these were held at bay while Jones' engineers prepared to destroy a very expensive target: the iron bridge over the Monongahela River.

This structure, the most expensive bridge on the entire railroad (it cost nearly half a million dollars to build), was 615 feet (187.5m) long and supported by tubular columns of cast iron resting on stone piers in the river. The engineers poured black powder into the hollow tubular structures and ignited fuses, but the large explosions did no damage to the large bridge. Jones ordered that the wooden parts of the bridge be burned. After this was done, a final attempt with black powder was tried, and by nightfall the last spans of the expensive structure lay in the water.

At this time, Jones headed east and marched directly at the large Union stronghold at Clarksburg, and turned only when his lead elements had struck the outer defenses. They struck hard at the railroad in the small town of Bridgeport, six miles (9.5km) from Clarksburg, and destroyed a train and all of the bridges and trestles they could locate nearby. Once this was accomplished Jones ordered a march toward Buckhannon, where he hoped to unite his force with that of Imboden.

Imboden had roamed through the region slowly, scouring the territory for supplies and horses for his command to take back to Virginia. He entered Buckhannon on April 29 while Jones was busily blasting away at the long bridge at Fairmont, and he waited for Jones' arrival. After a short period of rest, the commanders decided to call off their planned attack against Clarksburg, as the garrison had been reinforced, and Imboden was sent south toward Summersville with the wagon trains and captured livestock. Jones would continue operations against the railroad while attracting attention to his cavalrymen as Imboden's infantry marched slowly in the direction of safety.

Harman and his large detached force destroyed two bridges in the vicinity of West Union and captured ninety soldiers in the

While en route to a new assignment before the war, Confederate William E. Jones lost his wife when a huge wave swept her overboard. The loss deeply affected Jones, who was easily angered and became known as "Grumble" to his men. He served the Confederacy well until his own death during the Battle of Piedmont in 1864.

process of occupying the town. Jones moved farther toward the end of the B&O, to the Ohio River city of Parkersburg, but after receiving reports that the city had been reinforced by Ohio troops, he drew back from the planned attack there. In the vicinity of the small town of Cairo, his men leisurely burned three additional railroad bridges and destroyed a tunnel by filling it with cribbed wood and setting the wood on fire. The heat of the intense fires damaged the tunnel's roof and it caved in, blocking it from future train use for some time.

Immediately afterward, Jones marched his small army to Oiltown, the location of the Burning Springs oil field and the drilling operations there. On May 9, his soldiers completely smashed the field's drilling equip-

ment and set fire to the stored oil, destroying an oil refinery operation for the first time in warfare. Jones was elated with the damage he had created and wrote in his report:

All the oil, the tanks, barrels, engines for pumping, engine houses and wagons—in a word everything used for raising, holding, or sending it off was burned. The smoke is very dense and jet black. The boats, filled with oil in bulk, burst with a report almost equaling artillery, and spread the burning fluid over the river. Before night huge columns of ebon smoke marked the meanderings of the stream as far as the eye could reach. By dark the oil from the tanks on the burning creek had reached the river, and the whole stream became a sheet of fire. A burning river, carrying destruction to our merciless enemy, was a scene of magnificence that might well carry joy to every patriotic heart. Men of experience estimated the oil destroyed at 150,000 barrels.

Once they left the destruction of the oil field behind them, the Confederate column rode leisurely south until they reunited with Imboden on May 14 at Summersville. Imboden had chased the 91st Ohio Infantry and two companies of cavalry from the town during the evening of May 12, but Imboden's cavalry, commanded by his brother George, was able to capture the supply wagons belonging to the retreating Federal soldiers. Twenty-eight wagons filled with rations and supplies were a welcome addition to the scant food supplies that had been available to the Confederates for much of their march.

After a short period of rest, the soldiers of both columns made their way east through a wilderness area until they once again gained the relative safety of the Shenandoah

Valley. Jones and Imboden had achieved their purpose—and more.

As "Grumble" Jones reported to Lee:

In thirty days we marched nearly 700 miles [1,126km] through a rough and sterile country, gaining subsistence for man and horse by the way. At Greenland and Fairmont (and also at Bridgeport), we encountered enemy forces. We killed from 25 to 30 of the enemy, probably wounded three times as many, captured nearly 700 prisoners, with their small arms, and one piece of artillery, two trains of cars, burned 16 railroad bridges and one tunnel, 150,000 barrels of oil, many engines, and a large number of boats, tanks and barrels, bringing home with us about 1,000 cattle, and about 1,200 horses. Our entire loss was ten killed and 42 wounded, the missing not exceeding 15.

A very successful raid was concluded. Jones managed to divert large numbers of troops from their planned operations as the Union commanders scrambled to contain his movements. Fear was so great that two gunboats were sent up the Ohio River to Parkersburg to help contain Jones' regiments and prevent them from entering Ohio. Approximately twenty-five thousand Union troops were involved in actions designed to contain and engage Jones as he moved with relative impunity through western Virginia.

The Confederate commander's strategy of destroying the B&O at multiple points by burning bridges and destroying the tunnel made it difficult for Federal officers to concentrate their forces against Jones and Imboden at any single point. The additional tactic of dividing their men as they struck several targets simultaneously served to magnify their numbers in the view of their Union opponents. Reports of Jones' and Imboden's movements came from all quarters as panic only added false reports for the overall commander in the region, Benjamin F. Kelley, to consider.

Through leadership in the field and sheer audacity, Jones and Imboden had accomplished one of the boldest series of Confederate raids of the Civil War.

As the Union sought to counter the bold raids conducted by the Confederacy, Union cavalrymen began to appear in the field as Federal commanders. Cavalry units, with their speed and mobility, were best suited to such missions, and the Union army began to equip and deploy large cavalry elements to take on the Confederate raiders.

chapter 20

JOHN MORGAN RAIDS DEEPLY INTO THE UNION

> *"Having no fixed lines to guard or defined territory to hold, it was always my policy to elude the enemy when they came in search of me, and carry the war into their own camps."*
>
> —*John Singleton Mosby*

Cavalry raids were lightning strikes that often went deep into enemy territory in support of a larger army movement. Used as a diversionary tactic and part of an overall strategy, these raids could throw an enemy into confusion at a time when he most needed information about the plans and intentions of his opponent.

This was true during the summer of 1863 in Tennessee when Confederate General Braxton Bragg found himself vulnerable to well-executed simultaneous strikes by William S. Rosecrans from the direction of Murfreesboro and by Ambrose E. Burnside from the Ohio River. These blows were to fall on a weakened Bragg, as many of his men had been sent to reinforce Vicksburg, which was besieged by Grant and in danger of capture. In order to avoid a dual attack,

Bragg planned to fall back, withdrawing his forces to the vicinity of Chattanooga.

Bragg planned to cover his withdrawal by ordering Brigadier General John Hunt Morgan, an experienced raider, out on a raid into Kentucky with orders to destroy railroads, strike isolated Federal units, and threaten Louisville. The plan was well conceived, but it didn't fit Morgan's own plan. He wanted to go deeper into Federal territory by striking across the Ohio River, but Bragg wouldn't give his permission for the longer raid.

John Morgan had other ideas and decided to defy Bragg, an intention he kept to himself. He departed on his expedition on July 2, during Robert E. Lee's Gettysburg campaign, but there were no plans within the Confederacy to attempt to coordinate this raid with Lee's movements at Gettysburg.

Morgan departed from Burkesville, Kentucky, with 2,460 selected men from Kentucky and Tennessee regiments, which were divided into two brigades. One was commanded by Colonel Basil W. Duke, Morgan's brother-in-law, and the second was led by Colonel Adam Johnson. Scouts had been sent ahead all along the route to the Ohio River, where Morgan hoped to cross and then reenter Confederate territory by riding across West Virginia. The region was still disrupted by the Jones-Imboden Raid, and since Federal units were still reeling and disorganized, Morgan felt that he could traverse the region safely.

Once they crossed the Cumberland River at Burkesville, they sped across Kentucky and terrified the residents of Louisville but made no attempt to enter the city. The men he sent forward captured two riverboats, which were used to transport the entire command across the Ohio River at Brandenburg on July 8. The crossing was opposed by a Federal gunboat and Home Guards with a cannon located on the Indiana side of the river, but all of Morgan's men were safely across by midnight. Morgan made sure that

PAGE 311: John Hunt Morgan became a hero to the Kentuckians who supported the Confederacy. After organizing his Kentucky Rifles, he and his men slipped away from Lexington as Kentucky's neutrality came to an end. He raided successfully far and wide, but his effectiveness lessened after he married in 1862. Disobeying orders, he crossed the Ohio River on his great raid, but landed in a Federal prison at its conclusion. LEFT: General Braxton Bragg had served ably as an officer in the Mexican War and he enjoyed some success in the western theater of operations during the Civil War. His audacious invasion of Kentucky in 1862 was coordinated with Lee's movement into Maryland, but Bragg's efforts were overshadowed by Lee's battle at Antietam. Later, Bragg fought well at Chickamauga, but a series of errors resulted in significant losses.

none of his men would begin to think of returning to Kentucky: he had the boats burned behind them. They rode deep into Indiana with Federal cavalry in pursuit as infantry and Home Guard units marched about in attempts to block the raiders. Both Indiana and Ohio were up in arms, and every move Morgan made had to account for local defense units as Union army cavalry brigades closed in on his rear. Detachments were sent out to burn bridges in attempts to delay pursuit, to confuse Union pursuers as to their actual course, and to magnify, as much as possible, their numbers.

The night of July 13, Morgan swung past Cincinnati, actually transiting the outskirts of the city, but did no real damage—other than cause the townspeople considerable emotional distress. By July 18, his lead elements had reached the Ohio River near Buffington Island, where he planned his crossing. Not only was the selected ford guarded by Union troops, but high water had made any attempt at crossing dangerous, even by daylight. With the cavalry brigades and infantry units closing in from the rear, Morgan chose to fight instead of surrender.

Dense fog covered the area at first daylight, and in the engagement that developed the Union forces were supported by two gunboats that began shelling Morgan's positions. Under intense pressure, the Confederates began to break and Morgan lost his wagons, artillery, and several hundred of his men, all of them captured along with his brother-in-law, Colonel Duke.

RIGHT: *John Hunt Morgan's lightning-fast raids soon earned him the moniker "The Thunderbolt of the Confederacy," as Union forces were seldom able to predict where or when he would strike next. Careful scouting operations and well-planned, well-executed attacks made him one of the South's most feared raiders.*

RIGHT: *Basil Duke, Morgan's brother-in-law, was an excellent officer and strategist who was invaluable to Morgan in the planning of his raids. After Duke was captured at the conclusion of their raid across Ohio, Morgan became increasingly ineffective. It became obvious to many observers that Duke had played a pivotal role in Morgan's operations.*

MORGAN'S INDIANA AND OHIO RAID
July 2–26, 1863

1. On July 2 with 2,460 mounted troopers Morgan crossed the rain-swollen Cumberland River below Burkesville, Kentucky. After he brushed aside Union pickets that guarded the ford, he headed northward toward Columbia, Kentucky.

2. Union forces offered their first concentrated resistance near where Morgan had chosen to ford the Green River. Unable to dislodge the defenders, Morgan broke off the engagement, bypassed them, and headed toward Lebanon.

3. On July 8 Morgan crossed the Ohio River at Brandenburg in steamboats captured by his scouts the day before. Union pursuit forces arrived just as Morgan's rear guard crossed over the river.

4. At Corydon, Indiana, Morgan encountered and routed a force of 500 armed civilians. From this point on, Morgan was constantly ambushed by small groups of civilians and local militias.

5. On July 13 the raiders crossed over the Whitewater River into Ohio, and passed just to the north of Cincinnati.

6. On July 14 Morgan skirmished with a small force of ambulatory wounded Union soldiers at Camp Dennison, just east of Cincinnati. He then proceeded on to Williamsburg and rested his command for the first time since they entered Ohio.

7. A diversion and forage expedition led by Basil Duke split off from the main force of raiders and headed for the town of Ripley.

8. Union gunboats and pursuit forces attacked and captured many of Morgan's raiders as they attempted to cross the Ohio River at Buffington Island. Morgan and a few hundred raiders escaped the trap.

9. The surviving Raiders wandered west, then north through Ohio, toward Pennsylvania, clashing with Union pursuit forces and local militias.

10. Surrounded, Morgan and what was left of his command surrendered on July 26 near the town of Salineville, Ohio.

Morgan's raiders struck swiftly at their selected targets, like this attack on Washington, Ohio. The sudden appearance of Morgan's men struck terror into local defenders, who often fled or surrendered.

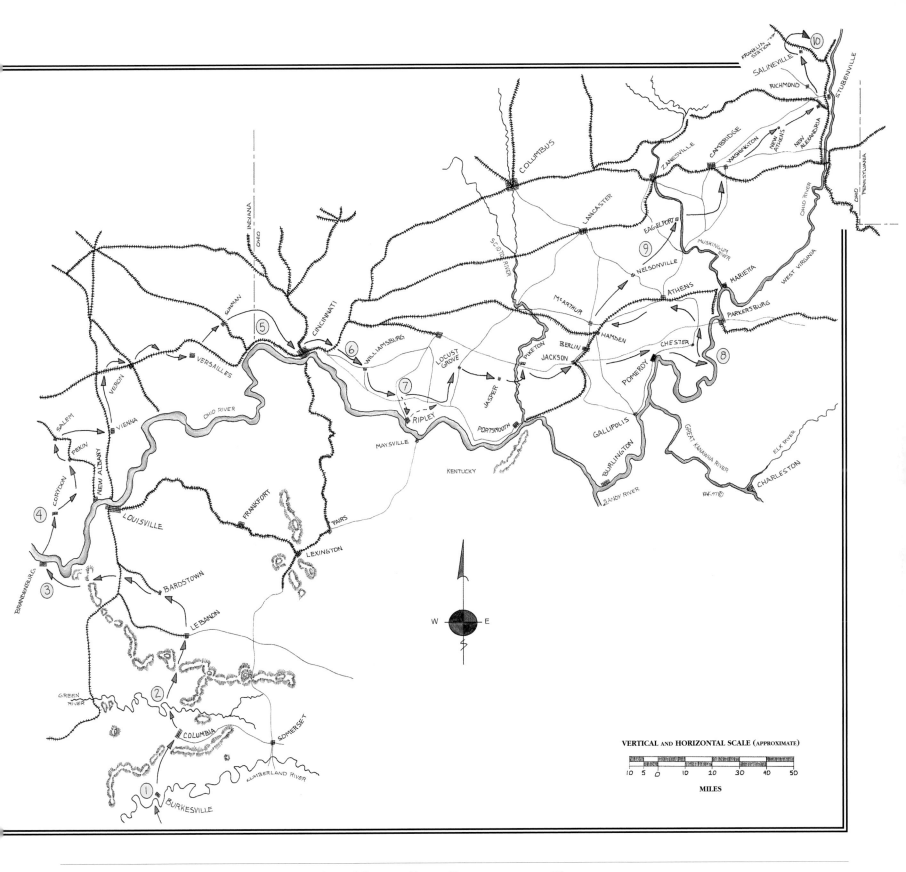

JOHN MORGAN RAIDS DEEPLY INTO THE UNION

315

JOHN MORGAN RAIDS DEEPLY INTO THE UNION

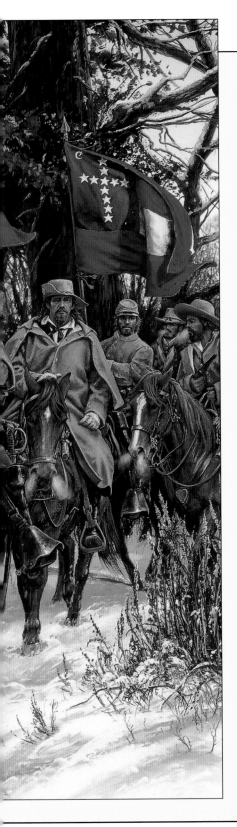

John Hunt Morgan's Career as a Raider

John Hunt Morgan gained his initial military experience during the Mexican War. Promoted to first lieutenant, he fought in the battle of Buena Vista. After the war, he returned to Kentucky, where he began a peacetime career as a businessman.

He had a successful career, but remained interested in military affairs. He organized the Kentucky Rifles in 1857, and they remained pro-Southern during the political crises that led to armed conflict. As Kentucky's attempts to remain neutral began to fail, he and his men slipped away from Lexington to join up with the Confederate army near Bowling Green, Kentucky, on September 20, 1861. They were forced to withdraw from Kentucky in early February, and Morgan was promoted to full colonel as a result of the raids he had led

John Hunt Morgan was an effective and courageous leader, but it is doubtful that he would have performed as well without the guidance of his brother-in-law, Basil Duke (marching beside him, at left) and his uncle, Thomas W. Hunt (behind him). The trio is depicted here leading over one thousand troops though the snow-covered hills of Tennessee in December 1862.

behind Federal lines. Morgan was a skilled raider who was in command of a group of brave, skillful riders, led by himself and disciplined by Basil W. Duke, his brother-in-law and second-in-command. The two men complemented each other—each supplied what was lacking in the other. They became expert at the hit-and-run tactics typical of the Confederate raiders.

Morgan's men included some flamboyant characters, like his wiretap specialist, George "Lightning" Ellsworth, who tapped into Union telegraph lines to gain intelligence on their plans, and George St. Leger Grenfell, a British soldier of fortune who soon became one of Morgan's favorites. Another of his men was Champ Furguson, a Kentucky guerrilla who had developed a habit of killing Union prisoners—a practice Morgan made him promise to discontinue before allowing him to join his force.

Morgan and his men were at Shiloh on April 6–7, 1862, and Morgan assisted with rear guard actions at the end of the battle. This was the only major battle in which he directly participated, but he developed his 2nd Kentucky Cavalry Regiment into an excellent raiding force. He was soon to use it at Tompkinsville on July 9, 1862, where he reported:

I was aware that a considerable body of cavalry, about 380 or 400 strong, were stationed at this town, and I thought by a rapid night march I might succeed in surprising them. I left the river at 10 P.M. on the 8th instant, and at 5 A.M. this day I surprised the enemy, and having surrounded them, threw four shells into their camp, and then carried it by a dashing charge. The enemy fled, leaving about 22 dead and 30 to 40 wounded in our hands. We have 30 prisoners and my Texas squadron are still in pursuit of the fugitives. Among the prisoners is Major Jordan, their commander, and two lieutenants. The tents, stores, and camp equipage I have destroyed, but a valuable baggage train, consisting of some 20 wagons and 50 mules, is in my possession; also some 40 cavalry horses, and supplies of sugar, coffee, &c. I did not lose a single man killed, but have to regret that Colonel Hunt, while leading a brilliant charge, received a severe wound in the leg.... I also had three members of the Texas squadron wounded, but not seriously.

He continued with his raiding in the region, reaching the telegraph line along the Louisville & Nashville north of Tompkinsville, where he tapped the telegraph line. "Lightning" Ellsworth sent out a flurry of phony messages. The messages alerted commanders throughout the Ohio Valley and produced panic in both Louisville and Cincinnati, potential targets of the raiders. Morgan kept the pressure on by riding swiftly to the banks of the Ohio River between Louisville and Cincinnati.

On July 17, Morgan struck at a lightly defended Federal depot in the town of Cynthiana, south of Cincinnati, and captured or drove off the defenders as frightened Federal commanders fired off messages in all directions requesting reinforcements. Morgan was on his way back to the safety of Tennessee before any reinforcements arrived. The results of the raid were impressive: Morgan's raiders had covered over 1,000 miles (1,609km) in three weeks, and captured 1,200 prisoners and seventeen towns as he delayed the Union army advance against Chattanooga.

He led another raid as a part of Braxton Bragg's invasion in late summer 1862. On August 12, Morgan captured the garrison at Gallatin, Tennessee, and burned the depot and train trestles before pushing wagons filled with hay into a long tunnel. The burning hay ignited the supporting timbers within the tunnel, cracked rocks, and caused the tunnel to collapse—creating a barrier that would require a major effort to clear.

Morgan missed the culminating battle of Bragg's campaign at Perryville, Kentucky, on October 8, 1862, as a tactical stalemate developed and Bragg was forced by his heavy casualties to retreat. The grand strategy of bringing Kentucky into the Confederacy by force was dropped after Perryville. Morgan moved back through Kentucky independently of Bragg's retreating army, but he was back in the field once again by December.

His command had been assigned to disrupt the Federal supply lines between Louisville and Nashville and he once again set off on an independent raid. After a grim winter march, Morgan and his troopers—with an infantry element attached—struck hard at the Federal defenders, two thousand strong, at Hartsville, and captured the entire garrison.

John Morgan married a seventeen-year-old beauty on December 12, the day after he was promoted to the rank of brigadier general, and the aggressive commander was off on another two-week raid into Kentucky. He struck hard at the Louisville & Nashville Railroad, destroying miles of track and millions of dollars worth of military supplies and capturing nearly two thousand prisoners.

At this time in his military career, however, his leadership ability began to be questioned. Once he was wed to the beautiful Mattie Ready, his attention was clearly distracted from military operations. He actually disobeyed his orders when he embarked on his great raid across Ohio, which landed him in the Ohio Penitentiary, but he and seven of his officers managed a spectacular escape on November 27, 1863, and he returned to duty.

Morgan's reputation had been severely damaged following that raid, which nearly destroyed his entire command. He quickly set off on another raid, this time into nearby Kentucky in an attempt to salvage what was left of his military career. Some of his men plundered private property during this raid and Morgan minimized their actions. Basil Duke was still in prison, and Morgan missed the excellent advice he had received from his brother-in-law and advisor in the past. His tendency to disobey orders began to alarm his superiors.

He attacked successfully once again at Cynthiana, Kentucky, on June 11, 1864, where he captured the 600 Federal defenders, but he broke the cardinal rule of the successful raider by remaining at the site of his attack overnight. Having time to react to his presence, a large Union force struck Morgan the next day, and he suffered severe casualties. He was soon transferred to command in eastern Tennessee and western Virginia, but the charges by his superior officers continued and Morgan was relieved of his duties on August 22, 1864.

Characteristically, Morgan ignored the order that relieved him and on his own led his men against a large Union force moving toward his positions. He was killed at Greenville, Tennessee, on September 4, 1864—one week before a court of inquiry was to convene to review his suspension.

OPPOSITE: Having lost his first wife just before going off to war, Morgan was attracted to the lovely Mattie Ready of Murfreesboro. After they were married in December 1862, Morgan's effectiveness as a combat commander began to decline. Many people attributed this to the distraction provided by his lovely new wife, although it is equally likely that his performance was affected by the departure of his brother-in-law and advisor, Basil Duke.

JOHN MORGAN RAIDS DEEPLY INTO THE UNION

Colonel Johnson and many of the men of his brigade were able to escape from the trap between the Union army on one side and the swollen Ohio River on the other. After an eighteen-mile (29km) ride upstream, they attempted to swim their mounts across to West Virginia; 280 men arrived safely. Several men drowned in the attempt to reach the shore, and General Morgan was in the middle of the stream when the arrival of a gunboat and its shelling forced him to return to the Ohio side of the river.

Johnson and the few survivors who made it across the Ohio River were helped by Confederate sympathizers along the river, but the arrival of West Virginia troops in the area forced them to move quickly into the interior of the new state. They evaded any further contact with Union troops in the area and were able to slowly cross the area to enter the safety of eastern Virginia.

Morgan and the survivors of the fight at Buffington Island were able to evade capture, but each day more men were lost. After a full week, Morgan and the rest of his men surrendered near East Liverpool, Ohio. He had led the Union army on quite a chase, but in the end, he lost most of his command without having accomplished a great deal.

Morgan was imprisoned in the Ohio Penitentiary at Columbus, along with sixty-eight officers from his command. On November 27, he and seven of his officers were able to escape from their cell through a tunnel they had laboriously dug over a period of twenty days with two small knives. After escaping, they separated and Morgan and Captain Thomas H. Hines calmly boarded a train in Columbus for Cincinnati, where they crossed into Kentucky. By December 5, Morgan and Hines were back in the vicinity of Burkesville and soon were able to link up with a part of Morgan's command that had not taken part in the disastrous raid. They crossed into Tennessee on December 13 but

OPPOSITE: Union newspapers and periodicals often carried illustrations of wartime events, such as this one titled "John Morgan's highwaymen sacking a peaceful village in the West," published in 1862. Such propaganda resulted in hardened attitudes toward Confederates, and captured raiders were normally condemned to state prisons—as were Morgan and those of his men who survived the raid across Ohio. ABOVE: Bold John Hunt Morgan was a cavalier from Kentucky's Bluegrass region. Quickly deciding to cast his lot with the Confederacy, Morgan embarked on a career as a dashing and successful raider. Unfortunately, he lacked the ability to accept the degree of supervision required to conduct large, coordinated campaigns, and his daring raid across Ohio ended in disaster.

had to continue to evade Federal cavalry patrols, one of which recaptured the unfortunate Captain Hines.

Morgan was back in the Confederacy, but he was given no command until April 1864. He lost his life in a clash with Union forces on September 4, 1864, while on an expedition into the interior of Tennessee.

chapter 21

JOHN MCCAUSLAND BURNS A PENNSYLVANIA TOWN

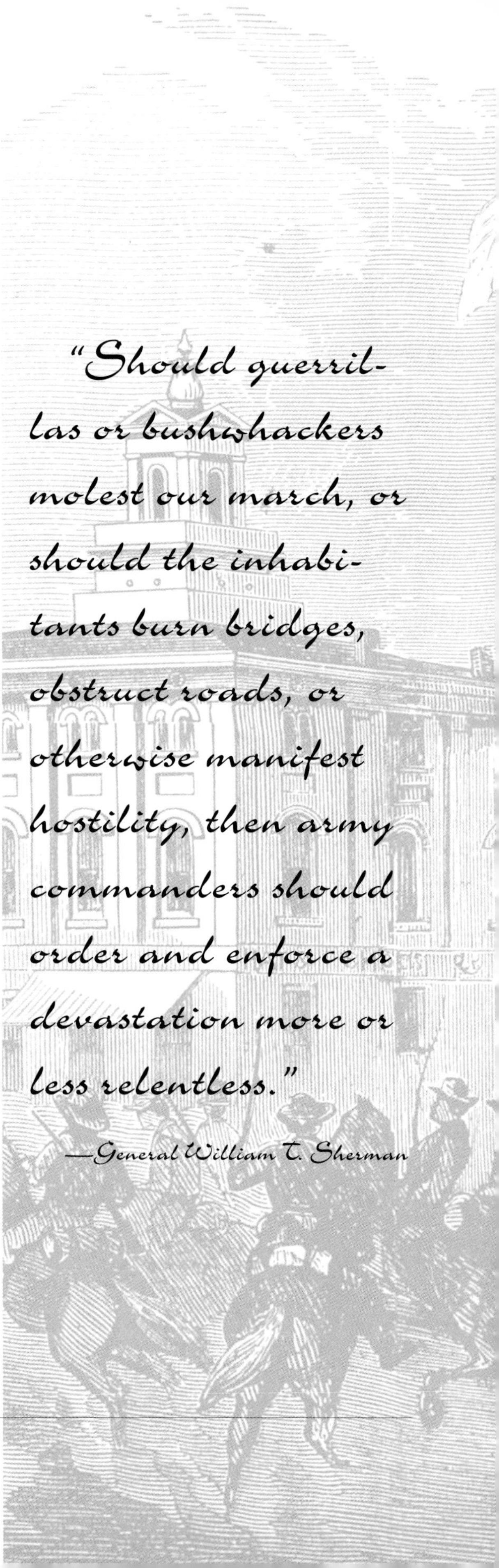

> "Should guerril-
> las or bushwhackers
> molest our march, or
> should the inhabi-
> tants burn bridges,
> obstruct roads, or
> otherwise manifest
> hostility, then army
> commanders should
> order and enforce a
> devastation more or
> less relentless."
>
> —*General William T. Sherman*

As the Union casualty lists from combat during the first three years of the war grew, anger and the desire to inflict punishment on the South grew also, along with resentment for their "great crime" of secession. This became especially true in the Shenandoah Valley of Virginia, where Federal invasions had been met by Confederate armies while "bushwhackers" and "guerrillas" attacked the rear areas of the Union commands. Captured and forced to take an oath of loyalty to the Union on their release, the guerrillas nonetheless usually returned to their partisan warfare. Gradually the Union army began to develop a merciless attitude toward them and their supporters. By 1864 it was common for Federal patrols to set fire to any property of secessionists found in the immediate vicinity of a bushwhacking attack. Cruelty was matched by cruelty, and the violence worsened as raid was followed by reprisal.

One of the most relentless of the Federal commanders—at least where the destruction of civilian property was concerned—was General David Hunter, a Virginian who chose to remain loyal to the Union. He was placed in command of the Shenandoah Valley after Major General Franz Sigel was defeated at New Market, and Hunter took his duties and orders quite seriously. On July 17, he received a message from the Union army's chief of staff, General Henry Halleck, that changed the focus of the war considerably.

Hunter's own chief of staff, David Hunter Strother, wrote in his diary:

July 17, Sunday....Received a tele-
gram from General Halleck informing

General Hunter....He was to devastate the valleys south of the railroad as far as possible so that crows flying over would have to carry knapsacks. This need not involve the burning of houses, dwellings. I have begged off Charles Town being burnt for the third time.

Strothel wrote of the following two days:

July 18, Monday....The house of Andrew Hunter was burned yesterday by Martindale. I am sorry to see this warfare begin and would be glad to stop it, but I don't pity the individuals at all. A war of mutual devastation will depopulate the border counties which contain all my kindred on both sides of the question. I would fain save them but fear all will go under alike in the end.
July 19, Tuesday....Orders given to burn the houses of E.J. Lee and Alex. Boteler. Martindale went forward to execute it. His description of the women and the scene is heart-rending.

PAGE 323: Brigadier General John McCausland had served at the Virginia Military Institute, where he taught mathematics under Thomas J. Jackson, later to be known as "Stonewall." As the war opened, young McCausland was ordered to western Virginia to recruit men to defend the state's border with Ohio. Later, he would be assigned the command of a cavalry brigade, and with this, he was able to delay the Union attack on Lynchburg—winning a golden sword and silver spurs from the city's grateful citizens. He received less welcome treatment at the hands of the Union army once he ordered the burning of Chambersburg. LEFT: The Civil War took a dramatic turn toward unrestrained violence during the campaign of spring 1864. Henry Halleck, the Union army's chief-of-staff, sent orders to his commander in the Shenandoah Valley, David Hunter, to begin the devastation of the region. His cruelty provoked fierce reprisals, and a cycle of barely restrained violence began to emerge.

David Hunter, known as "Black Dave" even to his own men, had been back in the region as commander only since July 15. In that short period of time, the face of warfare in the Shenandoah region began to change considerably. David Strother had been correct: a war of mutual devastation was about to begin. The local Confederate commander was Jubal Early, a man who would not stand for the destruction of civilian property without ordering a response.

Brigadier General John McCausland, a Confederate cavalry commander from West Virginia, was assigned to Early's command, and he later described a dispatch he received from Jubal Early: "I opened it and when I read those first lines I nearly fell out of the saddle. He ordered me in a very few words to make a retaliatory raid and give the Yankees a taste of their own medicine."

John McCausland, an aggressive officer still in his twenties at this time, was himself called "Tiger John" by his men. He was an experienced opponent of Hunter as he had managed to keep his small cavalry brigade in front of Hunter's invading army after "Grumble" Jones' blocking force was defeated in the battle of Piedmont. With the death of Jones, the way was cleared for Hunter to strike deep into central Virginia. He selected the industrial city of Lynchburg as his target, but McCausland was able to delay his progress through an extended series of hit-and-run attacks that began to deplete Hunter's army of both food and ammunition.

David Hunter, known as "Black Dave" even to his own men, responded to Halleck's orders to begin the destruction of the Shenandoah Valley area with ferocious enthusiasm. Having lost in his attack on Lynchburg—primarily due to the unrelenting efforts of John McCausland—Hunter reappeared in the region after Early's unsuccessful attack on Washington and renewed his old habit of burning dwellings that had no military significance.

Once Early was able to reinforce the doomed town's garrison, Hunter was forced to flee into the isolated mountains of southern West Virginia, where his men began to starve and were hit by repeated attacks by local Partisan Rangers.

McCausland was presented with a gold-inlaid sword and a pair of silver spurs by the grateful citizens of Lynchburg for saving the town, and Early was able to begin a long march back down the Shenandoah Valley along the route taken toward Lynchburg by Hunter. Hunter's retreat into southern West Virginia left the entire Shenandoah Valley without Federal defenders, and Early, quick to take advantages, marched confidently into the power vacuum.

Soon he and his small army were fighting at Monocacy, Virginia, only a short march from the defenses of Washington, D.C. Had it not been for the spirited delaying action fought that day by Union General Lew Wallace, it is quite likely that the North's capital city would have been captured, even if only briefly, during an election year when the Northern Democrats had nominated a peace candidate, former general George Brinton McClellan.

During this attack, McCausland led the advancing army and managed to enter the defensive works at Georgetown. He came closer to the Washington Monument than any other Confederate officer during the war.

Union General Lew Wallace ensured a Union victory for Grant at Fort Donelson in 1863 as he rapidly moved his division to contain an aggressive Confederate breakout attempt led by John McCausland. Wallace probably saved Washington, D.C. (and Lincoln's re-election) when he protected the city from occupation by Jubal Early's small army during the summer of 1864. During his successful defense against Early at the battle of Monocacy, Wallace was attacked by John McCausland. Lew Wallace later authored the classic novel, Ben Hur.

The small town of Chambersburg, Pennsylvania, with its gaslights burning, must have shone like a gleaming jewel as McCausland's men rode within sight. It was immediately occupied, and calls for the leading citizens of the town to assemble went out, but they refused to comply with the ransom order, either having sent much of the town's money to safety or relying on the nearby presence of Averell's cavalry division to save them from Early's terrible order.

Early decided to mount a reprisal expedition, and chose McCausland, a fighting general, to head it.

In his *Memoirs,* published after the war, Early wrote:

> *The town of Chambersburg in Pennsylvania was selected as the one on which retaliation should be made, and McCausland was ordered to proceed, with his brigade and that of Johnson and a battery of artillery, to that place, and demand of the municipal authorities the sum of $100,000 in gold or $500,000 in U.S. currency, as a compensation for the destruction of the houses named and their contents; and in default of that payment, to lay the town in ashes. A written demand to that effect was sent to the authorities, and they were informed what would be the result of a failure or refusal to comply with it; for I desired to give the people of Chambersburg an opportunity of saving their town, by making compensation for part of the injury done, and hoped the payment of a sum would have the effect of causing the adoption of a different policy.*

The two cavalry brigades and the artillery battery that would make the raid were prepared swiftly, and they began their long march northward on July 28. McCausland estimated the distance from the closest Confederate territory, Martinsburg, to Chambersburg to be seventy miles (113km). The cavalry crossed it quickly and arrived on the hills overlooking Chambersburg in the early hours of July 30, 1864.

Chambersburg would have appeared lovely from those hilltops in the early morning as darkness was setting. The relatively wealthy town had gaslit streets and was visible from some distance at night. The town's citizens would have been sleeping peacefully, under the impression that they were safe. Although the town had been occupied twice during the war up to the that point, it had sustained only minimal damage.

The war was about to touch the sleepy town in an entirely unfamiliar way, however: hard men were approaching to extort a ransom from the townspeople. Other Maryland towns had recently paid for their safety: Frederick had paid Early $200,000 following the successful conclusion of the battle of Monocacy, with the shrewd city fathers delaying payment until it was decided who would win the battle. Prior to this, Early had dispatched John McCausland to capture Hagerstown with verbal orders to collect $200,000 there as well.

McCausland returned with $20,000 and some supplies, and is reported by several historians to have erroneously dropped a decimal point, but the former mathematics professor was unlikely to have made such an error. It is more likely that McCausland decided not to burn Hagerstown for its lack of financial support for the Confederacy, and that he experienced a severe dressing-down from Early for his humanity. With Chambersburg, there would be no mathematical or judgemental misunderstanding

JOHN McCAUSLAND BURNS A PENNSYLVANIA TOWN

between them: Early gave McCausland written orders that contained no latitude for interpretation, and the town was doomed unless it paid the demanded ransom.

A member of the raiding party, Fielder Slingluff, wrote an article based on a letter he had written to a Chambersburg resident at the time of the raid. In part, he wrote:

...you would like to know if the men...justified the burning of your town, in their individual capacity, irrespective of the orders from headquarters under which they acted. I must say to you frankly that they did, and I never heard one dissenting voice. And why did we justify so harsh a measure? Simply because we had long come to the conclusion that it was time to burn something in the enemy's country. In the campaign of the preceding year, when our whole army had passed through your richest section of country, where the peaceful homes and fruitful fields only made the contrast with what he had left the more significant, many a man whose home was in ruins chaffed under the orders from General Lee, which forbade him to touch them, but the orders were obeyed, and we left the homes and fields as we found them, the ordinary wear and tear of an army of occupation excepted. We had so often in our eyes the reverse of this wherever your army swept through Virginia, that we were thoroughly convinced of the justice of stern retaliation.

The twenty-eight-year-old McCausland had been ordered to collect $100,000 in gold or $500,000 in Union "greenbacks"—illustrating the inflated value of paper money at that point in the war. Chambersburg was prosperous, and the townspeople might well have been able to pay the ransom that would have saved their town, but they chose to defy the threat.

It is no pleasure to me to recall the scenes of those days, nor do I do so in any spirit of vindictiveness, but I simply tell the truth in justification. We had followed Kilpatrick (I think it was), in his raid through Madison, Greene and other counties, and had seen the cattle shot or hamstrung in the barnyards, the agricultural implements burned, the feather beds and clothing of the women and children cut in shreds in mere wantonness, farmhouse after farmhouse stripped of every particle of provisions, private carriages cut and broken up, and women in tears lamenting all this. I did not put down anything I did not see myself. We had seen a thousand ruined homes in Clark, Jefferson and Frederick counties—barns and houses burned and private property destroyed—but we had no knowledge that this was done by "Official Orders." At last when the official order came openly from General Hunter, and the burning done thereunder, and when our orders of retaliation came they were met with approbation, as I have said, of every man who crossed the Potomac to execute them.

Of course we had nothing personal against your pretty little town. It just happened that it was the nearest and most accessible place of importance for us to get to. It was the unfortunate victim of circumstances. Had it been further off and some other town nearer that other town would have gone and Chambersburg would have been spared.

As it was, the town had several opportunities to save itself. McCausland sent a copy of the written demand into the town and rode there to personally request that the ransom be paid. Slingluff wrote of the response McCausland received: "They treated it as a

The destruction of Chambersburg was nearly total as flames consumed almost nearly three-quarters of the entire town. There was no military advantage to be gained by the burning, and McCausland was soon indicted for arson—a charge he felt was entirely unfair, as Sheridan and Sherman were burning far more than a single town.

JOHN MCCAUSLAND BURNS A PENNSYLVANIA TOWN

When Confederate cavalry rode into the "Diamond," Chambersburg's town square, on July 20, 1864, they intended to ride out with the ransom demanded by Jubal Early. The Confederate soldiers had also witnessed the "heart-rending scenes" described by Early as his army retraced the route taken by "Black Dave" Hunter. They were in the mood to burn something, and Chambersburg had the misfortune to be the first town they encountered.

joke, or thought it was a mere threat to get the money, and showed their sense of security and incredulity in every act."

The townspeople had good reason to feel that they were secure. General William W. Averell's combat-experienced cavalry division had arrived at Greencastle and was only ten miles (16km) away as McCausland delivered his ransom demands. McCausland was also aware of Averell's presence, as one of the Union commander's men had been captured. McCausland, however, was also aware that he had only a limited period of time before Averell's hardened troopers would be charging over the nearby hills.

McCausland actually went into the Diamond, as the town square was called, and approached at least one citizen, Mr. W. Douglas. Douglas wrote:

He took me by the arm, and leading me out into the Diamond, said: "Are you sure you have not seen your

public men? I should be very sorry to carry out the retributive part of the command of my superior officer." And as we walked to the Court House, he said: "Can't you ring the Court House bell and call the citizens together and see if this sum of money cannot be raised?"...He then ordered some of his men to open the Court House with the butts of their muskets and ring the bell. Then several of our citizens came and engaged in conversation with General McCausland, when I left, going to my hotel to notify my mother of the coming storm and save some articles of value to no one but family.

The threat of Averell's arrival combined with the uneventful previous occupations of the town and the fact that most of the available money was in the local banks doomed the town. As well, the general attitude of the town's citizens did little to endear them to

their temporary occupiers, who were called "Damned Rebs" and ordered to get out of town. One member of the town council said that the citizens wouldn't pay five cents! Their fate was sealed.

Details were sent into the middle of the town and fires were set. In a few minutes, the courthouse and the town hall were both in flames and the fire began to spread rapidly. The main portion of the town was enveloped in flames within ten minutes. The horrific scene was described by J. Scott Moore, one of the cavalrymen present:

The conflagration at its height was one of surpassing grandeur and terror, and had the day not been a calm one, many would have been licked up by the flames in the streets. Tall, black columns of smoke rose up to the very skies; around it were wrapped long streams of flames, writhing and twisting themselves into a thousand fantas-

tic shapes. Here and there gigantic whirlwinds would lift clothing and light substances into the air, and intermingled with the weird scene could be heard the shrieks of women and children. Cows, dogs and cats were consumed in their attempt to escape. It was a picture that may be misrepresented, but cannot be heightened, and must remain forever indelibly upon the minds of those who witnessed it.

Three-fourths of the town was destroyed in the huge conflagration. One section was spared when officer Colonel William Peters refused to set it aflame. He was later arrested, but returned to his regiment at Moorefield a few days later.

There were remarkably few deaths during the raid and the burning of the town. Daniel Parker, an elderly former slave (he "filled the measure of patriarchal years,"

OPPOSITE: William Woods Averell had proven himself to be an effective raider, but he was severely criticized after the burning of Chambersburg. Camped only ten miles (16 km) away, Averell didn't ride to save the town. He may have been arranging a massive ambush, but, regardless, most historians agree that he should be excused of blame: there had been no burnings on Union soil up to this point in the war, and he had no way to anticipate that Chambersburg was in mortal danger. He would, however, avenge Chambersburg with his surprise attack on McCausland's entire command at Moorefield, West Virginia. RIGHT: Confederate General Jubal Early, the commander in the Shenandoah region, began to receive appeals for assistance that were, as he described them, "truly heart-rending" and he ordered a retaliatory attack. Having successfully extorted a ransom from Frederick, Maryland, and a small ransom—through error only $20,000 instead of $200,000—from Hagerstown, Early ordered a raid into Pennsylvania. John McCausland was ordered to collect a ransom from the citizens of Chambersburg to pay for damages done by Union raiders or he was to burn the entire town.

JOHN McCAUSLAND BURNS A PENNSYLVANIA TOWN

according to newspapers reporting the destruction), died as a result of the raid. Two Union soldiers were shot to death in a drugstore by the enraged owner. Two Confederate officers lost their lives. One, Calder Bailey, was drinking heavily and was left behind; an enraged mob shot and wounded him, forcing him to take refuge in the cellar of a burning building; when he emerged to escape from the blistering heat, he was beaten to death with clubs.

The other Confederate officer, Henry K. Cochrane, was captured by Thomas H. Doyle, who gave his prisoner fifteen minutes to pray before shooting him. This nonjudicial execution and the killing of Bailey were widely reported in the North, where the population accepted the acts, essentially murders of prisoners, without question. Chambersburg was as legitimate a military target as were the homes and farms in the Shenandoah Valley that were being burned, but the Northern population viewed the two acts differently: burnings in the South were acts of reprisal designed to punish their Southern cousins for the crime of secession, but the destruction of Chambersburg was viewed as an act of arson done by criminal elements.

The raiders withdrew slowly from the area, probably wondering why they hadn't been attacked by the nearby Averell and his cavalry division. Averell was an unusual commander and a complex character, who was capable of valiant efforts, but seemed to "run both hot and cold" at times. He had led the winter attack all the way across West Virginia's mountains to strike deep in the Confederacy's rear areas, but he was also capable of indecisiveness at times, a fact that

OPPOSITE: The destruction in Chambersburg was nearly total, but only one citizen lost his life, an elderly black man who may have suffered a heart attack. Unfortunately, history has made light of the nonjudicial executions of captured Confederates from the raiding force.

would limit his military career in only a few months. Several attempts to contact Averell were made, and he was found sleeping beside a fence line. While he was only ten miles (16km) from the doomed town, Averell did not ride to the rescue.

In fairness to Averell, he and his cavalry division had just arrived in the area after a season of extremely hard marching and fighting. He had fought McCausland and had developed respect for the fighting ability of the west Virginian and his men. Averell wrote of the campaign he had just completed: "This command has marched 1,400 miles [2,253km] since the 1st of May, without a remount, and without a halt sufficiently long to set the shoes on my horses."

While resting his command, Averell must have believed that McCausland would occupy Chambersburg only temporarily before evacuating the town and retreating back along rural roads to rejoin Early's army near Martinsburg. There is no way Averell would have suspected that Early had ordered the town burned, as the Southern army, unlike the Union army, had never burned anything prior to this.

McCausland's force retreated rapidly from the town. Soon thereafter in Hancock, Maryland, McCausland demanded an additional ransom of $30,000, but the Maryland contingent with his command assigned guards to each building in the town to prevent burning or looting. They continued on to the federal garrison town of Cumberland, Maryland, where the commander, General Benjamin F. Kelley, prepared to meet him. McCausland ordered his men forward in an attack, but with heavy resistance in his front and Averell's cavalry riding toward his rear, the Confederate commander was forced to cross the Potomac and ride for the relative safety of the mountainous region.

McCausland continued to fight as his men rode. They destroyed a bridge in the

"I have the best possible reason for knowing the strength of the Confederate army to be one million men, for whenever one of our generals engages a rebel army he reports that he has encountered a force twice his strength. Now I know we have a half a million soldiers, so I am bound to believe that the rebels have twice that number."

—President Abraham Lincoln, 1862

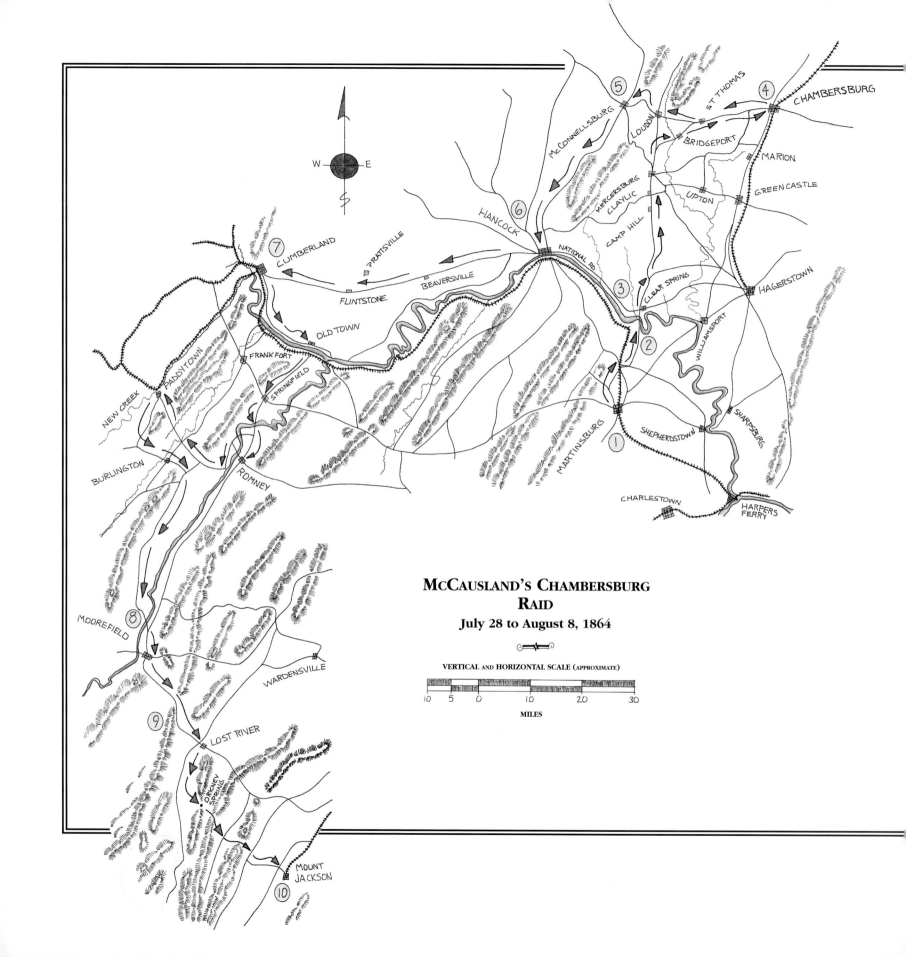

McCausland's Chambersburg
Raid

July 28 to August 8, 1864

VERTICAL AND HORIZONTAL SCALE (APPROXIMATE)

10 5 0 10 20 30

MILES

1. On July 28, 1864, McCausland departed Martinsburg, West Virginia, with two brigades of artillery. His destination was Chambersburg, Pennsylvania; his orders were to collect monetary restitutions for Union raids in the Shenandoah Valley or burn the town.

2. At first light on July 29, Confederate scouts, who were pre-positioned the night before, surprised and captured Union pickets at McCoy's Ford on the Potomac. With the ford secured, McCausland's main body crossed over.

3. When the raiders reached the National Road, McCausland sent scouts toward Cumberland and Hagerstown to drive back Union pickets and to mask his real destination. McCausland passed through Clear Springs and headed north on the road to Mercersburg, en route to Chambersburg.

4. Early on July 30, McCausland arrived at the outskirts of Chambersburg. The town was secured with very little opposition. When the ransom was not met, McCausland ordered the town burned.

5. The raiders camped over night at the town of McConnellsburg.

6. On July 31, the raiders stopped again to rest at Hancock, Maryland. An attempt was made to collect a ransom, but before the money could be raised, Union forces attacked Confederate picket posts outside of town. After a lively fight, McCausland moved toward Cumberland by the National Road.

7. McCausland attacked Union infantry that blocked his way at Cumberland. When pursuit forces approached from Hancock, McCausland disengaged and headed south to Old Town, where he re-crossed the Potomac.

8. On August 7, Union pursuit forces caught up with McCausland as he rested at Moorefield. Union cavalry dressed in Confederate uniforms, known as "Jessie Scouts," rode directly into McCausland's camp and opened fire. At the same time, regular Union cavalry attacked down the road from Romney.

9. Fragmented after their defeat at Moorefield, McCausland's remaining troopers traveled on separate roads as they made their way southeast to Mount Jackson.

10. On August 8, the remnants of McCausland's command reached Mount Jackson.

vicinity of Romney and ordered an attack against the Union garrison at New Creek, Averell's former base of operations. The defenders lost seventy-five men before McCausland ordered his men to retire in the direction of Moorefield.

The Confederates had ridden sixty miles (96.5km) since they last encountered Averell's advance units at Hancock, and they went into camp for four days to rest and recuperate after the mind-numbing ride they had just experienced. Scout reports told of Averell doing the same thing in the vicinity of Hancock and the men began to relax.

McCausland's scouts, left along the Romney road, began to report the movement of Averell's men into the area and told McCausland that he could anticipate an attack at daylight on August 7. A warning was sent to the commander of the Maryland brigade, Bradley Johnson; orders were sent to at least a part of his command to prepare their mounts for quick use, and a patrol was sent out in the night. Unfortunately, no warning of the probable approach of Averell was given to subordinate commanders, and many of those weary officers returned to their blankets.

Averell used his Jessie Scouts, the gray-clad riders who had been instrumental in the success of his winter raid against the Confederate depot at Salem. These men managed to capture both the patrol ordered out on the Romney road by Johnson and the Confederate advance pickets—without a shot being fired. After learning the password, the location of the picket reserve, and the name of the picket reserve's commanding officer, these same scouts, reinforced by volunteer cavalrymen also wearing Confederate uni-

forms, rode to the picket post, calling, "Lieutenant Bonn, you are relieved." This was the command that they were awaiting, but they soon found themselves taken prisoner; still not a shot had been fired.

As the prisoners were taken to the rear, the disguised Federal patrol rode directly to the perimeter of Bradley Johnson's brigade camp and, pretending to be the returning patrol sent out earlier on the Romney road, entered. One group rode directly to the McNeil home, where Johnson was sleeping, while another rode into the center of the perimeter, searching for Harry Gilmor. They began shooting from within the interior of the Confederate camp—while wearing gray uniforms—and as complete confusion developed among the Confederates, Averell ordered a general attack against Johnson.

Hit suddenly by an entire Federal division of cavalry while their commander was being routed out of his bed inside the McNeil home, the Confederates were rapidly overrun as Averell's men continued their charge to the fords of the South Branch of the Potomac and the location where McCausland's brigade was encamped. Only hard fighting at the fords saved McCausland from complete destruction as small groups of Confederate cavalrymen galloped to what safety they could find on their own.

Chambersburg had been avenged by a cavalry charge that was the greatest surprise attack in the history of the North American continent, a charge that had been set up by the actions of a unique group of scouts. These men would be involved in additional daring operations against the Confederacy as the Union army continued to develop into a highly trained fighting force.

chapter 22

Jessie Scouts Capture Harry Gilmor

Hanse McNeil was one of the Confederacy's most ingenious partisan leaders. He had been a successful farmer and livestock breeder who entered the service of Virginia even though he was personally opposed to secession. He was living in Missouri at the outbreak of the war and was soon captured, but after escaping he returned to the vicinity of Moorefield, Virginia, where he raised a Partisan Ranger company and began to conduct operations against the nearby Baltimore and Ohio Railroad, the most vulnerable of the Union's supply arteries. Most of its rails ran through Virginia, and its trains, filled with supplies, coal, and troops, were often attacked by Virginia's raiders.

McNeil learned a great deal about the psychology of the young Union soldiers who were sent out in small groups to guard critical points along the railroad. In one attack, he called out to the young Federal soldiers that he would parole every man who surrendered and they could go home. The tactic, surprising as it was, worked, and McNeil's twenty-four men captured seventy-two Union troops. He began to use this tactic in a more wholesale way: he left signed parole forms with local farmers, and any Union soldier who wanted to go home could simply trade for one of the forms, complete it, and depart for home and family until exchanged.

As the spring campaign began in 1864, McNeil became more than simply an irritant to Benjamin F. Kelley, the local Federal commander, the unfortunate man responsible for the safety of the railroad. On May 3, McNeil and sixty of his men climbed aboard a train that had been stopped, placed a pistol to the

"The military value of a partisan's work is not measured by the amount of property destroyed, or the number of men killed or captured, but by the number he keeps watching."

—John Singleton Mosby

PAGE 339: *Major Harry Gilmor slipped across the Potomac River from Maryland on August 30, 1861, and joined Turner Ashby's Virginia cavalry. He served as a scout during Jackson's incredible 1862 Shenandoah Valley campaigns, but he best served the Confederacy as a raider with an independent command. Gilmor was one of those rare officers who seemed to thrive on leading his men into combat. ABOVE: Gilmor's nemesis throughout the latter part of the war came in the form of Jessie Scouts, Union soldiers wearing Confederate uniforms as they searched for Confederates. Gilmor knew a great deal about Jessie Scout operations and organized hunts for these daring Federal soldiers. One of the best of the Jessie scouts was Archibald Rowand, pictured here with a group of Medal of Honor winners. Rowand is in the back row at the far right.*

head of the engineer, and rode in style to the interior of Piedmont, one of the major maintenance installations on the railroad.

By the time reinforcements could arrive from the Federal post at nearby New Creek, the entire yard at Piedmont was in ruins. Several thousand feet of track had been torn from cross ties, and buildings, machine shops, and nine precious locomotives had been destroyed. McNeil's nearby rear guard had also managed to strike effectively by capturing and burning three additional trains and capturing one hundred men. It became

obvious to Kelley that McNeil had to be eliminated if the railroad was to be operated in safety.

If, as John Mosby stated, the value of a guerrilla could be measured by the number of men kept watching for him, Hanse McNeil was becoming invaluable to the Confederacy. The Federal War Department shortly ordered eleven regiments into positions along the B&O at a time when the Confederacy was seriously debating the usefulness of its Partisan Rangers and ordered all of them to disband. The order, however, exempted the

two most effective units that were operating in northern and northwestern Virginia: McNeil and Mosby would be allowed to remain in the field.

McNeil soon fell in combat and the source of the wound remains a Civil War mystery. In early October, he led an attack on a bridge near Mount Jackson and was mortally wounded by a shot that came from one of his own men, a guerrilla who had apparently been reprimanded for stealing chickens. But George Valentine, the man who did the shooting, may have had a different motivation than revenge over the dressing-down he received for chicken theft.

Hanse McNeil, like many of the other effective Confederate commanders, led his men by example as well as by orders, and was in the front of the attack at Mount Jackson when he was killed. Valentine shot him from the rear and fled the scene. Later, Valentine was identified as a Jessie Scout, a fact that leaves only two possibilities. One, Valentine shot McNeil and deserted to Sheridan's Shenandoah army to gain some degree of safety and volunteered to serve as a Jessie Scout. Sheridan had several deserters from the Confederate army within his "scout battalion." Two, there is an excellent chance that George Valentine, actually a Jessie Scout at the time of the shooting, had enrolled as a Partisan Ranger and rode with McNeil until he had an opportunity to kill him. McNeil had become a serious problem for the Federal commanders to manage and he had to be eliminated—through one method or another—and it is entirely plausible that an operation designed to kill the partisan leader had been developed within Sheridan's headquarters.

Having lost a key commander, the Confederate command turned to Harry Gilmor, a Baltimore native who was quite familiar with railroad operations. After blocking the tracks of the ever-threatened B&O in early 1864, Gilmor's raiders boarded the train and robbed the passengers at gunpoint, collecting pistols, watches, coats, and money. After another robbery, Gilmor was ordered before a court-martial, and though he returned to duty, the actions of Gilmor and his men resulted in the decision of the Confederate Congress to disband its partisans. With the killing of Hanse McNeil, the obvious choice of commander for McNeil's and Woodson's partisans was Harry Gilmor.

It was, however, the Jessie Scouts—now assigned under the command of Philip Sheridan—and their new commander, Major

Major Harry Gilmor was a cool, dashing, and reckless Confederate cavalry officer who represented the last connection between the Confederacy and Maryland. Once Brigadier General Bradley Johnson had been assigned to command a prisoner-of-war camp, Gilmor became the only prominent Marylander left in the Confederate army. This fact, his knowledge of Jessie Scout operations, and his new assignment as a threat to the Baltimore and Ohio Railroad made him a primary target.

General Philip Sheridan was the answer Lincoln and Grant had been seeking to eliminate the Confederate threat to Maryland, Pennsylvania, and Washington, D.C. Soon after he was given command, Sheridan defeated Jubal Early at Winchester in late summer 1864. His next major objective was to eliminate the Confederate raiders operating near his base areas. Gilmor was near the top of his list.

Henry Young, who would have the responsibility of bringing Gilmor and his raiders under control. Curiously, the operation that took shape inside Sheridan's headquarters closely resembled one of the explanations for Valentine's act against McNeil.

Small, highly mobile, two-man Jessie Scout teams were sent into Hardy County, Virginia, in an attempt to locate Gilmor. A second, larger team of scouts—disguised in Confederate uniforms—prepared to ride behind Confederate lines to capture the new partisan commander. The final aspect of the plan involved experienced Federal cavalrymen, handpicked from several commands, who would arrive at the scene of Gilmor's capture and serve as security escorts. The entire Federal capture plan was far more detailed and involved than the hasty plan thrown together by Andrews, which had resulted in failure in Georgia in early 1862. Sophistication had entered into federal planning, and officers, men, and a female agent who were capable of carrying complex plans through to completion had been located by this point in the war. The problem was as old as the military itself: the target had to be located and its position fixed, and sufficient force had to be moved to the target's vicinity to eliminate it.

Youthful Archibald Rowand, one of Averell's former scouts, of the 1st West Virginia Cavalry, and another scout were selected to perform the reconnaissance inside the Confederate stronghold of Moorefield. Having been in the battle that destroyed much of McCausland's command after the burning of Chambersburg, Rowand was quite familiar with the region. He was well versed in the names of Confederate commanders and their units, and he had survived a hostile interrogation after being captured in his Confederate uniform as Averell maneuvered toward Lynchburg with Hunter. In short, Rowand was excellent at what he did.

John H. "Hanse" McNeil was a bold Confederate Partisan Ranger who had led numerous successful attacks against Union facilities associated with the critical Baltimore and Obio Railroad. While leading an attack on a covered bridge at Mt. Jackson in October 1864, he was mortally wounded by one of his own men, George Valentine, who shot him in the back and who was later reported to be a Jessie Scout. Harry Gilmor replaced McNeil and soon was the target of the Jessie Scouts.

This was a major operation, and a second Jessie Scout team—composed of Nick Carlisle, a Virginian, and Sergeant Mullihan of the 17th Pennsylvania—was also sent into Moorefield to look for signs of Gilmor. Reports exist that Sheridan also sent an unnamed female agent into the Confederate stronghold as well. The Union commanders in the region were determined to remove Harry Gilmor before he began damaging them as McNeil had.

Rowand and his companion reported back to Sheridan's headquarters in Winchester on February 3, 1865, and the female agent confirmed their reports that Gilmor was in Moorefield on the following day. The first part of the operation was complete: Gilmor had been located.

A force of twenty Jessie Scouts was assembled quickly from the men at Sheridan's headquarters, and they prepared to ride on February 4. Rowand, now familiar with Moorefield, would lead the operation back in the capture attempt, even though he had just finished an exhausting fifty-eight-mile (93km) winter ride the previous day. A composite force of three hundred volunteer cavalrymen, under the command of Lieutenant Colonel E.J. Whitaker of the 1st Connecticut Cavalry, would form the security element for the entire operation.

The cavalry element of the raid would follow several miles in the rear of the disguised Jessie Scouts, giving the appearance that they were tracking the Confederates as they rode to sanctuary in Moorefield. The scouts told one of two stories when questioned along the route: they were responding to the call from Gilmor for additional recruits, or they were from the Lost River picket post and were delivering a warning to Gilmor about the approach of the Union cavalrymen. In either case, the presence of Whitaker and his men in their rear gave credibility to their stories.

Once the Jessie Scouts entered the town of Moorefield in the early-morning darkness of February 5, only a short time was needed to locate the house where Gilmor was staying. The Scouts' commander, Henry Young, and a few Jessies quietly climbed the stairs and entered the bedroom where Gilmor was sleeping. Contrary to the reports of several historians who have written that Gilmor was in bed with a woman, he was in fact sharing a bed with his cousin, Hoffman Gilmor, who was also captured. Gilmor wrote about his capture:

My cousin, H——— G———, was in bed with me, when the door suddenly opened, and five men with drawn pistols, and although dressed as Confederates, I saw at a glance what they were. But it was too late for a fight, for they had seized my pistols, lying on a chair under my uniform. "Are you Colonel Gilmor?" said one of them. I did not answer at first; I was glancing around to see if there was any chance of escape. My attention was arrested by feeling the muzzle of a pistol against my head, and hearing the question repeated. "Yes, and who in the Devil's name are you?" "Major Young, of General Sheridan's Staff." "All right. I suppose you want me to go with you?" "I shall be happy to have your company to Winchester, as General Sheridan wishes to consult with you about some important military matters."

The difficult portion of the operation was now to begin. Young and his men had secured their captive, but they were deep within Confederate-controlled territory and Gilmor's men were roused. Three made a sudden charge against the capture party as Gilmor was "introduced" to Whitaker, and the long ride back to Winchester began.

Whitaker placed a force of thirty-eight men, fifteen of whom were armed with Spencers, in the back of the column to act as a rear guard. They held off repeated Confederate advances and retained their prized prisoner before stopping for the night. During this stop, Gilmor reported that he was closely guarded by a man who had served in the Confederate army under him before deserting to the Union army. This Jessie Scout, a Confederate deserter dressed in a Confederate uniform, was taking enormous risks with his life: if captured in either uniform he would be hanged, either as a deserter or as a spy.

En route to Winchester and Sheridan, the Jessie Scouts encountered and captured another of their enemies, Captain George Stump, who was near his father's home on the Romney road. Several accounts exist about this event, but what is certain is that George Stump did not survive his meeting with the Jessie Scouts. According to one story, he was executed at the order of Young when it was determined that he was "too sick to ride," and Young ordered his scouts to "make him sicker." Another account, related by Rowand, tells that Stump refused to give his parole and attempted to snatch Young's pistol from its holster. Young had him shot to death for his efforts. A third report exists in which Young gave Stump an opportunity to ride swiftly away before his scouts opened fire, but Stump was killed as he departed. Regardless of the execution details, George Stump found little mercy at the hands of the Jessie Scouts that night near Romney. As guerilla fighters, the scouts expected no mercy if captured, and gave little to their enemies.

Harry Gilmor was delivered to General Sheridan in Winchester on Monday, February 6. There, he was confined in handcuffs to a small hotel room. The operation to secure Gilmor had begun on January 31, when

Rowand rode for Moorefield. Within a week, the Jessie Scouts had ridden 232 miles (373km) over bad mountain roads in the worst of deep winter conditions to deliver Gilmor to Winchester. Archibald Rowand wrote about the daring expedition in a letter to his father:

...our trip was a perfect success. Succeeded in capturing the notorious Harry Gilmor and fifteen men of different commands. On Tuesday I was ordered to go with one man to Moorefield. By the order of Gen. Sheridan, went to Moorefield and returned on Thursday, reported to the General the whereabouts of Harry Gilmor and command. The General requested me to send in a written report to be filed. On Saturday morning a force of cavalry (300) and twenty scouts left this place for Moorefield, distant fifty-eight miles [93km]. Traveling all night, we arrived at Moorefield Sunday morning just before day. Leaving the town surrounded by a strong picket, we struck the South Fork river road....

Dashing across the fields, we surrounded the Williams' house and caught one of Rosser's men. Major Young went on to Randolph's and there caught Harry in bed. He was a little astonished, but took things coolly. You may be sure that we gave him no chance to escape.

Henry Halleck sent a telegram with directions for the imprisonment of Gilmor: "Major Gilmor will be sent to Fort Warren for confinement. A special guard will be selected to take him there." Sheridan's Jessie Scouts, including Major Young, personally escorted Gilmor to prison in Boston Harbor, allowing him no chance to escape.

Lieutenant Colonel Edward W. Whitaker led the Union extraction force that included men from his regiment, the 1st Connecticut Cavalry, during the Jessie Scout operation that netted Harry Gilmor for Sheridan. The hazardous mission, fifty-eight miles (93 km) deep inside Confederate territory, was achieved without serious losses to the Union cavalrymen.

A Prisoner and His Captor

Harry Gilmor was one of the few Civil War soldiers who later wrote about his own wartime capture. The Confederate soldier and his captor, Major Henry Young of Sheridan's Union scouts, quickly developed a bond verging on actual friendship that was based on their mutual respect for each other's courage and character.

Gilmor wrote about those cold February days:

> *I had not gone half a mile [0.8km] before Major Young thought it best to put me on a more indifferent horse, saying, "Colonel, I can not trust you on such a splendid animal, for you know that you will leave us if you get the smallest chance." He was right, for I was already on the look-out for a break in the fence to make the effort.*
>
> *My feelings can not be imagined as I passed through Moorefield, and saw the ladies run out into the street—some of them weeping—to bid me good-by, and express their sorrow for my situation. I tried to be cheerful, but it was hard to bear.*

Major Gilmor was extremely proud of his service to the Confederacy and posed for this post-war photograph after he had regained all of the weight he had lost while a prisoner of war in Boston Harbor. His officer's jacket was too tight to be buttoned for the portrait session.

We took the river road to Romney, to get on the Northwestern Turnpike to Winchester. H—— [Hoffman, Gilmor's cousin] and I rode at the head of the column with Colonel Whittington [Whitaker], while some of the other prisoners were kept in the centre by the provost guard. These prisoners were about a dozen or so of Rosser's and Imboden's men, picked up by them as they had gone along.

Night came on soon after leaving Romney, and, though the weather was intensely cold, and the horses very tired, we pushed on six or seven miles [10–11km] farther, when we halted for an hour to refresh both man and horse. The colonel, Major Young, the surgeon (Dr. Walls), H——, and I, with a guard of about ten men of the squad, went to a house near by for supper, and then we continued on our way to Winchester.

The night was so very cold that most of us had to dismount and walk. In passing through the mountain, I watched closely for an opportunity of breaking away and plunging down the steep hill-side; but four men were constantly near me with pistols drawn and cocked, and no chance appeared until we got within two or three miles [3–4km] of Big Capon River. Here Major Young asked the colonel to turn me over to him, and let him push rapidly ahead to Winchester; but the colonel refused, and the Major, becoming angry, took all his men, the scouts, off with him to Winchester. These were the only men I cared for, and I felt certain now of making my escape.

We were then some distance ahead of the main column, and when Young and his men left us there were none in sight except the colonel and his orderly, the surgeon, H——, and myself. We halted, and the orderly was sent back to hurry up a fresh guard for me. The doctor and H—— were on their horses, while the colonel and I were standing in the road in advance of them. The place, too, was a good one, on the side of a small mountain, and I made up my mind to seize the colonel before he could draw his pistol, throw him down, and make my escape. I was then about three paces from him when I formed this plan, had moved up closer to carry it into effect, and was just about to make the spring, when I was seized with an unacountable fit of trembling, and could not move. It was not fear, for although the colonel was even a larger man than myself, powerfully made, and apparently a cool head, I knew that my success was certain; for who could stand such a sudden shock as he would certainly have received? I had been standing there for some time, and was very cold, but I never trembled like that except when I had an ague-chill. I can not account for it; all I know is, that to keep him from noticing it, and not dreaming that any of his scouts would return, I put my hand on H——'s horse, and at length quieted my nerves, when suddenly up dashed four scouts. The snow was so deep they gave no sound of their approach. They had been sent back by Major Young for my guard. My heart sank within me; but I determined not to enter Winchester without making a strong effort to escape....We reached Winchester about noon, when I was separated from the other prisoners and taken to a small room in the hotel, destitute of furniture except a chair and the frame of an old bedstead. It was severely cold, but I was allowed no fire. Two sentinels, kept in the room, were instructed by the lieutenant to shoot me if I passed a line chalked on the floor.

The lieutenant gave me a pair of his own blankets, or I would have had none, for I gave mine to H——. I asked the provost marshall for something to lie upon, but he sent, instead, handcuffs. A number were brought before a pair of the "ruffles," as they were called then, was found to fit, and for the first time, I found myself in irons. I asked by whose authority I was subjected to this indignity, and was told that it was by the order of General Sheridan. I knew it was useless to appeal to him, and so spent an hour in cursing the crew, and wound up by flinging in a few lively epithets at the head of the guard, rather ungenerously, for it seems they were ordered to hold no conversation with me, and consequently could not reply.

One of the scouts (White), a decent, brave man, brought me every day a glass of toddy; but apart from this, I had only common army rations. I was allowed to see no one, although several ladies went to Sheridan and begged to be permitted to visit me. . . .

On the morning of the third day Major Young informed me that I was to be taken to some other prison, but he would not tell me where. The irons being removed, I found about twenty-five cavalrymen ready to escort me to Stevenson's Depot, where I was to take the cars to Harper's [sic] Ferry. Major Young had seven or eight of his scouts with him, and informed me that they would accompany me to the fort where I was to be confined. I guessed at once that Fort Warren was to be my prison, and, not long after, the major confirmed my suspicion. From first to last, he was as kind to me as it was possible for him to be, but, at the same time, he watched me like a hawk, and was always ready to draw his revolver. He told me frankly that he would not trust me far, for he knew that I would take desperate chances to escape. He did not iron me, as he had been ordered, nor did he ask me for my parole of honor, but I did not make a movement that was not quickly seen.

On arriving at Harper's Ferry, we had some difficulty in getting through the crowd assembled to meet us, and at one time it looked rather squally, for they threatened me with violence. Major Young, perfectly cool, waved them aside with his pistol at full cock, and whispered to me, in event of attack, to take one of his pistols and shoot right and left. "They will have," said he, "to walk over my dead body before they touch you." The cowardly scoundrels made a good deal of noise, but, finding they made no impression, began to slink off, when a tall, vulgar-looking lieutenant of artillery, somewhat intoxicated, cried out at the top of his voice, "I say, Gilmor, where is the watch some of your thieves stole from me on the Philadelphia train?"

Without deigning to utter a syllable, Major Young gave him a powerful blow across the mouth with the barrel of his pistol, which knocked him from the low platform. The fellow got up, with blood streaming out, and slunk off without another word. This stopped all the talk about taking me from Major Young . . . we left in the cars, reached New York the same evening, traveled all that night, and arrived in Boston at 7 A.M. on the 10th of February, 1865.

The major escorted me to the United States Hotel, where I should have enjoyed a good breakfast but for the crowd of men and women huddled together, gazing at me from every direction.

Major Young kindly accompanied me about town to make some purchases, and then conducted me to my prison home. Its gates closed upon me, and I had struck my last blow for the South. Though fully entitled to my exchange as a regularly commissioned officer, it was soon quite apparent that the government designed, if possible, to keep me back among those from whom this right was to be arbitrarily withheld. . . . . and, at length, on the 24th of July, 1865, the action of the President on officers of my rank brought the order with which my captivity was to end, and having complied with the regulations prescribed, I was paroled and released on that day.

Major Henry Harrison Young returned to duty as chief of Sheridan's scouts, and by the time Gilmor was released, had been sent to Texas with Sheridan and four (or possibly six) of his scouts, a group that included the brave man who provided Gilmor with a daily "toddy"—Sergeant Jim White.

They were ordered into Mexico—wearing their old Confederate uniforms—to collect information on the status of the Confederate soldiers who escaped across the international border to the French, Austrian, and Belgian army units that were supporting Emperor Maximilian and the Imperial Mexican army. Young was Sheridan's go-between with the camp of Benito Juarez and his Liberal army seeking to overthrow Maximilian, and several trips were made into northern

Mexico by the Union officer and his scouts. At one time, Young, Sheridan, and Grant in Washington discussed a plan to abduct the imperial garrison commander in Matamoros, Mexico, much like they had done with Gilmor.

Young was reported killed while leading a river crossing at the Rio Grande in late 1866 and his body was never recovered for burial. It was left to Jim White to complete the final mission of Sheridan's scouts.

Once Maximilian had been captured, he was tried by Juarez's officers at Querétaro, a city located 100 miles [161km] north of Mexico City. The former emperor was condemned

Major Henry Harrison Young served bravely with the 2nd Rhode Island Infantry Regiment, but the life of an infantry officer was too routine for him. His talents as a scout were discovered by Sheridan, who made him his assistant aide-de-camp and chief scout. Young led the deep penetration raid that resulted in the capture of Harry Gilmor, later captured Brigadier General Felix Barringer, and accompanied Sheridan to Texas at the end of hostilities with a few of his scouts—including Arch Rowand. Young died in Mexico in November 1866, while on a mission for Sheridan, but his service record describes a retroactive mustering out of service— back to July 15, 1865. His service in Mexico, which cost him his life, was classified secret by the army.

to death by firing squad—as he had done with many of his captives—and Secretary of State Seward, in Washington, began to receive pleas from European governments to intercede on their behalf to save his life.

Seward had no representative in Mexico, as the "Minister to Mexico" was located in New Orleans where he remained in contact with Juarez's officers. Having no way to deliver a diplomatic note deep within the interior of central Mexico, Seward or his minister requested assistance from Sheridan's headquarters and Sheridan called for Sergeant Jim White.

White was sent across the Gulf of Mexico on the steamer *The Black Bird,* and after landing at Tampico, he rode on horseback across Mexico, possibly still wearing the old Confederate uniform the scouts had used as disguises during the Civil War, and delivered Seward's message. Unfortunately for Maximilian, the request for mercy had no effect on Juarez's generals and the emperor was executed.

White was just as he was described by Harry Gilmor, "a brave, decent man" who risked his life for his country long after the Civil War was over. He delivered his message to Querétaro in early 1867—completing the last mission of Sheridan's scouts.

chapter 23

JOHN YATES BEALL'S MARITIME RAID

"Nor must Uncle Sam's web-feet be forgotten. At all the watery margins they have been present. Not only the deep sea, the broad bay, and the rapid river, but also up the muddy bayou, and where the ground was a little damp, they have been and made their tracks."

—Abraham Lincoln

The United States was developing into a powerful commercial maritime force on the world stage. Large numbers of ships carrying the freight and raw materials necessary to keep the war machine well oiled sailed the world's oceans. The Federal navy was sufficiently strong, relative to their Confederate opponent, in the initial stages of the war to begin the imposition of a blockade that was designed to bring the South to its knees through economic deprivation. Primarily agricultural, the Southern economy depended heavily on imports of manufactured goods from the North and Europe. Trade was necessary for the survival of the South and the access to trade was blocked. This was something that would not go unchallenged by the Confederacy. Raiders soon went to sea, and other operations were also under way.

One of the raiders who was less well known than some of the Confederates who covered the wide oceans as commerce raiders and nearly wrecked the Union's maritime industry was John Yates Beall, a former infantryman who had served in the Stonewall Brigade and been severely wounded.

Soon after recovering, he served the Confederacy as a secret agent in Iowa. Fearing that he would be discovered, he fled to Canada. He quickly contacted the Confederate government's representatives as he began to develop a plan for a stunning raid on Federal interests.

Lying in Sandusky Bay on Lake Erie was Johnson's Island, now used by the Federal authorities as a prison for Confederate officers who fell into their hands. Beall thought that a raid on the island to free the prisoners

captured for their pay. Privateering so closely resembled open piracy that it had been outlawed by most of the seafaring nations. Those undertaking it knew they could expect harsh penalties if captured.

This, of course, didn't deter Beall, and he recruited a lieutenant, Bennett G. Burleigh, and other men who would participate in several successful attacks in the Chesapeake Bay region in 1863. His raids included cutting the cable to the eastern shore and destroying the Federal lighthouse near Cape Charles. After capturing two small open boats, the seaborne guerrillas began to raid in earnest. In a short time, Beall and his men had captured and destroyed a dozen ships with their own two. They captured a large sloop loaded with sutler supplies for the Federal garrison at Port Royal, South Carolina, and attempted to run the blockade in order to sell the prized booty in Richmond. Unfortunately for the privateers, a Federal gunboat fired on them, setting fire to the ship. Although they lost most of the cargo, they escaped capture until the Union authorities ordered three infantry regiments, an artillery battalion, and ten gunboats into the Chesapeake—a massive force to stop the "pirates."

They were soon captured and sent in chains to Fort McHenry, where they were tried as pirates. They would have been hanged except for the intervention of the Richmond authorities, who placed an equal number of captured Union soldiers and officers in chains and threatened to give them the same treatment that was given to the captured privateers. Washington, under the threat of retaliation, held them as ordinary prisoners of war and exchanged them on May 5, 1864.

Beall went directly to Richmond to review his old plan for action on the Great Lakes with the Confederate authorities. By 1864 the end for the Confederacy was much

and set them loose in Ohio would tie down large numbers of Union troops. The troops would attempt to recapture the prisoners, preventing them from joining in the fight against the Confederacy. Beall traveled to Richmond and discussed his proposal in person with Stephen R. Mallory, the Confederate secretary of the navy.

Secretary Mallory thought the plan feasible but doubted that it could be carried out from neutral Canada without damaging the Confederacy's relationship with Great Britain. He suggested an alternative: privateering in the shipping lanes of the Chesapeake Bay. The suggestion led to a commission for Beall in the Confederate navy. He was now an "acting master," and was given a few pistols and swords. Beall was required by the commission to recruit his own men, but they couldn't be subject to military service, and as privateers they would have no salary and would be dependent on the "prizes" they

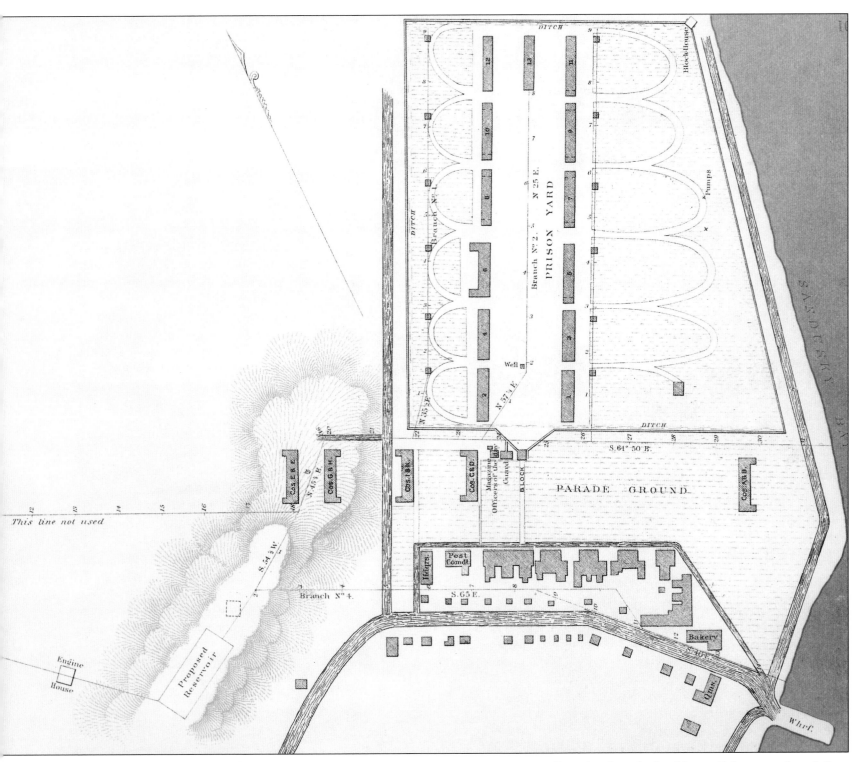

The prison camp at Johnson's Island was well organized, but because it lay within a deep bay, Beall's raiders hoped to be able to sail close enough to shell the Union guards and permit a mass escape.

Prison guards, both Union and Confederate, were under orders to fire at any prisoner who stepped across a marked "dead line." Federal guards were ordered to fire at any exposed light within a barracks after "lights out," and many prisoners lost their lives to shots fired suddenly through barracks windows.

seemed more appropriate to the officers in the Southern government. The letter contained instructions for Dahlgren to kill Jefferson Davis and other members of the Confederate government. Real or fraudulent, the letter was accepted at face value by many Confederates, and clandestine projects were approved more quickly than ever before. Beall's plan was ratified and he was once again off to Canada.

He envisioned a full campaign on Lake Erie. First, he proposed to capture the USS *Michigan,* a fourteen-gun warship—the only warship allowed by a treaty on the lake. Once the *Michigan* was in his possession, the lake cities would become easy prey for his men to attack as they pleased. The destruction being felt by the South would be felt in the far North.

The second phase of the campaign involved a raid on the original target in Beall's plan: the prison on Johnson's Island. Due to the captured warship, there would be little opposition. Once the prisoners (all officers) were set free, local Copperheads—Northerners who supported the South—would provide them with mounts and arms, and they could flee toward the safety of Virginia by passing through the new state of West Virginia. Beall and his men would then be able to steam at will on Lake Erie and shell Sandusky, Cleveland, and Buffalo if they chose to do so.

Burleigh, his old lieutenant from the Chesapeake raiding days, was the first to join Beall in the new venture, and together they located additional men from Confederate sympathizers and escaped prisoners who had found refuge in Canada. One of the Confederate commissioners in Canada, Jacob Thompson—the recent secretary of the interior under Buchanan—was the primary secret agent of the Confederacy in Canada, and he identified an agent of his who would prove useful as the plan developed.

more apparent and many similar operations began to be acceptable to the government. Following the discovery of a revealing letter on the body of Union officer Ulric Dahlgren, who was killed on a raid against Richmond, unconventional operations against the North

"War is cruelty and you cannot refine it."

—*General William T. Sherman*

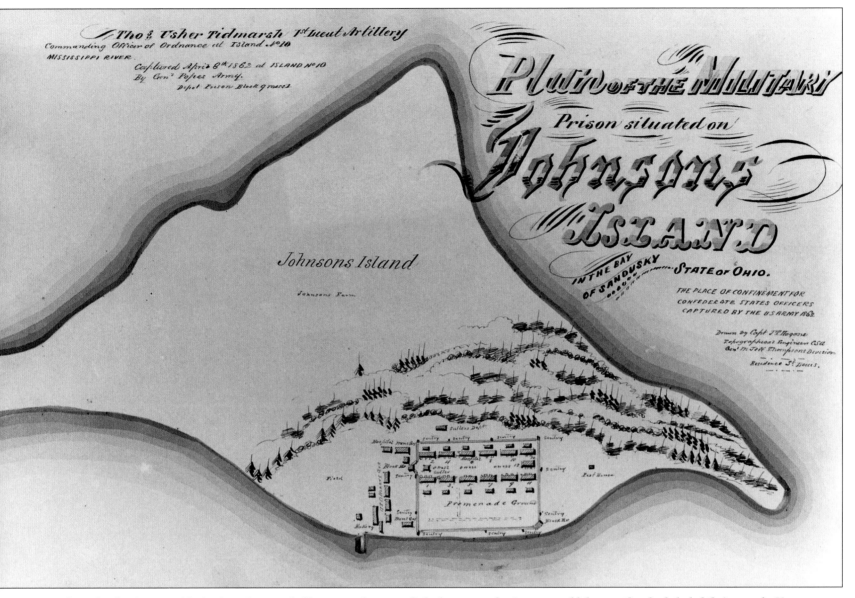

The following text appears within the map illustration:

Tho.ᵘ Usher Tidmarsh 1ˢᵗ Lieut Artillery
Commanding Officer of Ordnance at Island Nº 10
MISSISSIPPI RIVER.
Captured April 8ᵗʰ 1862 at ISLAND Nº 10
By Gen.ˡ Popes Army.
Depot Prison Block 9 mess.

Johnsons Island

Johnsons Farm

PLAN OF THE MILITARY
Prison situated on
Johnsons
ISLAND
IN THE BAY
OF SANDUSKY ———— STATE OF OHIO.
THE PLACE OF CONFINEMENT FOR
CONFEDERATE STATES OFFICERS
CAPTURED BY THE U.S ARMY 1862

Drawn by Capt J.T Hogane
Topographical Engineer CSA
Gen.ˡ M Jeff Thompsons Direction
Residence St Louis.

Johnson's Island was an ideal prison. Surrounded by water, there was little that escaped prisoners could do once they had eluded their guards. Many attempts were made, including that of a few brave souls who tried to walk across the frozen lake to reach Canada, but few men were able to get off of Johnson's Island without being exchanged.

Captain Charles H. Cole, a former member of Nathan Bedford Forrest's command, had been living in a hotel in Sandusky, posing as a wealthy young man from Philadelphia. He had spent freely, made friends with the officers guarding the prisoners on Johnson's Island, and developed good relations with the officers assigned to the *Michigan*. Like any good friend, he had been taken on tours of the ship and the prison where he had used money to recruit assistants for his espionage activities. Thompson was right: this man would be very useful to the plot to take control of Lake Erie.

Cole planned a great party at his hotel—to be held while the ship's captain and a group of his agents were away—and invited all of his Federal friends. Those Union officers not drunk would be drugged. Once this was accomplished, Cole was to fire a flare to signal Beall and the prisoners on the island

U. S. S. WOLVERINE (FORMERLY U. S. S. MICHIGAN.)
OLDEST IRON GUN BOAT IN THE WORLD. BUILT IN 1843.

The USS Michigan *was the only warship permitted on Lake Erie by an international treaty. Beall's plan included its capture, after which they would sail it to shell Johnson's Island before moving on to shell both Sandusky and Cleveland, Ohio.*

that the officers were under his control. At that point, Beall would move with his men to take over the *Michigan* and fire a shell into the island's officer's quarters. The twenty-five hundred prisoners would move against their surprised guards, who had few officers to direct a response. It was a good plan with a high probability of success.

The raid began to unfold gradually as the steam ferry *Philo Parsons* departed from Detroit on her daily run to Sandusky. One of her passengers that day was Burleigh, and

when the ferry docked briefly at Sandwich, on the Canadian side of the lake, Beall and two others came aboard. Later, at Amherstburg, sixteen other raiders boarded with a large trunk as their only piece of baggage. At about 5:00 P.M., after the *Philo Parsons* made its last stop before arriving in Sandusky, the disguised Confederates made their first move. Beall held a pistol at the head of the ferry's helmsman while Burleigh and the others herded the frightened passengers into rooms.

The ferry was landed at an island to take on wood and prisoners when they saw a second ferry, the *Island Queen,* approach. Beall and a few others leaped aboard from the upper deck of the *Philo Parsons*. Soon, shots were fired, the engineer of the *Island Queen* was wounded, and the second ferry was held by the Confederate raiders. The raiders were now within ten miles (16km) of the *Michigan* and all eyes strained to locate the signal flare to be fired by Captain Cole when the Union officers at his party were under his control.

The *Island Queen* was taken into deep water and allowed to sink slowly as the raiders cleared the decks of the *Philo Parsons* for action. Freight was thrown overboard as the ferry quietly slipped closer to Sandusky and the *Michigan*. As the warship's lights came into view, everyone began to realize that the signal from Cole was long overdue and the nearly foolproof operation was in danger of premature discovery.

Shortly afterward, the Confederate crewmen mutinied, refusing to go forward against a warship that might have learned of their approach. Only Beall, Burleigh, and one of the crew were willing to continue. Beall forced each of the men to sign a declaration that they would not continue before he reversed his course, admitting to himself that his long-hoped-for raid had failed.

Cole, one of Thompson's best agents, had been exposed. The captain of the *Michigan* had returned to the ship one day earlier than planned and had received a telegram from Detroit that explained the entire plot. Cole had been arrested.

In custody and facing capital charges for espionage, Cole quickly became an informer and exposed everyone involved. Arrests were swift, and the plot, only recently felt to be foolproof, had fallen to pieces.

Beall continued to attempt sabotage operations from Canada. He was arrested on December 16, 1864, when his team attempted to derail a train. He was tried as a spy by a military commission at Fort Lafayette. Found guilty, he was sentenced to death and hanged on Governor's Island in New York Harbor on February 24, 1865.

John Beall had attempted to bring the Civil War to a population that had been insulated from the destruction and violence seen throughout the South, particularly in his native Virginia. Had Charles Cole been able to gain control of the officers who were invited to attend his party in Sandusky, the

outcome might have been quite different, and the single warship allowed on Lake Erie could have devastated important Federal and state military and industrial facilities along the lakeshore. This strong blow for the Confederacy against the Union would have occurred in September 1864, just two months

prior to the general election in which Lincoln would face McClellan, a peace candidate. The presence of the Confederate navy on Lake Erie would have certainly been on the minds of many voters as they made their final decision within the privacy of the poll booth.

Unbelievable suffering occurred at Johnson's Island during the terrible winters. These men are walking beside the prison's dead line during a winter storm that left even the men inside their barracks freezing.

The Controversial Raid on Richmond

A report prepared by a secret agent working for the Union army may have sparked one of the most controversial operations of the Civil War—one that would have ramifications far beyond the battlefield. Joseph H. Maddox had reported that Richmond was nearly defenseless, and that one or two thousand cavalrymen "could land on the Pamunkey at dark and ride in unmolested and take Davis." While the report would be widely ignored, by February 1864, it seems that one man took it seriously and prepared to take advantage of the reported weakness in Richmond's defenses.

The winter fighting season had come to an end when the new commander of the Army of the Potomac and victor at Gettysburg, General George Meade, ordered his army to move north of the Rapidan River and enter winter quarters in the vicinity of Culpeper, Virginia. It was during this period that a brigadier general named Judson Kilpatrick, a cavalry commander in the Army of the Potomac, was able to gain the ear—temporarily—of Abraham Lincoln.

Kilpatrick managed to convince Lincoln that a division-sized raid into Richmond was entirely feasible, and the president approved the plan; General Meade seems to have grudgingly agreed. Before long, Kilpatrick was prepared to move, and a flurry of orders and reports began to flow from the Union commander's headquarters. One announced the contemplated move:

> *February 28, 1864.*
> *Major-General WARREN, Commanding Second Corps:*
>
> *The major-general commanding directs me to inform you that General Kilpatrick will move to-night, cross the Rapidan at the lower fords, and turning the enemy's right flank operate in his rear. He will be absent several days. He will withdraw all the supports and reserves of his picket-line, but will leave his pickets.*

Another dispatch advised the overall army commander, Henry Halleck, of the planned move and asked that General Benjamin Butler, commanding an army near Fort Monroe, be advised that Kilpatrick could arrive there without announcement as he withdrew from the vicinity of Richmond.

> *February 29, 1864—10 A.M.*
> *(Received 11.30 A.M.)*
>
> *Maj. Gen. H.W. HALLECK, General-in-Chief:*
>
> *A cavalry expedition left last evening with the intention of attempting to carry Richmond by a coup de main, General Kilpatrick in command. If successful, expects to be there by tomorrow P.M., March 1, and may the next day be in the vicinity of General Butler's outposts and pickets. Will you please notify that officer, that his advanced posts may be warned?*
>
> *GEO. G. MEADE*

Judson Kilpatrick had proposed to capture Richmond by a surprise attack with his small but highly mobile force as he freed the estimated fifteen thousand prisoners of war believed to be held in the immediate area of the Confederate capital. As part of the agreement he had made with Lincoln, Kilpatrick promised to distribute thousands of leaflets promising a general amnesty to those Virginians who were willing to take an oath of allegiance to the Federal government.

On the night of February 28, 1864, Kilpatrick's thirty-five hundred men recrossed the Rapidan River and rode south, hoping to be in and out of Richmond before the Confederate army could react to their presence. At Spotsylvania Court House, Kilpatrick split his force, sending a separate five-hundred man force under the command of Colonel Ulric Dahlgren in a wide swing to the west.

It was this portion of the raid that created a controversy that is still argued over today. Colonel Dahlgren was the son of Rear Admiral John Dahlgren, the inventor of the heavy and much-used Dahlgren gun. Ulric Dahlgren was only twenty-one years old—among the youngest colonels in the Union army—and he was on the operation in spite of the loss of one of his legs in fighting at Hagerstown at the end of the Gettysburg campaign. His part of the raid was complex: he was to ride to the south of Richmond, enter the city, and free the prisoners while Kilpatrick rode against the city's northern defenses and drew the Confederate reserves toward the main force.

At first, the raid went according to plan. Kilpatrick pushed his force all through the first night and the following day as the weather changed for the worse. Exhausted horses fell and never rose as the commander known to his men as "Kill Cavalry" began to live up to his name.

The Union cavalrymen stopped just short of

Richmond's defenses on March 1, but there was no sign that Dahlgren had entered the city as he had been instructed before he rode away from the main column at Spotsylvania Court House. The Union soldiers continued to skirmish with the Confederate defenders for most of the day as they waited for the arrival of Dahlgren's small column, but there was no sign of them, so Kilpatrick withdrew his men a few miles and set up a temporary camp. Confederate pursuers, under General Wade Hampton, arrived during the night and began to drop artillery rounds into Kilpatrick's camp. The Union cavalrymen withdrew even farther from the city as they were fired on by Hampton's men, but there was still no word on the fate of Dahlgren. The mystery was soon resolved as three hundred of Dahlgren's men rode into Kilpatrick's temporary camp. One of the officers who rode with Dahlgren reported:

Ulric Dahlgren, the son of Rear Admiral John Dahlgren, was one of the youngest colonels in the Union army. He lost a leg due to wounds suffered at Hagerstown during the final stages of the Gettysburg campaign, but this injury didn't stop him from leading his cavalrymen. He was killed in a raid that may have been intended to decapitate the Confederacy of its leadership.

We left division headquarters at Stevensburg, Va., at 6 P.M. February 28, 1864, and marched to Ely's Ford, which we reached about 11 P.M. We crossed the river, and a party of the Fifth New York Cavalry, under Lieutenant Merritt, and Hogan, the scout, captured the

enemy's picket-post, 1 officer and 14 men, belonging to a North Carolina regiment of cavalry. The colonel then pressed on to Spotsylvania Court-House, which he reached at early dawn on the 29th February, marched on in the direction of Frederick's Hall till 8 A.M., when he halted for fifteen minutes to feed the horses; then

pressed on again to within three-fourths of a mile [1.2km] of Frederick's Hall Station, which we reached about 11 A.M.

On the road we captured 16 artillery soldiers belonging to the Maryland Battalion. They told us that at the station there were three different camps, eight batteries in each, in all about ninety-

six guns; that there was a regiment of infantry near at hand and a battalion of sharpshooters in each camp. Here we captured also 12 artillery officers on court-martial—1 colonel, 1 major, and 8 or 9 captains. What information they gave to Colonel Dahlgren I am unable to state, but he determined not to attack the camp and moved around them, cutting the railroad and telegraph about 1 mile [1.6km] south of the station.

We now pushed on to the South Anna, which we crossed about 10 o'clock on the night of the 29th instant. It was raining and so intensely dark that it was almost impossible to keep the column closed up, and some 50 men were lost in the darkness, but joined us again in the morning near Goochland Court-House. About 2 a.m. the colonel halted. The name of the place I am unable to state, but think it was about 9 miles [14.5km] from Goochland. At daylight of the morning of the 1st of March we marched on toward the James River and stopped for a few minutes near Horton's house, on the

Dahlgren (top row, third from right) with a group of officers in a photograph taken at Army of the Potomac headquarters, Falmouth, Virginia, in 1863.

canal, about 21 miles [46.7km] from Richmond. Here Colonel Dahlgren gave me orders to take the detachment (100 men) of the Second New York Cavalry, the ambulances, prisoners, led horses, [etc.], and proceed down the canal, destroying locks, burning mills, canal-boats, and all the grain I could find; that when I came to Westham Creek I should send the ambulances, prisoners, [etc.], under guard to Hungary Station, there to join General Kilpatrick and the main column; that I was then to proceed down the river road or the canal, as I might see fit, while he, with the main portion of his command, was to cross the James River at a ford which his guide was to show him, release the prisoners, and enter Richmond by, I believe, the Mayo Bridge. Here I was to join him, if possible; if not, make my way to Hungary Station and join General Kilpatrick. He then divided the torpedoes, giving me one box, some

turpentine and oakum. He then started ahead of me. I struck the canal and moved down along its bank, sending the ambulances, [etc.], under guard of Lieutenant Randolph and 20 men, on the river road, with orders to join me at Manakin's Bend. Along the canal I destroyed six flourishing grist-mills, filled with grain and flour, one saw-mill, six canal-boats, loaded with grain, the barn (also well filled) on Secretary Seddon's plantation, coal-works at Manakin's Ferry, and Morgan's Lock just above. Here I found that there were neither canal-boats, locks, nor mills on the canal till the Three-Mile Lock, i.e., 3 miles [4.8km] from Richmond. I could not bring the ambulances on the tow-path, so I took the river road again, reaching which I was surprised to find the tracks of Colonel Dahlgren's party, and farther on the dead body of a negro hanging from a tree on the road-side. It seems that Colonel Dahlgren intended to cross the James River by a ford, to which his guide (this negro) promised to guide him. There was nei-

ther ford nor bridge; the guide had known it, and in his indignation the colonel hung him.

Colonel Dahlgren, finding there was no way to cross the James save by a very small scow, abandoned the project and proceeded to the cross-roads, about 8 miles [13km] from Richmond, I think near Short Pump. Here I joined him about 3.30 P.M. He now sent off the ambulances, prisoners, led horses, [etc.], under guard and in charge of the signal officer. That is the last I saw of them....

...The movements of Colonel Dahlgren and Major Cooke, after our separation, are better known to you than to myself. With regard to the address and memoranda of plans alleged by rebel papers to have been found on Colonel Dahlgren's person, I would state that no address of any kind was ever published to either officers or men; that none of Colonel Dahlgren's plans, save what I have mentioned in the first part of my report, were ever made known to either officers or men in the expedition, and that I know it was not Colonel

Dahlgren's intention to kill Jeff. Davis, in case he could be captured. The following is a list of killed, Wounded, and missing as accurately as I can get it: One officer killed, 4 officers missing, 194 enlisted men killed, wounded, and missing. Of this number about 60 are believed to be either killed or wounded.

Dahlgren had come quite close to Richmond before losing patience with his guide, Martin Robinson, and ordering him hanged. After the leading portion of his command became separated from the rest of his force, Dahlgren rode into an ambush that cost him his life. The ambush was reported by the officer who was in command of the Confederate force:

According to instructions I have the honor to report the facts concerning the little fight we had with the raiding party of the enemy around Richmond on the 5th day of March. I was informed by Lieutenant Pollard, of the Ninth Virginia Cavalry, that the enemy were advancing through King William County. I immediately ordered my men to report for duty, and succeeded in assembling 28 at King

and Queen Court-House. Lieutenant Pollard came up in their rear, and engaged their rear guard near Bruington Church, skirmishing for several miles. They halted and fed near Mantapike. The portions of the different commands were then collected together and put in ambush to await the advance of the enemy. After an hour or two's rest they moved on slowly. Our fire was reserved until the head of their column rested within a few yards, when they opened fire, which was instantly returned. Colonel Dahlgren fell dead, pierced with five balls. We captured 92 prisoners, 38 negroes, a number of horses, arms, [etc.]

Dahlgren was dead, his men killed, captured, or scattered. It was, however, not the audacity of the raid that created the controversy that survives to the present. When Dahlgren's body was searched, papers thought to be orders were found. These orders indicated that an escalation of this type of warfare was being considered by the Union army at this time.

Colonel Dahlgren had written to his father prior to the raid and, in part, the letter stated

that "if successful, it will be the grandest thing on record," indicating that more than simply freeing prisoners and spreading leaflets was intended. The papers, in Dahlgren's handwriting, indicated that the goal of the raid was the burning of Richmond and the killing of the Confederate leadership. A great outcry developed in the Confederacy and charges of atrocities were leveled at the Union army, but the army's leadership denied any involvement in Dahlgren's plan, if the papers were actually authentic.

Many historians feel that the escalation to this type of warfare was to result later in the Confederate Secret Service Bureau's plans to kidnap President Lincoln—a plot that eventually led to Lincoln's assassination.

In March 1864, General Lee left his temporary headquarters at Clark's Mountain to meet with Confederate President Jefferson Davis in Richmond. After the failed Federal raid, Lee returned to Clark's Mountain to prepare for a larger Federal advance.

Bibliography

Naval Warfare

Bearss, Edwin C. *Hardluck Ironclad*. Baton Rouge, La.: Louisiana State University Press, l966.

Beers, Henry Putney. *Guide to the Archives of the Government of the Confederate States of America*. Washington, D.C.: National Archives and Records Service, l968. (NARS Pub. 68-15).

Beers, Henry Putney, and Kenneth W. Munden. *Guide to the Federal Archives Relating to the Civil War*. Washington, D.C.: National Archives and Records Service, l962. (NARS Pub. 63-1).

Boatner, Mark M. III. *The Civil War Dictionary*, rev. ed. New York: David MacKay Co., 1988.

Canney, Donald L. *The Old Steam Navy*. 2 vols. Annapolis: The Naval Institute Press, 1990.

Coggins, Jack. *Arms and Equipment of the Civil War*. New York: The Fairfax Press, 1983.

Evans, Clement A., ed. *Confederate Military History*. 13 vols. rpt. Secaucus, NJ: Blue & Grey Press, n.d.

Gibbons, Tony. *Warships and Naval Battles of the Civil War*. New York: W. H. Smith Publishers, Inc., 1989.

Hewitt, Lawrence L. *Port Hudson: Confederate Bastion on the Mississippi*. Baton Rouge, La.: Louisiana State University Press, 1987.

Horan, James D. *Confederate Agent*. New York: Crown Publishers, 1956.

Johnson, Robert U., and Clarence C. Buel. *Battles and Leaders of the Civil War*. 4 vols. New York: The Century Co., 1887.

Jones, Virgil Carrington. *The Civil War at Sea*. 3 vols. New York: Holt, Rinehart & Winston, 1961.

Lord, Francis A. *Civil War Collector's Encyclopedia*. Secaucus, New Jersey: Castle, 1982.

Lucas, Daniel B. *Memoir of John Yates Beall*. Montreal, Que.: John Lovell, 1865.

Mahan, Alfred Thayer. *Gulf and Inland Waters*. New York: Charles Scribner's Sons, 1883.

Manucy, Albert. *Artillery Through the Ages*. Washington, D.C.: Government Printing Office, 1949.

Maury, Richard L. *A Brief Sketch of the Work of Matthew Fontaine Maury*. Richmond, Va.: Whittet & Shepperson, l915

Miller, Francis T., ed. *The Photographic History of the Civil War*. 10 vols. New York: The Review of Reviews, 1912.

Milligan, John D., ed. *From the Fresh Water navy: 1861–64*. Naval Letter Series: Volume Three. Annapolis, Md.: Naval Institute Press, 1970.

Nash, Howard P. *A Naval History of the Civil War*. New York: A. S. Barnes, Co., 1972.

Perry, Milton F. *Infernal Machines: The Story of Confederate Submarine and Mine Warfare*. Baton Rouge, La.: Louisiana State University Press, 1965.

Porter, David D. *Naval History of the Civil War*. rpt. Secaucus, N.J.: Castle, 1984.

Ripley, Warren. *Artillery and Ammunition of the Civil War*. 4th ed. Charleston, S.C.: The Battery Press, 1984.

Scharf, J. Thomas. *History of the Confederate States Navy*. Baltimore, 1887. rpt. New York: The Fairfax Press, 1977.

Silverstone, Paul H. *Warships of the Civil War Navies*. Annapolis, Md.: The Naval Institute Press, 1989.

Stern, Philip Van Dorn. *Secret Missions of the Civil War*. New York: Rand McNally, 1959.

U.S. Department of the Interior. National Park Service. *The Story of a Civil War Gunboat: USS Cairo*. Washington, D.C.: Government Printing Office, 1971.

U.S. War Department. *The War of the Rebellion. Official Records of the Union and Confederate Armies*. 73 vols. Washington, D.C.: Government Printing Office, 1880–1901.

———. *The War of the Rebellion. Official Records of the Union and Confederate Navies*. 31 vols. Washington, D.C.: Government Printing Office, 1895–1929.

———. *The Ordnance Manual for use by the Officers of the United States Army*. 3rd ed. Philadelphia: J. P. Lippincott & Co, 1862.

Wideman, John. *The Sinking of the USS Cairo*. Jackson: University Press of Mississippi, 1992.

Daring Raiders

Beymer, William G. *On Hazardous Service*. New York: Harper and Brothers, 1912.

Brown, James E. "Life of Brigadier General John McCausland," *West Virginia History*, Vol. IV, No. 4, July 1943.

Early, Jubal; *Jubal Early's Memoirs*, Nautical and Aviation Publishing, Baltimore, 1989.

Gilmor, Harry. *Four Years in the Saddle*. New York: Harper and Brothers, 1866.

Hoke, J. *Reminiscences of the War*. Chambersburg, Pa.: privately printed, 1884.

Jones, Beuhring H. *The Sunny Land*. Baltimore: Innes and Company, 1868.

Lewis, Thomas. *The Shenandoah in Flames: The Valley Campaign of 1864*. Time-Life, 1987.

McCausland, John. "The Burning of Chambersburg," *Annals of the War, Written by Leading Participants, North and South*. Times Publishing, 1897.

Moore, Frank. The *Rebellion Record*. New York: G.P. Putnam, 1862.

O'Connor, Richard. *Sheridan, The Inevitable*. Indianapolis, In.: Bobbs-Merrill, 1953.

Reader, Frank S. *History of the Fifth West Virginia Cavalry*. New Brighton, Pa., 1890.

Sheridan, Philip H. *Personal Memoirs of P.H. Sheridan*. New York: Charles L. Webster and Company, 1888.

Stutler, Boyd B. *Civil War in West Virginia*. Charleston, WV: Educational Foundation, 1963.

Sutton, Joseph J. *History of the Second Regiment, West Virginia Volunteers, During the War of the Rebellion*. Portsmouth, Ohio, 1892.

Wallace, Lee. *A Guide to Virginia Military Organizations*. H.E. Howard, Inc., 1986.

CRUCIAL LAND BATTLES

Fort Donelson

Cooling, Frank. "West Virginians at Fort Donelson, February 1862," *West Virginia History*, vol. XXVII, no. 2. January 1967.

Force, M.F. *From Fort Henry to Corinth: Campaigns of the Civil War Series*. New York: Charles Scribner's Sons, 1881.

Phillips, David L. *Tiger John: The Rebel Who Burned Chambersburg*. Gauley Mount Press, 1993.

United States General Staff School. *Fort Henry and Fort Donelson—1862*. Fort Leavenworth, Kans.: U.S. General Services School, 1923.

Wallace, Lew. "The Capture of Fort Donelson," *Battles and Leaders*. Ed. Ned Bradford. New York: Penguin Group, Meridian Books, 1989.

Pea Ridge

Mulligan, James A. "The Siege of Lexington," *Battles and Leaders*, vol. 1.. Ed. Robert U. Johnson and Clarence C. Buel. 1887.

Sigel, Franz. "The Flanking Column at Wilson's Creek," *Battles and Leaders*, vol. 1. Ed. Robert U. Johnson and Clarence C. Buel. 1887.

_____. "The Pea Ridge Campaign," *Battles and Leaders*, vol. 1. Ed. Robert U. Johnson and Clarence C. Buel. 1887.

Snead, Thomas L. "The First Year of the War in Missouri," *Battles and Leaders*. Ed. Robert U. Johnson and Clarence C. Buel, vol. 1. 1887.

Antietam

Cox, Jacob D. "The Battle of Antietam," *Battles and Leaders*. Ed. Ned Bradford. New York: Penguin Group, Meridian Books, 1989.

Hill, Daniel H. "The Battle of South Mountain, or Boonsboro," *Battles and Leaders*, vol. 1. Ed. Robert U. Johnson and Clarence C. Buel. 1887.

Longstreet, James. "The Invasion of Maryland," *Battles and Leaders*. Ed. Ned Bradford. New York: Penguin Group, Meridian Books, 1989.

Vicksburg

Grant, Ulysses S. "The Vicksburg Campaign," *Battles and Leaders*. Ed. Ned Bradford. New York: Penguin Group, Meridian Books, 1989.

Lockett, S.H. "The Defense of Vicksburg," *Battles and Leaders*, vol. 3. Ed. Robert U. Johnson and Clarence C. Buel. 1887.

Morgan, George W. "The Assault on Chickasaw Bluffs," *Battles and Leaders*, vol. 3. Ed. Robert U. Johnson and Clarence C. Buel. 1887.

Soley, James R. "Naval Operations in the Vicksburg Campaign," *Battles and Leaders*, vol. 3. Ed. Robert U. Johnson and Clarence C. Buel. 1887.

United States War Department. "General Reports—Vicksburg," *The War of the Rebellion*, vols. 24 and 25. 1893.

Gettysburg

Alexander, E. Porter. "The Great Charge and Artillery Fighting at Gettysburg," *Battles and Leaders*. Ed. Ned Bradford. New York: Penguin Group, Meridian Books, 1989.

Hunt, Henry J. "The First Day at Gettysburg," *Battles and Leaders*. Ed. Ned Bradford. New York: Penguin Group, Meridian Books, 1989.

_____. "The Second Day at Gettysburg," *Battles and Leaders*. Ed. Ned Bradford. New York: Penguin Group, Meridian Books, 1989.

_____. "The Third Day at Gettysburg," *Battles and Leaders*. Ed. Ned Bradford. New York: Penguin Group, Meridian Books, 1989.

Imboden, John D. "The Confederate Retreat from Gettysburg," *Battles and Leaders*, vol. 3. Ed. Robert U. Johnson and Clarence C. Buel. 1887.

Kershaw, J.B. "Kershaw's Brigade at Gettysburg," *Battles and Leaders*, vol. 3. Ed. Robert U. Johnson and Clarence C. Buel. 1887.

Longstreet, James. "Lee's Invasion of Pennsylvania," *Battles and Leaders*, vol. 3. Ed. Robert U. Johnson and Clarence C. Buel. 1887.

Melcher, H.S. "The 20th Maine at Little Round Top," *Battles and Leaders*, vol. 3. Ed. Robert U. Johnson and Clarence C. Buel. 1887.

United States War Department. "Gettysburg," The *War of the Rebellion*, series 1, vol. 27. 1897.

Monocacy

Early, Jubal. "Early's March to Washington in 1864," *Battles and Leaders*. Ed. Ned Bradford. New York: Penguin Group, Meridian Books, 1989.

_____. *War Memoirs*. Ed. Frank Vandiver. Bloomington, Ind.: Indiana University Press, 1960.

Gordon, John B. *Reminiscences of the Civil War*. New York: Charles Scribner's Sons, 1903.

United States War Department. "Monocacy," *The War of the Rebellion*, series 1, vol. 27. 1897.

Peachtree Creek

Cox, Jacob D. *Atlanta*. New York: Charles Scribner's Sons, 1882.

Hood, John B. "The Defense of Atlanta," *Battles and Leaders*. Ed. Ned Bradford. New York: Penguin Group, Meridian Books, 1989.

Howard, Oliver O. "The Struggle for Atlanta," *Battles and Leaders*. Ed. Ned Bradford. New York: Penguin Group, Meridian Books, 1989.

Johnston, Joseph E. "Opposing Sherman's Advance to Atlanta," *Battles and Leaders*, vol. 4. Ed. Robert U. Johnson and Clarence C. Buel. 1887.

Sherman, William T. "The Grand Strategy of the Last Year of the War," *Battles and Leaders*, vol. 4. Ed. Robert U. Johnson and Clarence C. Buel. 1887.

United States War Department. "Atlanta Campaign," *The War of the Rebellion*, series 1, vol. 38. 1893.

Five Forks

Porter, Horace. *Campaigning with Grant*. New York: The Century Co., 1897.

_____. "Five Forks and the Pursuit of Lee," *Battles and Leaders*, vol. 4. Ed. Robert U. Johnson and Clarence C. Buel. 1887.

Sheridan, Philip H. *Personal Memoirs of P.H. Sheridan*, vol. 2. New York: Jenkins and McCowan, 1888.

Sulivane, Clement. "The Evacuation," *Battles and Leaders*, vol. 4. Ed. Robert U. Johnson and Clarence C. Buel. 1887.

Tremain, Henry E. *Last Hours of Sheridan's Cavalry*. New York: Bonnell, Silver & Bowers, 1904.

INDEX

PHOTO CREDITS

AP/Wide World Photos: p. 126 top

Archive Photos: p. 58 top, 251 inset, 253, 263, 321 right

©Chris Bain: pp. 100 bottom left, 101 bottom right

Courtesy of the Anne S.K. Brown Military Collection, Brown University: p. 35 inset

Brown Brothers: pp. 25 right, 115, 133 inset, 134 top, 136 left, 144-145, 157 top, 160 top right, 162, 177 left, 181 right, 190 right, 201, 203 top, 217 top, 225 right, 231 top, 232, 258, 259, 266, 293, 311 inset

Eleanor S. Brockenbrough Library, The Museum of the Confederacy, Richmond, VA: p. 82 bottom

Corbis: pp. 17 top, 19, 23 right, 24 right, 25 left, 28 bottom, 30, 31, 32, 36, 37, 38 right, 39 both, 50 left, 51 bottom, 59, 64 both, 69 left, 76 both, 77 top, 87, 88 left, 94 right, 95, 98 all, 100 bottom right, 107 right, 111 middle and right, 112 right, 113 top, 114 bottom, 117, 119 inset, 123 top, 129, 136 right, 146-147, 155 right, 156, 158, 159 left, 160 bottom, 163 top, 165, 175, 178 bottom, 183 top, 185 inset, 187 bottom, 189, 193, 199, 200, 205 inset, 206 right, 213 right, 216 bottom, 219 inset, 226, 227 top, 230, 235 inset, 239 left, 242 right, 252, 255, 291 inset, 312, 320-321, 333

©Tom W. Freeman, Courtesy of SM & S Naval Prints, Inc., Forest Hill, MD: pp. 5, 130-131, 174, 186, 192, 214, 215, 224-225, 228-229, 236-237, 244-245 both

©Hal E. Gieseking: p. 56

Battle Diagrams and Map Illustrations by Robert Keene: pp. 27, 40, 57, 84, 270-271, 280-281, 306-307, 314-315, 336-337

Frank Leslie's Illustrated Newspaper: pp. 180-181, 249, 327, 331; background: pp. 20-21, 34-35, 44-45, 60-61, 70-71, 90-91, 104-105, 118-119, 132-133, 150-151, 166-167, 184-185, 204-205, 218-219, 234-235, 250-251, 274-275, 310-311, 322-323, 338-339

Library of Congress: background: pp. 302-303; pp. 2-3, 45 inset, 46-47, 51 top, 55, 56 top, 58 bottom, 61 inset, 63 both, 60-61, 69 right, 71 inset, 74, 81, 82 top, 88-89, 113 bottom, 114, 122 both, 123 bottom, 137, 138, 147 right, 155 left, 163 bottom, 168, 169 bottom, 170 center, 171, 182, 188, 194 left, 202, 203 bottom, 206 left, 209, 211 both, 217 bottom, 231 bottom, 233 bottom, 238, 256, 309, 323 inset, 332

Library of Congress, Courtesy of the Museum of the Confederacy: pp. 248, 276, 346, 351 inset

Library of Congress/National Archives, Courtesy of The Museum of the Confederacy, Richmond, VA: p. 325

©Eric Long Photography: p. 103

Painting by William R. McGrath, Courtesy WRM Graphics, Inc., Cleveland, OH: pp. 141, 142-143, 148-149, 196-197, 208, 210, 212-213, 220-221, 240-241

Massachusetts Commandery Military Order of the Loyal Legion and the US Army Military History Institute: pp. 284, 288-289 both, 292 both, 305, 314 top, 324, 326, 328-329, 330, 334, 340, 341, 343, 345, 356, 359, 360-361

The Museum of the Confederacy, Richmond, VA: pp. 261 top, 279 right, 287, 294 top, 298-299, 300, 308, 355

National Archives: pp. 140, 154, 157 bottom, 164, 169 top, 170 right, 222, 227 bottom, 233 top, 239 right, 243

National Archives, Courtesy The Museum of the Confederacy, Richmond, VA: p. 303 inset

National Portrait Gallery, Washington, D.C./Art Resource, NY: pp. 107 left, 342

New York Public Library Picture Collection: pp. 260, 294 bottom, 307 right, 314 bottom

North Wind Picture Archives: background: pp. 350-351; pp. 28 top, 38 left, 43, 73, 78, 102, 111 left, 135, 139, 143 right, 151 inset, 153, 159 right, 160 top right, 172, 173, 176, 177 right, 178 top, 183 bottom, 187 top, 190 left, 191, 207 both, 216 top, 223, 228 left, 261 bottom, 262, 267, 268, 352, 354, 357

©Aloysius T. O'Donnell: p. 94 left

Courtesy of the Pejepscot Historical Society, Brunswick, ME: p. 126 bottom

Paintings by Gordon Phillips: pp. 246-247, 296-297, 313

The Rhode Island Historical Society: pp. 349

George Rinhart/Corbis: p.301

Courtesy Beverly R. Robinson Collection/U.S. Naval Academy Museum, Annapolis, MD: pp. 29, 46 top, 66 left

Stock Montage: p. 33

Paintings by John Paul Strain: pp. 316-317, 362-363

Superstock: pp. 91 inset, 99 inset, 152, 167 inset, 194-195, 170 left; AKG Berlin: p. 21 inset; H. Lanks: p. 128

©Don Troiani: pp. 96, 100 top, 127 bottom, 134 bottom, 161,

Painting by Don Troiani, Southbury, CT: pp. 14-15, 24, 42, 48, 54, 68, 72, 77 bottom, 79, 80, 83, 85, 86, 99, 101, 109, 116, 121, 125, 127, 295

UPI/Corbis: pp. 17 bottom, 277

U.S. Army Military History Institute: p. 275 inset, 278, 282-283, 319, 339 inset

U.S. Government Printing Office: p. 179; copy photography by Christopher Bain: p. 242 left

Courtesy of the Valentine Museum/Cook Collection: pp. 16, 25 center, 50 right

Courtesy the Virginia Military Institute: p. 93 all

Courtesy VMI Public Relations Office; Painting by Benjamin West Klinedinst depicting the charge of VMI cadets at the Battle of New Market(the mural is affixed to the wall of VMI's Jackson Memorial Hall); from THE CIVIL WAR: SHENANDOAH IN FLAMES, photograph by Michael Latil ©1987 Time-Life books. Inc.: p. 92

Washington Government Printing Office: pp. 22, 23 left, 26, 41, 52, 62, 75, 97, 106, 110, 124, 257, 353

Courtesy of the West Point Museum, United States Military Academy, West Point, NY: p. 18

Courtesy of the Western History Collection, University of Oklahoma Library: p. 53

Frank and Marie-Terese Wood Print Collections, Alexandria, VA: background: pp. 290-291; pp. 65, 112 left, 114 top, 254, 264-265 both, 269 both, 271 right, 272-273 both, 279 left, 304